TRANSFORMATIVE SOCIAL WORK

D1564979

TRANSFORMATIVE SOCIAL WORK

PRACTICES FOR ACADEMIC SETTINGS

EDITED BY
JAN FOOK AND
DANIELLE JATLOW

Columbia University Press
New York

Columbia University Press
Publishers Since 1893
New York   Chichester, West Sussex
cup.columbia.edu

Library of Congress Cataloging-in-Publication Data
Names: Fook, Jan, editor.
Title: Transformative social work : practices for academic settings /
edited by Jan Fook, Danielle Jatlow.
Description: New York : Columbia University Press, [2023] | Includes
bibliographical references and index.
Identifiers: LCCN 2023028507 (print) | LCCN 2023028508 (ebook) |
ISBN 9780231207003 (hardback) | ISBN 9780231207010 (trade paperback) |
ISBN 9780231556767 (ebook)
Subjects: LCSH: Social work education. | Social service—Practice.
Classification: LCC HV11 .T6923 2023 (print) | LCC HV11 (ebook) |
DDC 361/.06071—dc23/eng/20230831
LC record available at https://lccn.loc.gov/2023028507
LC ebook record available at https://lccn.loc.gov/2023028508

Cover design: Noah Arlow
Cover image: Shutterstock

CONTENTS

III. SPECIFIC MODELS AND STRATEGIES

I

THE THEORETICAL, CULTURAL, COMMUNITY, AND UNIVERSITY CONTEXT

INTRODUCTION

What Is a Transformative Approach in Social Work?

JAN FOOK AND BRENDA SOLOMON

The global political scene changes moment by moment, and therefore so must the politics and theories that inform how social work is taught and practiced. In the few years before we wrote this book, we underwent a global pandemic, witnessed an international spread of the Black Lives Matter movement, and, in some Western countries at least, wrung our hands at the horror of the Russian invasion of Ukraine. It seems necessary, in this climate, to revisit what words like *transformative social work* mean. What relevance do these words have, especially in institutions of higher education that are traditionally somewhat removed from everyday responsibilities?

The intention of this book is to revisit the "transformative" perspective and to explore how it plays out in academic social work settings. This focus was chosen because so little has been written not only about how "transformative" ideas are enacted in universities but also about the actual practice of such a perspective, given the temptation in higher education to privilege theoretical thinking.

While a number of books have developed the transformative approach in social work practice (e.g., Schott & Weiss, 2015), very few detail what the approach looks like in academic circles. Although transformative approaches are popular with social work educators, there is little scholarship about how these approaches play out in academic life more broadly, including their impacts on different types of pedagogical and curriculum engagement and different topic areas; on how academic social work departments are managed; and on how academic relationships with academic and administrative colleagues, students, and managers within the university, as well as professionals and community members outside the university, are maintained outside the classroom. This book aims to fill that gap by addressing specific, concrete ways that the transformative approach has been implemented in academic social work settings, including education, administration, research, management, and outreach. The hope is to contribute to a broader ranging and more systematic understanding of how transformative perspectives play out throughout the academic and professional contexts in which social work education is delivered. This should contribute to a more intentional practice of being transformative which is relevant to many professions, not just social work.

The chapters in this book have been chosen to address all of the major aspects of academic practice: teaching and learning; management; research; administration and external outreach. It is our hope that this breadth of focus will stimulate thinking about how we practice transformatively not only in the classroom but rather throughout the context of our academic work lives. Chapters were chosen to represent a variety of authors, perspectives, and writing styles. In offering this diverse, multi-perspectival resource, we are modeling one way to think about and enact transformative approaches in the academic workspace.

In addition, there is a need to revisit how the academy contributes both to the specific geographic and professional communities in which our institutions are located and, more broadly, to the populations we serve. Recent global events highlight the necessity for universities to be actively involved in issues that reach far beyond their traditional borders. Increasing fiscal tightening has led governments and members of the public to question the role of the university in civic life, and of the role of higher education in preparation for life more generally, beyond a concrete focus on employment (Barnett, 2012; Collini, 2012; Docherty, 2011). How do social work academics contribute to these conversations, and how can their contributions be informed by transformative principles?

Finally, this book addresses transformative approaches in the international context. How to practice and work transformatively is becoming an increasingly complex question, with growing calls to develop ways of working that are relevant to local cultures and contexts (Fook, 2023). This is especially pertinent for the social work profession, which must always be locally relevant but still subscribe to universal principles. Accordingly, this collection draws on contributions from several countries (Australia, Canada, the United Kingdom, the United States, and Israel), offering both a comparative and a universal contemplation of what constitutes a transformative approach to practice in academic settings in each context. The original impetus for this book came from the long-standing experience of members of the Department of Social Work at the University of Vermont, a department that has long prided itself on offering a distinctively transformative social work program. There is, however, equal and substantial input from other national and international colleagues. The book not only addresses a current gap but also helps to develop the transformative approach by documenting like-minded practices across the globe.

AIMS OF THE BOOK

This book is aimed at social work educators and students who wish to further develop their academic practice from a transformative perspective by thinking through how social work education plays out in an increasingly neoliberal academic environment. Specifically, it will:

- Provide detailed examples of how transformative perspectives translate into specific academic practices
- Discuss the experience of trying to practice transformatively in academic settings, especially those that may feel increasingly at odds with these perspectives
- Raise significant issues and tensions in the academic practice of transformative social work that require acknowledgment and further work
- Inspire and stimulate further thinking and development of transformative perspectives, particularly in challenging environments
- Inspire and stimulate further thinking about innovative roles academics can take to contribute to local and global communities
- Provide a number of different perspectives (ranging from student to faculty member, practitioner, administrative staff member, and

manager, and encompassing a variety of country contexts) in order to paint a complex picture of the issues, challenges, and possibilities
- Provide some guidelines for how a transformative perspective might be applied differently in different contexts

We—Brenda and Jan, the authors of this introduction—bring two differing perspectives to the content. We hope that readers' understanding of what *transformative* means will be enriched by the dialogue between our viewpoints. Part of this dialogue is explicating a historical understanding of how the term *transformative* developed in relation to the specific context in Vermont, written about by Brenda, a long-standing member of faculty in the University of Vermont's Department of Social Work, who was active in shaping the term to encompass the varying perspectives of the faculty at the time. This is juxtaposed against meanings gleaned from relevant literature and from writings developed in international contexts, written about by Jan, who recently migrated to the United States to take up the position of professor and department chair at the University of Vermont. We hope that these perspectives will provide a historical, national, and local context for the ideas presented in this book.

THE USAGES OF *TRANSFORMATIVE* IN SOCIAL WORK

CULTURAL AND HISTORICAL CONTEXTS

The term *transformative social work* is not clear-cut and well-defined. When I, Jan, first took up my position at the University of Vermont, I was puzzled as to why we did not just use the term *critical social work*, a theoretical perspective with which I was very familiar. As far as I was concerned, there was a huge body of social work literature that identified itself this way, arising in the 1970s and reaching a peak in the 1990s. It first appeared as "radical" social work, originating through the writings like those of Bailey and Brake (1975) in the UK. I credit myself (Fook, 1993) and Jim Ife (1997) with furthering this tradition as it later morphed into "critical social work" in the early 1990s, led from Australia. Theoretical bases shifted from Marxist ideologies in the 1970s to reliance on the more broadly "critical" school, with its analyses of power and its postempiricist leanings. This tradition also embraced feminist analyses in the 1980s. While I still personally subscribe to a broadly critical approach in this tradition, my approach is also informed by the move to embrace more ostensibly postempiricist thinking, including postmodern and poststructural perspectives (e.g., Pease & Fook, 1999; Fook, 2002, 2023).

I recognize now that my work was deeply influenced by the academic culture of the country of my birth, Australia, and that, in turn, Australia's colonized academic culture was derived from the country of its origin, the United Kingdom. I have written elsewhere (Fook, 2023) about how my own social work education was profoundly British even though its Britishness was—unhelpfully—not acknowledged at the time! My understanding of academic social work was formed in the 1970s, and when I came to do my own first piece of research for a master of social work degree, I reviewed almost exclusively British literature on what was at the time termed "radical social work." So, I had formed the unquestioned idea that different perspectives within social work practice were based primarily on academic theory.

Coming to work in the American context was initially deeply dismaying and not a little annoying, since I already had clear and definite ideas about what should constitute sound academic thinking. It was hard for me to be patient and suspend my judgment, but eventually I absorbed enough of the unarticulated culture of a different country to enable me to understand its different academic context. I have learned that, although we seem to assume that all Western academic cultures are based on similar premises, that is not entirely the case. I have also been forced to recognize that the ways terms are used and understood are formed by national and local cultures as well as historical and political influences. Far from seeing "theory" as something that remains abstract and untouchable, I now realize the need to appreciate the genesis of meanings and their significance to the local people who use them. I have also come to appreciate how even the idea of "theory" carries different significance in different places.

In a later section, Brenda will describe the meaning of the term *transformative* as it developed at the University of Vermont about twenty years ago. We decided it was important to include this history, given that the Department of Social Work has long held a distinctive transformative perspective that has been recognized as marginal to the mainstream.

Brenda will illustrate how the use of the term emerged and the social and political reasons why it was crafted as it was. I hope this will convey a greater understanding of how theory and theoretical perspective must be appreciated in relation to specific contexts. This is perhaps a lens that can inform a more complex understanding of all of the chapters in this book.

USAGE OF THE TERM *TRANSFORMATIVE* IN SOCIAL WORK LITERATURE

A quick overview of social work literature indicates that the term *transformative* is used in quite a general way to refer to change. The term, of course, does not originate with the social work profession and is probably most identified with the discipline of education. It is therefore relevant to quote from one of the seminal works in that field: "Fostering transformative learning is seen as teaching for change—a practice of education that is predicated on the idea that students are seriously challenged to assess their value system and worldview and are subsequently changed by the experience" (Quinnan, 1997, p. 42; quoted in Taylor, 2009, p. 3). Taylor (2009) goes on to explore the association of "transformative learning" with experience, critical reflection, dialogue, a holistic orientation, an awareness of context, and authentic relationships. It is instructive to note that all these ideas and concepts recur or are implied in most of the literature that pertains to transformative social work. In a later work, Cranton and Taylor (2012, p. 7) outline the dominant perspectives in transformative learning: "Transformative learning is described as cognitive and rational, imaginative and intuitive, as spiritual, as related to individuation, as relational, and as relating to social change." The elements of transformative learning as described in each of these lists are all present in this book. The concept of relationality in particular is understood to be integral to the transformative perspective on learning (McNamee & Moscheta, 2015) and is an idea central to most of the chapters in this volume.

The principle of change being associated with transformation is fundamental to the work of Stanley Witkin, one of the most prolific writers on transformative perspectives in social work. Witkin (2017, pp. 13–14) also emphasizes the idea of change as being central to the idea of transformation, although all of his work is based on a theoretical framework of social constructionism, which he uses to challenge the epistemological bases of social work. This theoretical approach accords with Mezirow's acknowledgment of the basis of transformative learning as "constructivist" (Mezirow, as referred to in Cranton & Taylor, 2012, p. 5).

Overall, though, it appears that the term *transformative social work*, or transformative perspectives in social work, has a more generic meaning and is mostly associated with theories or frameworks based on critical perspectives. Webb (2019, p. xxxiii) says: "It is now accepted that critical social work is a generic term—for an approach to practice, policy and research—that draws on critical theory and progressive Left thinking to promote social and economic justice through transformational change and insurrection." Key ideas in critical theory are an analysis of power and how inequities are created and maintained, which is foundational to making more equitable social changes. A skepticism toward purely empirical ideas of knowledge creation and a questioning of deterministic notions of the nature of people and social systems are also important (Fook, 2023). Echoes of all of these ideas can be found in many of the common terms associated with transformative social work, such as *social justice* and *human rights*, also called *freedoms* (Borenstein et al., 2021). Much of the social work writing focuses on critical reflection as transformative learning (e.g., Bay & MacFarlane, 2011; Beres & Fook, 2020). Indeed, the idea of reflection, or reflective practice, has become almost synonymous with the term *transformative learning* in social work (Stone & Harbin, 2016). Another commonly occurring term associated with transformative perspectives is *anti-oppressive* (Caron et al., 2020), which is in turn associated with critical perspectives.

In closing this section on the different usages of the term *transformative* in social work, it is important to note that there are newer developments in social work thinking that must affect our understanding of what transformative means. These newer developments may be said to be even more transformative in that they lead us to question the cultural and epistemological foundations of our thinking, thus enabling even more radical levels of change. For this reason, we are happy to include in this volume some writings from students, who are very much engaged with contemporary thinking, particularly in relation to the need to develop ecological social work (e.g., Boetto, 2017) and the transformative changes that this implies in terms of our relationship to our environment in all its forms.

In addition, there is a need to incorporate a decolonizing analysis (Clarke & Yellow Bird, 2021), which also implies the need to question our foundational cultural thinking in order to plumb, in depth, how our assumptions about our being and our knowledge need to be transformed. In particular, it is crucial to include indigenous ways of knowing and being, which are radically different from Eurocentric ways of knowing and being. Lastly, we need to incorporate an analysis of how anthropocentric views (Bozalek & Pease, 2021) also need to be broadened and transformed in order for us to create a society and an environment that include all forms of life. Many of the perspectives of ecological, decolonizing, indigenous, and nonanthropocentric thinking are interrelated, and embracing these more recently developed frameworks will carry the transformative agenda even further.

THE DEVELOPMENT OF THE CONCEPT OF TRANSFORMATIVE SOCIAL WORK AT THE UNIVERSITY OF VERMONT

I (Brenda) will begin by providing some context to my own thinking about transformative perspectives before I detail how the term came into use at the University of Vermont. My social work training and development took place in the United States during the late 1980s and early 1990s. During that time, I, like others, found inspiration from British and Canadian social work scholars. They took a broader philosophical view of human suffering and an expansive interest in the human capacity for meaningful relationships. I found that this set the terms for a social work practice keenly attuned to the connections among people in their everyday lives, social theories, and political claims making. I had been taken with the profession's role in social movements during the 1960s and 1970s, from deinstitutionalization to community action to civil rights and women's rights. Looking back, what most strikes me about my training is that it was buttressed by a sentiment that the proliferation of social programs during the 1960s and 1970s was cause for later civil unrest. A clear governmental reaction to the inroads made by social activists, social work scholars, and others during that earlier period was well felt in social work education. As I entered my MSW program, despite a focus on policy, what held currency was the ascension of family systems theory and related therapies. Thus, it was via a kind of radical interest in family process that social relations were examined. Critical analysis adjusted to meet the times, and a good portion of it focused on the family.

Thus, the critical view of social process was very much focused on one of the smallest concentric circles (the family) emanating from a person in their environment and was very much contained within the professional space of a therapy session. Nevertheless, I was taken with the radical assertions by individual therapists of notoriety and other thinkers whose ideas were brought to bear on the therapeutic context. I was reading June Jordan (1985, 1992, 1993), Mimi Abramovitz (1996), Frances Fox Piven and Richard Cloward (1971, 1977), and bell hooks (1981, 1984, 1990), among others, and living through the imperative that the AIDS epidemic presented to our profession, bolstering the call for marginalized perspectives to be aired in the open.

When I started teaching social work and became a student of sociology for my doctoral studies, I felt at home somewhere between social work and sociology. As I looked for social work teaching positions in the late 1990s, that liminal interest was recognized and welcomed in only a few spaces. One of those spaces was the social work department at UVM with its own critical take on the state of the profession and social work education. While there were others in the department doing work that contributed to the critical approach of the programs, it was Stan Witkin's (2011, 2014, 2017; Witkin & Saleebey, 2007) instruction regarding constructionist social work combined with Marty Dewees's (2005a, 2005b; Berg-Weger et al., 2015) constructionist practice approach, Susan Roche's (2007; Roche et al., 1999) feminist articulation, and Suzy Comerford's (2005, 2008, 2018) application to the disenfranchisement of marginalized groups that met my interests as an institutional ethnographer/sociologist/social worker in 1999.

Witkin's contributions as a scholar to critical social construction in the United States is unparalleled. Along with his good friend and scholar, Dennis Saleebey, of strength-based approach notoriety, he established what they termed an "anti-conference" for social work academics. This gathering provided a supportive discussion space for (often lone) social constructionist/postmodern scholars in social work departments at various universities in the United States. I recall his being amazed by how much interest there was in what became known as the Vermont meetings each fall. Initially U.S.-focused, they later expanded to include a substantial contingent of international scholars. These annual meetings and the network that supported them were subsequently dubbed the Transforming Social Work (TSW) practice, education, and inquiry gatherings, and the organizing group became the Global Partnership for Transformative Social Work (www.gptsw .net); the group still meets today.

As these meetings formed, they came to play a more coherent role in bringing together a community of scholars to share critical constructionist approaches toward transformative change. Our department became known as one of the rare examples of a social work academic unit teaching critical social construction in the United States. However, the specific orientation had yet to be officially named.

Finding an umbrella term that properly recognized this critical stance and at the same time fulfilled accreditation requirements was tricky. It felt necessary to move beyond a critique of knowledge production to encompass a process of substantive and sustainable change to enable a more established approach to practice. That realization, along with our associated success with the Vermont meetings, moved us toward an identification with transformative change.

At the time, ironically, the term *transformative* was not one that people in the department used to identify their work. Perhaps it was the experience of linking arms with a group of like-minded scholars from around the world that fortified us to claim such a position, in contrast to what was accepted and promoted in the profession as we knew it in the States. The term *transformative social work* stuck, was embraced, and continued to serve us well. The task then became one of ensuring that our curriculum became worthy of the term. In the first year of our two-year MSW program, we focused on introducing a context for teaching and practicing transformative social work by way of three philosophical orientations: (1) a strengths-oriented approach; (2) a critical constructionist perspective; and (3) the promotion of social justice and human rights.

These three philosophical strands do not adhere to any one social work theoretical approach but do set out the broad terms of engagement. Intertwined, these philosophical strands form a commitment to the traditions of our profession and the relational, profound, and generative elements of transformative social work. Transformative social work explores the promise of social work as:

- A *relational* practice that provides welcoming and reliable contexts for individuals of all ages, families, groups, communities, and organizations to explore the unprecedented challenges they face with dignity and respect
- A *profound* practice that understands and engages an ever-broader array of viable solutions to inform substantive change
- A *generative* practice that meets the challenges of people through a full range of interventions in policy, practice, and research that seek national and global as well as local influence

A transformative social work engagement with human suffering and social problems places UVM social work graduate students at the intersection of innovative theorizing, creative policy and practice advances, and the assemblage of viable contexts for help to individuals, families, and local and global communities (University of Vermont Social Work Department, 2010).

The aim of a specialized practice in transformative social work is to create a context in which students can be aware of and critically examine the accepted notions and practices in which their personal and professional lives are embedded. This examination is meant to create opportunities to engage power toward a practice in everyday life and in social work that is liberating, is inclusive, promotes self-direction, and is better for more people, more often.

We intend to create a learning context in which students are able to participate in producing knowledge in the places they occupy with the people they aim to help and, further, in the marketplace of ideas about our profession to make a way forward for humans and other animals and the planet.

A RECENT FORMULATION

Recently, the department has expanded with new faculty. As this has happened, we have attempted to reconfigure the existing conceptualization to incorporate the thinking of a newer faculty group. To this end, we have attempted to tie together the various philosophical and theoretical strands and to define some of the newer key concepts and theoretical developments that are involved in a transformative approach. The following statement is based on an international definition of social work:

Social work is a practice-based profession and an academic discipline that promotes social change and development, social cohesion, and the empowerment and liberation of people. Principles of social justice, human rights, collective responsibility and respect for diversities are central to social work. Underpinned by theories of social work, social sciences, humanities and indigenous knowledge, social work engages people and structures to address life challenges and enhance wellbeing. The above definition may be amplified at national and/or regional levels. (International Federation of Social Workers, 2014)

Following is our current document, which is a continuing work in progress:

- Our understanding of social justice means that we seek to critique, challenge, and change, in profound ways, all social inequities that manifest at personal, interpersonal, social, and structural/institutional levels, in ways that are transformative.
- Social justice encompasses many forms of justice (social, economic, racial, environmental, and political).
- A transformative approach to social justice must include sound knowledge of what is being critiqued, so that viable alternative practices can be posed and enacted.
- With respect to issues of diversity, we are particularly committed to racial justice and to ensuring that diverse racial and cultural perspectives are recognized and understood in relation to how the social work profession and its practice are conceptualized. We pay attention to analyses that recognize the influence of colonizing practices and regimes in underpinning different current cultures in the Western world and, in particular, how these have influenced our framing of the social work profession and practices.

- An international and global perspective ensures that we focus on issues that concern all human and nonhuman animals within our shared environment. Thus, our focus is not just on human rights but on the rights of all beings within our shared contexts. We therefore seek to embrace newer theoretical approaches to social work in a postanthropocentric world (e.g., critical posthumanism). In addition, we incorporate existing theoretical approaches that enhance our understanding of how we adhere to social justice principles. These include the strengths perspective (focusing on people's capabilities rather than deficits); critical social work approaches (incorporating an analysis of how power inequalities are constructed and maintained and providing a blueprint for social change); feminism (an analysis of how gender inequalities are maintained); social constructionism (an understanding of how we make knowledge, and therefore power inequalities and social differences, particularly through language and discourse); and anti-oppressive social work approaches (aimed at reducing oppression of marginalized people).
- These perspectives give rise to particular principles guiding the way we relate to one another and also the practices and skills we believe are important:
  - A critical stance involves the ability to "think underneath" and question (not take for granted) current social arrangements.
  - A critical stance leads to new paradigms and possibilities for envisioning society and relations within it and, therefore, an openness and generous embracing of personal and social change.
  - A critical stance involves the ability to analyze and think critically but also the ability to critically reflect and learn from experience. The two sets of skills complement each other but are not a substitute for each other. Both are important for responsive and responsible social work practice.
  - A relational approach means that the following principles are important:
    - How we understand different opinions and perspectives and can debate these in respectful and nonviolent ways
    - A sense of community, collaboration, and relationship—an ongoing commitment to learning from one another and a willingness and an ability to negotiate differences

- ° Humility—cultural, personal, and political
- ° The ability of individual students and faculty to understand and appreciate, in a critically reflexive way, their own identities (including ways of knowing, being, and doing) and how they can develop this understanding to make unique contributions as social workers and members of civil society

CONCLUSION

While we have established that the term *transformative* in social work does not have universally agreed or clear-cut meanings, it is commonly understood to refer to conditions that bring about fundamental change. This change is underpinned by values and principles of equity, inclusion, social justice, and human rights. Epistemologically, it implies a constructivist approach to knowledge, relationally created and maintained. The approach to learning is therefore reflective, incorporating and valuing personal experience as a source of knowing in conjunction with other forms of knowledge transfer and creation. It also shares common principles with social work approaches such as a strengths-based perspective that focuses on human strengths rather than pathologies. The critical aspects of a transformative perspective imply a principle of analysis that is mindful of social inequities and the processes of power creation that sustain them and that seeks to make social change on this basis. From this perspective, newer social work theories that incorporate environmental, decolonized, indigenous, and postanthropocentric analyses are crucial, as such approaches integrate a deep-seated questioning of fundamental epistemologies and worldviews.

The chapters in this book address aspects of these transformative perspectives as they apply in different areas of academic practice. All seek to forge new ground, with outlines of specific new theoretical approaches, the development of new concepts, illustrations of specific experiences and practical suggestions that arise from these, and specific suggestions for classroom strategies that are based on a remaking of traditional conceptions of learning. We have deliberately included different writing styles and formats in order to allow different voices and perspectives to be expressed in ways most relevant to the authors. There are fairly conventional academic pieces that argue for and describe certain approaches and ideas. There are also reflective pieces that attempt to convey insights developed though personal experience. Several chapters convey their content through an interview format. There are authors from different countries and backgrounds, with different roles in the academy (administrators, managers, students, and faculty). We hope that the volume compiled in this way will speak to a range of audiences and perspectives and thus model its own diversity.

We hope the book is interesting, engaging, perhaps a little controversial, and most of all inspiring! As social workers, we can and should contribute to all aspects of academic life; this book is our contribution to supporting us in doing so.

REFERENCES

Abramovitz, M. (1996). *Regulating the lives of women: Social welfare policy from colonial times to the present*. Boston: South End.

Bailey, R., & Brake, M. (Eds.). (1975). *Radical social work*. London: Edward Arnold.

Barnett, R. (Ed.). (2012). *The future university*. New York: Routledge.

Bay, U., & MacFarlane, S. (2011). Teaching critical reflection: A tool for transformative social work. *Social Work Education*, 30(7), 745–758, https://doi.org/10.1080/02615479.2010.516429.

Beres, L., & Fook, J. (Eds.). (2020). *Learning critical reflection: Experiences of transformative learning*. London: Routledge.

Berg-Weger, M., Dewees, M. P., & Birkenmaier, J. (2015). *The practice of generalist social work*, 3rd ed. New York: Routledge.

Bhopal, K. & Shain, F. (2016) "Educational exclusion: towards a social justice agenda" in K. Bhopal & F. Shain (eds) *Neo-liberalism and Education*, London: Routledge, pp. 1–5.

Boetto, H. (2017, January). A transformative eco-social model: Challenging modernist assumptions in social work. *British Journal of Social Work*, 47(1), 48–67, https://doi.org/10.1093/bjsw/bcw149.

Borenstein, J., Frederico, M., & McNamara, P. (2021, March). Creating "deep knowledge" and transformative change: A critical social work approach to researching formal kinship care. *British Journal of Social Work*, 51(2), 733–751, https://doi.org/10.1093/bjsw/bcaa173.

Bozalek, V., & Pease, B. (2021). *Post-anthropocentric social work: Critical posthuman and new materialist perspectives*. London: Routledge.

Caron, R., Ou Jin Lee, E., & Sansfaçon, A. P. (2020). Transformative disruptions and collective knowledge building: Social work professors building anti-oppressive ethical frameworks for research, teaching, practice and activism. *Ethics and Social Welfare*, 14(3), 298–314, https://doi.org/10.1080/17496535.2020.1749690.

Clarke, K., & Yellow Bird, M. (2021). *Decolonizing pathways towards integrative healing in social work*. London: Routledge.

Collini, S. (2012). *What are universities for?* London: Penguin.

Comerford, S. A. (2005). Engaging through learning—learning through engaging: An alternative approach to professional learning about human diversity. Social Work Education, 24(1), 113–135, https://doi.org/10.1080/0261547052000325017.

Comerford, S. A. (2008). The challenge of providing culturally and linguistically accessible human services in rural and increasingly diverse communities: A case example from a small New England state. *Journal of Immigrant and Refugee Studies*, 4(3), 97–114, https://doi.org/10.1300/J500v04n03_05.

Comerford, S. A. (2018). An autoethnography of a neurotypical adoptive mother's journey through adoption into the world(s) of intellectual variety in the early years of the U.S. education system. *Qualitative Social Work*, 18(5), 772–786, https://doi.org/10.1177/1473325018766708.

Cranton, P., & Taylor, E. W. (2012). Transformative learning theory: Seeking a more unified theory. In E. W. Taylor, P. Cranton, & Associates (Eds.), *The handbook of transformative learning* (pp. 3–20). San Francisco: Jossey-Bass.

Dewees, M. (2005a). *Contemporary social work practice*. New York: Routledge.

Dewees, M. (2005b). Postmodern social work in interdisciplinary contexts. *Social Work in Health Care*, 39(3), 343–360, https://doi.org/10.1300/J010v39n03_08.

Docherty, T. (2011). *For the university*. London: Bloomsbury.

Fook, J. (1993). *Radical casework*. Sydney: Allen & Unwin.

Fook, J. (2002). *Social work: Critical theory and practice*. London: Sage.

Fook, J. (2012) *Social Work: A Critical Approach to Practice* 2nd ed. London: Sage

Fook, J. (2016) *Social Work: A Critical Approach to Practice* 3rd London: Sage

Fook, J. (2023). *Social work: A critical approach to practice*, 4th ed. London: Sage.

Gergen, K.J. (1994) *Realities and Relationships: Soundings in Social Constructionism*. Cambridge, Harvard University Press,

hooks, b. (1981). Ain't I a woman? Black women and feminism. Boston: South End.

hooks, b. (1984). Feminist theory: From margin to center. Boston: South End.

hooks, b. (1990). Yearning: Race, gender, and cultural politics. Boston: South End.

Ife, J. (1997). *Re-thinking social work: Towards critical practice*. Melbourne: Addison-Wesley Longman.

Jordan, J. (1985). *On call: Political essays*. Boston: South End.

Jordan, J. (1992). *Technical difficulties: African-American notes on the state of the union*. New York: Pantheon.

Jordan, J. (1993). *Technical difficulties: New political essays*. Trafalgar Square.

Lather, P. (1991). Deconstructing/Deconstructive Inquiry: The politics of knowing and being known. *Educational Theory*, 41(2), 153–173.

McNamee, S., & Moscheta, M. (2015, Fall). Relational intelligence and collaborative learning. *New Directions for Teaching and Learning, 2015*(143), 25–40. https://doi.org/10.1002/tl.20134.

Pease, B., & Fook, J. (Eds.). (1999). *Transforming social work practice: Postmodern critical perspectives*. Sydney: Allen & Unwin.

Piven, F., & Cloward, R. (1971). *Regulating the poor: The functions of public welfare*. New York: Pantheon.

Piven, F., & Cloward., R. (1977). *Poor people's movements: Why they succeed, how they fail*. New York: Pantheon.

Roche, S. E. (2007). Postmodern call and response in the modernist university. In S. Witkin & D. Saleebey (Eds.), *Transforming social work: Re-shaping the canon in inquiry, practice, and education*. Washington, DC: Council on Social Work Education.

Roche, S. E., Dewees, M., Trailweaver, R., Alexander, S., Cuddy, C., & Hady, M. (Eds.). (1999). *Contesting boundaries in social work education*. Washington DC: Council on Social Work Education.

Schott, E., & Weiss, E. L. (2015). *Transformative social work practice*. London: Sage.

Stone, C., & Harbin, F. (2016). *Transformative learning for social work*. London: Palgrave.

Taylor, E. W. (2009). Fostering transformative learning. In J. Mezirow, E. W. Taylor, & Associates (Eds.), *Transformative learning in practice* (pp. 3–17). San Francisco: Jossey-Bass.

University of Vermont Social Work Department. (2010). *Master of Social Work self-study*. Submitted to the Council on Social Work Education as part of program reaccreditation.

Webb, S. (2019). Critical social work and the politics of transformation. In S. Webb (Ed.), *The Routledge handbook of critical social work* (pp. xxx–xliv). London: Routledge.

Witkin, S. L. (2011). *Social construction and social work practice: Interpretations and innovations*. New York: Columbia University Press.

Witkin, S. L. (Ed.). (2014). *Narrating social work through autoethnography*. New York: Columbia University Press.

Witkin, S. L. (2017). *Transforming social work: Social constructionist reflections on contemporary and enduring issues*. London: Palgrave.

Witkin, S. L., & Saleebey, D. (2007). *Social work dialogues: Transforming the canon in inquiry, practice, and education*. Washington, DC: Council on Social Work Education.

1

REVISITING TRANSFORMATIVE
THINKING IN SOCIAL WORK

ANNA GUPTA

T his chapter explores two contemporary examples of transformative thinking in social work: the Poverty Aware Paradigm (PAP) (Krumer-Nevo, 2020) and the Capability Approach (CA) (Sen, 2005; Nussbaum, 2011). As a British academic, I do not regularly use the term *transformative social work*; the terms more commonly used in the United Kingdom are *critical social work* and *anti-oppressive practice*. I have identified the PAP and CA as transformative approaches as they both, in complementary ways, further our understanding of social work that promotes social justice and human rights. A theme linking these two approaches is that of poverty. This is the central reason that I developed my academic interest in both these approaches, and I include in this chapter reflection on my journey in understanding the transformative potential of these two approaches. My professional and academic interest is in child and family social work, and this chapter focuses on the application of these approaches to child protection work in England. I start by reflecting on why two contemporary transformative approaches are needed to reinvigorate attention to poverty in social work debates in the first half of the twenty-first century.

Social work has always been defined by its focus on individuals within their social contexts. However, the relationship between an individual and society and whether personal problems should be understood in terms of individual factors, social problems, or a combination of the two have been and continue to be highly contested. Hardy (2015) argues that individual-ism and social reform have vied for prominence throughout the history of social work and that the debates have been influenced by wider poli-cies. Evans (2015), drawing on the work of C. Wright Mills (1959), traces this back to debates surrounding the origins of social work in the United Kingdom in the late nineteenth century, when the Charities Organisation Society (COS) viewed poverty as a private problem, a tragedy, or a per-sonal failing requiring individualized support or guidance, whereas the settlement movement saw poverty as a public issue, a reflection of social disadvantage amenable to social and political action.

These debates, always present in social work discourses, have come to the fore once again in the years following the global financial crisis of 2008. The neoliberal project of relying on individual responsibility and self-sufficiency, reducing the welfare state, and opening opportunities for competition in a free market was well underway prior to 2008 (Hardy, 2015). Following the financial crisis, however, many countries across the world implemented stringent "austerity" policies, increasing poverty and hardship for many marginalized individuals and families, with the bank-ing crisis providing an "alibi" for "wide-ranging, radical and ambitious reforms" as part of this ideological project (Hall, 2011, p. 21). Wacquant (2010) argues that the small-state ideology of neoliberalism is leading to more intensive and punitive interventions in the lives of some marginal-ized groups that is "not a deviation from, but a constituent component of, the neo-liberal leviathan" (p. 201). The relationship between the state and those who are marginalized is therefore characterized by both intrusive and neglectful responses, creating high challenge/low support social envi-ronments (Wacquant, 2010). Social work has not been immune to these developments, with supportive roles being increasingly replaced by more punitive surveillance, primarily of people living in challenging socioeco-nomic circumstances (Cummins, 2016).

What happened within the English child protection system exempli-fied Wacquant's ideas about punishing the poor. In "austerity" England in the second decade of the twenty-first century, many families were having their welfare benefits cut and children's centers, youth clubs, and other family support services were closing, while at the same time the number of children on child protection plans and in out-of-home care was increas-ing (Featherstone et al., 2018). The work of the Child Welfare Inequalities

Project (CWIP) demonstrated a clear link between deprivation and a child's chances of being on a child protection plan or in out-of-home care (Bywaters, 2016). However, poverty remained the "elephant in the room" (Gupta, 2017), with tackling poverty and inequality not considered "core business" for child protection social workers or policy makers; the profession itself had incorporated "wider social and political discourses about the failing poor and the toxicity of needs" (Morris et al., 2018, p. 370). Academics in other countries, including New Zealand, the United States, Australia, and Israel, similarly argued that child welfare and protection systems were not only insufficiently resourced but also harmful and discriminatory, mainly toward society's most marginalized and deprived families (Dettlaff et al., 2020; Keddell, 2018; Saar-Heiman & Gupta, 2020).

In this context, I undertook research exploring the impact of poverty on children and families and their experiences of the child protection system, with the aim of facilitating more humane and socially just policies and practices. One of the projects, a participatory research project with ATD Fourth World, an international anti-poverty human rights organization, involved workshops bringing families living in poverty who had experienced child protection interventions together in dialogue with social work practitioners and academics. The family members spoke about shaming processes associated with living in poverty and how these were compounded by punitive child protection responses, how fear and blame permeated the system, and how material hardship and poor housing went unacknowledged (Gupta et al., 2018).

Discussions with professional audiences regarding poverty and child protection met some resistance and criticism. To some critics, we were stigmatizing people in poverty; to others, including the government minister responsible for children's services at the time, we were "excusing" parents for abuse and neglect of their children (Gove, 2013). However, many social workers shared a similar disquiet about how families in poverty were experiencing the child protection system, recognizing the harm of poverty and related structural inequalities but feeling powerless to address them. Over the past few years, and particularly since the pandemic that shone light on a British society riven with deeply entrenched structural inequalities (Marmot et al., 2020), there has been a much more positive reception to the idea that poverty matters; however, in the face of continuing severe constraints on resources, there remains much fatalism as to what social workers can do about it. Both the PAP and the CA offered ways of thinking beyond poverty as a structural problem, a macro issue, to one that social workers undertaking casework can utilize to develop transformative practice.

THE POVERTY AWARE PARADIGM

The PAP was developed in Israel by Professor Krumer-Nevo with the aim of constructing a comprehensive theoretical framework to challenge the individualistic and conservative ideology dominating policy, research, and practice regarding poverty (Krumer-Nevo, 2020). The PAP offers theoretical, ethical, and practical principles for social work with families living in poverty. The paradigm has three interrelated parts—ontology (what is the nature of poverty?), epistemology (what kind of knowledge is needed when working with people in poverty?), and axiology (where should a social worker position herself ethically when working with people in poverty?)—that together influence and are influenced by practice (Krumer-Nevo, 2016).

When addressing the ontological questions, PAP challenges the conservative paradigm so dominant in social work that views "poverty as the sum product of the psychological, moral, behavioural and cultural pathologies or deficits of poor people" (Krumer-Nevo, 2016, p. 1795). Instead, PAP builds on and extends a structural analysis of poverty not only as a lack of material and social capital, such as adequate housing, health care, and education, but also as a lack of symbolic capital, manifested in stigmatization, discrimination, "othering," and lack of voice (Lister, 2004). PAP regards poverty as a violation of human rights. People in poverty are perceived in PAP as resisting poverty in daily decisions, in explicit and implicit ways. What can seem from the outside a poor choice or decision may in fact be rational or adaptive in the context of insufficient and precarious resources (Krumer-Nevo, 2020). For me, this resonated with the narratives of the ATD Fourth World families when they spoke about the psychological as well as the material impact of poverty on their lives and how their struggles, skills, and contributions so often go unrecognized (ATD Fourth World, 2019).

According to the PAP framework, poverty is a material predicament that has strong relational and symbolic components. Drawing on the work of Lister (2004, 2013), Krumer-Nevo developed the wheel of poverty. The first or inner circle represents poverty as a lack of material capital. The second or middle circle represents the lack of social capital as a result of unequal and unjust distribution, resulting in limited social opportunities. The third or outer circle relates to poverty as a lack of symbolic capital, manifested in the dehumanization and "othering" of people in poverty. (Krumer-Nevo, 2016). Lister (2013, p. 112) describes poverty as being not only material disadvantage and economic insecurity but also "a shameful social relation, corrosive of human dignity and flourishing, which is experienced in interactions with the wider society and in the way people in poverty are talked about and treated by politicians, officials, professionals, the media, and sometimes academics." The inclusion of relational and symbolic aspects in the definition of poverty adopted by PAP highlights the micro level of poor people's everyday experiences, in which they feel the effects of power and powerlessness. One mother from ATD Fourth World summarized her experiences of parenting in poverty under the gaze of social work services:

> Poverty is living day to day and making ends meet. The money you have is not enough to provide for your kids. My daughter was bullied at school for her clothes and not having the right fashions; she stopped attending school and I was threatened with prison. I don't like borrowing from family and friends so I asked for help from social services. Then a social worker came around, checked my cupboards and made me feel I had done the wrong thing by asking for help. (Gupta, Blumhardt, & ATD Fourth World, 2016, p. 164)

This understanding of the symbolic violence people in poverty experience implicates social workers. Practice within the PAP framework requires critical reflection on how practices can perpetuate (and resist) dominant discourses that encourage us to see people in poverty as "them—not like us," compounding shame and humiliation. The PAP regards active rights-based advocacy as a crucial strategy to address the lack of symbolic capital that many families in poverty experience, challenging views that this can create dependency (Krumer-Nevo, 2020).

Adopting a poverty lens can open possibilities for questioning taken-for-granted assumptions and create social work practices that promote rights.

In relation to epistemology, the PAP takes a critical constructivist approach that focuses on reality being socially constructed within contextual power relationships and processes (Krumer-Nevo, 2016). Working within the PAP entails social workers creating relationship-based knowledge, with power relationships as the context in which reality and knowledge are constructed. Workers need to acknowledge and question the different status of knowledge of professionals compared to that of families living in poverty, and how this reflects material and symbolic power differentials. According to the PAP, to understand service users' subjective experiences, social workers should gather knowledge through diverse interactions in the real context of their lives (Saar-Heiman & Krumer-Nevo, 2020). This involves incorporating an understanding of how poverty and other intersecting structural inequalities, such as race, gender, and disability, frame the lives of clients in the context of the communities in which they live.

In relation to axiology, the premise of PAP emphasizes the ethics of solidarity. As Krumer-Nevo (2016, p. 1802) explains, "solidarity is achieved through an active effort to include the other in the 'we', based on the acknowledgement of the differences between us in terms of power, history and social position" and requires specific awareness of the effects of power and othering on professional practice. Pervasive views, perpetuated by neoliberal politicians and the right-wing media, that blame individuals for their poverty can make solidarity with service users challenging. However, paradoxically, "standing by" can make disagreeing and being critical easier and more effective as service users feel cared about and the contexts of their lives better understood (Krumer-Nevo, 2016). Aiming to connect the material and emotional aspects of life through a combination of relationship-based and rights-based practice is central to the PAP.

Participants in the ATD Fourth World workshops noted the importance of such relationships:

> If actually you've got at least one person in authority that you feel is on your side and who does recognise you, that actually can be quite a turning point.

Social workers are perhaps one of the most intimate relationships [individuals] have with the state, and it's someone who has a lot of power over them . . . if that person is not treating them with recognition and respect, what it's doing to their self-esteem, their sense of themselves, regardless of the success of the social work relationship, is actually terribly damaging. It's reinforcing all the negative stuff they're seeing in the media or hear politicians talk. (Gupta et al., 2018, pp. 254–255)

The PAP is a generic framework for social work with any client group. Together with Dr. Saar-Heiman, I explored what it might mean for child protection practice, where risk dominates and children's rights are often juxtaposed against parents' rights. The Poverty Aware Paradigm for Child Protection (PAPCP) is an analytical framework that rejects the dominant risk paradigm in child protection, in which risks to children are seen as located within individual families and caused by actions of parents or guardians, with little attention to the social and economic contexts of families' lives (Saar-Heiman & Gupta, 2020).

From an ontological perspective, PAPCP takes a wider view of risks to children's well-being to include social harms and policies and practices that contribute to such harms. Poverty affects all dimensions of children's development and needs to be viewed as societal neglect that requires redistributive national economic and social policies, along with a child protection system that actively engages with family poverty. A review of the literature on the relationship between poverty and child abuse and neglect, updated in 2022, highlights how economic conditions are inextricably connected to parental problems such as mental health, substance misuse, and domestic abuse (Bywaters & Skinner, 2022). Poverty works directly through material hardship or lack of money and indirectly through parental stress and neighborhood conditions (Bywaters et al., 2016). Poverty is not a background factor or "the wallpaper of practice" (Morris et al., 2018) but is implicated in innumerable ways in the lives of families and the decisions made every day by social workers. These ideas about systemic causation require us to move away from models of assessment that focus on individual blame and responsibility and to think in contextual, interactional, and dynamic ways about families' lives (Featherstone et al., 2018). An activist from ATD Fourth World explains:

> I am supporting a couple of families where, being aware of social work practice, it's clear that there is material deprivation, but there's also severe depression from the mother and that is raising questions over whether she can look after the children. So it's not clear cut what the issues are at play there. If the child is taken away, no one will say because of material deprivation, but will say that the mother can't cope because of mental health. But it's not that simple, there are many factors building up and material deprivation can play a huge role. Parents are judged because of the way they are suffering for things sparked by material deprivation. (Gupta et al., 2016, p. 169)

PAPCP similarly draws upon a critical constructionist approach to knowledge, where the interrelatedness of power and knowledge is highlighted and "risk" placed within a social context (Saar-Heiman & Gupta, 2020). Some of the suggestions made for practice within a PAPCP include:

- Recognizing the importance of values, ethics, and human rights, with social workers needing to ask themselves: What are my values and beliefs regarding poverty? What are the implications for my practice?
- Developing an understanding of lived experiences, spending time in homes and communities
- Incorporating social and economic contexts into all assessments and interventions in ways that recognize the complex interrelationships among poverty, other intersecting forms of structural inequalities such as racism, and problems facing the individual members and family—a nuanced multifactor analysis
- Providing practical help and proactive advocacy, recognizing the connections between the material and the emotional
- Recognizing and challenging "microaggressions"—often small, seemingly innocuous, shaming and othering practices
- Maintaining a relationships-based practice that acknowledges macro-level power dynamics and their impact on micro-level interventions—on the relationship with the social worker but also with family, friendship networks, and community

On an organizational level, recommendations include undertaking an audit, ideally with families, that aims to "poverty-proof" policies and practices. Wider transformative change is also encouraged through policy practice, working alongside families in poverty to raise awareness and coconstruct knowledge and services. PAPCP offers a wider political and social justice agenda for deconstructing risk (Saar-Heiman & Gupta, 2020).

In summary, based on an understanding of the political nature of the knowledge construction and interpersonal encounters between social workers and service users, PAP and PAPCP propose possibilities for transformative social work practice within a social justice and human rights framework. As Boone, Roets, and Roose (2018, p. 12) state:

> Social work has to take on an active role in challenging injustices in the different domains of social justice by engaging in reframing and projecting individual and collective concerns and lifeworlds of people in poverty from the private sphere of commodities and market relations, on the one hand, and family and personal relations, on the other, into the public forum of political debate.

THE CAPABILITY APPROACH

Whereas the Poverty Aware Paradigm was developed as a transformative approach for social work, the Capability Approach (CA) was conceived by the Nobel prize–winning economist Amartya Sen and further developed by the feminist philosopher Martha Nussbaum. It provides a theoretical framework concerning well-being, human development, and social justice. The CA has been incorporated into academic and policy discourses in development studies and other disciplines, with some consideration beginning to be given to its relevance to social work. The CA recognizes that people are not equally placed to realize their capabilities because of structural inequalities such as class, race, gender, and disabilities, and tackling these is central to the CA's theory of social justice (Carpenter, 2009).

My thinking about how the CA could offer transformative possibilities for social work with children and families also began with my interest in understanding the experiences of families living in poverty and developing more effective and humane practices of working with them. The CA offers a framework that clearly establishes the structural basis for poverty and challenges neoliberal ideas that blame individuals for their socioeconomic circumstances. Within the CA, poverty is regarded as a capability depriver because it interferes with a person's ability to make valued choices and participate fully in society (Sen, 1999). Like the PAP, the CA places centrally the need to acknowledge both the material and the affective consequences of poverty and inequality. Poverty is not just a lack of material resources; as Sen explains, it leads to the deprivation of certain basic capabilities, "from such elementary physical ones as being well nourished, being adequately clothed and sheltered, avoiding preventable morbidity, and so forth, to more complex social achievements such as taking part in the life of the community, being able to appear in public without shame" (Sen, 1995, p. 15). Shame is individually felt but socially constructed, imposed on people in poverty by dominant discourses and dealings with others, including public services (Chase & Walker, 2013).

The CA calls for consideration of the role of social institutions in contributing to the development of individual freedoms or "capabilities" to live the life the person values and has reason to value (Sen, 2009). People differ in their ability to convert means into valuable opportunities (capabilities) or outcomes (functionings). Even with the same set of personal means, differences in one's capabilities to function can arise for a variety of reasons, or "conversion factors," including personal, sociostructural, cultural, and institutional factors (Robeyns, 2005). The CA is predicated upon a contextual notion of causality that is flexible enough to incorporate both individual and social causes into social analysis (Smith & Seward, 2009). As opposed to a very narrow view on the prevention of harm, the CA focuses on the promotion of human dignity and flourishing: the capabilities that people have to choose between different kinds of life that they may value and have reason to value. The CA provides a lens for poverty analysis that emphasizes its ethical dimension, stressing the intrinsic importance of the promotion of people's capabilities as part of a broad theory of social justice that promotes human dignity for all.

The CA highlights that whether individuals have certain capabilities depends not only on individual features like skills and competences but also on the external conditions in which they find themselves—the norms, institutions, and social structures that provide the context and influence their ideas and actions (Nussbaum, 2011). An analysis of the child protection system in England based on the CA suggested that policies that increase poverty and inequality serve to reduce the means available to families, while cuts to local authority and community-based family support services diminish conversion factors that would enhance capabilities in these adverse circumstances. Families involved in the child protection and family court systems then face a "triple jeopardy" of punitive practices that fail to recognize the socioeconomic context of their lives (Gupta, Featherstone, & White, 2016). The analysis suggested an urgent need for a refocusing of the relationship between agency and structure, so that parenting practices are not reduced to simple assessments of poor choices but families' lives, as well as policy and practice responses, are contextualized. While there is a need for the state to impose limits on some parental rights and freedoms to protect the capabilities and rights of children, social institutions also have a responsibility to promote children's and parents' human rights (Nussbaum & Dixon, 2012).

The capability for "voice" is an important concept in the CA. On an individual level, the CA proposes an understanding of empowerment as the process of expanding an individual's well-being, freedom, or set of valuable capabilities to live the life they value and have reason to value (Keleher, 2014). According to the CA, capability necessarily involves having agency and opportunities to influence decisions and circumstances that affect one's own life and, as Hickle (2020) argues, is central to the development of trauma-informed practices that promote well-being and flourishing. The CA distinguishes between power *over* others and power *with* others; it encourages relational thinking about people and their capabilities (Entwistle & Watt, 2013), valuing individuals' and families' strengths, hopes, and aspirations. What would not only help them to parent their children safely but also enable them to flourish?

The lack of family members' voice in child protection processes leads to a sense that they are being treated as "less than human" (Smithson & Gibson, 2017). In the ATD Fourth World workshops, child protection meetings were highlighted as spaces where parents felt particularly powerless and voiceless. One participant explained: "You sit at the table and listen, but you are not allowed a choice or an input that's going to have any impact. So you are sat there observing what everyone else is doing with your life, and your children's lives on the basis of strangers around the table. It is degrading, humiliating. Everything is taken away from you" (Gupta et al., 2015, p. 137).

Sen's (1992) notion of "informational basis of judgement in justice," or IBJ, emphasizes the selection of some sources of information over others and how facts and values are entwined in the design and implementation of public policies. From a social policy perspective, Bonvin (2014, p. 240) argues that the CA requires championing "the capability for voice of those who are all too often excluded from public discussion, especially the most disadvantaged and vulnerable as socio-economic inequalities often translate into participative inequalities." In relation to child protection policy and practice, attention must be paid to whose voices are privileged in policy making and practice decisions, with the aim of promoting participation as intrinsically and instrumentally valuable. In recent years, much has been learned from successful participatory approaches such as children-in-care councils and parent advocacy programs (e.g., Thomas & Percy-Smith, 2012; Tobis, 2013).

In summary, the CA has the potential to offer an overarching framework for socially just policy and social work practice development that challenges the ascent of neoliberalism and the individualization of risk and, therefore, warrants further attention (Den Braber, 2014). As a normative framework for social work practice consistent with the "Global Definition of Social Work" (International Federation of Social Workers, 2014), the CA has the potential to offer the following:

- A conceptual framework for social work—the goal of social work being the promotion of well-being, capabilities, and human dignity, not just a narrow remit of protection from harm
- A theory for ethical practice—facilitating questioning and dialogue by social workers such as: Why am I doing what I am doing? How does my use of power promote or diminish capabilities?
- A qualitative evaluative instrument: Is what I am doing in practice effective in terms of improving well-being and capabilities?
- A multidimensional framework predicated upon a contextual notion of causality—a framework that incorporates both individual and social causes into social analysis

- Relational rather than individualistic thinking about people and their capabilities—an understanding that capabilities are dynamically shaped by interactions between individuals and their environments, including their social relationships

CONCLUSION

In this chapter I have explored two contemporary examples of transformative thinking in social work: the Poverty Aware Paradigm (PAP) and the Capability Approach (CA). The discussion has focused on child protection policy and practice, primarily in England. However, both approaches have relevance and, I would argue, much to offer social work within a social justice framework across different organizational settings and service user groups. Specifically in relation to work with individuals and families in poverty, both approaches recognize the material and affective impact of poverty, the social construction of shame, and the role of social institutions in mitigating the impact of poverty and promoting well-being and human rights. Both approaches require attention to power in professional relationships and the coproduction of knowledge and services with marginalized individuals, families, and communities.

REFERENCES

ATD Fourth World. (2019). *Understanding poverty in all its forms.* https://atd-uk.org/projects-campaigns/understanding-poverty/.

Boone, K., Roets, G., & Roose, R. (2018). Social work, participation, and poverty. *British Journal of Social Work, 48*(8), 2381–2399.

Bonvin, J. P. (2014). Towards a more critical appraisal of social policies: The contribution of the capability approach. In H.-U. Otto & H. Ziegler (Eds.), *Critical social policy and the capability approach.* Leverkusen, Germany: Barbara Budrich, 231–248.

Bywaters, P. (2016). Inequalities in child welfare: Towards a new policy, research and action agenda. *British Journal of Social Work, 45*(1), 6–23.

Bywaters, P., Bunting, L., Davidson, G., Hanratty, J., Mason, W., McCartan, C., & Steils, N. (2016). *The relationship between poverty, child abuse and neglect: An evidence review.* York, UK: Joseph Rowntree Foundation.

Bywaters, P., & Skinner, G. (with Cooper, A., Kennedy, E., & Malik, A.). (2022) *The relationship between poverty and child abuse and neglect: New evidence.* London: Nuffield Foundation.

Carpenter, M. (2009). The capabilities approach and critical social policy: Lessons from the majority world? *Critical Social Policy, 29*(3), 351–373.

Chase, E., & Walker, R. (2013). The co-construction of shame in the context of poverty: Beyond a threat to the social bond. *Sociology, 47*(4), 739–754.

Cummins, I. (2016). Reading Wacquant: Social work and advanced marginality. *European Journal of Social Work, 19*(2), pp. 263–274.

Dean, H. (2013). The translation of needs into rights: Reconceptualising social citizenship as a global phenomenon. *International Journal of Social Welfare, 22*(S1), S32–49.

Den Braber, C. (2014). The introduction of the capability approach in social work across a neoliberal Europe. *Journal of Social Intervention: Theory and Practice, 22*(4), 61–77.

Dettlaff, A. J., Weber, K., Pendleton, M., Boyd, R., Bettencourt, B., & Burton, L. (2020). It is not a broken system, it is a system that needs to be broken: The upEND movement to abolish the child welfare system *Journal of Public Child Welfare, 14*(5), 500–517.

Entwistle, V. A., & Watt, I. S. (2013). Treating patients as persons: A capabilities approach to support delivery of person-centered care. *American Journal of Bioethics, 13*(8), 28–39.

Evans, T. (2015). Introduction: Policy and social work. In T. Evans & F. Keating (Eds.), *Policy and social work practice.* London: Sage, 11–21.

Featherstone, B. Gupta, A., Morris, K., & White, S. (2018). *Protecting children: A social model.* Bristol, UK: Policy Press.

Gupta, A. (2017). Poverty and child neglect—the elephant in the room? *Families, Relationships and Societies, 6*(1), 21–36.

Gupta, A., & ATD Fourth World. (2015). Poverty and shame: Messages for social work. *Critical and Radical Social Work, 3*(1), 131–139.

Gupta, A., Blumhardt, H., & ATD Fourth World. (2016). Giving poverty a voice: Families' experiences of social work practice in a risk-averse system. *Families, Relationships and Societies, 5*(1), 163–172.

Gupta, A., Blumhardt, H., & ATD Fourth World. (2018). Poverty, exclusion and child protection practice: The contribution of "the politics of recognition & respect." *European Journal of Social Work, 21*(2), 247–259.

Gupta, A., Featherstone, B., & White, S. (2016). Reclaiming humanity: From capacities to capabilities in understanding parenting in adversity. *British Journal of Social Work, 46*(2), 339–354.

Gove, M. (2013). Getting it right for children in need. Speech to the NSPCC. https://www.gov .uk/government/speeches/getting-it-right-for-children-in-need-speech-to-the-nspcc.

Hall, S. (2011). The neo-liberal revolution. *Soundings, 48*, 9–27.

Hardy, M. (2015). Discretion in the history and development of social work. In T. Evans & F. Keating (Eds.), *Policy and social work practice.* London: Sage, 22–43.

Hickle, K. (2020). Introducing a trauma-informed capability approach in youth services. *Children & Society, 34*(6), 537–551.

International Federation of Social Workers (2014). *Global Definition of the Social Work Profession.* Available at: https://www.ifsw.org/what-is-social-work/global-definition-of-social-work/.

Keddell, E. (2018). The vulnerable child in neoliberal contexts: The construction of children in the Aotearoa New Zealand child protection reforms. *Childhood, 25*(1), 93–108.

Keleher, L. (2014). 'Sen and Nussbaum: Agency and capability expansion. *Ethics and Economics, 11*(2), 54–70.

Krumer-Nevo, M. (2016). Poverty-aware social work: A paradigm for social work practice with people in poverty. *British Journal of Social Work, 46*(6), 1793–1808.

Krumer-Nevo, M. (2020). *Radical hope: Poverty-aware practice for social work.* Bristol, UK: Policy Press.

Lister, R. (2004). *Poverty.* Cambridge: Polity Press.

Lister, R. (2013). Power, not pity: Poverty and human rights. *Ethics and Social Welfare, 7*(2), 109–123.

Marmot, M., Allen, J., Goldblatt, P., Herd, E., & Morrison, J. (2020). *Build back fairer: The COVID-19 Marmot Review.* www.health.org.uk/publications/build-back-fairer-the-covid-19-marmot-review.

Mills, C. W. (1959). *The sociological imagination.* New York: Oxford University Press.

Morris, K., Mason, W., Bywaters, P., Featherstone, B., Daniel, B., Brady, G., Bunting, L., Hooper, J., Mirza, N., Scourfield, J., & Webb, C. (2018). Social work, poverty, and child welfare interventions. *Child & Family Social Work, 23*(3), 364–372.

Nussbaum, M. (2011). *Creating capabilities: The human development approach.* Cambridge, MA: Harvard University Press.

Nussbaum, M., & Dixon, R. (2012). Children's rights and a capabilities approach: The question of special priority. *Public Law & Legal Theory Working Papers No. 384.* Chicago: University of Chicago Law School.

Robeyns, I. (2005) The capability approach: A theoretical survey. *Journal of Human Development, 6*(1), 93–117.

Saar-Heiman, Y., & Gupta, A. (2020). The poverty-aware paradigm for child protection: A critical framework for policy and practice. *British Journal of Social Work, 50*(4), 1167–1184.

Saar-Heiman, Y., & Krumer-Nevo, M. (2020). "You decide": Relationship-based knowledge and parents' participation in high-risk child protection crisis interventions. *British Journal of Social Work, 50*(6), 1743–1757.

Sen, A. (1992). *Inequality reexamined.* New Delhi: Oxford University Press.

Sen, A. (1995). The political economy of targeting. In D. Van de Walle and K. Nead (Eds.), *Public spending and the poor* (pp. 11–24). Washington, DC: World Bank.

Sen, A. (1999). *Development as freedom.* Oxford: Oxford University Press.

Sen, A. (2005). Human rights and capabilities. *Journal of Human Development, 6*(2), 151–166.

Sen, A. (2009). *The idea of justice.* London: Allen Lane.

Smith, M. L., & Seward, C. (2009). The relational ontology of Amartya Sen's capability approach: Incorporating social and individual causes. *Journal of Human Development and Capabilities, 10*(2), 213–235.

Smithson, R., & Gibson, M. (2017). Less than human: A qualitative study into the experience of parents involved in the child protection system. *Child & Family Social Work, 22*(2), 565–574.

Thomas, N., & Percy-Smith, B. (2012). "It's about changing services and building relationships": Evaluating the development of Children in Care Councils. *Child & Family Social Work*, *17*(4), 487–496.

Tobis, D. (2013). *From pariahs to partners: How parents and their allies changed New York City's child welfare system*. Oxford: Oxford University Press.

Wacquant L. (2010). Crafting the neoliberal state: Workfare, prisonfare, and social insecurity. *Sociological Forum*, *25*(2), pp.197–220.

2

TRANSFORMATIVE SOCIAL WORK CONTRIBUTIONS AT THE EXECUTIVE LEVEL

WANDA HEADING-GRANT AND JAN FOOK

Social workers possess a range of skills and orientations that translate well into other roles. Social work is an interdisciplinary profession that functions at many different levels, and it is important to document how a social work orientation might be practiced at senior levels in the university. Academic practice, after all, extends all the way to the top, yet many social workers seem little aware of how management, including senior management, roles can be performed in ways that are informed by social work values and make use of social work skills. Additionally, being relational is the key to being transformative, especially in relation to diversity, equity, inclusion, and belonging (Brown, 2018).

Perhaps our focus on client work and direct practice trains our gaze toward student-related work rather than toward the organization (especially at top levels) that provides the service that sustains the environment that frames the experiences of individual staff, students, and faculty.

In this chapter, therefore, we attempt to extend the gaze of a transformative social work lens to the top of the university as an organization. The chapter presents the thinking of Wanda Heading-Grant, a woman of Black/African American heritage who has held senior executive positions at the University of Vermont (UVM) and now Carnegie Mellon University (CMU). Wanda offered her views in a conversation with Jan, and here we present her thoughts in answer to some key questions.

Jan: *Tell me what "transformative social work" means to you.*

I think the age-old social work adage of "starting where people are at" comes to mind first of all. Asking what people's strengths are and how you do things with, not to, people are important starting questions in a transformative approach. This also involves leading, following, listening, caring, empathizing, and simply inviting the person you want to support into the process with you. The person you are trying to support gets to "pick the menu at the table" once they are invited to the table. I like to use the term *moving the needle*, which is what we are trying to do in being transformative. Another way of putting it is that to move the needle, people are invited to the party and they also get to dance—this is "inclusive excellence," especially if they get to dance the way they want to, and develop the playlist. It is also true belonging: eventually they can own going to the next step. I believe that using a strengths-based approach in doing inclusion and equity work can be transcending. A strengths-based approach, as we know it in social work (Saleeby, 2013), focuses on the strengths that clients possess rather than pathologizing them or the problems they experience. This is similar to the transformational approach of asset framing, which doesn't look at what we think are someone's challenges or assume deficits about them but rather focuses on their values. This transformational approach, highlighted by thought leaders such as the late Ralph Ellison (1964) and Trabian Shorters (2015), can leverage and multiply reach and outcome, especially when dealing with matters of social justice and equity.

Jan: Tell me about your leadership roles and how they developed?

I started my early career as a social worker and worked briefly in clinical social work, although I had an interest in working with older people, an interest I had noticed in the presence of older people in my own family. I came to UVM because Counseling and Psychology Services wanted a clinical social worker; I applied because the work schedule would be more accommodating to supporting my spiritual background (I was a committed member of my church). I was hired; however, I found this work not as stimulating as my earlier hospital work, partly because it was not as crisis focused. Around that time, I was second-guessing the change from working in a hospital to working in a higher education setting. UVM was interested in hiring someone with a social work background in the Affirmative Action and Equal Opportunity Office, and this work appealed to me, especially as they clearly wanted to hire someone who could listen, triage a situation quickly, and make people feel valued. I felt that my skills and mindset were a perfect fit for the assistant director's job.

I then served as interim director of the AAEO when the director left, knowing the AAEO business was very helpful in advancing my career. I particularly liked this work as I could be relational and see where systems were broken to effect change. I became the permanent executive director after successfully leading the institution through an important audit. That change in direction from clinical to administrative work led to a few other positions at the university. As politics within and outside the university shifted, it was decided to appoint a vice president for human resources, diversity, equity and inclusion responsible for areas such as AA/EO, benefits, compensation, labor relations, identity centers, and professional development. When I took on this position, it was a major shift for me. It rapidly expanded my sphere of influence (I had a team of fifty-eight people), and it meant I could have a different kind of impact on critical climate and personnel matters, such as health care, retirement, sexual harassment processes, and employee assistance programs. This role expanded my ability to get things done more quickly. I was responsible for several job duties related to organizational development, recruitment and staffing, employment law, performance management, employee relations, and compensation and benefits. In addition, I provided management, leadership, and direction to the HR staff, supporting one of my core values, "people first."

That position had a significant impact on where I am now as chief diversity officer for Carnegie Mellon University (CMU). In this position, much of the work is the same and much of it is different—different colleagues, private versus public, more of an urban setting, and the position was a newly created one. I see my success as being very much about relationships—about making people feel they are valued and showing care; for example, I would send personal notes to people after an event. Showing respect for others and upholding them as human beings goes a long way, especially when working to move the needle on inclusive excellence.

Since starting at CMU, I have been reflecting more on my approach. When I value people's strengths, I think about cultural humility— understanding my own cultural background but also valuing and welcome other people's culture, which is just as important to them. I try to be self-reflective and critical of myself but also to model self-care for myself and other people. I have very much appreciated the excitement at CMU about me and this inaugural position.

Jan: *What particular aspects of these roles have you felt you have brought a transformative social work lens to?*

There was a particular situation involving students who were protesting and demanding specific changes involving diversity, equity, inclusion, and belonging. They, along with some of their allies (students, faculty, staff, and others), staged a sit-in inside one of the main university buildings and also organized a street blockage. The "rubber really hit the road" over this situation and made me think about "walking my talk"—I had to think a lot about my cultural and emotional intelligence; my own social identity as a woman, a person of color, and a first-generation college student; and what it was like for me. It raised a lot of issues for me from my own background which made me identify with the students to some extent. Yet as a leader, I felt honesty and courage were needed. I asked myself what critical thinking was needed to support everyone in this situation. In that moment, the phrase "to whom much is given much is expected or required" rang loud and clear in my head. There was a lot of emotion swirling around, and rightfully so.

I had to remember that there was no courage without vulnerability. I believed that there would be no resolution without empathy and cultural humility. Any uncomfortableness and fear would have to take a back seat. In that moment, I had to remind myself how important it was for me to be an equity-minded leader. Administrators in challenging situations must draw on and apply many tools and resources. They must lead with their whole self. For this social worker at heart, it was natural for me to exercise a holistic approach. I think it is important for many executive leaders to practice this behavior.

I aligned my approach in leadership with one that listened to understand and engaged the voices that wanted and needed support, regardless of my feelings about the way things were unfolding. It was important to let those students share their voices and listen to others (leadership, faculty, and staff) who were making themselves available and vulnerable to create change that supported a welcoming, safe, and inclusive work and learning environment—and to recognize what emotions and feeling were guiding me so that I could contribute to the solution and promote restoration with a clear mind. I guess in the end I led with my heart, soul, and mind. There was no doubt that relationships, not transactions, would be the key to moving the needle.

Jan: *How has your transformative approach helped you work with your colleagues at the executive level?*

It has allowed me to have "appropriate patience." This work is so complex that you can easily run out of steam, so you need more realistic expectations. Paying attention to my peers and their work at national-level organizations helps me put things in perspective. Sometimes the journey takes longer than expected. Recognizing this pushes me to be more reflective, and it helps me to understand that sometimes the issues and solutions are right in your face.

My cousin often shares a story that helps to illustrate this idea. She is waiting for the big payoff from a particular slot machine after she has had some "luck" at that machine. She is waiting and hoping for a larger payout. She finally realizes it is possible that the machine has already distributed the big payout for that moment in time. The big payoff is subjective. This may not be a typical example when thinking about a transformational approach, but it makes me think about the importance of how I process a situation and think about outcomes in terms of process, progress, and value. James Clear (2018), in his book *Atomic Habits*, writes about building new habits. In my cousin's case, she needed to learn how to walk away from slot machines, especially when she was ahead. For me, it became important to notice every step along the way so that I might see the wins toward advancing inclusive excellence. I did this by writing in a journal, once a day, about one effort I engaged in. I noticed that the small things can be quite monumental.

I have had to become more reflective about my work, acknowledge all the issues on the table, and try to understand when the work is at its "hottest." I can more fully understand when and why systems break down. It has become clearer through some of the bad experiences that you must always take into account the different voices and histories around you to help you determine where to make change. Sometimes I just need to follow and not necessarily lead.

A colleague recently spoke to me about being a senior executive and a mature manager. He believes that people recognize my skill in building trusting relationships. I often see my leadership as involving mostly "honey" with a little bit of "salt." The "honey" is about helping people to feel valued, that they are invited into my space—people being attracted to my way of being (that's the social worker in me). I lead with an ethic of care. I am relational and developmental (at least they think I am!). I attribute this to my social work background, which enhances the chances of success, or at least a chance at better thriving.

I also like to have some fun in my work. [Jan: You enjoy doing what you do?] I like injecting humor in my work—"humor at the table." I have a sense that has grown over the years, and I now feel I can be less controlled about this. For example, I took a lot of photos at UVM, which other members of the executive started doing—it was something distinctive about me that people could identify with. I was called "the selfie queen."

A few years ago, at the president's retreat, I instituted a campaign called "fully engaged," which was about being flexible, adaptive, and creative and working in the space you are in at that moment. As an example, referring back to the student protest I spoke about earlier, I remember that there was so much fear about what people would think. I realized that one of my colleagues (a white woman) needed my help, my voice, so there was a moment of decision to go along or not. I was a Black woman and a mother who could not imagine what would happen if those students were arrested. I was also trying to reconcile the different perspectives at the table (student affairs; diversity, equity, inclusion and belonging [DEIB]; safety; compliance). I could identify with the students, with the administration, and with many who were just in between. There was a lot of emotion pushing toward varied actions, and I needed to have much compassion.

Jan: *Can you describe your identity as a leader and how your transformative lens is incorporated into this? You have answered some of this already, of course, but it would be good to just reemphasize some of the key ideas.*

Relational and *developmental* are key words that spring to mind. I would also say I feel good about being in service to others. Brene Brown (2018), a social work and research professor, speaks about being a servant leader and how courage is the foundation of servant leadership. The idea that leading by following manifests in engagement, innovation, creativity, productivity, and trust really resonates with me. It is through this lens that I believe I have partnered with others and been successful.

I work on fear regularly so that I am not paralyzed by the unfair, biased, or discriminatory situations that I may have to deal with or experience. It's like strengthening a muscle so that you are prepared to deal with the weight of the good, the bad, or the ugliness of a situation.

I believe I am compassionate, a visionary. As I get older, I talk about myself as a "cultural architect," building anchors and pillars on which ideas can be sustainable. Others also see me as hands-on, so I can be involved in concrete ways while also providing a loftier vision. I believe I naturally share with others and also mentor. I like to use the term *sponsorship*, which means that I like to use what influence I have to try to get others to partner with me. This can help by giving all involved some "street cred" in one another's sphere of working.

I don't necessarily plan to do this, but I often find myself in the middle of initiatives. I try to be true to myself, so I like to lead others but also take care of myself. This doesn't always involve a plan—sometimes it just involves being myself, so it's more about my personality. However, I find that when I am myself, I am more down to earth and people trust me better. In some ways I "don't give a damn," which is seen as my having grit and fortitude. This also means I try not to let people take too much of me when I feel I don't have much more to give. I have realized over the years that I do say yes a lot, and this can pull me in lots of different directions. At the same time, though, when you have given a lot, it can pay off because you build many trusting relationships.

In some ways, I can sum up my approach to my work as "I am in everybody's business"—and the great thing is that they want me there!

REFERENCES

Brown, B. (2018). *Dare to lead*. New York: Random House.
Clear, J. (2018). *Atomic habits*. New York: Avery.
Ellison, R. (1964). *Shadow and act*. New York: Knopf Doubleday.
Saleeby, D. (2013). *The strengths-based perspective*. New York: Pearson.
Shorters, T. (2015). *Reach: Stories by Black men*. New York: Simon & Schuster.

3

MANAGING A TRANSFORMATIVE DEPARTMENTAL CULTURE

JAN FOOK

Being a department chair is a challenging position at the best of times. It is of course the frontline management position, and there seem to be increasing inroads into the autonomy of such a position, given the trend toward more centralization of power and decision making within the university (Docherty, 2011; Barnett, 2012). In addition, managing the changes expected from individual faculty and staff can be difficult, given their varying ages, expectations, and statuses. Rapid changes in the university system can easily expose generational differences among faculty, and systemic changes can also affect pay and status differences between faculty and staff. Individual faculty, staff, and departments within universities that have known a relatively stable background may find the nature and rate of current changes to be drastic and may resist changes that feel too discomforting or completely at odds with a formerly comfortable culture. The recent experience of the pandemic can result in new inequities (Khilji & List, 2021). Under all these changing conditions, it is more challenging to think through, and enact, ways of managing that preserve a sense of transformative values and to have a clear sense of what transformative actions might look like under rapidly changing regimes.

In this chapter, I attempt to outline some of the challenges I have experienced as a department chair and the approaches to management I have tried to use to maintain a sense of social justice and steer a department through rapidly changing and rocky times. I will organize the chapter around two major issues that emanate from the changing contexts in which we work, particularly in the United States: the increasing polarization of perspectives and the rise of metrics. I finish with a section that outlines my own contextual approach to management.

POLARIZATION OF PERSPECTIVES AND MAINTAINING RELATIONALITY

The challenges involved in maintaining and developing a transformative culture have clearly become both broader and more localized. In terms of broader challenges, how can relationality be maintained under pandemic conditions when people are physically distanced and socially isolated? One of the chapters in this book (chapter 5) discusses the challenges of maintaining a welcoming and inclusive physical and social space in the department. This was much easier to do without pandemic restrictions, when the department space could be used for all sorts of social gatherings, formal and informal. As we return to more in-person conditions, we are confronted with the need to revisit how this is done and how pandemic conditions may have changed our values and expectations regarding face-to-face work. Among the social justice implications of these issues is how to analyze and understand the way remote working affects different groups differently (e.g., people with young children, people without efficient computer equipment or internet connections, people who commute great distances) and what policies are equitable regarding who is allowed to work remotely, and how often.

Perspectives can be polarized along many different lines. Clearly political differences are most easily identifiable, but fault lines also occur in terms of gender, race, and other identities such as class and religion. I will touch on these in the following discussion.

The increased polarization of political perspectives, made more evident by the events following the murder of George Floyd in 2020 and the international spread of the Black Lives Matter movement, has had parallels in the classroom. Reasoned debate has been difficult to sustain, given the tendency to take passionate sides and oppositional positions, exacerbated by the extreme polarization modeled in the life of the United States at a national level. The warring nature of political debate, brought to life by the Capitol Hill insurrection in early 2021 after the election of Joe Biden over Donald Trump, has found its way into the classroom—not with the exact same politics in leftist Vermont but with its tendency to make political difference a life-or-death issue.

In an empirical study of five hundred social work students in the United States, Flaherty et al. (2013) drew attention to how, in social work, students who self-identify as politically conservative are more likely to report that they perceive the classroom environment as less conducive to debate (p. 1). The chasm between different political persuasions is fairly evident in a state like Vermont, where, although the overall political ethos is commonly regarded as left-leaning (it is the home state of Senator Bernie Sanders, after all), a good deal of the population lives in rural areas and is likely to hold opposing political views. Additionally, Vermont is known as a predominantly white state; most of our class cohorts have only one or two students of color, and our faculty and staff group in social work has included only one person of color, for only a few years. Over the past thirty years or so, until very recently, the percentage of faculty/staff of color has therefore been less than 10 percent; in the student body, the percentage of people of color has averaged about 3–4 percent. These two issues (politics and race) mean that, besides the general difficulty of maintaining open debate in the classroom and the department, because people of color are vastly outnumbered, it can be difficult to create spaces for debate in which issues such as racism can be raised equally from different perspectives.

Sometimes these differences are expressed as a kind of standoff between genders and races, with white men seen as privileged oppressors whose views in a leftist environment are, accordingly, often unwelcome. This may mean that white men cease to express their views and engage actively in debate, or that they preface everything they say with an apology for being white and male or, at best, qualify everything they say with that caveat. For some faculty and students, these issues translate as simply trying to "flip" the privilege by privileging the views of Black, indigenous, and other people of color (BIPOC) and women instead. This, however, may mean that more conservative or racist views, which do need to be aired, debated, and challenged, may be held in secret and not open to scrutiny.

How to work with such differences and allow as much open debate as possible, while also acknowledging that having some views expressed (especially if they are perceived as racist) may be experienced as hurtful or offensive by some people from racialized backgrounds, is a major issue for educators and managers. Alternatively, for students coming from a more conservative political angle, feeling attacked or personally vilified is probably not conducive to the best learning possible. This involves a number of different facets. First is the issue of how much students should be "coddled." This is highly controversial, as a common response to the extreme polarization of views has been to try to censure unwanted views and to create "safe spaces" within universities. Associated with this idea is a perceived need to protect some students from harm. I believe this is the imperative behind giving "trigger warnings" (National Coalition Against Censorship, 2020) before a sensitive topic is introduced. However, these concerns have resulted in what some claim to be a coddling of thinking (Lukianoff & Haidt, 2018), whereby universities have moved to ban the expression of certain views, leading to a culture in which only certain standpoints are approved and protected. Some claim that this tendency has resulted in "indoctrination" rather than education (Naudé, 2021).

I see another problematic tendency associated with polarized thinking: the tendency to conflate an individual person and their identity with the broader social, systemic, or structural phenomena with which they are perceived to be associated. By this I mean the tendency to assume, for instance, that an individual BIPOC (Black, indigenous, person of color) woman, must have the same experiences, needs, desires, and wants as BIPOC people (and women) have more broadly. This effectively depersonalizes or deindividualizes the woman, seeing her only in terms of her race. This is a form of "othering" (Fook, 2016), whereby people are categorized on the basis of a feature that differentiates them from the norm. In this way, they are constructed as "different" by definition, leaving the way open for them to be discriminated against in other ways.

This type of thinking also plays out within departments, among individual faculty and staff. Often it can be underpinned by differences of opinion about how gender and racial diversity are handled in the classroom. Sometimes an instructor prefers a more direct approach, whereby politically "unacceptable" views are challenged head-on. For example, an instructor may introduce a course by challenging the privilege of white men and continue with this type of analysis as a fundamental framework for the course. Other faculty members may prefer a more "soft-edge" approach that seeks to articulate and examine reflexively the genesis of all perspectives. These different approaches in the classroom can play out within departments in terms of disagreements about how to handle diversity, especially racial/cultural differences. Sometimes faculty who do not subscribe to the former approach (an upfront confrontation with politically conservative views) may be labeled as politically conservative themselves and, therefore, as potentially racist and acting against the interests of BIPOC people. Sometimes these accusations can even be leveled at other faculty of color. This type of thinking can make for potentially unbridgeable chasms between BIPOC faculty of different racial backgrounds and can mirror culture wars that occur at the national level.

These polarized differences also play out with regard to how activism is viewed. Activism is a way of being that is strongly congruent with a transformative perspective, but I have sometimes seen a downside to this. An activist stance can be implicitly pitted against a more reflective stance, unhelpfully polarizing opinions. There may be a tendency to teach content such as critical frameworks (assuming that this is needed for activism) as opposed to process (as implied in the teaching of reflective/reflexive skills). An effective social worker needs both activism and reflection, but when such views are polarized, it is all too easy to personalize the conflict (those who support activism versus those who support reflection) and to see the two positions as mutually exclusive. It is hard to achieve a collective team spirit when personal philosophical differences are easily weaponized. Perhaps such phenomena have been exacerbated by pandemic conditions, with fewer chances to relate informally and a seeming imperative to battle opposing dangerous viewpoints.

These conflicts are a reminder of how complex political, racial, and gender issues are, and that a tendency to polarize is extremely problematic for the social work educational endeavor. I have often observed that students on placement, especially young women, feel as if they have failed because they did not immediately act to challenge a racist comment from an older colleague or even a supervisor. It is as if they have polarized the possibilities for action: either challenge/change as an activist or passively do nothing and be complicit in the racism. The latter is conceptualized as failure, regardless of circumstances. In other instances, students may perceive a polarization between professionals and clients and cannot square their identity as a person who has experienced, for instance, mental illness, with their identity as a professional, therefore also seeing themselves as a failure, as someone who cannot possibly be a social worker.

From a transformative standpoint, the recognition of the complexity of human lives—personal, emotional, and social—is crucial to a theoretical stance that recognizes multiple viewpoints. Although intersectionality is now a commonly accepted concept in social work higher education (Kendall & Wijeyesinghe, 2017), I often observe, in my own experience of the classroom and departmental discussions, that social class and religion are missing from the analysis. It is also interesting that it is assumed that all the aspects of intersectionality are points of privilege (as in Kendall & Wijeyesinghe, 2017) against which social workers should analyze themselves, instead of acknowledging that many faculty, students, or workers may actually come from nonprivileged backgrounds. Such assumptions potentially construct a polarized divide between an idealized conception of professional and academic social workers, who are effective activists, and ordinary people from all walks of life who struggle to uphold their caring values within varying life circumstances.

It is important, in this context, to discuss social class differences. In my experience, differences related to class often show up very distinctively in the classroom. Although it is clearly acknowledged that students from working-class backgrounds are disadvantaged in the educational system (Duckett, 2021), it is all too easy to see this as mostly economic. But cultural factors associated with class can be experientially discriminatory. For example, class factors are present in terms of verbal expression (e.g., in the degree of swearing or the degree of comfort with verbal expression) or just in familiarity with professional labels and terminology. It is easy to make assumptions that people who swear are somehow more crass or aggressive; indeed, I have witnessed this as a judgment of Australian colleagues (in Australia swearing is much more common than I have seen in higher education in the UK, Canada, or the United States). With regard to verbal comfort, I have seen it assumed that there is a problem with students who don't speak up, who are therefore judged negatively as nonassertive (Fook, 2014). It is important to recognize that the sort of space that is created is crucial to encouraging faculty and students to express their views; "lack of assertion" may be a response to how the learning environment is experienced. Compounding the situation for working-class students, at least in Britain, is the fact that elites still dominate at higher levels (Todd, 2021). This means that the people deciding the criteria for success are liable to do so in terms of their own class/culture familiarity, thereby maintaining cultural reproduction of middle-class professional values. This, of course, runs counter to transformative values of equity and inclusion.

In my own classroom, and indeed in my relations with students, faculty, and staff, I try to make explicit my own class and cultural background in order to give context to my ideas and interactions. Elsewhere (Fook, 2014, 2023) I have outlined in a little detail my background as a later-generation Australian-born Chinese woman from a lower-middle-class family, raised as a fundamentalist Protestant. My class background contributes to my relative lack of expressivism (compared to colleagues in the United States), but it has also helped me to understand (if slowly) how much of what I observe about ways of relating is almost purely cultural in origin. This latter stance helps me suspend judgment. I also try to be deeply embedded in critical reflection, which insists that I try to think and act beyond cultural restrictions (by first suspending judgment) and assist students of critical reflection to do the same (Fook & Gardner, 2007).

My own background has made me acutely aware of the nuances and complexities of race. My early religious upbringing contributes to my sense of difference in the world in a way that compounds my racial appearance. Being raised as a third-generation Australian-born Chinese Seventh-Day Adventist in white Australia gave me a marginal identity from early on. But these experiences also highlighted to me how much more complex a person I am than my racial appearance. My partner of nearly five decades appears as a white man, but he was raised (largely in a Catholic monastery) by a Japanese mother in post–Korean War Australia. He combines an odd mix of cultures, but in ways that are unseen and unassumed because of his appearance. I am in fact more "Australian" than he, yet people make the opposite assumption when they see us. I also have white Jewish friends, who can tell me a lot more about racism on an institutional level. And most of my family in my generation have mixed-race children and are themselves part of a mixed-race couple. Fixed racial categorizations, which are often integral to the many polarizations around racial issues, thus run the risk of denying or dismissing much of what I am as a person, and of what other people are as whole human beings.

Add to this the complications of religious, class, and cultural upbringing, and the whole picture becomes much messier, yet more interesting. It provides a platform for deeper and more fulfilling engagement, and for better relationality.

Flaherty et al. (2013, p. 17) summarize beautifully the challenges of this complexity for educators:

> Educators must be cognizant of the immense power imbalance that exists between instructor and student, and of how intimidating it can be to be in the minority, including the political minority. Students do not come to us as blank slates. They arrive with an array of strengths and limitations, skills and deficits, deeply held beliefs and tentatively held notions. They may be unprepared to articulately defend some ideas, and may not have been previously challenged to do so. As social work educators, it is our responsibility to model critical reasoning and constructive debate, and to promote a classroom atmosphere that encourages students to take intellectual risks, while still adhering to the profession's commitment to social justice. In doing so, we must also be willing to defend our ideas and positions against reasoned challenges without resorting to dogma or intimidation.

It is from such a place as this that I seek to create a classroom, and a departmental space, that allows for differences and nuances of opinion and of identity. It is perhaps not a "safe" space that I strive for, but a more "courageous and generous" space—one in which multiple divergent and contradictory views can be aired, and experiences noted, without the imperative for judgment but, instead, a commitment to deep listening with a view to understanding. This is in line with the best of "transformative" values.

With this in mind, we have begun a process of sharing our own philosophical positions in the department and in our teaching, as part of an overarching review of programs in the department. These views are being collated into collective documents that do not seek to represent consensus but try to include and fully represent the individual views of each faculty member. It is enlightening to read these and to realize how much of what is written shares common fundamental values but also captures individual approaches and ways of expressing them. Producing these documents is an exercise in airing different views in a relational way.

THE NEOLIBERAL AGENDA AND
THE RISE OF METRICS

As many of the chapters in this volume claim, there are certainly more neo-liberal influences creeping into the university. This is indicated by the broad shift toward the marketization of education and a decrease in self-manage-ment, concomitant with policies of austerity and an emphasis on financial management. Under such regimes, a social justice agenda is threatened (Bhopal & Shain, 2016, pp. 1–2). Among corresponding phenomena is the increasing use of metrics to inform decision making. This manifests in all sorts of decisions at the strategic and more individualized levels. For instance, we are often presented with endless tables and comparative statis-tics to illustrate trends in student application numbers and enrollments. The volume of data presented in these ways, without a corresponding degree of attention to what the statistics and trends actually mean, indicates a privileg-ing of statistics without a translation into strategy and meaningful actions.

The dominance of metrics in decision making is also demonstrated in faculty evaluations. Faculty are assessed annually in terms of agreed criteria, and the quality of their performance is rated according to rubrics and scores, which are then used to determine pay increases. Relative per-centages of workload are also determined by metrics, and this means that any other activities that are needed for a department and university to run effectively either go unaccounted for (because they are not easy to metricize) or do not get done by some people (because they don't see a metricized reward). These necessary activities must then be performed by those who are willing, so workloads become unfairly balanced. Examples of such activities are reference letters requested by students; consultations requested by potential partners in the professional community regarding curriculum or program development; development of strategic objectives relating to diversity and equity; and program and curriculum review, additional to normal teaching obligations. Ironically, it is these activities that may be necessary for transformative work to happen.

As Collini (2012, p. 120) so eloquently states, "Not everything that counts can be counted." The challenge for a department manager in this environ-ment is to create ways in which things that are important are still factored in. It needs to be made clear how things that ultimately count are accounted for, thereby building a framework that allows them to increase.

A CONTEXTUAL APPROACH TO MANAGEMENT
IN A TRANSFORMATIVE DEPARTMENT

As a manager of a transformative department, I must constantly make decisions about what practices and policies must be implemented, and how, in order to preserve our faculty's and staff's sense of values and integrity and, at the same time, keep our department in good standing so that we receive the resources needed to do our best job. How do we maintain individual and social health and self and community care in this environment?

The main principle that guides my approach to management is based on the recognition that individual faculty and staff are largely not responsible for the contexts in which they work, in particular the way the university as an organization functions. This means not that individuals lack agency, but that the broader parameters of that agency are often predetermined. Nonetheless, individual faculty and staff are also part of the context, and changes in the way they work and relate to one another will also bring about changes in the context. I try to remind people that although we are not responsible for the whole university environment, we are responsible for creating a microclimate within it. In short, it is important to identify and remember the ways we can and do have agency within a broader context.

Along with this principle, I try to remind myself not to "blame the victim," the individual staff or faculty member, but to broaden my focus to the contexts in which people work and to understand how these contexts influence how people do their jobs, how they respond to one another, and the systems and processes they must negotiate to get their jobs done. In some ways, this is a type of relational approach at the organizational level. As department chair, I see my responsibility as trying, as far as possible, to create a climate, or microclimate, that enables people to do their jobs to the best of their ability. Part of this is recognizing that not everyone is good at everything they are required to do, so getting as good a fit as possible with people's skills, talents, passions, and values is more important than getting everyone to conform to organizationally derived standards. As far as possible, I try to accommodate individual needs and wishes and to create ways in which departmental goals can be achieved with this in mind. This involves a lot of struggle on my part to find creative options, and perhaps a little manipulation of the system, but I find that being relational with the next level of management above me does a lot to enable cocreation of strategies that work for us all.

I find, though, that it is sometimes difficult, in a department and with a group of people who have, over a long period of time, developed practices and ways of thinking that were relevant in a different era, to keep assessing whether these ways need to be reworked in a changing environment. I believe it is always important to keep revisiting these questions, especially when we work in environments that are constantly changing. Over the past few decades, I have developed an approach that I have termed *contextual practice*, a sort of critical poststructural approach to social work practice (Fook, 2002, 2012, 2016, 2023) that takes into account working with, and within, changing contexts. It relies on a sense of how one is influenced by context and on weighing up what is relevant, or likely to be relevant, in that context, as opposed to applying a predetermined strategy to all situations. I believe that a contextual practice approach could be relevant to academic practice in these times when many of our basic assumptions about how people and organizations should work are being relentlessly overturned.

One set of strategies I have developed as part of this approach is to become a kind of mediator and translator. This involves trying to present new ideas in terms of how they compare to past ideas, "translating" them in terms of the current context. I am hopeful that this helps ensure that we have what we need to do the sort of job we want but, at the same time, moves us along so that we can take on the best of the new ways that are being proposed. For example, what experiences have we taken from the restrictions of the pandemic, and how can what is good about these be preserved in the way we continue to work? What have we learned about flexible working and teaching, and how can this be incorporated in an ongoing way? I hope that in this way we can update our notions of what it is to be good and caring academic and staff people within an environment that seems to be increasingly outside our control.

Performing this translator role requires maintaining and profiling a strong sense of transformative values of social justice and inviting faculty and staff to analyze how proposed new practices may or may not threaten these. There is sometimes a tendency for new practices to be debunked simply because they are new (or perhaps mistakenly based on an over-reliance on metrics) rather than assessed though a detailed analysis of how a new practice may actually work for some people or groups and not others. Ironically, not all new practices disadvantage marginal groups but may work, for example, in favor of newer academics. An example of this is transparency of expectations regarding the numbers and types of research outputs expected. Such transparency can be helpful to newer faculty members who are finding their footing in the academy, whereas for long-established faculty, used to a lack of clarity about these standards, such certainty can be experienced as threatening. It is helpful under these circumstances to think through what a stance of social justice looks like for whom. Rather than a one-size-fits-all approach, a critical stance that recognizes different interest groups and different power bases and experiences is crucial.

The mediator role also involves taking short-, medium-, and long-term views all at once. Sometimes this involves "losing the battle to win the war" (i.e., balancing short-term gains against possible longer-term wins). One of the challenges in a department with a long-established history is to try to assess when collective decisions, reactions, and judgments are being made in terms of past experience as opposed to current or even future possibilities. There may be a tendency to see even minor changes as "the thin end of the wedge" because of an established suspicion of any changes, a result of harmful experiences in the past.

Second, my approach in this type of neoliberal climate is a strong sense of prioritizing. Most of us experience the neoliberal university as one in which there is always too much to do and not enough time or resources to do it. I simply acknowledge this and try to instill a sense of firm values by which faculty and staff can decide where best to put their energies. The following questions can help:

- Who will be affected, e.g., the department, my colleagues (who), students (exactly which ones), and in what ways (short-/long-term effects, small- or large-scale effects, implications) if I do or do not do what is being asked?
- How will social justice be affected, in terms of who is affected and how?
- Will the energy spent on resisting the request be worth whatever gains I hope to make?

- What else will I have to neglect in order to spend energy resisting this request?
- What is my bottom line in terms of my values here, and does complying with this request threaten that bottom line and how?

A third principle, which I have already touched on, is to be mindful of multiple perspectives and interests and that other people's perspectives and interests may differ markedly from my own. This is particularly important when tempted to take extreme, perhaps even polarized, positions, especially when it is all too easy to frame people in a relatively powerless group (e.g., students or junior faculty) as "victims" and those in more powerful groups (managers) as "oppressors." Understanding the different usages of power, and that power is neither finite nor enacted in one way, is vital to negotiating ways of working that function well for as many people as possible. Working relationally is a keystone of functioning in an academic setting, but it is all too easy for faculty who believe themselves to be the sole purveyors of social justice to construct people with more power than themselves as necessarily opposed and, therefore, as deserving of having oppositional tactics used against them. A manager, or department chair, can easily become caught in the middle. I find that a constant understanding of the different cultures involved, with a translation of each set of cultures to the others, is crucial to taking a department forward and also to achieving the social justice goals of the institution.

Finally, a stance of reflexivity has been necessary to defuse polarized and oversimplified approaches, both for myself and for the people in the department. Reflexivity—being mindful of one's own position and biases and where these come from, in order to more fully appreciate other perspectives—has been an invaluable reminder to me, especially as someone from a different country and culture trying to manage a department with a workplace culture solidified some time ago. I mentioned in the introduction that I had to learn about and understand the history of the department and the experiences that had led to the development of current thinking about transformative social work. I add to this the culture of the country, the thinking about theory, and the approach to relating to students. While much of it is, and will remain, foreign to me, it is nonetheless important that I understand the counterinfluence of my own thinking and background vis-à-vis that of my colleagues, some born and raised in the United States and longtime Vermont residents, others who bring backgrounds from further afield. There is a mix of urban- and rural-based practices, generational and gender-based differences, and racial, ethnic, and class-based cultures that interact in the context we are trying to create in the department. This understanding allows me to make decisions about how the culture of the department needs to develop in the future, in order to create an environment in which different cultures can feel welcomed and included. I can see what is more personally based, what is a matter of national or regional culture, and what I need to translate to all parties about understanding one another in order to find ways of functioning that work as well as possible for all of us.

An example of this challenge is how to formulate orientation events for new students and closing events for graduating students. What degree of information giving, mixed with relational exercises, will send the right messages to new students? What sort of informal and fun activities will strike the right celebratory tone for students leaving? How can these events be organized in a way that people from different backgrounds and expectations will find inclusionary? These are concrete questions whose answers embody the lived culture of the department—and who can say what is experienced as transformative by everyone? It is one of my biggest challenges as department chair to assist faculty to understand and accept one another's different cultures in order to create an environment that will be experienced as inclusive, and indeed transformative, by as many different groups as possible.

CONCLUSION

How do we negotiate the many challenges thrown up by changes in the current political and cultural climate? While a set of values inimical to a transformative perspective is relatively easy to state, how these play out in the day-to-day experience of creating a classroom and departmental environment is relatively complex. Taking into account the influence of global and national trends and how they have affected higher education, I have first tried to outline what some of these are and how I have experienced them in my role as both a social work educator and a department chair.

I have detailed some of the experiences related to the increasing polarization of perspectives, among both students and faculty, particularly in relation to issues of gender, race, and class. Given these tensions and the need for a reflexive stance, I have made suggestions about creating open spaces for debate. I have also discussed the rise of the use of metrics within the university and how to maintain a sense of transformative values in an environment where it feels as if those values are being constantly challenged by forms of management based on measurement. I have attempted to provide some guidelines about how to survive as a successful department in such a changing regime while constantly redefining what social justice might mean and being mindful of multiple and divergent perspectives. Strategies include taking on a translator type of role; prioritizing in terms of social justice principles; and being able to update a transformative perspective constantly by incorporating new learning from changing circumstances. Fundamental to all of this is an ability to be reflexive—to understand where your own (and others') thinking and behavior come from—and to adapt your own response accordingly, through a deep appreciation of different perspectives. This is a must for relational, and therefore transformative, practice.

REFERENCES

Barnett, R, (ed) (2012) *The Future University*, New York & London: Routledge

Bhopal, K., & Shain, F. (2016). "Educational exclusion: Towards a social justice agenda." In K. Bhopal & F. Shain (Eds.), *Neo-liberalism and education* (pp. 1–5). London: Routledge.

Collini, S. (2012). *What are universities for?* London: Penguin.

Docherty, T. (2011). *For the university*. London: Bloomsbury Academic.

Duckett, I. (2021). Class and education. *Academia Letters*, article 739. https://doi.org/10.20935/AL739.

Flaherty, C., Ely, G. E., Meyer-Adams, N., Baer, J., & Sutphen, R. (2013). Are social work educators bullies? Student perceptions of political discourse in the social work classroom. *Journal of Teaching in Social Work, 33,* 59–74. https://doi.org/10.1080/08841233.2012.750259.

Fook, J. (2002). *Social work: critical theory and practice*. London: Sage.

Fook, J. (2012). *Social work: a critical approach to practice*. London: Sage.

Fook, J. (2014). Learning from and researching (my own) experience: A critical reflection on the experience of social difference. In S. Witkin (Ed.), *Narrating social work through autoethnography* (pp. 120–140). New York: Columbia University Press.

Fook, J. (2016). *Social work: A critical approach to practice* (3rd ed.). London: Sage.

Fook, J. (2023) *Social work: A critical approach to practice* (4th ed.). London: Sage.

Fook, J., & Gardner, F. (2007). *Practising critical reflection*. Maidenhead, UK: Open University Press.

Kendall, F., & Wijeyesinghe, C. L. (2017). Advancing social justice work at the intersections of multiple privileged identities. *New Directions for Student Services, 2017*(157), 91–101. https://doi.org/10.1002/ss.20212.

Khilji, S., & List, C. (2021). Humanizing to address the grand challenge of rising inequalities: Leadership in a post-COVID world. *Academia Letters*, article 215. https://doi.org/10.20935/AL215.

Lukianoff, G., & Haidt, J. (2018). *The coddling of the American mind*. New York: Penguin.

National Coalition Against Censorship. (2020). What's all this about trigger warnings? https://ncac.org/resource/ncac-report-whats-all-this-about-trigger-warnings.

Naudé, A. (2021). Academic inquisition: Are universities centres of higher education or higher indoctrination? *Academia Letters*, article 130. https://doi.org/10.20935/AL130.

Todd, S. (2021). *Snakes and ladders: The great British social mobility myth*. New York: Penguin.

4

DEVELOPING A TRANSFORMATIVE
APPROACH AS A WHOLE DEPARTMENT

KEN BECHTEL, KATE BALL CLEM, JAN FOOK,
AND BC GARVEY

I t is all too easy to assume that academic practice is centered on the work of faculty and that the administrative work of staff is marginal and should remain somewhat hidden in the academic enterprise. This view can give rise to unwelcome tensions between faculty and staff, with an accompanying assumption that staff are less valued in the academic hierarchy. Yet from a transformative perspective, relations should be as equitable as possible. However, this equitability is hard to build and maintain within a broader university culture that is itself hierarchical and perhaps becoming more so (Bleiklie, 2012). Although the tensions are acknowledged as a part of university culture, there is not much literature that explores the nature of this hierarchical relationship, the tensions that exist between administrative and academic employees (Hyun & Oliver, 2011), and what can be done to improve the situation (Harrill et al., 2015). However, there is literature that clearly acknowledges the vital role of staff in the student experience (Kutchner & Kelschink, 2016; Masserini et al., 2019), and in this day and age, when the income from student enrolment is mandatory for some universities to stay afloat, there should be more concern to improve the staff experience. Some literature indicates more specific benefits of staff involvement in what might be seen as more "academic" affairs. For example, it is important to include staff when developing statements of support for diversity and inclusion work, department goals, and strategies for achieving them. They are often the forward faces communicating values and implementing them with students and the general public (Clauson & McKnight, 2018). In addition, staff who teach students to interact with administrative processes are teaching valuable skills for navigating other organizations after graduation. A department that makes staff work and voices visible sets a different tone for higher education (Strayhorn, 2015).

For social work programs seeking U.S. Council of Social Work accreditation, it should be noted that staff are an integral aspect of the implicit curriculum (that is, the messages conveyed by the overall learning environment, not specific to the classroom or formal syllabi). Student interactions with staff, the helpfulness that staff communicate to students, and the overall social and physical environment that staff create in a department (and the broader university community) may all be experienced by students to be as important as classroom teaching and interactions with faculty. Yet it is easy for academic faculty to assume that the formal role of teaching constitutes the main aspect of a program and to devalue the role and input of staff.

In this chapter, we reflect on how these inequitable relations might be transformed. We also offer some concrete ways staff roles can be conceptualized so they are seen as integral to the work of the department. Our hope is that this will not only improve the workplace experience for staff but also transform the culture of the departmental workplace. Our focus will lead us to consider the academic department as a whole, including students, staff, faculty, and departmental culture as well as the physical space.

The central questions we examine in this chapter are: How can we transform departmental culture and arrangements in a way that attempts to equalize the power imbalances between staff and faculty groups? How do we need to reframe the various aspects of the relationship between faculty and staff in order to transform departmental culture?

We will begin with a brief introduction to our roles and history in the department, then move on to consider some of the "sticking points" in trying to develop a transformative culture, how these might be reframed, and how a transformative department might look.

The content for this chapter was discussed in a lengthy conversation among three of us (Ken, Kate, and Jan). We also had assistance with the chapter from our departmental research assistant, MSW student BC Garvey.

Besides assisting us by locating relevant literature, BC has been assisting our staff in preparing administrative materials for student use. Including their perspective has helped immensely in designing materials that speak directly to student needs, and for this reason we have felt their employment in this way is potentially transformative. There is a section at the end of the chapter written by BC to spell out the nature of their experience. We will attempt to condense the themes that emerged but also preserve some of the conversational quality. We hope this will communicate the spirit of the conversation in the way it was intended. The intent of this chapter is not to "preach" about right or wrong ways of doing things but simply to express something of the experience of administrators in trying to uphold the academic ideals of transformative social work, in the hope that it can stimulate some further thinking and reflections about how we can keep transforming our relationships and arrangements.

INTRODUCTION TO THE DEPARTMENT

The social work department at the University of Vermont was established in 1974 and later expanded to include graduate studies in 1989. It is currently located administratively within the College of Education and Social Services, which is largely dominated by programs in education but also houses programs in developmental studies as well as counseling. The department currently has approximately ten full-time academic faculty and a host of part-time faculty, as well as two staff positions. For much of its history, the majority of full- and part-time faculty have been women. The department offers a bachelor of social work (BSW) program and a master of social work (MSW) program. There are approximately 180 social work students enrolled in any one year. The department occupies a wing of the main building of the university (the building that houses the university executive). Most offices in this wing are occupied by social work faculty and staff, but some are also occupied by other college staff (e.g., the director of diversity, the college publicity officer, and staff people who handle graduate administrative matters and student services). The wing also includes a conference room (available to the whole university) and a student lounge, as well as a large open space with couches and armchairs that invite casual conversation. So the space feels very much like a social work space but also one in which it feels important to welcome others. This is a significant aspect of creating a transformative space, which we will refer to in the body of the chapter.

Because of the long history of the department (and the long history of the core faculty and staff members), it is sometimes difficult to envision what changes can and should be made. Nevertheless, changes will be necessary, especially given the recent influx of a substantial number of new faculty. This history serves as a backdrop to the comments in this chapter.

THE HISTORY AND ROLES OF EACH PERSON

Kate: "My official title is business manager, and I see myself as handling resourcing for the department—obviously finances but resources more generally (like space and HR). I have been in this role for over twenty years and originally worked at UVM in the printing office, so I already knew some systems at UVM. The college was looking for someone who could work with figures (which incidentally I can do, though I am not officially trained in financial management—my degree was in English and psychology!). I have seen a lot of evolution during my time in the department. When I first started in the position, I was also a student at the time and it was difficult to maintain my student role, but also, with my student hat on, I noticed that the department was very good at student advising. Lots of changes in staffing at UVM have meant that my role has had to become very relational."

Kate later related how she felt a student had captured her role well when she spoke about her as "the keeper of the hearth." We will elaborate on this in a later section.

Ken: "I have been at UVM since 2006. I work as the academic support person for the three programs: BSW, MSW, and field education. My role has changed over time as different faculty have left and staff positions have shrunk. This has meant I have had to keep adding new aspects to my role, which has also meant learning more, often without a transition period. Not only have I developed new relationships with different people, but I have had to be very adaptable and look for the positives in the change. This makes the job interesting—I do enjoy talking to people (as long as they are in a good mood!). More on this later."

Jan: "I came to UVM in 2019 as the chair of the department, from the UK. This was my first time working and living in the United States. I would describe my role as a mix of administration, management, academic work (research and teaching), and academic leadership. I don't think this role is well understood by faculty, nor are the difficulties in juggling the four aspects. Adapting to the UVM culture has been a huge challenge (since I came from overseas with different academic systems) but right away, on meeting Ken and Kate, I realized that they would be my quiet guides and supports—people who understood the culture (having had to navigate it for many years) but also had a keen desire for change because they could envisage new possibilities and because they had the overview of the department and where it fitted in the broader university system and culture. As staff I knew they had to constantly navigate the whole system to make things work, whereas individual faculty tended to be more autonomous in their work and had the relative luxury of being able to be more blinkered, allowing them to focus on their individual responsibilities. As chair, whose role it is to ensure the safety and well-being of the whole department within the institutional context, my experience has been that I could not do my job well without the insights, caution, diplomacy, and generosity of the business manager and the academic support person."

Jan: *Since you have both worked here for a substantial period of time, can you tell me what keeps you here?*

Both Ken and Kate would say that their working relationship sustains them in their jobs. Both have seen a lot of change and have worked with successive chairs with widely varying approaches. They described themselves as "having to find a way to be here." Ken characterized one of his sayings that helped him get through tough times as being from Mister Rogers: "Look for the helpers." (Fred McFeely Rogers, also known as Mister Rogers, was an American television host. He created and hosted the preschool television series *Mister Rogers' Neighborhood*, which ran from 1968 to 2001. Many of his sayings became iconic in the memories of young Americans. His work was recently featured in the 2019 movie *A Beautiful Day in the Neighborhood*, starring Tom Hanks.)

Ken and Kate see themselves as being good at supporting each other. Kate spoke of the awareness they had of each other's lives and in particular of the quality of her supervisory experience with Ken as a person who has "so many qualities."

Both described the way they felt they had acted as a "retreat" or "sanctuary" for a past chair (a little like the way I recognized they would be a support for me as chair when I started in that role). In some ways, it may be that providing this sort of support for the chair also risks misunderstanding, or at least a downside in relation to other faculty. They described how, if they try to discuss each other's roles or actions with faculty, they are often accused of being "defensive." I would suggest that perhaps, in a broader national culture that seems dead set on polarizing many issues, the chair and the two administrative staff people are seen as one group pitted against the faculty group. In these instances, it seems convenient to forget that the chair is also an academic with teaching responsibilities, who may simply have a different perspective because they also have to take administrative issues, and the university as an organization, into account. A "whole department" mindset can be quite different from a faculty mindset. Assumptions about the academic and administrative roles being completely oppositional and mutually exclusive are certainly problematic in terms of forging a more equitable culture. We will return to this point further on.

Jan: *What is your own take on transformative social work; what do you mean and understand by it?*

Interestingly, both Ken and Kate went straight to their experience of the pandemic to begin to answer this question. "We had to be transformative because of the pandemic." "You can't go through a hard thing without learning from it. We had to change so much of what was important." As an example, they spoke about realizing the importance of the accessibility of information, so they made a decision to revolutionize the way they presented information to both faculty and students. They developed online presentation packages using Microsoft Sway to capture the important processes and to link related tools for many administrative aspects of the work (e.g., how to weigh different types of scholarships and how to apply for them, how faculty can access professional development funds). The beauty of Sway is that it is accessible, is easily utilized from various mobile devices, and supports clear, concise presentation of information and related web links. Ken and Kate also described an aspect of the experience of going through the pandemic as a "chance to practice change" (because change was thrust upon everyone and the whole institution). This experience of being able to drive change can be very empowering for staff: "a chance to do change more independently shifts confidence and so it is easier not to put up with so much 'guff' the next time."

When they spoke about transformative social work, they understood that this is better achieved the more people are involved and that either you could advocate for change or you could just sit and listen to people in relative silence. Ken described learning to do this listening over a period of time, applying it to listening to faculty, and also appreciating the interconnectedness of everything.

The conversation morphed into a discussion of how the expectations of staff knowledge has increased over time and that, in some ways, this requires staff to be transformative in the sense of having to be adaptable and flexible (because sometimes faculty are not). This involves needing to develop new sets of skills and to communicate changes to faculty, who sometimes do not engage. So their staff job becomes one of trying to "put things together in a process way to get it to work."

Jan: *What are some of the sticking points you have observed in trying to develop a more equitable culture?*

Some of these issues have already been picked up in the foregoing discussion, but the issue of difficulties encountered by faculty who are resistant to change is an ongoing one. It is difficult for staff who are not recognized as "experts" or are seen as subordinate to faculty to bring about change, and therefore there is a huge need to strategize about how to do this. It is also more difficult for staff because, although it is conventional for faculty to speak more directly to one another, such directness is not always seen as acceptable (given their inequitable position) for staff.

The issue of staff being categorized as a group naturally in opposition to faculty is a problematic one that we have touched upon earlier. "Sometimes people don't get that you are different from your job." Often social workers seem to have a depersonalized attitude to administration/management (Skaggs, 2015) that accords with the tendency to categorize people into boxes (roles). In some ways, there has been a tendency for Kate to be seen as the "gatekeeper" and Ken as the "gopher." Neither of these categorizations seems very transformative in the sense of a more complex understanding of how organizations work or respect for the importance and autonomy of their respective roles. I have experienced this as chair, being seen as powerful and therefore (I imagine) without the same right to respect or empathy as an equal human being. Presumably this kind of thinking is associated with so-called transformative ideologies that are suspicious of power and inclined, as a flip side, to characterize faculty as "powerless" and as "victims" (Carvalho & Videira, 2019). Staff are not even included in this hierarchical perspective; again, it is perhaps the tendency to polarize that minimizes the complexity of different positions and perspectives.

Kate made a nice distinction in describing some faculty ways of relating to staff as either "delegatory" or "deferential," as seen in the way faculty refer students to consult with Ken or Kate. A delegatory style would involve a more dismissive attitude, implying that it is not the job of the faculty member to address the inquiry, that it is beneath their level. In these instances, a faculty member might not even attempt to impart the relevant information or even bother to find it. A deferential style, on the other hand, would involve the faculty member trying to address the inquiry but then referring the student to the relevant "expert" staff member to corroborate and/or add further information. The latter feels more like a collaboration, rather than a "passing off," between faculty and staff member.

Both Ken and Kate feel that students come first, but it can be difficult with some students who sometimes act as though they see staff people as "storekeepers," just there to serve student needs. This may be related to a similar attitude that sometimes occurs with faculty, that staff are more like "servants." Ken and Kate refer to the front of Ken's office—Ken works in a space behind a desk that is open to the general office space (now behind a Perspex screen because of COVID), which means that he can be seen constantly and appears available for every query—as "Ken's drive-up window." This phrase communicates something about how easy it may be to take Ken and his position for granted. It may also communicate to students, perhaps through faculty behavior, that it is OK to see Ken this way. As chair, I recall one student being very annoyed at Ken because paper coffee cups were not supplied in the department—this is in a department where students already have their own lounge, access to a microwave and electric kettle, and a cupboard supplied (by faculty and staff) with food. It is helpful to reflect on how students received the message that such expectations were OK and to speculate on whether a student would have expressed this same annoyance to a faculty member. It may also be instructive to reflect on a "culture of entitlement" (Webb, 2018) that is perhaps not confined to students of social work. Webb suggests that this may be related to the culture surrounding consumerism in higher education.

Ken and Kate also noted gendered expectations as playing a role in divisions within the department. Given the history of the department, it was often perceived that men were privileged: there have been very few full professors in the department, and for many decades the only full professor was a man. For most of the department's forty-eight-year history, the vast majority of staff and faculty have been women. Understandably, feminist frameworks have informed the transformative perspectives of the faculty.

Both Ken and Kate reflected that these divisions probably played a role in creating tensions that obscured or limited the positive impact the department would have liked to have, because people did not appear to collaborate easily. "Joining together would have had a lot more impact."

Ken and Kate noted other tensions when it came to their perceptions of differing expectations for staff as opposed to faculty. They felt that "staff have to be perfect—we are the safety net," whereas often it felt as though faculty were not honest, or expected to be honest, about their own shortcomings or aware of how the department as a whole functions (and how their shortcomings might affect the smooth running of the department). Staff may feel that they have to be "apologists" for the department. This division was also felt in relation to pedagogic discussions, where staff felt that faculty considered it "weird" if they were involved. Other examples included staff being seen simply as a cog in the infrastructure, rather than valued for their unique perspective, or faculty not sharing important information that staff might have needed to perform their roles effectively (the assumption being that faculty did not consider staff roles important enough to require the information).

Jan: *What would a transformative department culture and space look like?*

The resounding response to this was "modeling social engagement . . . trying to establish more personable working relationships between staff and faculty." This would "lower the tensions, help people be more relaxed [with one another] and enable better working at a collective level." In a transformative culture, the responsibility for establishing good working relations would be the joint concern of both faculty and staff, with reciprocal interest in the roles and stressors experienced by all.

This relational theme came through when they referred to the "Ken and Kate" routine—that is, how they both tried to engage with different visitors to the department in different ways, but the underlying intention was always to be welcoming and to see this engagement as a type of "recruitment" to the department. With students this might take the form of trying to "talk students down from their anxiety," helping them think through how to navigate different administrative aspects of the department or the university.

Ken and Kate offered some suggestions about how faculty might show some curiosity about their work, thereby communicating that staff work was valued and contributing to equalizing the relationship. For example, faculty might reflect on questions such as "How do I think the staff person feels about their job? What have I learned (as a faculty person) from a staff person? What do I think staff need? What would make this space/process feel more comfortable to me, and how should I communicate that?"

"The department is how we all interact as a department" is the underlying principle that should spark interest from faculty about the staff experience and perspective. A strategy that staff often have to use to gain consideration of their needs is to try to spark the empathy of an individual faculty member. But in a department that operates from a transformative perspective, there should be natural empathy and consideration for all the different roles that must be performed in order to ensure that the department runs for the benefit of all—students, staff, and faculty.

With regard to a transformative departmental culture, staff should be included in related strategizing, such as diversity, equity, and inclusion work. Since staff are the face of the department (in information, materials, and relationships), this is where a welcoming and inclusive attitude is first experienced by the public, prospective students, faculty, and staff. An important aspect of transformative work at the organizational level is being mindful of teaching, learning, and modeling how to work effectively with administrative systems. In the words of Ken and Kate: "Staff who teach students to interact with administrative processes are teaching valuable skills for navigating in their own organizations after graduation. A department that makes staff work and voices visible sets a different tone for higher education."

In a transformative culture, the staff role can be conceptualized as "navigators and translators of systems." In this sense, systems benefit from staff input in their customer-facing roles. Some staff roles act as a bridge between communities and the policies and systems they must adhere to and work within. In these roles, staff can act as educators who teach faculty and students, and each other, required systems and valuable skills. They strive to remove institutional barriers to success however they can. They can model for students (and faculty) how to work with challenges in the following areas: navigating bureaucratic requirements; creating opportunities for empowerment (e.g., identifying tools and resources for students and faculty to pursue their own goals); and identifying and addressing inequities in administrative processes, such as institutional bias and the disempowering experience of paperwork.

A transformative approach also involves recognizing that staff are in a position to create a collaborative environment, perhaps more so than faculty, given that staff are more likely to be physically present for a longer time than faculty. Staff see their jobs as critical to the mission of higher education. They are perhaps in the best position to help by modeling accessibility and compassion for the difficulties individual students and faculty must navigate.

A further crucial element of a transformative departmental culture is to consider the whole context of departmental interactions. From this perspective, how the physical space of the department is maintained and managed can support transformative values. Both Ken and Kate described how it was extremely important to them to make the space a welcoming one, accessible not just to members of the department but to the whole college. Not only do other college members have their personal offices in the space, but there is also common space, including a student lounge, a sitting area, and a conference room available to the whole university. They described how happy they felt when people from outside the department came and sat in the space and held lively conversations with department members. Being able to share the space meant a lot. Some of how this was brought about was relatively simple. The three of us reminisced how we had chosen a paint color for the conference room and for Ken's office area: the color, called "reflecting pool," was chosen through enthusiastic consensus by several of us when, after we had leafed through pages of boring and uninspiring colors, this characterful, vibrant, yet subdued and relaxing mid eau-de-nil (light turquoise) hue leaped out. We simultaneously uttered a collective "yes." Somehow that color, along with the new orange Turkish-inspired rug and a few other intentional decorating choices, has turned the space into a place where people want to be. These touches further fed other concrete additions such as a common free food cupboard and homely contributions from different faculty members, turning the space into a collectively created place in which we hope many different people can find a relaxing, welcoming spirit. As Kate says, these interior design efforts are a result of the "emotional labor" that goes into "inclusive caretaking." This inclusive caretaking is integral to the heart and soul of being transformative, leading to a space that is designed and cared for by more than just the staff who sit in it each day.

Comments from BC:

It's been a tremendous opportunity to be a part of this departmental project. As noted, there can be a disconnect among the three major components of academic department: faculty, staff, and students. In a traditional sense, based in systems theory, faculty and staff operate the department as a mechanism for facilitating the transformation from student to professional (Bess & Dee, 2008). Students have little say in the way the system works: they choose to attend, they choose their courses, and they choose to do the work, but the way the overall system operates and develops is out of their hands. In this way, higher education will always remain hierarchical to some degree and therefore not entirely equitable. This is why decentralizing departmental dominance with the inclusion of a master's student research assistant into the fine-tuning of the department is so radical.

The last time I was in a departmental office at a higher education institution, I was working as a financial aid counselor at a college in Buffalo, New York. I obtained my education master's in higher education administration and was eager to make a difference in the lives of my students. I learned a lot about the realities of day-to-day departmental work, faculty-staff relations, and the breadth of student needs. Having since returned to school for my MSW, I was delighted that the social work department viewed my experience as a strength that could benefit the entire department. I set to work improving the website and informational materials, optimizing their accessibility for modern college students. The latitude

I was given to do this work and the feeling that I was truly heard and respected are indicative of this department's dedication to transformative work beyond the classroom by weaving it into every aspect of departmental operations.

CONCLUSION

We end this chapter with an invitation to reconsider and reconceptualize the staff role and relations among staff, faculty, and students within the department (and university) from a transformative perspective. This involves not seeing the staff role as one that is qualitatively different from, subordinate to, or less important than that of an academic role, but one that works alongside the faculty in a complementary way to enable success for all people in the organization. Staff are enablers and empowerers, skilled in systems and bureaucratic procedure. They have an overview of the whole organization and processes (which individual faculty often do not have) and can therefore assist in successfully negotiating the system and empowering faculty and students. Because they are often the front face of the university to prospective students and families, they are crucial in terms of recruitment and retention. They hold key information and are therefore central to creating a collaborative work and study environment. We close the chapter with an invitation for faculty and students to give careful consideration to how staff roles enliven and enable the educational experience. This may mean a more mindful understanding of the details of staff roles and more mindful ways of relating in order to achieve a more equitable approach to faculty-student-staff relations. Especially transformative may be a greater awareness of how subtle inequities between faculty and staff are reinforced. The recent effect of the pandemic on flexible work practices provides useful fodder for further reflection. For instance, how equitable are requirements to be present for in-person work between faculty and staff? What messages are being communicated about equity when faculty, who are relatively privileged, complain about work conditions and requirements to staff who enjoy less flexibility and receive a lower salary?

REFERENCES

Bess, J. L., & Dee, J. R. (2008). *Understanding college and university organization: Theories for effective policy and practice*. Sterling, VA: Stylus.

Bleiklie, I. (2012). Collegiality and hierarchy: Coordinating principles in higher education. In A. R. Nelson & I. P. Wei (Eds.), *The global university* (pp. 85–104). New York: Palgrave Macmillan.

Carvalho, T., & Videira, P. (2019). Losing autonomy? Restructuring higher education institutions governance and relations between teaching and non-teaching staff. *Studies in Higher Education, 44*(4), 762–773. https://doi.org/10.1080/03075079.2017.1401059.

Clauson, C., & McKnight, J. (2018). Welcome to campus: Planning for diversity, inclusion, and equity. *Planning for Higher Education, 47*(1), 39.

Harrill, M., Lawton, J. A., & Fabianke, J. C. (2015). Faculty and staff engagement: A core component of student success. *Peer Review, 17*(4), 11–14.

Hyun, E., & Oliver, S. (2011). Comprehensive curriculum reform in higher education: Collaborative engagement of faculty and administrators. *Journal of Case Studies in Education, 6*, 1–20.

Kutchner, W., & Kleschick, P. (2016). Mentoring in higher education administration. *College and University, 91*(4), 41–44, 46. Retrieved from https://login.ezproxy.uvm.edu/login?url=https://www.proquest.com/scholarly-journals/mentoring-higher-education-administration/docview/1845129505/se-2?accountid=14679

Masserini, L., Bini, M., & Pratesi, M. (2019). Do quality of services and institutional image impact students' satisfaction and loyalty in higher education? *Social Indicators Research, 146*, 91–115. https://doi.org/10.1007/s11205-018-1927-y.

Skaggs, M. L. (2015). *The great divide: The perceptions and dynamics of the faculty and staff professional relationship* (Doctoral dissertation, Western Kentucky University). http://digital commons.wku.edu/diss/74.

Strayhorn, T. L. (2015). *Student development theory in higher education: A social psychological approach*. New York: Routledge.

Webb, M. K. (2018). *The impact of consumerism on student learning in higher education* (Doctoral dissertation, University of South Alabama).

5

ANTI-RACIST PRACTICES IN ACADEMIA

Transformative Perspectives on Administration

LAURA S. ABRAMS, DOMINIQUE MIKELL MONTGOMERY,
JASON ANTHONY PLUMMER, GERRY LAVIÑA,
NANA SARKODEE-ADOO, LATOYA SMALL,
AND NICOLE VAZQUEZ

On May 25, 2020, the videotaped murder of George Floyd by four Minneapolis, Minnesota, police officers catalyzed a global protest movement for racial justice. This wave of activism centered the voices of Black Lives Matter (BLM), a movement that originated in the United States in 2013 to challenge pervasive and systemic racism and anti-Blackness. BLM rejects a color-blind racial narrative (Obasogie & Newman, 2016) that underlies liberal and neoliberal institutions associated with the profession of social work, and with American higher education more broadly. Black students and allies at schools of social work around the United States challenged faculty to commit to anti-racism in the profession. Students argued that because of social work's (neo)liberal orientation and connections between social control and policing, the profession has largely upheld white supremacy rather than dismantled it. Social work faculty were thus challenged to examine implicit and explicit racism operating in their own organizations.

A commitment to anti-racist education and practice has recently emerged as a more explicit mandate in U.S. social work. However, social work education and social work organizations as a whole tend to center respect for diversity and multiculturalism, and this "race-neutral" approach serves to uphold racial hierarchies by rendering them more invisible (Lopez, 2003). An anti-racist approach to education recognizes the existence of racism and anti-Blackness within the United States as a feature of contemporary social infrastructure and rejects public policies and social welfare practices that purport to be race-neutral (Abrams & Moio, 2009; Orbe, 2018).

Critical race theory argues that racism is structural and interpersonal and that it can be internalized (Jones, 2000; Taylor, 2016). For social work programs to become anti-racist, it is not simply a matter of adding mate-rial to the foundation curriculum. Educators and administrators must also be critical about how they as individuals reproduce whiteness and white supremacy through the neoliberal ethos of social work and the practices involved in their teaching and training. Moreover, educational organizations need to take a deep look at their own practices of racial exclusion and hierarchy in order to move toward a more transformational approach to organizational change. Higher education is deeply embedded in racial hierarchy and anti-Blackness, and social work education is no exception (Haley, 2020).

This chapter illustrates how one social work department in the United States coalesced around organizational transformation on multiple levels. We present the background and context of our efforts, describe how our coalition emerged, and detail our accomplishments and barriers. We con-clude with lessons learned from organizational transformation and offer our personal reflections on the process from our different standpoints.

The context of this chapter is the University of California, Los Angeles (UCLA) Department of Social Welfare. UCLA is ranked the leading pub-lic university in the nation and is a large Tier 1 research institution (U.S. News and World Report, 2023). Situated on a campus of nearly 45,000 undergraduate and graduate students, the Department of Social Welfare includes thirty faculty (of various ranks and appointment types) and approximately 250 graduate students pursuing MSW and PhD degrees. Since 1995, the Department of Social Welfare has been housed in a larger School of Public Affairs, alongside the Departments of Urban Planning and Public Policy. The racial composition of the social welfare student body is 13 percent Black, and the faculty are 16 percent Black. While the department has significantly increased the numbers of students and fac-ulty of color in the past twenty-five years, Black students and faculty have remained a small minority, and for many years students have criticized the department for anti-Blackness and racism (Callender et al., 2007).

We write this chapter as a coalition of administrators (Laura is the department chair (and full professor) and Gerry is the director of field education), faculty (Latoya), PhD students (Dominique and Jason), alums (Nicole), and MSW students (Nana, now an alum). Our working group, which included the authors in addition to PhD student Victoria Copeland, MSW student (now alum) Jameelah Howard, and alum Evin Capel, formed in the summer of 2020 to meet student demands to address racism and anti-Blackness. Here we offer our collective story.

RESPONSE TO THE MURDER OF GEORGE FLOYD

When Minneapolis police officers murdered George Floyd on May 25, 2020, Los Angeles was in the midst of a COVID-19 stay-at-home order and final exams were looming. UCLA social welfare students, who had already been in isolation for ten weeks, were suddenly bombarded with news and recurring video footage of law enforcement officers murdering a Black man, an injustice far too familiar to Black students. Over the next few days, Black students took part in classes and conversations in which students and faculty alike did little to address what was happening outside of the classroom space. When faculty and staff finally addressed Floyd's murder and the subsequent protests, classroom conversations were filled with increased tension, white guilt, and little to no reflection on individual actions and systemic practices that perpetuate anti-Black beliefs, including in social work. On social media, classmates spoke negatively of protests or made collective decisions about student needs without centering Black students' experiences. For Black social welfare students, that week felt extremely isolating and highlighted some of the subtle racism that existed within our own department. When an email finally came from department and school leadership five days after the murder, it spoke to the burden of students of color more broadly, not the specific experiences of Black students. For Black students who had experienced that week and years of racial trauma, this singular email was not enough.

After a particularly painful conversation related to the protests among the students, Black social welfare students began conversing with one another about their lack of support from classmates, faculty, and staff. Black students wrote to the department chair, Laura, and to the Luskin School dean expressing their current state of emergency and profound disappointment in the silence and lack of support offered specifically for Black students. Students felt as if they were expected to carry on as normal, but could not because of their overwhelming grief and outrage.

Laura responded with an apology and offered to meet with students that week. The department also quickly organized various virtual gatherings to process the national events, including a space for Black students and faculty, a space for non-Black allies, and a general space for all students. Black students used this space for collective healing and to draft a list of "Expectations for a Racially Just Climate in the Social Welfare Department." At the first meeting between administrators and the Black students, the students presented this document. To us as administrators, some demands seemed unattainable within the constraints of the university; others were well within reach. We felt a sense of urgency and quickly gathered data that students had requested regarding admissions and funding, among other items; discussed the list of expectations with the entire faculty in a Zoom meeting; and prepared for a second meeting with the Black students.

For the second meeting, Laura prepared a presentation on the list of expectations, including what seemed possible and not possible within each area of concern, and what the department had done in the past on these issues. This meeting was uncomfortable and rife with tension. After three extensive remote meetings between Black students and faculty/administrators, we all agreed on a departmental action plan and the faculty voted unanimously in favor of the plan (see table 5.1). The action plan did not meet all of the students' expectations for a racially just climate, but it touched upon all areas of the request: (1) visibility and funding of Black students in social welfare (e.g., funding more fellowships for Black students); (2) recruitment, admissions, and scholarly trajectories for Black students and faculty (e.g., reporting on admissions of Black students and hiring students as outreach workers); (3) decolonizing the curriculum (for this task, we hired Nicole, Evin, and Jameelah as consultants to review and comment on our foundation curriculum); and (4) improving

TABLE 5.1 Anti-racism plan

Goal 1: Increase visibility and funding of Black students in social welfare

Short-term (2020–2021)	Longer-range (2–5 years)
Set up a fund designated for Black student scholarships	Work with the development office to grow a fund for scholarships through direct appeals
Fund a committee to host events/trainings directly related to the Black community	Funding commitment for three years ($10,000 per year) for events/trainings
Hire students for outreach positions	Commit to hire outreach positions for 2021–2022 and evaluate results
Increase web visibility on Black student issues at Luskin and within social welfare	Consider center idea or partnerships with existing centers on campus

Goal 2: Enhance recruitment, admissions, and scholarly trajectories for Black students and faculty

Short-term (2020–2021)	Longer-range (2–5 years)
Admissions committee will draft language regarding increasing Black student recruitment and retention in applicant pool	Future joint hire in Black studies and/or in an area related to Black communities and social welfare
Plan at least one professional development event focused on Black PhD students	Continue to recruit and enhance lecturer pool
Recruit more Black lecturers for teaching pool	Expand Black faculty affiliates on campus
Consider joint appointments with Black scholars across campus	Investigate models for student involvement in admissions committees
Admissions audit of 2020 data; routine sharing of admissions data	

Goal 3: Decolonize the curriculum

Short-term (2020–2021)	Longer-range (1–3 years)
Hire summer researchers to assist with MSW and PhD curriculum review and recommendations	Partner with African American Studies to create a joint MA/MSW program
Craft an anti-racist competency and weave this goal into foundation courses and assignments	Assess outcomes for new competency

(continued)

TABLE 5.1 Anti-racism plan (*Continued*)

Goal 4: Improve climate and support for Black students

Short-term (2020–2021)	Longer-range (1–3 years)
Advocate for in-house mental health services	Secure more mental health support at Luskin through the dean's office
Provide frequent reminders to students regarding channels for reporting discrimination	Explore the potential for a restorative justice approach and training to address discrimination
Review Inter Group Dialogue (IGD) curriculum and train more PhD students and faculty in IGD	
Collaboration between faculty and students re: addressing climate (internal and external)	
Diversity Equity and Inclusion (DEI) and Black Caucus representatives to speak during student orientations	

the climate and support for Black students (e.g., advocating for designated Black student space). The plan included short-term and long-range actionable goals. With a plan in place, the challenge became how to carry out the work—which is how SWARC (the Social Welfare Anti-Racism Committee) was formed.

SWARC GROUP FORMATION AND PROCESS

Our process mirrored key stages of group norms and interaction: forming, storming, norming, performing, and adjourning (Tuckman & Jensen, 1977). The forming stage involves orienting the group to the issue, finding a purpose, testing roles and boundaries, and establishing interdependence between leaders and other members. Our group included a mix of department leadership, faculty, MSW and PhD students, and alumni. With some exceptions, many of us had not worked together or known each other beyond a surface level. We spent time orienting one another to our institution, with its limitations, and our various roles. Forming also meant that we were testing our boundaries with one another and finding our way as a group.

The storming phase includes explicit conflict, polarization, and resistance to group influence and established power differentials (Tuckman & Jensen, 1977). Our primary tension in SWARC was between students and administration, which was also layered with racial, role, and power differences. The two administrators in the group, Laura and Gerry, held the most power and were not Black; all of the students and alumni were Black or biracial. This storming also gave us the opportunity to work collegially, with less hierarchy, and to incorporate multiple viewpoints in the process. We had very real and direct expressions of positionality, with honest admissions of where our department had fallen short of truly embodying anti-racism.

In the norming phase, intergroup cohesion develops, new standards evolve, new roles are adopted, and tasks can focus the group. We began to feel more cohesive by focusing on the action plan and specific tasks. We also began to oscillate between seriousness and humor as we became more genuine with each other. Naming ourselves SWARC was significant in solidifying our mutual purpose and efforts. We also began to establish norms, such as students taking the role of facilitating meetings and setting agendas. As with any stage theory, there was movement back and forth between stages—for instance, storming over new issues that arose—but we also had a smoother return to norming as the group evolved.

In the performing phase, interpersonal structure and tasks are assigned, roles become flexible and functional, and group energy is channeled toward the task. The hard work of summer 2020 was tangibly directed into accountability to one another and our community, and continued on throughout the year. Each task was completed by committee, with multiple revisions and storming/norming, moving toward consensus on the final product, plan, or implementation. For example, in October 2021, we hosted a major event, "From Conversation to Practice: Making Black Lives Matter" that involved the entire social welfare community, including all faculty, staff, and students. We also worked together on public statements in response to racial violence and current events. We kept the work going with a tangible commitment to the anti-racism plan as an anchor.

The process of adjourning refers to task completion and often the breaking up or changes in the group. By June 2021, two of our core members were graduating; the group also needed to find some closure. Once we had all received COVID-19 vaccinations, we came together to film a video summarizing our accomplishments. The video was circulated throughout our community, our alumni, and externally to other social work programs. Two months later, we planned an in-person retreat where we reflected on what had been accomplished and where we had landed, and discussed what was next. The group brainstormed how to diffuse anti-racism into many school and department committees, yet we still wanted to continue SWARC in some form. This is not uncommon in intense group work; it is a recognition of the significance of the time together, while also acknowledging that the work is not yet complete.

BARRIERS TO ORGANIZATIONAL TRANSFORMATION

During our eighteen months of intensive work as a collective, we faced various challenges and barriers to our success. Perhaps the most significant barrier was time. During summer 2020, our productivity was at its highest. However, as the school year began, our frequent meetings were forced to become monthly. Despite our dedication, the reality was that SWARC work often had to take a back seat to our full-time roles as faculty, students, and alumni. While we were able to accomplish a great deal in a short period, time constraints were a primary barrier to sustained productivity.

The larger academy's ideas regarding what work is valuable had affected each of us as we attempted to prioritize SWARC work during the previous year and a half. We had all received subtle and sometimes not-so-subtle messaging that work aimed at tackling institutional racism is not deemed valuable within the academy. The undervaluation of this work also resulted in minimal compensation for it, with the exception of the contracted foundation-year curriculum review.

The context surrounding our action plan presented significant barriers to our progress in ways that we cannot address in this short piece.

These impacts ranged from the context of our school to the context of the state and the nation as a whole. Within our larger School of Public Affairs and the university, momentum addressing racism and anti-Blackness was slow. These differences in nimbleness resulted in our committee's adopting a strategy of focusing on what we could control within our department while advocating for larger changes at the School of Public Affairs, without tying our own progress to the larger changes.

In addition to time constraints and contextual limitations, we faced the challenge of building larger community support. We were all committed to this work being sustainable, which meant that our department's students, staff, and faculty had to think that the work was essential and that they played a role. We also wanted to ensure that we could move the work forward promptly while centering the voices of Black students and faculty. At times these goals conflicted, and as a group, we had to decide what direction to take. For example, after we shared the action plan with the whole school in a public meeting, white students began asking how they could support the work moving forward. At that time, SWARC had to consider a number of questions: What would it mean to include non-Black students in this work? What capacity did our committee have to create a pathway for more community members to be involved? What vetting, if any, should we do when welcoming more people to take the lead in this work? Ultimately, to build support, we launched a mini-grant program that provided all community members the opportunity to apply for funding to host events or trainings related to addressing anti-Blackness. While only a few community members applied, this was one essential way we attempted to build a culture of addressing anti-Blackness within our institution. We continue to strategize how we will increase community-wide support with these initiatives, particularly as we return to in-person activities.

As we continue this work, we will undoubtedly face more barriers. The barriers of time, context, and community support will not disappear. However, our commitment to this work and the power of the coalition we have built among students, faculty, and staff have allowed us to navigate these challenges. We hope these strengths will allow us to continue these efforts.

LESSONS LEARNED FOR ORGANIZATIONAL TRANSFORMATION IN SOCIAL WORK

Across the United States, social work institutions are being challenged to move beyond performative allyship and toward more concrete anti-racism work. This starts with examining our own organizations—institutions of higher education, social welfare institutions at large, and nonprofit organizations—to see how practices of white supremacy and anti-Blackness are embedded in the institutions themselves. Structural racism cannot be rooted out if it is left unseen or if we are blind to the many ways that anti-Blackness permeates social institutions (Olson, 2004; Taylor, 2016). From this case study, we have learned several lessons for transforming the university and achieving organizational change, as detailed below.

Sustained partnership among students, faculty, and administration is paramount. Faculty and administrators often take the stance that the faculty and administrators (who often rotate between groups) are the permanent members of the university, whereas students are "visitors," which renders their voices at times less meaningful. This stance effectively shuts down student voices in organizational change, thereby maintaining the status quo. Some of this sentiment had permeated our organization in relation to past anti-racism efforts. This movement was a turning point. While we recognize that students, faculty, and administrators hold different lenses and stakes in the organization, we learned that anti-racism work needs to be done collaboratively with sustained partnership among all three groups. To that end, breaking down power differentials, allowing time for a group dynamic to form, and truly listening to and hearing one another were critical.

Anti-racism organizational work needs to take a strong, unwavering stand. Anti-racism work is different from DEI or "diversity work." One issue that came up during the first year was the focus on anti-Blackness, with questions such as "what about other minoritized groups?" or "shouldn't we take a more intersectional approach?" While dealing with these questions with care, our coalition had to maintain our focus on anti-Blackness. We explained that centering the needs of Black people did not mean excluding or minimizing other needs. Given that race and racism in the United States are rooted in the Black/white binary and that anti-Blackness thus operates to justify a restrictive allocation of social and economic resources as well as social exclusion, conceptualizing the liberation project as addressing anti-Blackness has benefits for everyone (McGhee, 2021; Taylor, 2016; Zakaria, 2017). Creating ways for other groups of students and faculty to get involved in anti-racism efforts was one way that we kept our focus on anti-Blackness while still building community.

Organizational change efforts need funding and institutional support. Students asked for numerous ways of funding fellowships, jobs, and new faculty lines in the midst of a global pandemic, when new funding was far from guaranteed. As administrators, we realized that no sustained anti-racism effort could be maintained without financial backing. We used creative ways of financing students and obtaining new faculty positions. We created opportunities for Black students to be paid as outreach workers under work-study and with admissions and recruitment funds. We also applied for, and received, a new faculty line through the university's initiative on race, which will allow us to hire a new tenure-track assistant professor in Black studies. Other efforts for financing, such as creating a fellowship fund for racial justice, were less successful. The main takeaway is that institutional resources have to back up any type of organizational commitment to change.

Representation is essential. All too often, we hear from faculty that "we tried" or "there isn't a pipeline" when it comes to recruiting and admitting Black students or attracting Black faculty. One of the major lessons we learned camefrom student voices: representation and visibility are important in creating a climate that supports Black students and faculty. This means admitting and recruiting more Black students at all levels, making concerted effort to recruit Black faculty and lecturers, and increasing representation throughout the curriculum of Black authors, texts, and scholars. These changes will be incremental, particularly in transforming the curriculum, yet the lesson is key: representation is critical to fighting anti-Blackness within organizations of higher education, including social work.

CONCLUSION: PERSPECTIVES ON
ORGANIZATIONAL CHANGE

As individuals working together from different vantage points, racial groups, and positions of power, we conclude with brief narratives and our own perspectives. These narratives provide a glimpse into the emotional labor needed to sustain anti-racism work in higher education and the importance of building a coalition.

Laura: One of my main takeaways was understanding the difference between a professed commitment to anti-racism and concrete action. My initial reaction to the student expectations was a mixture of defensiveness (we already do so much!) and sadness/disbelief (how have we failed so miserably as an organization?). Part of me saw myself as having failed personally. As the only white member of SWARC, part of my learning curve in this process was to move past the complex emotions of defensiveness and guilt and to move toward concrete action. As the department chair, I often felt that it was up to me to move many pieces forward and that accountability and an eye toward incremental but also realistic change rested with me. Working closely with the students allowed me to get out of my own headspace and into a place of actionability. In my twenty years as a faculty member, I look at this process as the most transformative to date in my development as a leader.

Dominique: Participating in this committee was a profound learning experience, especially in my understanding of how to create organizational change focused on addressing anti-Blackness within the academy. During this process, what stood out most to me was the indisputable value of open dialogue among stakeholders, particularly between Black students and university leadership. However, understanding the value of open dialogue and creating it are vastly different tasks. Open dialogue requires that all parties involved be willing to speak their truth and actively listen and attempt to understand the views of others, despite all the barriers that make that extremely difficult. The complex histories among our members included mistreatment and misunderstandings, and current power imbalances resulted in significant mistrust that we had to manage constantly throughout our interactions. At times, open dialogue shut down, and I honestly began to question our chances of doing anything meaningful and the value of putting my physical and emotional energy into this work. However, our ability to reset and continue to strive toward open dialogue allowed us to create change that, despite our differences, we all viewed as important.

Jason: Initial meetings focused on what the department had done in the past for Black students. I took offense at this. First, no matter how nicely phrased, it was an attempt to negate my present concerns. Second, I felt it revealed a desire to focus on effort and not results. As a result, my work in this committee was focused on how we could measure our progress in ways such that subsequent cohorts could hold us accountable.

Gerry: I am an alum of this program and have been a field education faculty member in social welfare for thirty years. I have worked on anti-racism issues as a practicing social worker in a community mental health agency along with other helping professionals. I have worked on anti-racism in our institution along with students, staff, and faculty in our department and across campus, as well as with colleagues from other MSW programs. I have witnessed real systemic change happen, and I have seen individual beliefs altered. My professional and institutional memory and experiences, along with lived experience as a person of color within these institutions, provide me perspective and the reluctant acceptance that the arc is long. It is also exhausting to see that for every step forward we take a step or more back. As a social worker, I know that our work is sometimes incomplete, that it will be carried forth, and that it will take sustained effort and accountability to make sure we are truly taking more steps forward. The authenticity of this group is an example of possibilities for real change, with the opportunity to have real and hard discussions as individuals and as a group and to collectively concretize ideas into reality. Our work is not done, and it is our responsibility to make sure that what we started continues and real change is established.

Nana: It can be hard to be one person and know that the conversations you are having affect not only your greater cohort today but also the cohorts to come. Frequently, when participating in these conversations, I grappled with the immediate impact our conversations would have versus the long-term systemic change that was also needed. As the initial facilitator for these meetings, I often felt caught between wanting to be the "angry Black student" and playing the role of mediator. At times, it was difficult to empathize and uplift the experiences of students who have experienced harm in this space longer than I have, without adopting those experiences as my own. I frequently felt conflicted about my role on SWARC, particularly because so few of us were actually a part of the conversations affecting the other students and faculty around us, and I often felt concerned that I was speaking for a larger population than I had the right to. As I reflect on this experience a year later, however, I feel unwavering gratitude for this challenge and growth. I know there is much more that can be done and should have been done during this time, but I am proud of the progress that we did make and am very hopeful that it has set continued change into motion.

Latoya: My intention with this group was to help our students create meaningful change. To see the actions taken by our students, followed by the response from our department, was encouraging. For much of this process, I felt stuck between two worlds, being both a Black woman and a faculty member. I struggled with many of our group discussions, as I shared many of our students' concerns but also understood the power and limitations of our department. How does one function as an untenured faculty member, responding to student demands, managing my own experiences with institutional racism, and simultaneously collaborating with non-Black colleagues on sensitive issues around race? Addressing anti-Blackness in our program has felt both meaningful and performative, depending on the colleagues and students I spoke to; however, the work and commitment from this group remind me that although the road is long, change is possible.

Nicole: I held a unique perspective coming into the transformative challenge as an alum, a critical race practitioner, and a consultant. Assisting the department in facing its shortcomings around race was personal for me, particularly as an alum, as current student concerns echoed the concerns I had shared with my colleagues when I was a student in the department. I am hopeful for the future of the department and am confident about the success of their endeavor, as long as all faculty members engage deeply in their commitment and the efforts are sustained over time.

REFERENCES

Abrams, L. S., & Moio, J. A. (2009). Critical race theory and the cultural competence dilemma in social work education. *Journal of Social Work Education, 45*(2), 245–261.

Callender, S., Garcia, J., Oh, L., Sangalang, C., Solis, R., & Vazquez, N. (2007). *Critical race theory and social welfare.* Unpublished report, University of California, Los Angeles.

Haley, J. M. (2020). Intersectional and relational frameworks: Confronting anti-blackness, settler colonialism, and neoliberalism in US social work. *Journal of Progressive Human Services, 31*(3), 210–225.

Jones, C. P. (2000). Levels of racism: A theoretic framework and a gardener's tale. *American Journal of Public Health, 90*(8), 1212–1215.

Lopez, G. R. (2003). The (racially neutral) politics of education: A critical race theory perspective. *Educational Administration Quarterly, 39*(1), 68–94.

McGhee, H. (2021). *The sum of us: What racism costs everyone and how we can prosper together.* New York: One World.

Obasogie, O. K., & Newman, Z. (2016). Black Lives Matter and respectability politics in local news accounts of officer-involved civilian deaths: An early empirical assessment. *Wisconsin Law Review, 2016*(2), 541–574.

Olson, J. (2004). *The abolition of white democracy.* Minneapolis: University of Minnesota Press.

Orbe, M. (2018). "#BlackLivesMatter is racist; it should be #AllLivesMatter!": #AllLivesMatter as post-racial rhetoric. In S. E. McClure & C. A. Harris (Eds.), *Getting real about race* (pp. 305–317). Thousand Oaks, CA: Sage.

Taylor, K.-Y. (2016). *From# BlackLivesMatter to black liberation.* Chicago: Haymarket.

Tuckman, B. W., & Jensen, M. A. C. (1977). Stages of small-group development revisited. *Group & Organization Studies, 2*(4), 419–427.

U.S. News and World Report. (2023) Top public colleges and universities. https://www.usnews .com/best-colleges/rankings/national-universities/top-public.

Zakaria, R. (2017). *Against white feminism: Notes on disruption.* New York: Norton.

6

TRANSFORMATIVE JUSTICE IN PRAXIS

Creating the Alliance of Disability and Social Work

SARAH NUNES AND DIANE R. WIENER

T his chapter explores the creation, organizational structure, and future directions of a nonprofit entity, the Alliance of Disability and Social Work (ADSW), as illustrative of transformative justice in praxis. The importance of disability justice in social work education and practice is highlighted in order to situate the creation of ADSW (Sins Invalid, 2015). We review relevant literature to highlight the themes, gaps, barriers, and implications for the future of disability in social work that contributed to the authors' decision to found ADSW.

THE CREATION OF ADSW

ADSW began as a call to action. This chapter's coauthors created the organization together in direct response to gaps, barriers, and implications that we identified within the disability in social work literature. ADSW also arose as a consequence of our distinct and overlapping personal and

---

This chapter details the establishment of the ADSW from its origins until mid-2023. At the time of this book's going to press, the ADSW was in the process of changing its structure—from a nonprofit organization to a consultative, collaborative grassroots entity.

professional experiences. As discussed below, ADSW's focus is on social work education and practice. At the time of ADSW's genesis (at Syracuse University, in 2019), the coauthors were both affiliated with the Office of Interdisciplinary Programs and Outreach at the Burton Blatt Institute (Syracuse University College of Law). Sarah was a first-year MSW student working as a research assistant, and Diane served as a neuroqueer, gender-nonconforming research professor and associate director.

In March 2021, ADSW shifted its location to an independent one when it was granted nonprofit status at the New York State and federal levels. While ADSW was housed at Syracuse University, Sarah and Diane worked collaboratively to set up an advisory board (discussed below); when ADSW became a nonprofit organization, a board of directors was established.

Social work education is typically based on a medical model that does not lead social work students toward a deeper understanding of disability. Because the disability community is the largest community social workers serve, an in-depth and nuanced understanding of disability is crucial for social workers' and clients' success.

Social work students who learn solely or predominantly about the medical aspects of disability are thereby restricted in their understanding; importantly, this limitation has potential consequences for direct practice with clients and communities. Conceptualizing disability as solely medical or medicalized, rather than a complex set of cultural experiences, risks pathologizing the already often "othered" disability community (Bean & Krcek, 2012; Coriale et al., 2012; Dupré, 2013; Fuld, 2020; Gilson & Depoy; 2002; Gourdine & Sanders, 2002; Hallahan, 2010; Hearn et al., 2014; Judy et al., 2014; Kiesel et al., 2018, Kim & Sellmaier, 2020; Meekosha & Dowse, 2007; Morgan, 2012; Nunes, 2022; Pardeck, 2002; Quinn, 1995; Rees & Raithby, 2012; Smith et al., 2008; Stainton et al., 2010). ADSW will address these gaps in students' learning by partnering with universities and organizations to explore, review, and recommend revisions regarding social work and other educational curricula in order to center disability as a lived cultural experience and an aspect of intersectional identities.

Social work education does not often provide a robust discussion connected to disability as a lived experience and a cultural identity. Without a multifaceted and nuanced understanding of clients' experiences, social work students cannot effectively advocate, a cornerstone of the profession. Social work students who work from a disability justice perspective enhance their rapport-building skills and connection to communities, which are central to being an effective social work practitioner (Ballan, 2008; Bean & Krcek, 2012; Davis & Mirick, 2021; Gilson & Depoy, 2002; Kiesel et al., 2018; Kim & Sellmaier, 2020; Muyor-Rodríguez et al., 2019; Nunes, 2022; Poole et al., 2012; Rees & Raithby, 2012; Smith et al., 2008; Stainton et al., 2010; Wiener et al., 2009). ADSW will continuously center a disability justice framework in our dialogues and other interactions with social work students, practitioners, and educators.

Often, social work faculty desire to engage in discussion about disability equity, disability as culture and identity, and disability advocacy within the classroom and in the profession but lack knowledge about these topics. Those who seek to enact personal and institutional change cannot do so without first being equipped with the tools, resources, and knowledge necessary to incorporate disability equity, culture, identity, and advocacy into the classroom (Ballan, 2008; Davis & Mirick, 2021; Dunn et al., 2008; Nunes, 2022; Tator, 1996). ADSW has provided and will continue to provide professional development opportunities to students, practitioners, and faculty to augment their understanding and experiences of disability.

Various kinds of barriers exist to equitable access for disabled social work faculty, students, and practitioners. The social work profession is known for its gate-keeping practices; oppressive systems act to keep oppressive systems intact. The fact that disabled social work faculty, students, and practitioners do not receive equitable access in their employment and learning environments contributes to the undermining of their professional efficacy and financial solvency (Ballan, 2008; Coriale et al., 2012; Davis & Mirick, 2021; Dunn et al., 2008; Hearn et al., 2014; Kiesel et al., 2018; Poole et al., 2012; Stainton et al., 2010; Tator, 1996). ADSW was created for the purpose of addressing these systemic barriers.

Other themes in the literature underscore the presence of pervasive attitudinal barriers within social work education and practice that in turn reify large-scale systems of oppression (including ableism), thereby diminishing the professional efficacy and solvency of disabled faculty, students, and practitioners. Faculty, students, and practitioners are typically not "out" or open about their disability status, leading to isolation and marginalization within social work education and practice. Often, isolation and marginalization are magnified by hostile environments. Besides having detrimental effects on individuals and groups, these circumstances greatly diminish the promise of coming together to organize collectively. Furthermore, social work researchers, educators, administrators, and practitioners are inconsistent in their inclusion of disability identity as part of an understanding of and commitment to intersectionality. The patterns described herein are present on a global scale.

Despite thirty years of social work research on disability identifying these themes (including Ballan, 2008; Bean & Hedgpeth, 2012; Bean & Krcek, 2012; Cheatham et al., 2015; Coriale et al., 2012; CSWE, 2001; Davis & Mirick, 2021; Dunn et al., 2008; Dupré, 2012; Dupré, 2013; Džombić & Urbanc, 2009; Friedman, 2002; Fuld, 2020; Gilson & Depoy, 2002; Gourdine, 2002; Hallahan, 2010; John & Schrandt, 2019; Johnson, 2009; Judy et al., 2014; Kiesel et al., 2018; Kim & Sellmaier, 2020; Linton & Canales, 2018; Meekosha et al., 2007; Morgan, 2012; Muyor-Rodríguez et al., 2019; Nunes, 2022; Pardeck, 2002; Poole et al., 2012; Probst et al., 2015; Quinn, 1995; Rees & Raithby, 2012; Rueda et al., 2014; Smith et al., 2008; Stainton et al., 2010; Tator, 1996; Wiener et al., 2009), U.S. schools of social work have not consistently addressed the 2001 recommendation of the Council on Social Work Education (CSWE) Education and Policy Accreditation Standards (EPAS) to remediate social work curricula by incorporating disability literature, experiences, narratives, and diversity into classroom and field-based coursework. Additionally, CSWE has not outlined a specific plan for schools of social work to take immediate action to remedy the disability content disparities that exist within social work education.

We have reflected frequently on the legacy of social work and its troublesome history rooted in social Darwinism, eugenics movements, and complicity and engagement with carceral practices and institutions, as well as other practices and ideologies that inform the medical model of disability. These ongoing influences continue to hold sway in social work practice and education, affecting the lived experience of disabled social work clients, communities, students, faculty, staff, and practitioners. Our significant concerns about these themes, legacies, and patterns led, along with the reasons cited previously, to the creation of ADSW.

WHAT IS ADSW?

In addition to being a call to action, ADSW was created intentionally as a transformative entity. Our egalitarian approach to chairing our meetings, our flattened hierarchy with respect to decision making, the intersectional composition of our advisory board and board of directors, and our engagement with interdisciplinarity are all designed to influence and change positively the current landscape of disability in the social work profession. As part of ADSW's more egalitarian and less hierarchical approach, Diane and Sarah are currently exploring switching their respective roles as executive director and managing director. As they think creatively about what it means to colead an organization that actively seeks to distinguish itself from normative nonprofit structures (often, though not always, based on vertical hierarchies), their roles might change again every few years. Critical questions and explorations of equity, what it means to lead, and what it means to be leaders remain intertwined with feminist and disability praxis—all central to ADSW's values and mission.

As a nonprofit organization, ADSW will provide needed resources, professional development opportunities, consultation, and programming approaches to support disabled and nondisabled social work practitioners, educators, students, professional leaders, and others in working effectively with disabled clients and communities. As of this writing, ADSW has presented at programs and events hosted by the Social Work and Law National Symposium, the New York State Association of Probation Officers, the Association of Women in Psychology, NAADAC (the Association for Addiction Professionals), and the National Association of Social Work's (NASW) New York State Chapter (as part of an ongoing continuing education series) to begin to infuse communities connected with and adjacent to social work with a critical understanding of disability and disability justice that is intersectional and reflective.

As noted previously, ADSW started with an advisory board within the academic environment at Syracuse University. The advisory board comprises a diverse array of individuals, including social work practitioners, social work faculty members, art and design faculty members, advocates, and social work students. The board of directors is similarly variegated in its members' roles and orientations.

As part of our commitment to transformative justice in praxis, we reflected upon and continue to be intentional about creating inclusive power structures and identities within ADSW's leadership, approaches, and practices. As white Ashkenazi Jewish feminists, we actively created a leadership team that is diverse in myriad ways, with particular attention paid to pro-disability, anti-racist, pro-queer, anti-classist ethics and labor, and, more broadly, anti-oppressive values.

Disability rights movements (DRMs) have been criticized as white-centric (Northwest Health Foundation, 2020 Thompson, 2020). Arguably, DRMs continue to primarily serve and remain dominated by whiteness, are devoid of diverse disability representation, and actively contribute to the harm, undermining, and marginalization of disabled Black, indigenous, and people of color (DBIPOC). The ADSW advisory board and board of directors think critically and consistently about intersectional identities, power dynamics, and purposeful egalitarianism. We operate with a flattened hierarchy that is likewise reflective of our diverse leadership team's membership. ADSW's organizational culture aims to further the organization's autonomy, collaborative approaches, and progressive-minded, collective decision making.

ADSW meetings and discussions are consistently cofacilitated via a minimally hierarchical approach, often referred to affectionately as "the pancake." During all of our interactions, we openly acknowledged our positions of power, professional and personal, in relation to one another. In holding ourselves and each other accountable with kindness and assertiveness, we actively and compassionately challenge each other. Through this iterative process, we aim to reflect critically on how we may sometimes reenact systems of oppression in our own work. In turn, we address directly what we can do to disentangle, understand, and disrupt these habits, tendencies, and patterns.

During each ADSW meeting, we have "accessibility check-ins," reflecting on pragmatic communicative elements like language choices, pause time, and other aspects of engagement. Among other examples, during one of our virtual meeting accessibility check-ins, we addressed the digital brainstorming and "mind-mapping" tools we had been utilizing. We centered the voices and experiences of those on our team most affected, ultimately resulting in our not using those tools anymore and instead finding new approaches for increasingly effective and accessible collaborative communication that met everyone's needs and will likewise benefit our constituents in the short and long term. Additionally, we have in-depth conversations about race and disability, practicing our continuous commitment to be accountable to one another and the community at large by exploring and challenging our own biases.

As noted previously, disability justice is and will remain foundational to all of ADSW's structures and approaches. The "Ten Principles of Disability Justice" (Sins Invalid, 2015) help us to think and act critically about social work's legacies and current practices as we engage intersectionality and decenter whiteness and other privileged and oppressive identities and locations. Increasingly, activists emphasize disability justice as a model that is distinct from disability rights, which remains white-centric (Northwest Health Foundation, 2020; Thompson, 2020).

FUTURE DIRECTIONS OF ADSW

As a new organization, ADSW is growing and evolving. Currently, we are building our website; developing resources for our constituents; consulting with social workers at the macro, mezzo, and micro levels of practice; partnering with colleagues who work in solidarity with the principles of disability justice; and building our unique brand. ADSW's future directions will be rooted in bringing disability rights, cultures, and identities, within a disability justice activist framework (Sins Invalid, 2015), to the forefront of social work education and practice. Disability interconnects with myriad axes of difference, including but not limited to race, ethnicity, gender expression, class, sexual orientation, age, nationality, political beliefs, spirituality and secularism, geographic region, and size. We recognize vividly that experiences of disability are unique to each disabled individual's lived experience. Understanding and prioritizing the experience and expertise of disabled people within social work education and practice are and will remain the cornerstone of ADSW's transformative praxis.

REFERENCES

Ballan, M. S. (2008). Disability and sexuality within social work education in the USA and Canada: The social model of disability as a lens for practice. *Social Work Education, 27*(2), 194–202. https://doi.org/10.1080/02615470701709675.

Bean, K. F., & Hedgpeth, J. (2012). The effect of social work education and self-esteem on students' social discrimination of people with disabilities. *Social Work Education, 33*(1), 49–60.

Bean, K. F., & Krcek, T. E. (2012). The integration of disability content into social work education: An examination of infused and dedicated models. *Advances in Social Work, 13*(3), 633–647.

Cheatham, L. P., Abell, N., & Kim, H. (2015). Development and validation of the social worker's attitudes toward disability scale. *Journal of Social Work Education, 51*(2), 379– 397. https://doi.org/10.1080/10437797.2015.1012939.

Coriale, L., Larson, G., & Robertson, J. (2012). Exploring the educational experience of a social work student with a disability: A narrative. *Social Work Education, 31*(4), 422–434. https://doi.org/10.1080/02615479.2011.564611.

CSWE. (2001). *Issues of disability and disability–competent care social work curriculum: Educational resource database.* https://www.cswe.org/CSWE/media/Diversity-Center/DCC -Educational-Resources-Disability_Database-Accessible-11_6_18-FINAL.pdf.

Davis, A., & Mirick, R. (2021). Microaggressions in social work education: Learning from BSW students' experiences. *Journal of Social Work Education, 58*(1), 1–18. https://doi-org /10.1080/10437797.2021.1885542.

Dunn, P., Hanes, R., Hardie, S., Leslie, D., & MacDonald, J. (2008). Best practices in promoting disability inclusion within Canadian schools of social work. *Disability Studies Quarterly, 28*(1). https://doi.org/10.18061/dsq.v28i1.66.

Dupré, M. (2012). Disability culture and cultural competency in social work. *Social Work Education, 31*(2), 168–183. https://doi.org/10.1080/02615479.2012.644945.

Dupré, M. E. (2013). *Social work education and disability: A multicase study of approaches to disability in core and specialized curricula at three bachelor of social work programs* [Doctoral dissertation, University of Manitoba (Canada)]. http://search.proquest.com/docview/1512636922 /abstract/757C7BBCEC474018PQ/1.

Džombić, A., & Urbanc, K. (2009). Involvement of persons with disability in the education of social work students. *Ljetopis Socijalnog Rada, 16*(2), 375–394.

Friedman, B. D. (2002). Two concepts of charity and their relationship to social work practice. *Social Thought, 21*(1), 3–19. https://doi.org/10.1080/15426432.2002.9960304.

Fuld, S. (2020). Demarginalizing intellectual and developmental disabilities in graduate social work education. *Journal of Social Work Education, 56*(3), 508–518. https://doi.org/10.1080/1 0437797.2019.1656584.

Gilson, S. F., & DePoy, E. (2002). Theoretical approaches to disability content in social work education. *Journal of Social Work Education, 38*(1), 153–165. https://doi.org/10.1080/104377 97.2002.10779088.

Gourdine, R. M., & Sanders, T. (2002). Missed opportunities and unlimited possibilities: Teaching disability content in schools of social work. *Journal of Health & Social Policy*, *16*(1–2), 207–220. https://doi.org/10.1300/J045v16n01_17.

Hallahan, L. (2010). Legitimising social work disability policy practice: Pain or praxis? *Australian Social Work*, *63*(1), 117–132.

Hearn, C., Short, M., & Healy, J. (2014). Social work field education: Believing in students who are living with a disability. *Disability & Society*, *29*(9), 1343–1355. https://doi.org/10.1080/09687599.2014.935296.

John, A., & Schrandt, K. (2019). Social work practice with individuals with intellectual disability: Social work students' perspectives. *Journal of Social Work Education*, *55*(4), 724–735. https://doi.org/10.1080/10437797.2019.1611511.

Johnson, K. (2009). *Critical social work: Disabling discourses and enabling practices in disability politics* (2nd ed.). London: Routledge.

Judy, M., Carter, I., Hanes, R., McMurphy, S., & Skinner, S. (2014). Disability and social work education in the United Kingdom. *Canadian Journal of Disability Studies*, *3*(3), 53–82. https://doi.org/10.15353/cjds.v3i3.173.

Kiesel, L. R., DeZelar, S., & Lightfoot, E. (2018). Challenges, barriers, and opportunities: Social workers with disabilities and experiences in field education. *Journal of Social Work Education*, *54*(4), 696–708. https://doi.org/10.1080/10437797.2018.1507365.

Kim, J., & Sellmaier, C. (2020). Making disability visible in social work education. *Journal of Social Work Education*, *56*(3), 496–507. https://doi.org/10.1080/10437797.2019.1661899.

Linton, K., & Canales, C. (2018). Notes from the field: Continuing education for social workers on Autism, Intellectual Disability, and sexual health. *Professional Development: International Journal of Continuing Social Work Education*, *21*(2), 61–66.

Meekosha, A. P. H., & Dowse, D. L. (2007). Integrating critical disability studies into social work education and practice: An Australian perspective. *Practice*, *19*(3), 169–183. https://doi.org/10.1080/09503150701574267.

Morgan, H. (2012). The social model of disability as a threshold concept: Troublesome knowledge and liminal spaces in social work education. *Social Work Education*, *31*(2), 215–226. https://doi.org/10.1080/02615479.2012.644964.

Muyor-Rodríguez, J., Manzano-Agugliaro, F., & Garrido-Cardenas, J. A. (2019). The state of global research on social work and disability. *Social Work in Health Care*, *58*(9), 839–853. https://doi.org/10.1080/00981389.2019.1659904.

Northwest Health Foundation. (2020). *Disability justice: An audit tool*. https://www.northwesthealth.org/djaudittool.

Nunes, S. (2022, March). *Troublesome Histories and disablement: Legacies of psychology, social work, and other affiliated professions*. Paper presented at the meeting of Feminist Psychology in the Twenty-First Century, Association of Women in Psychology, Chicago.

Pardeck, J. T. (2002). Knowledge, tasks and strategies for teaching about persons with disabilities. *Journal of Social Work in Disability & Rehabilitation*, *1*(2), 53–72. https://doi.org/10.1300/J198v01n02_04.

Poole, J. M., Jivraj, T., Arslanian, A., Bellows, K., Chiasson, S., Hakimy, H., Pasini, J., & Reid, J. (2012). Sanism, "mental health," and social work/education: A review and call to action.

Intersectionalities: A Global Journal of Social Work Analysis, Research, Polity, and Practice, 1, 20–36.

Probst, B., Balletto, C., & Wofford, N. (2015). What they bring: How MSW students think about mental disorder and clinical knowledge. *Clinical Social Work Journal, 43,* 419–430.

Quinn, P. (1995). Social work education and disability: Benefitting from the impact of the ADA. *Journal of Teaching in Social Work, 12*(1), 55–71.

Rees, J., & Raithby, M. (2012). Increasingly strange bedfellows? An examination of the inclusion of disability issues in university- and agency-based social work education in a Welsh context. *Social Work Education, 31*(2), 184–201. https://doi.org/10.1080/02615479.2012.644946.

Rueda, H. A., Linton, K. F., & Williams, L. R. (2014). School social workers' needs in supporting adolescents with disabilities towards dating and sexual health: A qualitative study. *Children and Schools, 36* (2), 115–124.

Sins Invalid. (2015). *Ten Principles of Disability Justice.* https://www.sinsinvalid.org/blog/10-principles -of-disability-justice.

Smith, L., Foley, P. F., & Chaney, M. P. (2008). Addressing classism, ableism, and heterosexism in counselor education. *Journal of Counseling and Development: JCD; Alexandria, 86*(3), 303–309. https://doi.org/10.1002/j.1556-6678.2008.tb00513.x.

Stainton, T., Chenoweth, L., & Bigby, C. (2010). Social work and disability: An uneasy relationship. *Australian Social Work, 63*(1), 1–3. https://doi.org/10.1080/03124070903291886.

Tator, C. (1996). Anti-racism and the human-service delivery system. In C. E. James (Ed.), *Perspectives on racism and the human services sector: A case for change* (pp. 152-170). Toronto: University of Toronto Press.

Thompson, V. (2020). *About the founder.* Ramp your voice! https://www.vilissathompson.com /about.

Wiener, D. R., Ribeiro, R., & Warner, K. (2009). Mentalism, disability rights and modern eugenics in a 'brave new world', *Disability & Society, 24*(5), 599–610. https://doi.org/10.1080 /09687590903010974.

RESOURCES

Adjei, P. B. (2018). The (em)bodiment of Blackness in a visceral anti-Black racism and ableism context. *Race, Ethnicity and Education, 21*(3), 275–287. https://doi.org/10.1080/13613324.2016 .1248821.

Bashford, A., & Levine, P. (2010). *The Oxford handbook of the history of eugenics.* Oxford: Oxford University Press.

Bell, C. (2012). *Blackness and disability: Critical examinations and cultural interventions.* East Lansing: Michigan State University Press.

Ben-Moshe, L. (2020). *Decarcerating disability: Deinstitutionalization and prison abolition.* Minneapolis: University of Minnesota Press.

Ben-Moshe, L., Chapman, C., & Carey, A. (Eds.). (2014). *Disability incarcerated: Imprisonment and disability in the United States and Canada.* New York: Palgrave Macmillan.

Biklen, D., & Burke, J. (2006). Presuming competence. *Equity and Excellence in Education, 39*(2), 166–175. https://doi.org/10.1080/10665680500540376.

Blahovec, S. (2017, December 6). Confronting the whitewashing of disability: Interview with #DisabilityTooWhite creator Vilissa Thompson. *Huffpost*. https://www.huffpost.com/entry/confronting-the-whitewash_b_10574994.

Catapano, P., & Garland-Thomson, R. (2019). *About us: Essays from the disability series of the New York Times*. New York: Liveright.

Charlton, J. I. (2000). *Nothing about us without us: Disability oppression and empowerment*. Berkeley: University of California Press.

Clare, E. (2017). *Brilliant imperfection: Grappling with cure*. Durham, NC: Duke University Press.

Cone, K. (n.d.). *Short history of the 504 sit-in*. Disability Rights Education & Defense Fund. https://dredf.org/504-sit-in-20th-anniversary/short-history-of-the-504-sit-in/.

Couser, G. T. (1997). *Recovering bodies: Illness, disability, and life writing*. Madison: University of Wisconsin Press.

Crenshaw, K. (2016, October). *The urgency of intersectionality* [Video]. TEDWomen. https://www.ted.com/talks/kimberle_crenshaw_the_urgency_of_intersectionality/up-next.

Crenshaw, K., Gotanda, N., Peller, G., & Thomas, K. (Eds.). (1996). *Critical race theory: The key writings that formed the movement*. New York: New Press.

Crossman, A. (2019). *A biography of Erving Goffman*. ThoughtCo. https://www.thoughtco.com/erving-goffman-3026489.

Davis, A. Y. (2003). *Are prisons obsolete?* New York: Seven Stories.

Davis, L. J. (1995). *Enforcing normalcy: Disability, deafness, and the body*. London: Verso.

Davis, L. J. (2017). *The disability studies reader* (5th ed.). London: Routledge.

Dolmage, J. (2017). *Academic ableism: Disability and higher education*. East Lansing: University of Michigan Press.

Goffman, E. (1959). *The presentation of self in everyday life*. Garden City, NY: Doubleday.

Goffman, E. (1961a). *Asylums: Essays on the social situation of mental patients and other inmates*. Garden City, NY: Anchor.

Goffman, E. (1961b). *Encounters: Two studies in the sociology of interaction*. Indianapolis: Bobbs-Merrill.

Goodley, D. (2017). *Disability studies: An interdisciplinary introduction* (2nd ed.). London: Sage.

Groce, N. E., & Marks, J. (2000). The great ape project and disability rights: Ominous undercurrents of eugenics in action. *American Anthropologist, 102*(4), 818–822.

Hall, M. C. (2019, September 23). Critical disability theory. *The Stanford encyclopedia of philosophy*. https://plato.stanford.edu/cgi-bin/encyclopedia/archinfo.cgi?entry=disability-critical.

Hamraie, A. (2017). *Building access: Universal design and the politics of disability*. Minneapolis: University of Minnesota Press.

Hedva, J. (n.d.). Sick woman theory. *Mask Magazine*. http://www.maskmagazine.com/not-again/struggle/sick-woman-theory.

Kafer, A. (2013). *Feminist, queer, crip*. Bloomington: Indiana University Press.

Lebovic, M. (2020, May 9). Eighty years ago, lethal Nazi T4 center began euthanizing Germans with disabilities. *Times of Israel*. https://www.timesofisrael.com/80-years-ago-lethal-nazi-t4-center-began-euthanizing-germans-with-disabilities/.

Linton, S. (1998). *Claiming disability: Knowledge and identity*. New York: New York University Press.

McRuer, R. (2006). *Crip theory: Cultural signs of queerness and disability*. New York: New York University Press.

Metzl, J. (2009) *The protest psychosis: How schizophrenia became a Black disease*. Boston: Beacon Press.

Miserandino, C. (n.d.). The spoon theory [Blog post]. *ButYouDontLookSick*. https://butyoudont looksick.com/articles/written-by-christine/the-spoon-theory/.

Mitchell, D. T., & Snyder, S. L. (2001). *Narrative prosthesis: Disability and the dependencies of discourse*. East Lansing: University of Michigan Press.

National Association of Social Workers. (2021). *Code of Ethics*. https://www.socialworkers.org /about/ethics/code-of-ethics/code-of-ethics-english.

National Disability Rights Network. (2020, February 1). *Harriet Tubman: Disability rights in Black 2020*. https://www.ndrn.org/resource/drib2020-harriet-tubman/.

PhilPapers. (n.d.). *Linked bibliography for the SEP article "Critical disability theory" by Melinda C. Hall*. https://philpapers.org/sep/disability-critical/.

Piepzna-Samarashinha, L. L. (2018). *Care work: Dreaming disability justice*. Vancouver: Arsenal Pulp.

Price, M. (2011). *Mad at school: Rhetorics of mental disability and academic life*. East Lansing: University of Michigan Press.

Puar, J. K. (2017). *The right to maim: Debility, capacity, disability* Durham, NC: Duke University Press.

Ray, S. J., & Sibara, J. (2017). *Disability studies and the environmental humanities: Toward an eco-crip theory*. Lincoln: University of Nebraska Press.

Rembis, M., Kudlick, C. J., & Nielsen, K. (2018). *The Oxford handbook of disability history*. Oxford: Oxford University Press.

Roustabout Media. (2019, July 8). *Piss on pity: We will ride* [Documentary]. Vimeo. https:// vimeo.com/ondemand/pop1/328004608.

Saleebey, D. (2005). *Strengths perspective in social work practice* (4th ed.). Boston: Allyn & Bacon.

Samuels, E. (2017). Six ways of looking at crip time. *Disability Studies Quarterly, 37*(3). https:// dsq-sds.org/article/view/5824/4684.

Taylor, S. (2017). *Beasts of burden: Animal and disability liberation*. New York: New Press.

Waitoller, F. R., & Thorius, K. A. K. (2016). Cross-pollinating culturally sustaining pedagogy and universal design for learning: Toward an inclusive pedagogy that accounts for dis/ability. *Harvard Educational Review, 86*(3), 366–389.

Walker, N. (2022). *Neuroqueer: An introduction* [Web]. Neuroqueer: The writings of Dr. Nick Walker. https://neuroqueer.com/neuroqueer-an-introduction/

Wiener, D. R. (2005). Antipsychiatric activism and feminism: The use of film and text to question biomedicine. *Journal of Public Mental Health, 4*(3), 42–47. https://doi.org/10.1108 /17465729200500023.

Wiener, D. R. (2021a). Dis/ability and critical cultural studies. In *Oxford research encyclopedia of communication*. Oxford: Oxford University Press. https://doi.org/10.1093/acrefore /9780190228613.013.1006.

Wiener, D. R. (2021b). Utilizing disability studies and universal design for learning (UDL) as philosophical foundations for advising and supporting. In R. Wagner & C. Catalano, (Eds.), *Advising and supporting in student affairs* (pp. 233–251). Springfield, IL: Charles C. Thomas.

Wilson, R. A. (2021). Dehumanization, disability, and eugenics. In M. Kronfeldner (Ed.), *The Routledge handbook of dehumanization* (pp. 173–186). London: Routledge.

Wong, A. (Ed.). (2018). *Resistance and hope: Essays by disabled people.* Disability Visibility Project. https://www.smashwords.com/books/view/899911.

II

CORE CONCEPTS AND COURSES IN THE TRANSFORMATIVE CURRICULUM

7

REFLECTIONS ON A TRANSFORMATIVE RELATIONAL EXPERIENCE

DANIELLE JATLOW

This reflective chapter was written just after I returned from an impromptu trip to see my Nana toward the end of her life. During a meeting with a colleague, I was sharing how this critical visit with my grandmother was affecting me. I was particularly focused on how the time I spent with her was a catalyst for learning, growing, and developing in my roles as social work practitioner and as a newer social work educator. Reflection, exploration, navigation of uncertainty and unpredictability, slowing, honoring variation, holding complexity, and practicing patience and presence had become recentered in my various relationships. Jan encouraged me to write about this through a personal narrative.

AN UNEXPECTED VISIT TO NANA

My sister and I decided to fly down to Florida quickly following a troubling phone call with Nana in which she didn't sound like herself. Though she was 101 years old, she had been in pretty good health and living alone, which was her preference. We arrived late at night from Vermont and quietly slipped into her apartment, which she keeps open in case medical personnel have to enter unexpectedly. She was sitting at the edge of her bed, feet dangled over the side, and staring into the darkness. Her skin was gray, her eyes seemed tired, her body had become frailer, she moaned and seemed in pain. Her first words invited us to get her water so she could take her medication. She seemed relieved not to have to make her way to the kitchen. We gave her hugs, water, and meds and put her back to bed.

The next morning, in spite of Nana's reluctance, my sister and I took her to the doctor. The doctor, who had seen her just a month before, said that Nana had undergone significant decline since that last visit, but Nana couldn't clearly remember or articulate any changes she had experienced since her last medical appointment. It is possible she had fallen and had forgotten, or that COVID restrictions had increased her social isolation and decreased the remnants of her social connectedness (her card games were put on hold early on, most of her friends had passed away, and most family lived far and had been cautious about visiting during the pandemic). It's also very possible that Nana's body was starting to feel her 101 years and was preparing to make the final transition toward death. While my grandmother was in pretty good health overall—her vitals seemed stable, her faculties were mostly intact, and her blood work had not revealed any pathology—the doctor believed the decline would continue and in-home care was a necessity for Nana's safety and quality of life. So much of what my sister and I had observed in the past day was a labored existence—Nana was putting in a tremendous amount of effort just to navigate her activities of daily living in her apartment. Following the doctor's assessment and recommendations, we set up hospice care, recognizing it seemed hard to believe that she had, until now, been managing on her own.

I was relieved when both the hospice social worker and the hospice nurse came to the home to do their initial intake assessments the day after the doctor's appointment. The two hospice workers, from the same agency, stayed for about an hour each and engaged Nana in two different assessments, using tools and methodologies that led to different prognoses. I shared the results of the various assessments with my family. For some family members it was unsettling to have three different professionals (doctor, nurse, social worker) provide three different prognoses. While the lack of a clear prognosis and trajectory is familiar for many families, it doesn't often feel helpful to receive seemingly different assessment results and recommendations about the same person.

How much time can we expect Nana to live? How much support does she need right now, and how much support might she need in the near future? Should we be initiating a higher level of support now, or do we wait? What resources will this take, and how do we make a decision about what support she will need next week when family will be a little less available? The questions seemed loud, and the questions seemed pressured. Different responses surfaced. I noticed myself feeling a deep connection and compassion for the professionals trying to help my family make sense of an unpaved pathway ahead—one that would entail differentiated navigation of emotions, perspectives, decisions, and letting go. I also noticed I wasn't feeling anxious or conflicted about how three different professionals arrived at three different sets of recommendations for Nana's care moving forward.

Sitting with the complexity of human experience and all of the accompanying, ambiguity during these moments of decision is not an experience usually normalized or valued in places and spaces where people expect that training, education, skill, experience, and research should provide firm answers (Chappell Deckert & Koenig, 2019). Typically, people want answers and clarity. When decisions affect our loved ones, we are invested in doing what we think is best, and we need support from professionals and others to help us get there. However, this isn't always possible, and three or more of the most skilled and experienced providers might end up with different recommendations. Decisions and approaches are personal, unique, cultural, and spiritual; they require exploration, care, compassion, self-reflection, and self-awareness.

I could tell that all three providers brought expertise in their fields, tested tools, and compassion for my grandmother (Tanner, 2020). None of them truly knew or could predict with certainty when Nana might die, what would best meet her needs in the days ahead, and how she or my family and I were feeling (which was evolving and varied) about her transition toward death. Various prognoses from different experts in different fields and within fields can and do exist at the same time. It's a postmodern gift—and for people needing an answer, not without its challenges (Afrouz, 2021). Needing and wanting answers is typical and can be important for maintaining and upholding our proclivity toward certainty during uneasy times. What happens when we don't know? What feelings come up for us? Where do we feel that in our bodies, and how do we each face and move through that experience? What are the effects of increasing our awareness about how we move through discomfort—individually, within families, and collectively? How and when might we learn this, and who and what experiences will help us to move through this?

Clients are the experts on their own lives and experiences (Laird, 1995; Freeman & Couchonnal, 2006; Murphy et al., 2013). The professionals, who bring expertise, could offer my family their thoughts, considerations, perspective, and ideas, but I felt confident that they were all carrying some uncertainty in their certainty. All three of them were incredulous that Nana was 101 and doing so well. None of my family members thought this was unusual. All three of the professionals spent about an hour with Nana before making recommendations. In twenty-four hours, though, as I had witnessed during this critical time of assessment, one hour could look very different from the next. The varying recommendations were unsettling for some family members and, at times, even the providers. Nana could live for a day, a few months, another five years, or longer. It was hard to know. I didn't feel I needed to know, which allowed me to stay (for the most part) grounded and calm. Is it a privilege to feel comfortable with uncertainty? Many people sit uncomfortably in navigating diverse perspectives. I listened. I noticed. I reflected back and tried curiously to understand what each provider and family member was bringing to this complex situation. A person's experience moving toward death was shifting and changing in each moment, and it made sense that nobody and everybody should or could have "an answer."

Over several days, I was attentive. I really tried to see Nana. I wondered if she noticed me noticing, and I didn't think she did until she asked me if I might need to get back to my work (my computer was in the other room). I let her know I didn't have anything pressing, but I would let her rest. She closed her eyes. I might have been too attentive, and it was making her tired. I appreciated her gentle cue and let her sleep. During the previous few days, I had observed Nana experiencing millions of moments of varying levels of functioning, pain, movement, clarity, engagement, energy, and presence. In environments where "knowing" is valued, variation and inconsistency in human behavior are often perceived as faulty, contradictory, or challenging. If we *know* something, weaving in a contradiction can be hard, as it goes against what we have already determined. I have come to expect that variation and unpredictability are often the most authentic of human qualities. Being with Nana and holding the ambiguity of all the different moments she was experiencing provided clarity for me—she was very much living as she moved toward the end of her life.

The professional assessments were important, but their importance waned as I focused solely on being with Nana and making sure the qualities I wanted her to experience were in the room with us. The yearning to maintain control in the face of hard emotional experiences can pull humans toward reactionary and challenging places, leading toward anxiety, blame, disagreement, judgment, relational rupture, and more. It can distract people from feeling, being, and connecting. With all the opinions, assessments, emotions, and decisions, I was focused on how to be deeply *with* Nana during this visit. Most of our current professional environments and systems have been constructed to efficiently and productively oversimplify our understanding of people by placing us into categorical, linear, if-this-then-that scenarios—when really, during times of uncertainty or sadness or challenge, what I think we can benefit from most is presence, understanding, and tenderness.

Nana struggled to bend over to put on her undergarments. Together, my sister and I took turns helping her with this intimate task. We shared glances of comfort, acknowledging we were with Nana now, and thought about how she had been managing this on her own prior to our arrival. I remembered Nana doing this for us when we were little. We cleaned Nana's apartment, which had become slightly overrun by dust and stale air. We did laundry, washed and changed her sheets, made meals, and offered water. We held her hand, knowing that it had likely been months or years since she had experienced touch of any kind. Her skin seemed so thin that even a soft touch might cause a bruise, but it was worth the risk. I leaned toward more physical connection, not less, knowing Nana had been living alone for so long. Human touch can light up parts of the brain that other experiences cannot. As she moved toward death, I wanted her to recall and experience this connection, kinship, touch, and love.

Nana's naps punctuated most of the day, so when she woke, knowing my time with her was limited, I yearned to hear her stories and wanted her to know it was okay to talk about death and dying. Not everyone feels comfortable talking about death with the living, but we are all moving toward it. I wanted Nana to feel she didn't have to face death alone, and I worried that nobody had asked her how she was feeling about it. Nana had shared with many of us that she had been sad and lonely since my grandfather died, and she had also shared that she was ready to die. However, I didn't assume that she didn't have other feelings about facing death or actually dying. What were her wishes about dying? Did she want or need anything before she died? Did she have beliefs or ideas or hopes about what would happen after she died? Did Nana want me to ask her these questions, did she prefer to ponder them on her own, or was she content to move toward death without concern for the answers? I sat gently but curiously with Nana and let her have space to respond in whatever way suited her.

I asked if she would tell me stories from when she was younger, and she did—both beautiful and mostly difficult experiences growing up as the daughter of a bootlegger who died young. She also told stories about what it was like to be the daughter of a mother who struggled with mental health issues. I had so much I wanted to learn, but I also wanted to be thoughtful about which questions to ask and for what reason. Navigating my curiosities as both a granddaughter and a social worker kept me contemplative about the various hats social workers wear as they navigate relationships with family, friends, clients, and others. Nana kept repeating "I've lived a strange life," and I believed her without requiring more explanation than what I heard and listened for in her recollections.

Nana's stories opened a door to a time of her life that preceded her role as my grandmother. I thought about how little I knew about that earlier part of her life—I reflected on how many human relationships neglect space for exploration connected to the parts that are not adjacent to our own. I let myself imagine my grandmother as a younger person— as a child, an adolescent, a young adult, a woman prior to marrying my grandfather (deceased now for twenty years), a mother to my father and his brother, and more. I felt a tinge of intimate closeness and connection to the identities that Nana carried throughout her life. I felt distant from the depths of all the moments that comprised a full and dynamic life mostly lived in another era. Close and distant and everything in between, simultaneously—in this way, we exist in relationships.

LEAVING AND STAYING WITH

With so much unknown about Nana's care and health but with hospice set up, leaving her to head back to Vermont felt a little bit too soon for me. I extended my stay for a few more days. During those days, I let myself get as close to the fullest and most cherished moments of relationship as possible—savoring the minutiae of the activities of daily living, inquiring softly about events, experiences, and stories, noticing Nana's breath, seeing her eyelids open and shut, studying the lines on her face. I was maybe too aware of the subjective experience people have about choosing to see these types of moments as intimate and coveted, and I felt somewhat disappointed that others don't often relish in the intimacy. I lingered there because—*look at self first*—it brought me to my other relationships and what I had perhaps been overlooking, both over- and underemphasizing so much without realizing.

Being present in the caring helped slow time. In this slowing, I let myself look tranquilly at the imminent decision to return home to Vermont even though Nana was still living and needing care. Family members and other caretakers were going to be stepping in when I left. I unhooked from the need to know the outcome of what was pending, waiting, to come. To stay or go left little space for the immense possibilities that typically exist within the limitless bounds of human experience. I was curious about what it would mean to return home while also holding onto this brief visit and the generational bidirectional influence with and for her, and with and for me. No "right" answer can feel tumultuous, but there was an internal calm as I reflected on the time we shared.

Knowing is often mistaken for "simple" or "easy" or "right." The complexities and nuances of the art of human decision making are highly personal, intimate, and sometimes enigmatic to others (and often judged, moralized, or stigmatized). Understanding the strengths and limitations of each pathway, making an individualized or collectively informed (broadly defined and defined by those involved) decision, and being accountable to the wide range of consequences of choice are embedded in my social work practice (and perhaps, of course, an ongoing area for work in my own life experience). My time with Nana held a remarkable sacredness of both uncertainty and presence at this time toward the end of her life, and I wished it were longer, in fact forever, for her. I worked on making sense of leaving and staying—feeling the pull of connection here and the pull of connection there simultaneously.

RETURNING HOME

Engaging so closely with my Nana was with me as I stepped back to my family in Vermont, my social work classroom, and my social work practice. I carried the task of integrating the profundity of holding her so closely and intensely into the different relationships and roles I hold outside of my relationship with her. When I returned home to my family, I found myself lighter, slower, more present, more compassionate—for myself, for others. I thought about forgiveness and repair, being relationally close and far at the same time, and living and dying more than I had before I left. I stayed curious about this reflection and ways to turn my thinking and reflection into feeling and action. I felt thankful that being with Nana toward the end of her life had sparked this relational adjustment in me. Hoping to hang onto this openness, I felt like a parent watching a young child hold onto the very end of a string tied to a helium balloon. I knew the string could slip out of hand at any time. I wasn't anxious, but I definitely felt the tension.

We barely leave space to set intentions for what we want to hold onto and what we want to shed in our lives. In my social work practice, I provide my clients with an opportunity to think attentively and thoughtfully about this exact thing. Typical navigation of our busy lives doesn't usually privilege reflection, intention, thoughtfulness, and care. My time with Nana helped me stay focused on what matters most—not simply at the end of a life. Time is uncertain even when it doesn't feel that way. Who have we shared our moments, minutes, days, years, and lives with? What do we value, and how have we made space to connect with our most authentic selves? What have we learned from our proudest and our darkest experiences? How have we practiced loving ourselves, and how have we practiced loving others? How are we making sense of our lives while we are living so that we can, if possible, rest, feel content, when we are close to dying? What needs tending, nurturing, and nourishing in the moment, in the moments, in the days, in the years, and how will we make time to explore this? How are we cultivating compassion, deepening, loving, and intentionality as we navigate through joys, challenges, and the highs and lows of our time?

RETURNING TO THE CLASSROOM

Experiencing the range of human emotion with clients is transformative work. As my clients share and navigate thoughts, ideas, hopes, dreams, issues, struggles, complexities, choices, and emotion, I am changed, experiencing transformation in the process. The multidimensional and dynamic nature of the change and growth that happen within relationships is unteachable and often indescribable through our limited language. We share through words and sometimes through other means (creatively, artistically, spiritually, physically) as we reflect on our relational work (with self, in supervision, by way of consultation, and through other means). The essence and energy of what happens between client and social worker are right there interpersonally, and are also carried into every other relationship that the social worker and the client hold. Some call this concept a form of generalizability, but I feel it's more than that. Traditionally, most of the social work skills, concepts, and frameworks in the classroom underemphasize metamorphic human processes. This is social work—human work—after all.

I returned to the classroom from my time with Nana with a renewed pedagogical stance focused intensely on nurturing and honing purpose and meaning, intensifying curiosity, centering complexity (Iancu & Lanteigne, 2022), and recommitting to valuing utter presence and slowing within relationships as essential to social work skill and practice. I had been working too hard to separate out and clarify my social work practitioner self and my newer, developing social work educator self. Where had those messages come from, and what views had I constructed that dictated my leaning toward compartmentalization? Where else had I experienced this? I shed what I felt had been a required yet uncomfortable role shift and moved toward integration of these roles, coming to see my classroom as a coconstructed community space predicated on relationships, experiences, emotions, and values (some aligned, some differentiated, of course). In this way, I realigned internally and began to further trust my more authentic, congruent self.

Through this small change in perspective and identity, I became more deeply rooted in the social work principles that guide my social work practice while in the classroom space. I felt attuned with a collaborative, relational, inclusive community orientation where students and I are in the experience together, walking side by side, attempting to look in the same direction (Rollins, 2020). Share, learn, grow, manage discomfort, retreat, remain, experience joy, honor uniqueness and togetherness, hold grace, be real, open, changing—all through engaging in exploration of selves in relationship to others. It isn't easy. My hope is that students step into the process of developing self-meaning, sense of hope, authentic connection, interpersonal growth, and individualized and collective movement toward becoming—always striving to be evolving, developing versions of their social worker selves within this community context. In the transformative community space, I aspire for my students and me to critically reflect on and admire the complexities of our human experiences—all the things we know, all the things we don't know, and all the things we don't know we don't know—and to explore together the dynamic, multidimensional understandings of identities, positioning, privilege, and power in relationship, in community. I wondered how, through which methods, I could and would continue to develop in my roles and how to further hone my current exploration of self and others, building iteratively on methods I had already practiced and practiced and practiced. How might I shift into new levels of approaching, learning, and deepening? Which relationships and experiences would hold me accountable to this evolving exploration?

Many of our service systems and educational systems are set up to restrict or push against these types of foundational being and skill development in social work practice (Cabiati & Gómez-Ciriano, 2021; Dore, 2020). And while many or most students come to appreciate the transformative approach, they also have an understandable yearning and concern about acquiring more concrete skills, interventions, and answers. This yearning allows me to explore and grapple transparently with the conundrum of supporting students to be social workers who "know" as they step into a broad range of placements, programs, systems, and environments, and supporting students who practice cultivating ongoing self-awareness and critical thinking as they consider principles and practices based in postmodern, constructionist, strength-based, justice-oriented, transformative approaches to social work. Students will each want to, need to, and get to make decisions about who they are and what they bring to their clients and colleagues within the vast social work field. The possibilities are limitless for students to carry and hone their unique social work lens. What else might they want to consider and learn and practice? How might they stay curious, humble, and connected to their evolving stances and lenses as they navigate their various relationships, practice environments, and lives? How will they be supported to determine what they want to continue to sharpen and learn and shift?

While I was in Florida visiting my Nana, I wondered what my students might think of the diverse assessments, recommendations, and decisions we were contemplating as a family. How might my students step into the space with my grandmother and my family holding different perspectives and honoring "no one pathway" toward peace or wellness or health or comfort? How would they help my family sit in the discomfort of uncertainty and challenging emotional experience? Each person and professional will bring all that they uniquely bring—sometimes that is more than enough, sometimes it is enough, and sometimes, though hopefully not too frequently, it is not enough to enable people to make sense of the widest range of unifying and unique complex experiences. This is the integrated personal and professional practice work that continues on in our field.

My visit with Nana helped reaffirm the importance of finding calm, finding clarity, and continuing to cultivate curiosity and patience for myself and others during challenging and complex emotional experiences. Holding someone you love during a transitional or critical time— helping them and others (family members, hospice workers, doctors, social workers, friends, and more) move through the uncertainties of the events of living—helped me to further reflect on, acknowledge, and integrate the ways in which the conundrums and seeming contradictions of human experience are inherent, yet quieted and undervalued, in most arenas of social work practice and social work education. Conundrum and uncertainty, while central to our lives as people, are counter concepts to the "expert" environments within which we live, learn, and practice.

There will always be people who want answers to unanswerable questions. Finding authentic self and grounding amid change, transition, and the unknown is a social work skill, a social work educator skill, and a human skill. After all, the more things shift and change, the more we navigate the unknown, the more we are called to be in our humanity.

REFERENCES

Afrouz, R. (2021). Approaching uncertainty in social work education, a lesson from COVID-19 pandemic. *Qualitative Social Work*, 20(1–2), 561–567.

Cabiati, E., & Gómez-Ciriano, E. J. (2021). The dialogue between what we are living and what we are teaching and learning during Covid-19 pandemic: Reflections of two social work educators from Italy and Spain. *Qualitative Social Work*, 20(1–2), 273–283.

Chappell Deckert, J., & Koenig, T. L. (2019). Social work perplexity: Dissonance, uncertainty, and growth in Kazakhstan. *Qualitative Social Work*, 18(2):163–178. https://doi.org/10.1177/1473325017710086.

Dore, I. (2020). Social work on the edge: Not knowing, singularity and acceptance. *European Journal of Social Work*, 23(1), 56–67. https://doi.org/10.1080/13691457.2018.1463971.

Freeman, E. M., & Couchonnal, G. (2006). Narrative and culturally based approaches in practice with families. *Families in Society*, 87(2), 198–208. https://doi.org/10.1606/1044-3894.3513.

Iancu, P., & Lanteigne, I. (2022). Advances in social work practice: Understanding uncertainty and unpredictability of complex non-linear situations. *Journal of Social Work*, 22(1), 130–149.

Laird, J. (1995). Family-centered practice in the postmodern era. *Families in Society*, 76(3), 150–162. https://doi.org/10.1177/104438949507600303.

Murphy, D., Duggan, M., & Joseph, S. (2013). Relationship-based social work and its compatibility with the person-centred approach: Principled versus instrumental perspectives, British Journal of Social Work, 43(4), 703–719. https://doi.org/10.1093/bjsw/bcs003.

Rollins, W. (2020). Social worker–client relationships: Social worker perspectives. *Australian Social Work*, 73(4), 395–407.

Tanner, D. (2020). "The love that dare not speak its name": The role of compassion in social work practice. British Journal of Social Work, 50(6), 1688–1705. https://doi.org/10.1093/bjsw/bcz127.

8

TRANSFORMATIVE FIELD EDUCATION

A Relational Approach

JB BARNA

A transformative approach to social work invites social workers and social work educators to think about change from a critical (Fook, 2002) and social constructionist (Dean, 2012) perspective. I interpret this perspective as inviting us to consider how identity, power, and social arrangements affect the way we make sense of the world around us. It invites us to question what we know, and how, by examining language and dominant discourses. A transformative social work approach invites us to embrace relationships as foundational to authentic and profound work. It invites us to make explicit our own assumptions about ourselves, the people we find ourselves sitting with, the organizations within which we sit, and the systems that arrange how we do the sitting. This approach invites us to consider our values, their origins, and their impact on our work. In fact, given the social dilemmas of our time, a "reimagining" of field education practices (George et al., 2013) can benefit greatly from a transformative and relational approach to learning and doing. In this chapter, I will share some thoughts, ideas, and examples of ways we might center this approach within our field education programs.

Throughout the twenty years of my tenure as the coordinator of field education in the Department of Social Work at the University of Vermont, I came to understand that the development of students' skills, confidence, and social work identity was embedded in multiple levels of intentional relationships in their field experiences. Conversely, when students were struggling in their placements, I wondered (and therefore, explored) whether a relational quality was absent from the student placement. While we as field educators may take it for granted that relationships matter, I believe it is the intentional building and layering of these relationships that contributes to overall success for field students and field agencies.

It is important for me to be explicit regarding what I mean by a relational approach. I see this as an approach in which relationship is at the center of teaching and learning. I am talking not only about the relationship between student and field instructor but also about the students' relationship to themselves, to service users, to colleagues, to the specific field of practice in which they are engaged, and even to the profession as a whole. When we think about field education as the epitome of experiential learning, I believe we are called upon to focus on the entirety of the student experience. Often we privilege and focus on skills and competencies related to students' work with clients and service users when, in fact, their skills as members of organizations and collaborative teams, as well as their skills of deeply knowing themselves as social workers, are worthy of that same focus.

I believe we can do this most easily by grounding the learning process in the student *relationship* to the entire field experience. The language of relational field education, and the approach to which it refers, provides students with a home base to which they can always return. By helping students explore the contemplative questions below, we are framing their work as a combination of relationships that feeds into their identities as social work practitioners.

- What qualities do I bring to my relationship with my field instructor?
- What qualities do I bring to my relationship with the service users— the people with whom I sit and do my work?
- What qualities do I bring to my relationship with my colleagues?
- What qualities do I bring to my relationship to the field of practice within which I am engaged and even to the profession of social work as a whole?
- And finally, what qualities do I bring to my relationship with myself?

There is great benefit to starting with and centering relationship. Through this explicit naming and describing, we are stating how foundational relationship is to the practice of social work. Students can more easily identify their strengths, questions and curiosities, and places for growth and development when evaluation of their work is negotiated through these questions. These relational questions help with assessment of what is going well in a field placement and what needs more attention. This assessment and development of skills are laser focused on the ultimate goal of launching not just intelligent new social workers but competent, confident, and relational new social workers.

Because of this approach at UVM, I developed a prompted and relationally driven December conversation for field instructors and students. The origin story of this document comes from a realization, during my 2013 sabbatical, that we had students and field instructors doing what we called a Mid-Year Evaluation just three months into an almost nine-month placement (so, not actually midyear). As field coordinator, when I thought about what kind of intentional feedback students needed at this point in the academic year (late November/early December), I realized that it really came down to the relationships described in the questions outlined above. The following is an excerpt from the tool/assignment given to students and field instructors that reflects these ideas.

> **Introduction**: This December Conversation is a time for Field Instructors and students to take a deep breath, sit together for a bit, and reflect on your individual and joint beginnings. It concludes with you imagining your work together in the weeks and months to come. This dialogic and qualitative evaluation guidance has been designed to be more of an authentic and relational structured conversation than a numeric evaluation tool.
>
> The hope is that the experience of sitting together in this way will be far more dynamic than any written account of that conversation. However, as an academic program, the field instructor is required to write something about your conversation (a summary) and make a recommendation for the student's first semester grade. Additionally, it seems important that the student participate in the "writing" and "telling" of your evaluative experience together.
>
> **Discussion**: The discussion prompts below are meant to encourage reflection and conversation. Reading these ahead of the actual meeting time will give each of you a chance to prepare some initial thoughts

which, in all likelihood, will impact the depth and breadth of your generative "out loud" thinking and talking process.

I.   Please reflect together on the student-orientation period. Talk about both the formal agency-directed process and the student-directed process of curiosity and information-seeking.

II. Please reflect on and tell stories of your relationship with one another as student and Field Instructor. Also explore the nature of the student's relationships with other professional colleagues and what kinds of related goals the student might like to have as a social work collaborator.

III. Please share some specific examples of the student's relationship to the work of the internship. The student should comment from a self-reflective stance of skill progress, knowledge, and a depth of emotional understanding. This is a good time to consider how the complexity of the work provided opportunities for growth as a professional social worker, not just in terms of skill development, but also in terms of taking initiative, developing a social work identity and a personal self-reflective practice. It's also a place to notice assumptions, language, and times when questions complicated the taken-for-granted approaches to the work. Think, too, about the connections between field and classroom work.

IV. Please spend some time getting specific about your goals for your work moving forward—both as a student and as a Field Instructor/ student dyad. Please give voice to what's going well and to any lingering concerns. Consult the initial Learning Agreement to see if revisions are needed.

V.   Intentionally explore together the things that may have been left unsaid.

I used this tool for the last eight years of my time as field coordinator. Field instructors and faculty field liaisons who went through the transition (from the previous Mid-Year Evaluation to the current December Conversation) provided immensely positive feedback about this newly focused and relational evaluative tool. A colleague serving as a field liaison at the time expressed that, in her opinion, the new tool seemed to follow the natural course of how we begin any new endeavor together, thus modeling for students "what is possible" with social work colleagues going forward. Another appreciated how the academic expectations were "lifted up" as natural progressions in a much larger process. If we look at the opening questions for relational field education alongside the prompts within this tool, the overlap of ideas is clear.

In the sections that follow, I have chosen to expand on two of what I consider to be the most profound relational components of field education. The student relationship to field instructor and the student relationship to themselves were always central to the trainings and orientations I did with both field instructors and students.

STUDENT RELATIONSHIP TO FIELD INSTRUCTOR

Students, faculty, and field instructors have been known to identify field education as the place where classroom knowledge and experiences take flight. In fact, the Council on Social Work Education describes field education as "the signature pedagogy of social work education" (Wayne et al., 2010). Students often identify their field experiences as the time and place they see their identities as social workers come more brilliantly into focus. Field instructors, therefore, can play a key role as mentors to our students. It is not uncommon for these mentoring relationships to happen not only during the student's time in the field agency but also beyond their graduation and into their social work practitioner career. It has been relatively common for me to have unexpected casual conversations with current and past field instructors about the students with whom they have remained connected. These conversations are usually accompanied by very enthusiastic storytelling and easy smiles. It was apparent, in these cases, that the field instructor–student relationships mattered: the impact of the relationship lingered on and on.

So, in addition to spending time on the many intricate details of what it takes to be a field instructor (timelines, paperwork, requirements, etc.), I used these trainings to emphasize the field instructor's responsibility to intentionally build relationships with their students. I wanted them to consider how these mentoring and teaching relationships develop. Following are five examples from those trainings.

FIELD INSTRUCTOR RELATIONSHIP MINDSET

I generally started with asking field instructors to adopt the mindset that building student relationships with intention needs to be a central theme in their teaching. To illustrate this point, I often told this story from my own experience as a student in the first year of my MSW program. I shared that I had been struggling with something my field instructor, Margaret, said about me in a meeting in front of others. She shared some personal information I was not ready for others to know. When I went into our supervision meeting later that week, she asked me how I felt the meeting went. I lied and said I thought it went well. She replied with a single word: "Really?" I stuck to my story. She followed with, "I guess I was wondering if you had any feelings about the part of the meeting when I shared something personal without your permission?" At that point I said, "Well, I guess I was surprised, but it was fine. I'm fine." In other words, I lied again. She then said something like, "You know, JB, we have almost a full year of work together ahead of us. Telling one another the truth—no matter how hard—is going to be important to our relationship but more important, to your learning. Let's reschedule our supervision for a time tomorrow and let's both think about having this conversation in a different way at that point." I said it was fine again and I could be more honest in that moment. She was adamant that we "sleep on it," so I left after having only been in the room with her for a few minutes. To say this conversation changed my life as a social worker (and person) would be an understatement. Our relationship has continued for more than thirty-seven years—so much so that I keep a picture of Margaret and me on my desk at work. I feel that it continues to help me to know she is keeping an eye on me.

SETTING THE STAGE

Borrowing from Kathleen Crocket's (2002) collaborative supervision work, I also encouraged field instructors to write their students an actual letter before their first day in their field placements. I explained that the letter would probably say much of what had already been said in an interview and other previous planning meetings, but the intention of writing a letter was to set the stage that this field instructor-student relationship mattered. In other words, it showed that there was an implicit value being placed on the relationship. I encouraged field instructors to include things such as what a student could expect of weekly supervision, what the field instructors' supervisory style looked like, and something about how they were looking forward to learning and teaching with and from the student.

MODELING AS FIELD TEACHING METHOD

Additionally, I reminded (even warned) new field instructors that students are great observers, watching their every move not only during what are explicitly seen as "learning opportunities" but also during less explicit times. I liked to call those the in-between moments. I explained that students notice your tone when you talk to colleagues in the hallways and around lunch tables, what you say about clients before and after client meetings, how early/late you come to meetings, how late you stay at work after others have left for the day, and more. I usually laughed and told another story of my own student experience—that I was so enthralled with what and how my field instructor practiced social work that all I wanted to do after graduation was get a silver soft-top jeep, exactly like the one she drove. My intention during this part of the orientation was not to scare field instructors but to let them know the power of their relationship with a student who is eager to learn it all. And when I said "all," I was really trying to emphasize those in-between moments. It isn't simply about what we say aloud; it is also about who we are and how we show up in our practice settings that has an impact.

WARM AND WELCOMING STANCE AS ENGAGEMENT AND RAPPORT BUILDING

A rather simple gesture I encouraged was for field instructors to invite the student to lunch during the first week of placement. I talked about this because I have observed that not knowing the lunch culture is often a source of stress for our students. They want to know if they should bring their lunch or not; they want to know if people eat at their desks or eat together somewhere. Additionally, lunch can be an informal and even intimate time—a time when students can see their field instructors as real people. I would encourage field instructors to ask about their extra-curricular activities and other campus life experiences. Students are in a very exciting part of their social work journey when they are in their field placements, and they have a "big life" outside of the field experience. I have always believed this small gesture can show the student that, at the end of the day, we are all just human beings engaged in the work together and that our relationships with one another are bigger than the titles of student and field instructor.

CURIOSITY, VULNERABILITY, AND NOT KNOWING

While these actions are fairly concrete, perhaps the most important part of encouraging this relational approach to field instructor is being authentically curious about how the students are making sense of what they are seeing and doing. I explained that this curiosity can be powerful if pointed toward issues of social difference, long-held values and beliefs (and their origins), assumptions they might be unearthing, their relationship to power, their relationship to knowledge development and truth (or Truth), and more. It can reduce defensiveness and can allow the student to be vulnerable, take risks, and be comfortable "not knowing." Curiosity from a field instructor can enable students to think more deeply about themselves in the work—especially as it relates to the ways they are similar to and different from those with whom they work. Therefore, I very explicitly encouraged field instructors to center curiosity in their work with students.

STUDENT RELATIONSHIP TO THEMSELVES

A second profound relational component of field education—the students' relationship to themselves—builds nicely on the first component. I have observed quite a range of student ability on this component, often correlated with their previous experiences of vulnerability. Many social work students, for example, have been in positions of needing and asking for help themselves and, as a result, started from a particular place of knowing themselves. In my experience, they seemed less surprised by how "who they are in the world" may be affecting their practice. However, even for those who were less accustomed to this self-exploration, taking a stance of vulnerability did seem to resonate eventually with their desire to be attentive and effective practitioners. No matter the point from which they start, it is important that we explicitly talk about this journey of reflective practice as a value to hold close throughout the entirety of their social work career. Where they start is their unique launching point, and it is important that we make space for students to show up "exactly as they are" in these early moments. It's not just field instructors encouraging this work. Faculty in the social work classrooms play a role; faculty academic advisers play a role; the social environment of the academic department plays a role; field liaisons and seminar instructors play a role; and, of course, other students and colleagues play a role.

Developing a self-reflective practice is commonly used language in social work education and in the field of social work, but how that is understood and practiced can vary dramatically (Fook, 2002). After reviewing the syllabus for a field seminar some years ago, a student raised their hand and said, "Do you mean to tell me that you are going to grade us on our ability to be self-reflective because that's too personal—this isn't supposed to be therapy." Fortunately for me, another student responded before I could. She was eloquent and clear and said, "We can't avoid doing the very thing we ask our clients to do, can we?" At that point, I took a deep breath and chose to be patient with the process. I had faith that the student would eventually come around to the necessity and beauty of this social work practice value. Of course, critical reflection, just because it uses personal experience as a basis for learning, is not necessarily the same as therapy. However, there are and should be therapeutic outcomes of all good learning (Fook & Gardner, 2007, pp. 44–52).

I find myself frequently sharing that, in a field that is full of unpredictability, knowing ourselves intimately enough to not be surprised by our own in-the-moment engagement (reactions, decisions, and actions) gives us the best chance of being fully present for the experiences of the people with whom we were working. I follow with the question, "Is it not our goal to be fully present?" I also explain that this is not a simple task to be checked off a to-do list one time. Rather, this is a significant part of their social work practice. It is complicated, nuanced, and forever changing.

Students need help with this (as do the rest of us). It's become clear to me that structured methods of reflection are most helpful—any method that teaches students to have a deeper relationship with themselves through reflective practice is likely going to have a positive impact on the student as practitioner. Personally, I believe the teaching, learning, and practice of Jan Fook's model of critical reflection (Fook, 2002; Fook & Gardner, 2007) is incredibly impactful for both students and seasoned practitioners. By adding the critical perspective to reflection, students have the opportunity to truly unearth the assumptions, values, ideals, and thinking patterns that affect their practice. Students are encouraged to look at their identities and social context in relation to the identities and social context of those with whom they are working and, even more generally, how their identities over time have contributed to the beliefs and lenses that affect their practice engagement, assessment, planning, and evaluation.

Likewise, students are encouraged to look at their relationship with power and to develop their own analysis of power arrangements in agencies and organizations. Students are encouraged to look at language (theirs and others) and how that affects how they see a situation and what they take for granted as "knowing and knowledge." Finally, developing a critically reflective practice allows students to use past experiences as their teachers for future experiences in an extremely explicit manner—the process ends with them naming and identifying their own personal theory of practice.

Vulnerability is a key component in students' ability to develop an authentic and complex relationship with themselves (Béres, 2020). I believe that a deep and complex relationship with the self is essential for effective social work practice. A relational approach to field education, therefore, requires field instructors to be willing to work with students to see this as a significant piece of their learning. And dare I say that, in order to do so, field instructors must also have this same depth of relationship with themselves.

I've had many experiences with students and the critically reflective process through the teaching of the field education seminars. I always poll the students on their relationship with critical reflection. Most would say that in the past when they reflected on challenging situations, they were encouraged to go straight to how they "felt about" the situation and the analysis would often end there. The purpose of reflection, they were taught, was problem solving for the "next time" they encountered something similar. But when we talked about the process of critical reflection (as defined by Fook), one of the most common responses was that they did not realize how prevalent their assumptions were about the situation, the people involved, and themselves. A second common response was how powerful it was for them to consider their identities (race, class, gender, sexuality, ability) in relation to the identities of those with whom they were sitting. A third common response was how profound it was for them to explore how their personal values affected the situation and then to explore where those values came from.

Students have overwhelmingly appreciated participating in the critical reflection process. Perhaps the most salient and undeniable thread was their stated appreciation for their relationships with the other students in the classroom. They centered these relationships as foundational to their ability to receive and respond to the critical questions asked, their ability to take risks being open and raw with their emotions, and their willingness to see perspectives other than their own. They explained that their vulnerability to complicate their understanding of themselves was only possible because of those trusting relationships with the other students in the seminar.

A CRITICAL REFLECTION EXAMPLE FROM MELANIE

To underscore the relational approach to field education through a critically reflective process, I am sharing the experience of an undergraduate senior, Melanie, in our field experience seminar. In this process, students are asked to bring a critical incident to the group for discussion and exploration. A critical incident is an experience from their field placement that they are struggling to make sense of—a real, raw experience that they want to consider more deeply. It does not have to be an emergency or crisis; in fact, it can be quite benign (Fook & Gardner, 2007). Students are encouraged to bring incidents to the group that they can't stop thinking or worrying about.

The first part of the assignment involves presenting the critical incident and then engaging in dialogue related to the group's critical questions. A facilitator keeps the process moving by asking importantly timed process questions. All students are trained as facilitators in critical reflection, and all have multiple opportunities throughout the year to take their turn as facilitator. For the second part of the assignment, the student responds in writing to a series of reflective questions about the process, new learnings, and thoughts going forward.

Melanie was a first-semester senior BSW student. The critical reflection started with her describing the context of the incident (where her field placement was, a little bit about her role in the experience, and who else was present). She also explained why the incident was critical for her—in this case, because she still didn't understand why she acted the way she did and continued to have a physical sensation of discomfort when she thought about what had happened. Then she read aloud a brief description of the incident, which I am paraphrasing:

> I am interning at the family center, and one of my assignments is to attend the technology group for the families in our community who describe themselves as New Americans. Staff sit at the computers with whoever shows up, trying to help them navigate through some of their questions about the software or even basic computer skills. Most people who come want help understanding the communication software from their children's schools, job search engines, and how to find newspapers in their native languages. Relationships develop over time as we end up talking about other things that are going on in their lives and other areas in which they could use some support. This was my first time attending the group. When I walked in, I observed the people in attendance and chose to sit with three men looking at the same computer screen. I quickly realized that one of the men seemed to know more than the others and was showing them how to do some of what they were asking. I helped out a little, but it didn't seem as though they needed me all that much. I stayed with them throughout the group. There were many other people there that night, and most of them seemed like they needed a lot of help. There were not enough of us to go around. There were two women not too far from

where I sat, but I did not go over to them. When I left the center that night, I was very confused about my behavior. I was keenly aware that I chose not to help the women but instead stayed with the men.

After she read this to us, the facilitator followed the critical reflection process. She asked if there were any clarifying questions. There were a few but none of any major significance. The facilitator then invited the group to ask Melanie critical questions. The first question asked was about Melanie's identities in relation to the identities of those in the group. Melanie shared that there were people from several African countries, from Nepal, and from Vietnam. She then said that she identifies as a white cisgender queer woman. She also shared that the men she sat with told her their families had come to the United States from the Republic of Congo. When asked about the women's identities, she shared that she was not entirely sure; however, they were wearing head scarves. At this point, she was asked if she thought these identities had anything to do with why she sat with the men versus the women. This took Melanie a while to unpack. She first examined gender and age. Several questions that followed were related to her queer identity. It seemed that we weren't quite getting to the insight she was looking for. Then a student asked her about the role the women's headscarves might have played in her decision to not go toward them. Melanie paused and explained that the process was becoming emotional for her, and it was here that the conversation changed direction.

Melanie shared with the group something that most students did not know about her—that she was hard of hearing. She had hearing aids and read lips. She also shared that her quality of life had been significantly affected by the pandemic because of mask wearing. She was quite tearful and shared that maybe these women didn't get the help they needed from her because she was afraid that between the headscarves, the masks, and the noise in the room, she wouldn't be able to hear them. She also shared that one of the reasons this incident was confusing for her was that it is harder for her to hear lower-pitched voices (like those typical of men) and still she chose to sit with the men.

More questions were asked, and eventually Melanie shared that she has been wondering if, as someone with a disability, she can be a good social worker. She said she had never met another social worker who was hard of hearing. Students then began helping her deconstruct "good social worker" and "disability." At one point, a student very gently asked her if she believed that people with disabilities should not be social workers. Melanie sat straight up in her chair and said she had never thought of it that way—that "of course people with disabilities can be social workers . . . just maybe not me." And then she kind of laughed at herself. She also shared that she thought keeping her hearing loss "a secret" was not helping her in her social work practice. This was a big moment for Melanie.

We continued with the critical reflection process. She could easily answer the facilitator's next question: "Has anything shifted in your thinking about the incident?" She responded that her thinking had shifted; the story of the incident was thickened and complicated through the process of asking and responding to the group's critical questions. In the written part of the assignment, she explained that she was still a bit stunned that so much had not occurred to her in the moment that night, or even afterwards. She wrote about knowing that her hearing loss is incredibly complicated for her and that she is eager to do more work exploring the relationship between her hearing loss and her social work practice.

CONCLUSION

Making sense of who we are in our work as social workers can be incredibly interesting and rewarding. Ultimately it is our clients who benefit. Paying attention to our relationship with our "self" through a reflective process is key. Doing this in community with others can be dynamic; it can shift how we see ourselves and how we do the work. This kind of relational work does require some guidance and practice. Working with students in their field placements and field seminars provides a wonderful avenue for them to begin developing a relational and reflective social work practice. I have shared some overarching field education practices that have had an impact on our students' learning, our field instructors' practice, and my own. It is abundantly clear to me that field education benefits greatly from a transformative and relational approach to learning and doing.

REFERENCES

Béres, L. (2019). Reflections on learning as a teacher: Sharing vulnerability. In L. Béres & J. Fook (Eds.), *Learning critical reflection: Experiences of the transformative learning process* (pp. 123–138). London: Routledge.

Crocket, K. J. (2002). Introducing counsellors to collaborative supervision. *International Journal of Narrative Therapy and Community Work, 2002*(4), 19–24.

Dean, R. (2012). Becoming a social constructionist. In S. Witkin (Ed.), *Social construction and social work practice: Interpretations and Innovations* (pp. 72–102). New York: Columbia University Press.

Fook, J. (2002) *Social Work: Critical Theory and Practice*. London: Sage.

Fook, J., & Gardner, F. (2007). *Practicing critical reflection: A resource handbook*. Maidenhead, UK: Open University Press.

George, P., Silver, S., & Preston, S. (2013). Reimagining field education in social work: The promise unveiled. *Advances in Social Work, 14*(2), 642–657.

Wayne, J., & Raskin, M., & Bogo, M. (2010). Field education as the signature pedagogy of social work education. *Journal of Social Work Education, 2010*(46), 327–339.

9

ETHICAL CONSIDERATIONS ON RACISM

Strategies for a Transformative Anti-Racist Pedagogy

MERLINDA WEINBERG

In approaching the challenging topic of racism, this chapter offers some guidance by identifying ethical considerations and transformative pedagogical strategies to support critical anti-racist education. The question is, what can educators do to contribute to a transformative pedagogy for anti-racism in social work and ethics? As a white settler and educator, I reference some of my own struggles with these concepts as a contributor (however unwittingly) to white supremacy and my responsibilities to dismantle white dominance. There are those who argue that as a white person I have no right to speak about anti-racist pedagogy, a position with which I disagree. This issue requires debate, and I will return to it further on, as I think it is important to be open about the conflicts embedded in these ideas.

The scourge of racism has plagued social work since its inception. Despite the foundational value of social justice (International Federation of Social Work, 2014), the history of the profession is replete with troubling examples of racist policies and systemic injustice (Chapman & Withers, 2019; First Nations & Indigenous Studies, 2009; Hall, 2021; Miller & Garran, 2017).

Many thanks to my colleagues Dr. Carolyn Campbell and Dr. Jan Fook for their attentive and erudite suggestions for this chapter.

By *racism*, I am referring to the operation of power whereby individuals are positioned as superior and inferior, oppressing racialized populations (Carter, 2007; Winant, 2006). *Racialized* refers to processes whereby people are labeled as nonwhite (Gosine & Pon, 2011). While there is no biological basis for the concept of race, it has significant material impacts on people's lives. Racism is multifaceted and widespread, transforming over time. It is broader than between individuals. It operates at all levels of society, including institutions and ideologies, affecting those who are racialized on a regular basis but often unseen by whites (Feagin, 2013; Mills, 1997). It is a system of domination that privileges whites through sociopolitical, economic, and cultural structures.

Racism is an ongoing problem in social work today (Aldana & Vazquez, 2020; Blackstock, 2017; Iglehart & Becerra, 2011), in part because of the supremacy of whiteness. White supremacy is "a political system, a particular power structure of formal or informal rule, socioeconomic privilege, and norms for the differential distribution of material wealth and opportunities, benefits and burdens, rights and duties" (Mills, 1997, p. 3). These structures maintain the hegemony of whiteness and lead to oppression of racialized service users in social work.

One illustration in the United States, Canada, and the United Kingdom is the overrepresentation in child welfare of children of African descent and Indigenous children (Barn, 2007; Kim, 2017; Lash, 2017; Truth and Reconciliation Commission of Canada, 2015; Turner, 2016). In the United States, "Native American children were overrepresented in the foster care system at a rate of 2:1" (Kim, 2017, p. 3). In Canada, Black and Indigenous families are reported to child welfare at twice the rate of whites; these children reside longer in foster care and are less likely to be reunited with their families of origin (Adjei & Minka, 2018). In 2002, in England, 5.2 percent of children of African descent were in out-of-home care, compared to 2.6 percent of the general child population (Tilbury & Thoburn, 2009). A substantial body of research (Hallberg & Smith, 2018; Sawrikar, 2017; Thibeault & Spencer, 2019; Turner, 2016) proposes bias, racism, and structural inequalities as significant components of racialized children's disproportionality in child welfare.

In social work ethics, there is a gap between this problem and its framing in ethics literature. While there are exceptions (e.g., Dominelli, 2018; Miller & Garran, 2017), too many current-day discourses in ethics have highlighted "difference," "diversity," "ethnicity," or "culture," thereby whitewashing the cultural imperialism, coloniality, and racism that underpin the profession. To my consternation, as an academic whose interest is ethics, and as a white settler in Canada, I too minimized the persistence and extent of the issues until two research projects made this divide crystal clear (Weinberg & Fine, 2022). In my research, racialized participants immediately identified racism as an ethical concern while white participants did not.

DEFINITIONS OF ETHICS AND TRANSFORMATIVE PEDAGOGY

Ethics is a "conscious reflection on our moral beliefs" (Hugman, 2005, p. 1). One component of that reflection is how we treat others, particularly their difference from us, based on sociocultural categories such as race. Cornell (1992) suggests that an ethical relationship must avoid the harm that comes when individuals are not treated as unique.

Considering everyone as particular and distinct is a challenge for all of us, especially in social work. In relation to race, we must recognize the ingrained implicit biases we all hold (Banaji & Greenwald, 2013). Bias refers to the "tendency to favour one thing over another" (Jana & Freeman, 2016, p. 7). It is a survival mechanism that allows us, as a species, to determine quickly who is friend or foe, creating categories and permitting rapid judgments. But stereotypes about race, when accepted, can lead to biases toward others that we unconsciously maintain, treating individuals based on some general characteristic such as skin color and thereby causing harm. Stereotypes control what we see and how we interpret our world, potentially skewing assessments and practice based on these biases (Eberhardt, 2020).

Furthermore, the neoliberal values of efficiency and austerity that are at the forefront in modern-day social work (Rogowski, 2011) result in having to serve more people with fewer resources. These macro trends hamper workers from providing the comprehensive, individualized approach required for ethical treatment. At times racialized service users receive even fewer of the inadequate resources distributed. In the health system, for instance, racialized service users are underrepresented, and racism and bias are seen as contributing factors (Allan & Smylie, 2015; Brody et al., 2012; Feagin & Bennefield, 2014).

To change these disparities, we need transformative education. To transform is to cause an important and lasting change. But for transformative pedagogy, this change must be deeply political, in a direction that envisions our social world as one that is more socially just. This requires altering our discourses, our societal structures, our relationships, and our very selves.

How might we transform our approach to ethics and pedagogy to offer truly respectful, just, and healing relationships to racialized service users?

THEORETICAL CONCEPTS RELATED TO ANTI-RACIST EDUCATION

If we wish to contribute to a transformative pedagogy in social work and ethics, it is important to consider the following conceptual ideas.

CRITICALLY EXAMINING DOMINANT DISCOURSES

There is extensive denial by white individuals regarding racism (Rozas & Miller, 2009), including the acceptance of dominant discourses that support this denial. Whiteness is normalized and constructed as superior while being invisible for many white people. Thus, pedagogy must surface what has been unseen and confront denial (Lynch et al., 2017). To contest this normalization requires examining the taken-for-granted dominant discourses and asking a series of questions: Who constructed the dominant discourses? What was their intention and their stake in these constructions? Whose voices are missing? Whose knowledge counts, and whose does not?

A primary discourse in ethics has been to utilize codes for assistance in ethical quandaries (Hugman, 2005). Codes are based on a philosophical theory called deontology. The underlying premise of deontology is that individuals should be treated as ends, not means, using universal principles to guide practice. The theory suggests that these abstract principles should be applied similarly to everyone, to determine correct courses of action, regardless of context. Immanuel Kant was the key architect of deontology (Alexander & Moore, 2021). This was at the time of the Enlightenment, with its emphasis on intellectual reason and individualism. It was also a period of European empire building. Significantly, Kant was a driving force behind the development of a hierarchy of races (Mills, 2005) in which whites were at the top and racialized groups seen as not fully human (Bernasconi, 2002). One could speculate that Kant's "universal" principles did not include the perspectives of racialized individuals and served the interests of dominant European white men at a time of national expansion and colonization.

Can difference truly be understood and embraced by using universal principles that ignore the context and structures that are so salient in ethical deliberations? Whose notion of "universal" is being applied? Whose perspectives are being omitted? Relying on deontological theory as the foundational ethical discourse results in codes of ethics that are framed from the perspective of dominant white values. For instance, many people of African descent and Indigenous peoples put communitarian values ahead of those of the individual (Sewpaul & Henrickson, 2019). This becomes problematic when we use the "universal" principle of confidentiality, for example, to determine who receives information about a patient in the hospital when an extended family requests a report.

Dominant discourses lead to social rules, such as universal principles to guide ethics. These rules are necessary devices that allow people to go about their day without questioning every interaction, contributing to social stability. However, by the same token, they can lead to a level of thoughtlessness (Orlie, 1997). Even worse, they can result in maltreatment. Orlie refers to this as "ethical trespass," the harm that comes not from bad intentions but from our "participation in social processes" (p. 5). This is especially true for those individuals such as social workers who are the " 'responsible,' well behaved, predictable subjects of social order who reinforce and extend patterns of rule" (p. 23). Examples of social workers' involvement in patterns of rule include mechanisms of social control, such as apprehensions, and determinations of resource distribution.

UNDOING TESTIMONIAL AND HERMENEUTIC INJUSTICE

Ethical principles based on white supremacy lead to testimonial injustice when a speaker's credibility is questioned or disregarded based on their identity. Refuting a person's trustworthiness or reliability is a major component in the invisibility or negation of others. When people operate from a stereotype of the Other, the outcome may be inaccurate prejudgments about knowledge claims (Fricker, 2007). A white practitioner may perceive a racialized service user's account of an incident as "oversensitivity," denying the validity of the racialized client's observations. Or a racialized mother's perspective may be disbelieved in making determinations about a child's welfare. Given that generations of socialization and adoption of dominant discourses shape how all of us understand the world, in teaching students practice skills, what emphasis do we place on recognizing implicit bias and white supremacy, resulting in the minimization of other perspectives?

When testimonial injustice occurs, those who are marginalized become disadvantaged in knowledge production. This is known as hermeneutic injustice, meaning a bias in whose interpretation is taken as "truth" in the construction of knowledge. For example, Indigenous peoples' worldviews have always centered on a deep understanding of the intricate and essential interplay between humans and their environment. But the acceptance and utilization of the theoretical approach "people-in-environment" has historically required endorsement from the dominant group to gain credence in social work, denying centuries of Indigenous knowledge.

INCORPORATING AN UNDERSTANDING
OF HISTORY AND CONTEXT

A transformative ethics must consider the history both of the social work profession and of marginalized services users and their relationship to providers. The history of social work's complicity in the supremacy of whiteness must be seen and accepted, since this history contributes to the construction of the helping relationship today. As mentioned previously, research suggests that the underrepresentation of racialized people in health care directly relates to their distrust of a system in which they were historically horrifically mistreated and their ongoing differential treatment based on structural racism today (Allan & Smylie, 2015; Brody et al., 2012; Feagin & Bennefield, 2014).

Histories of multigenerational trauma for racialized groups also need acknowledgment and reparations. For instance, for Indigenous peoples in Canada, forced separation into residential schools, the erasure of one's language and culture, and horrendous abuse and loss of life, as indicated by the unmarked graves now being uncovered, can profoundly damage how an individual and family see the world. These traumas can disrupt attachment and affect coping mechanisms, unintentionally influencing future generations (O'Neill et al., 2018).

Besides confronting history, analyzing context is also crucial in morally fraught situations. Context is "the background and set of circumstances and conditions that surround and influence particular events and situations" (Finn & Jacobson, 2008, p. 43). It includes sociopolitical, cultural, legal, institutional, and policy components. It extends to examining both individual racism and the structural disadvantages that figure prominently for racialized groups.

An illustration of a worker attempting to do this was the manager in one study (Weinberg, 2021), who struggled with apprehending a child from a First Nations mother. In his deliberations, he was cognizant of the complexity of removal, given the history of colonialism, genocide, and distrust of white government officials. This recognition is a necessary precursor to reducing ethical trespass that a universalistic approach does not furnish.

USING THE WHOLE SELF, INCLUDING EMOTIONS

Transformative ethics encompasses utilization of the whole self. We must examine our own standpoints of privilege or disadvantage, our most valued beliefs (Sakamoto & Pitner, 2005), and the ways they have unwittingly contributed to systemic injustice.

Because racism is ongoing and pervasive, all of us must be open to the possibility of collusion. Challenging the myth of our implicit righteousness and moral goodness is essential. We need to recognize that we will all engage in ethical trespass. This is inevitable, given the supremacy of whiteness and the socialization processes in which we are all embedded. Whites in particular have a disproportionate obligation because they have been structurally and culturally advantaged. This is not a static advantage, however, because socioeconomic position, gender, and religious status, for example, are dimensions of identity that are fluid and dependent on context, thus shaping in a particular instance one's advantage or disadvantage, regardless of race or ethnicity. I will elaborate on the ramifications of this below.

Recognizing my own minimization of the problem of racism in ethics as a white academic was a necessary step for me. This was an uncomfortable realization, but crucial for transformative education generally, and ethics in particular. White people, especially, must see themselves as implicated in modern-day systemic racism, whether intended or not.

Here I want to refer back to my initial statement about the debate regarding my right to speak about anti-racist pedagogy as a white settler. In my own experience, I have encountered hostility and challenge regarding this issue. I have been somewhat nonplussed by these reactions, since my desire to discuss these issues arises directly from my extensive research on ethics, imbuing me with an urgency to address the very worrying racial gap I have encountered in the way social workers think about ethics. From this perspective, I wish to suggest that focusing on one racial group over others, or categorizing the rights of one over others, does not seem a complex enough response, given that we all exist in the same cultural and structural stew and may internalize many of these aspects differently.

Furthermore, it may not just be whites who can perpetrate racist acts or be unwittingly racist. Racialized individuals may also be infected by the toxicity of racist tropes and have unconscious biases (Banaji & Greenwald, 2013). This is not to direct blame at any of us; it is to acknowledge a collective responsibility to be mindful of our own implicit biases, advantages, and disadvantages and committed to changing these in ourselves and others. Social transformation will more likely occur if all of us, advantaged and disadvantaged, are involved in this change.

From an ethical standpoint, a recognition of emotional discomfort is an important indicator that something may be morally fraught, whatever one's social location. Emotions make individuals "attentive to how the *other* perceives the situation [and] link our perception of the situation to that of the other involved in it" (Vetlesen, 1994, p. 166). They contribute to an understanding of what is salient for others interpersonally. They are an element of empathic attunement, a primary skill in relationship building.

Affect is also essential to the ethical judgment necessary to undo racism. Some theorists suggest that affective evaluations are primary and intuitive, with moral reasoning following to justify actions taken (Monin et al., 2007), especially in situations of moral infraction, such as racism. Therefore, cognitive approaches using decision-making models based on codes miss the crucial element of emotions in ethical judgments that must be included in transformative pedagogy.

Critical reflection can be employed when our sense of discomfort arises (Fook & Gardner, 2007). Seeing ourselves as lifelong learners is part of this process by recognizing that knowledge is always partial and shaped by our own positioning. Therefore, engaging in a continual reflexive process and operating from a stance of "informed not-knowing" (Keenan, 2004) to seek others' perspectives are components of a transformative ethics. However, racialized individuals legitimately resist being positioned as having to be educators for whites. This is ultimately white people's responsibility.

Overcoming the barriers of discomfort, guilt, shame, and anxiety are essential. One component of what racialized people need from whites is an openness to feedback, however uncomfortable, without turning to behaviors that shut down conversation (such as crying) or defensive claims ("you're making a big deal about nothing") (Diangelo, 2018). Whites need to focus more on listening and less on pontification or justification. Racialized individuals, too, need to avoid defensiveness when their own racism is identified. Forgiving and acceptance of ourselves, while developing stances of openness, humility, and curiosity, are what we need.

COMPLICATING BINARIES

People as good or bad. Part of the challenge is to confront notions of good and evil. Social workers enter the field wanting to do good; they resist viewing themselves as racist and thus being seen by themselves or others as immoral. In part, this perception results from defining racism as individual isolated acts, rather than understanding that racism operates not just at micro levels but also, significantly, at systemic and epistemological levels (Delgado & Stefanic, 2017). It can result in color-blindness or aversive racism—the racism of those who profess a belief in egalitarianism but hold unconscious racist views (Dovidio & Gaertner, 1986). The notion of ethical trespass is relevant here because it helps people understand that sometimes our harm exists outside of malicious intent or may be due to factors outside our control.

Assigning blame for the existence of racism, while necessary, is ultimately less useful than orienting toward taking responsibility to eradicate it. Bravery against the tide and the discomfort of owning up to our own racism are indispensable assets.

White versus racialized identities. While I have been primarily discussing race in a binary way (racialized versus white), I want to complicate this picture by further developing the notion of identity. The idea of viewing people as white or racialized is useful because, through this categorization, we can see the material effects of racism. This is theoretically necessary and politically expedient because it allows for an analysis of power and for efforts toward social transformation.

However, social categories do not account for heterogeneity within a social group. There is a danger in the single articulation (Adichie, 2009) because it creates stereotypes and is always incomplete. "Race" is a social construction; it shifts over time and context. For example, in some historical periods, the Irish and Jews were not perceived as "white" (Menakem, 2017). Additionally, our identities are defined by multiple social locations: age, gender, class, etc. Much more complex than a single feature, they are fluid, ever-changing, always becoming. Individuals can fit within overlapping categories, calling for an intersectional approach to identity (Crenshaw, 1991). Which dimension is primary will vary over time through our interactions with others, how we are seen by others, but also how we see ourselves, and through societal structures.

Whites committed to racial justice. Our present world seems more polarized than ever. This contemporary bifurcation is partially a by-product of neoliberalism, which systemically supports and consolidates difference to ensure the continuance of the ruling elite (Garrett, 2010). This has led to identity politics, through which marginalized groups use their commonality for self-empowerment and to overcome oppression.

It has also engendered some rejection of whites' participating in attempts to shatter racism. As mentioned earlier, there are those who perceive the very notion of being a white anti-racist as an oxymoron (Kim, 2010). Given the benefits that I, as a white woman, might inevitably derive from the structures of white supremacy, some say there is no way to maintain my identity and be an anti-racist. At a conference in which I was a presenter, the keynote speaker said that white folks who worked in this area were frauds. People with these views reject the idea of someone like me, a white settler, undertaking anti-racist work. They question my legitimacy and my right to address the topic. This is one more bifurcation that oversimplifies identity and diminishes struggles against racism.

Part of their concern might legitimately be "Will my voice take up too much space and detract from their perspectives?" Another disquiet is the rightful anger racialized individuals feel about expectations of gratitude for my anti-racist work, a dimension of the powerlessness of being racialized.

While I appreciate these apprehensions and know that I will at times "get it wrong" in anti-racist efforts, I think we need a more nuanced approach. We must recognize the complexity of identity. I am marginalized in other aspects of my identity, perhaps giving me some empathy for anti-racist struggles. For instance, I suspect that my religious beliefs (part of intersectionality) have contributed to my determination to work toward social justice.

Moreover, I do not believe that things can be accomplished without bringing those who are dominant into the anti-racist struggle. Early in the women's movement, men were not allowed any role. It took years to recognize that for gender equality to occur, allies were indispensable. Changing the definition of healthy masculinity required men as partners in that fight. More recently, the witnessing of the murder of George Floyd and the resulting Black Lives Matter movement have sparked global awareness of racism, from whites as well as those who are racialized.

Nonetheless, the role of allies must always be negotiated and open to critical reflection. Racism will not be upended without whites being prepared to question and unsettle their privilege and power, changing the very structures upon which white supremacy rests.

THESE CONCEPTS IN THE CLASSROOM

What does transformative pedagogy look like in the classroom? A starting point is the examination of white supremacy and telling the truth about its history and continuance in social work.

I do not support a "safe" classroom. I believe it needs to be "safe enough," setting the conditions for risk and civility (Barrett, 2010), because transformation is uncomfortable, requiring exposure and leading to uncertainty and anxiety. Racialized students in particular need support because they have so often felt marginalized, betrayed, and maligned in academic settings. It is crucial that racialized students are able to give voice to their experiences. At the same time, racialized individuals rightly do not want to have to represent their whole group nor provide the additional labor of being the educators when this is emotionally taxing and not solely their responsibility.

Instructors have an ethical obligation to ensure that risk is tolerable and does not lead to more harm. Guidelines for trust and repair must be established (Diangelo, 2018; Gehl, n.d.; Leonardo & Porter, 2010). When microaggressions or critical incidents occur in the classroom, they must be addressed, foremost to protect marginalized students but also as teachable moments.

As a white professor, I try to be a model of risk and openness, acknowledging my own trespasses. With a guest expert in critical reflection, I used the example of my shame staying silent at a dinner party when someone referred to Muslim students as "towelheads." I explored what led to my inaction, including my guilt and the disruption of my "innocence," change I would want to make going forward, and the connection to social work practice. When derogatory language occurs in a classroom, it must be confronted but can also serve as a learning opportunity (Walker et al., 2018).

Seeking the subordinated discourses is a crucial component. This can be accomplished by including more diverse content and presenting marginalized discourses in curricula. Tactics include bringing in the expertise of the Other, storytelling, and films. These approaches begin to correct for hermeneutic injustice regarding whose knowledge counts. Additionally, telling the truth about the profession's complicity and exposing racist social work narratives, both past and present, are necessary elements for transformative pedagogy.

Active engagement rather than passive theoretical approaches is key. Experiential exercises move students past cognitive processes to engage the whole self, potentially leading to deeper change. There are reams of wonderful materials available on anti-racist education and curricular design to support experiential learning (Campbell & Baikie, 2013; Craig et al., 2021; Csiernik & Hillock, 2021; Hamilton-Mason & Schneider, 2018). In my class, a white student undertook a critical reflection about being pushed and harassed in a bar when she was assumed to be an "Arab." Her enhanced empathy for the racism experienced by racialized individuals and the complexity of identity were two of the learnings from this process.

Transformation must move in two directions: first, within the individual, but second, outward, at the macro level. Racism must be tackled structurally, including at the university level. Besides exploring the mechanisms by which white supremacy is maintained, we need to undo those mechanisms. Ethics is inherently political. It involves a commitment to social justice, because our deeds matter more than our intentions (Orlie, 1997). Students need training about macro structures to understand the connection between power and politics, and to begin work toward systemic change. Once critical consciousness has developed, advocacy and activism are indispensable for transforming society.

CONCLUSION

Only through the goal of nonviolative relationships with those who are racialized can the profession move toward a transformative ethical anti-racist pedagogy. Reckoning with our white supremacist past and critically examining the ongoing dominant discourses (such as the development of codes) that result in epistemic injustices are necessary steps. Political action to undo white supremacy must follow. A society that is not racially just is an unethical society.

We must be open, self-reflective, and brave, using our hearts as well as our minds, while resisting the bifurcations so prevalent in our modern world. Creating courageous and tenacious classroom spaces is indispensable. These steps can begin to build a transformative anti-racist pedagogy.

REFERENCES

Adichie, C. N. (2009). The danger of a single story. TED Talk. https://www.ted.com/talks/chimamanda_ngozi_adichie_the_danger_of_a_single_story.

Adjei, P. B., & Minka, E. (2018). Black parents ask for a second look: Parenting under "white" child protection rules in Canada. *Child and Youth Services Review*, *94*, 511–524. https://doi.org/10.1016/j.childyouth.2018.08.030.

Aldana, A., & Vazquez, N. (2020). From color-blind racism to critical race theory: The road towards anti-racist social work in the United States. In G. Singh & S. Masocha (Eds.), *Anti-racist social work: International perspectives* (pp. 129–148). London: Red Globe.

Alexander, L., & Moore, M. (2021, Summer). Deontological ethics. In Edward N. Zalta (Ed.), *The Stanford Encyclopedia of Philosophy*. https://plato.stanford.edu/archives/sum2021/entries/ethics-deontological/.

Allan, B., & Smylie, J. (2015). *First Peoples, second class treatment: The role of racism in the health and well-being of Indigenous peoples in Canada*. Toronto: Wellesley Institute.

Banaji, M. R., & Greenwald, A. G. (2013). *Blindspot*. New York: Delacourt.

Barn, R. (2007). "Race," ethnicity and child welfare: A fine balancing act. *British Journal of Social Work*, *37*, 1425–1434. https://doi.org/10.1093/bjsw/bcm145.

Barrett, B. J. (2010). Is "safety" dangerous? A critical examination of the classroom as a safe space. *Canadian Journal for the Scholarship of Teaching and Learning*, *1*(1). https://doi.org/10.5206/cjsotl-rcacea.2010.1.9.

Bernasconi, R. (2002). Kant as an unfamiliar source of racism. In J. K. Ward & T. L. Lott (Eds.), *Philosophers on race: Critical essays* (pp. 145–166). Oxford: Blackwell.

Blackstock, C. (2017). Does social work have the guts for social justice and reconciliation? In E. Spencer, D. Massing, & J. Gough (Eds.), *Social work ethics: Progressive, practical, and relational approaches* (pp. 115–128). Don Mills, ON: Oxford University Press.

Brody, H., Glenn, J. E., & Hermer, L. (2012). Racial/ethnic health disparities and ethics: A need for a multilevel approach. *Cambridge Quarterly of Healthcare Ethics*, *21*, 309–319. https://doi.org/10.1017/S0963180112000035.

Campbell, C., & Baikie, C. (2013) Teaching critically reflective analysis in the context of a social justice course. *Reflective Practice*, *14* (4), 452–464. https://doi.org/10.1080/14623943.2013.806299.

Carter, R. T. (2007). Racism and psychological and emotional injury: Recognizing and assessing race-based traumatic stress. *Counseling Psychologist, 35*(1), 13–105. https://doi.org/10.1177/0011000006292033.

Chapman, C., & Withers, A. J. (2019). *A violent history of benevolence.* Toronto: University of Toronto Press.

Cornell, D. (1992). *The philosophy of the limit.* New York: Routledge.

Craig, S. L., Gardiner, T., Eaton, A. D., Pang, N., & Kourgiantakis, T. (2021). Practicing alliance: An experiential model of teaching diversity and inclusion for social work practice and education. *Social Work Education, 41*(5), 801–819. https://doi.org/10.1080/02615479.2021.1892054.

Crenshaw, K. (1991). Mapping the margins: Intersectionality, identity politics and violence against women of color. *Stanford Law Review, 43*(6), 1241–1300. https://doi.org/10.2307/1229039.

Csiernik, R., & Hillock, S. (Eds.). (2021). *Teaching social work: Reflections on pedagogy and practice.* Toronto: University of Toronto Press.

Delgado, R., & Stefanic, J. (2017). *Critical race theory* (3rd ed.). New York: New York University Press.

Diangelo, R. (2018). *White fragility.* Boston: Beacon.

Dominelli, L. (2018). *Anti-racist social work* (4th ed.). London: Palgrave Macmillan.

Dovidio, J. F., & Gaertner, S. L. (Eds.). (1986). *Prejudice, discrimination, and racism.* London: Academic.

Eberhardt, J. L. (2020). How racial bias works—and how to disrupt it. TED Talk. https://www.youtube.com/watch?v=rVNb53lkBuc.

Feagin, J. R. (2013). *The while racial frame* (2nd ed.). New York: Routledge.

Feagin, J. R., & Bennefield, Z. (2014). Systematic racism and U.S. health care. *Social Science and Medicine, 103*, 7–14. https://doi.org/10.1016/j.socscimed.2013.09.006.

Finn, J., & Jacobson, M. (2008). *Just practice: A social justice approach to social work* (2nd ed.). Peosta, IA: Edie Bowers.

First Nations & Indigenous Studies. (2009). Sixties scoop. *Indigenous Foundations,* University of British Columbia. https://indigenousfoundations.arts.ubc.ca/sixties_scoop/.

Fook, J., & Gardner, F. (2007). *Practising critical reflection: A resource handbook.* Maidenhead, UK: Open University Press.

Fricker, M. (2007). *Epistemic injustice: Power and the ethics of knowing.* New York: Oxford University Press.

Garrett, P. M. (2010). Recognizing the limitations of the political theory of recognition: Axel Honneth, Nancy Fraser and social work. *British Journal of Social Work, 40*, 1517–1533. https://doi.org/10.1093/bjsw/bcp044.

Gehl, L. (n.d.). *Ally bill of responsibilities.* http://www.lynngehl.com/uploads/5/0/0/4/5004954/ally_bill_of_responsibilities_poster.pdf.

Gosine, K., & Pon, G. (2011). Experiences of racialized child welfare workers in Toronto, Canada. *Journal of Progressive Human Services, 22*(2), 135–159. https://doi.org/10.1080/10428232.2011.599280.

Hall, R. E. (2021). Social work's feminist façade: Descriptive manifestations of white supremacy. *British Journal of Social Work, 52*(2), 1055–1069. https://doi.org/10.1093/bjsw/bcab093.

Hallberg, R., & Smith, C., of Barnes Management Group. (2018). *Understanding social work and child welfare: Canadian survey and interviews with child welfare experts.* Ottawa: Canadian Association of Social Workers.

Hamilton-Mason, J., & Schneider, S. (2018). Antiracism expanding social work education: A qualitative analysis of undoing racism workshop experience. *Journal of Social Work Education, 54*(2), 337–348. https://doi.org/10.1080/10437797.2017.1404518.

Hugman, R. (2005). *New approaches in ethics for the caring professions.* New York: Palgrave Macmillan.

Iglehart, A. P., & Becerra, R. M. (2011). *Social services and the ethnic community* (2nd ed.). Long Grove, IL: Waveland.

International Federation of Social Work. (2014). Global definition of social work. https://www.ifsw.org/what-is-social-work/global-definition-of-social-work/.

Jana, T., & Freeman, M. (2016). *Overcoming bias.* Oakland, CA: Berrett-Koehler.

Keenan, E. K. (2004). From sociocultural categories to socially located relations: Using critical theory in social work practice. *Families in Society, 85*(4), 539–548. https://doi.org/10.1177%2F104438940408500412.

Kim, H. (2017, Spring). The Indian Child Welfare Act and the need for reform. *Health Law Litigation,* 19368380, 14(1).

Kim, K. J. (2010, November 11). The white anti-racist is an oxymoron: An open letter to "white anti-racists." *Live Journal.* https://ontd-feminism.livejournal.com/438107.html?.

Lash, D. (2017). *"When the welfare people come": Race and class in the U.S. child protection system.* Chicago: Haymarket.

Leonardo, Z., & Porter, R. K. (2010). Pedagogy of fear: Toward a Fanonian theory of "safety" in race dialogue. *Race Ethnicity and Education, 13*(2), 139–157. https://doi.org/10.1080/13613324.2010.482898.

Lynch, I., Swartz, S., & Isaacs, D. (2017). Anti-racist moral education: A review of approaches, impact and theoretical underpinnings from 2000 to 2015. *Journal of Moral Education, 46*(2), 129–144. https://doi.org/10.1080/03057240.2016.1273825.

Menakem, R. (2017). *My grandmother's hands.* Las Vegas, NV: Central Recovery.

Miller, J. L., & Garran, A. M. (2017). *Racism in the United States: Implications for the helping professions* (2nd ed.). New York: Springer.

Mills, C. W. (1997). *The racial contract.* Ithaca, NY: Cornell University Press.

Mills, C. W. (2005). Kant's *Untermenschen.* In A. Valls (Ed.), *Race and racism in modern philosophy* (pp. 169–193). Ithaca, NY: Cornell University Press.

Monin, B., Pizarro, D. A., & Beer, J. S. (2007). Deciding versus reacting: Conceptions of moral judgment and the reason-affect debate. *Review of General Psychology, 11*(2), 99–111. https://doi.org/10.1037/1089-2680.11.2.99.

O'Neill, L., Fraser, T., Kitchenham, A., & McDonald, V. (2018). Hidden burdens: A review of intergenerational, historical and complex trauma, implications for Indigenous families. *Journal of Child and Adolescent Trauma, 11,* 178–186. https://doi.org/10.1007/s40653-016-0117-9.

Orlie, M. A. (1997). *Living ethically, acting politically.* Ithaca, NY: Cornell University Press.

Rogowski, S. (2011). Managers, managerialism and social work with children and families: The deformation of a profession? *Practice: Social Work in Action, 23*(3), 157–167. https://doi.org /10.1080/09503153.2011.569970.

Rozas, L. W., & Miller, J. (2009). Discourse for social justice education: The web of racism and the web of resistance. *Journal of Ethnic and Cultural Diversity in Social Work, 18*(1–2), 24–39. https://doi.org/10.1080/15313200902874953.

Sakamoto, I., & Pitner, R. O. (2005). Use of critical consciousness in anti-oppressive social work practice: Disentangling power dynamics at personal and structural levels. *British Journal of Social Work, 35,* 435–452. https://doi.org/10.1093/bjsw/bch190.

Sawrikar, P. (2017). *Working with ethnic minorities and across cultures in Western child protection systems.* New York: Routledge.

Sewpaul, V., & Henrickson, M. (2019). The (r)evolution and decolonization of social work ethics: The Global Social Work Statement of Ethical Principles. *International Social Work, 62*(6), 1469–1481. https://doi.org/10.1177/0020872819846238.

Thibeault, D., & Spencer, M. S. (2019). The Indian Adoption Project and the profession of social work. *Social Service Review, 93*(4), 804–832. https://doi.org/10.1086/706771.

Tilbury, C., & Thoburn, J. (2009). Using racial disproportionality and disparities indicators to measure child welfare outcomes. *Child and Youth Services Review, 31,* 1101–1106. https:// doi.org/10.1016/j.childyouth.2009.07.004.

Truth and Reconciliation Commission of Canada. (2015). *Honouring the truth, reconciling for the future: Summary of the final report of the Truth and Reconciliation Commission.* https:// ehprnh2mwo3.exactdn.com/wp-content/uploads/2021/01/Executive_Summary_English _Web.pdf.

Turner, T. (2016). *One vision one voice: Changing the Ontario child welfare system to better serve African Canadians.* Toronto: Ontario Association of Children's Aid Societies.

Vetlesen, A. J. (1994). *An inquiry in the preconditions of moral performance.* University Park, PA: Penn State University Press.

Walker, L. A., Davis, D. K., & Lopez, M. (2018) The impacts of processing the use of derogatory language in a social work classroom. *Journal of Ethnic and Cultural Diversity in Social Work, 27*(1), 41–53. https://doi.org/10.1080/15313204.2017.1417943.

Weinberg, M. (2021). Exacerbation of inequities during COVID-19: Ethical implications for social workers. *Canadian Social Work Review, 37*(2), 9–15. https://doi.org/10.7202/1075117ar.

Weinberg, M., & Fine, M. (2022). Racisms and microaggressions in social work: The experience of racialized practitioners in Canada. *Journal of Ethnic & Cultural Diversity in Social Work, 31*(2), 96–107. https://doi.org/10.1080/15313204.2020.1839614.

Winant, H. (2006). Race and racism: Towards a global future. *Ethnic and Racial Studies, 29*(5), 986–1003. https://doi.org/10.1080/01419870600814031.

10

TRANSFORMATIVE LEARNING
IN SOCIAL WORK

A Critically Reflective Process to Affirm My Indigenous

Worldview as a Child Welfare Intern

TIFFANY TUTTLE

his account of a critical reflection is included here to illustrate a
process of transformative learning. The chapter initially focuses
on worker safety in child welfare and uncovers deep-seated fears
brought to the forefront of my consciousness during my field placement
in the Department for Children and Families (DCF), Family Service
Division (FSD). I explore historic traumatic events experienced by the
Dakota Nation and share a Dakota worldview and perspective for social
work practice. This exploration led to an affirmation of my indigenous
values and the development of an indigenous framework to integrate with
my social work approach. The chapter closes with insights gained in my
transformative learning process.

In this chapter, I use Fook and Gardner's (2007) model of critical reflection, which was designed with the intention of "unsettling" practitioners'
implicit assumptions to incorporate multiple perspectives in professional
practice. The process helps professionals critically examine a critical incident or "specific and concrete practice experiences to devise new practices and approaches to practice."

Fook and Gardner's critical reflection method involves a two-stage
process. In stage one, I discuss a critical incident in social work practice,
specifically in child welfare. The outline of the critical incident is preceded

by background information to provide context and is followed by a discussion of why I chose to reflect upon that critical incident. In stage two, I discuss the main assumptions that emerged from my reflection, observations about the two-stage process of reflection, and new thinking and ideas for practice that emerged from the second stage. As this work is also about transformative learning, I share insights gained in this critically reflective process at the end of the chapter.

BACKGROUND: WORKER SAFETY
IN CHILD WELFARE

Shortly after turning fifty, in May 2020, in the early months of the COVID-19 pandemic, I left my profession as a massage therapist and yoga teacher and entered a Master of Social Work (MSW) program. This course of study was made possible by the Child Welfare Training Partnership Scholarship program between my university and the Department for Children and Families. This traineeship, commonly referred to as the Title IV-E scholarship, is funded by the U.S. federal government through the Social Security Act. My Title IV-E contract required me to take a Child Abuse and Neglect course during my first semester of the MSW program, to complete an internship in child welfare with the Family Service Division during my second year of the program, and to be employed in child welfare work within FSD for three years upon graduation.

When I signed the Title IV-E Educational Assistance Agreement, I was unaware of the prevalence or the degree of worker safety issues inherent in the child welfare profession. In my first semester in the MSW program, as required by my contract, I registered for the Child Abuse and Neglect course. During our last class of the semester, the professor held a memorial for a well-loved child welfare social worker, Lara Sobel, who had been shot and killed "as she left her office" in Barre, Vermont, on August 7, 2016. According to the police, Lara "was ambushed by a mother who was angry about losing custody of her daughter" (Donoghue & Burbank, 2016).

Two of my classmates in the Child Abuse and Neglect course, also Title IV-E students, were existing FSD employees on educational leave. Both knew Lara well. One of them had worked closely with Lara in the Barre office and was working late with her when the tragic incident occurred. For those classmates who knew and loved Lara, spending our final Child Abuse and Neglect class memorializing her was difficult but healing. For me, it was disturbing. As a youth, I had witnessed numerous violent and life-threatening incidents. My cousin, my uncle, and my father each died because of gun violence. As a ten-year-old girl, I just missed a bullet when guns were fired in my living room. I was troubled when I realized that I had entered a binding contract with serious risks of harm.

During the spring term of the first year in the MSW program, one of my Title IV-E classmates picked me up for our only in-person course, which we attended fully masked and with six feet of social distance. I owned a small condo in a low-income development I'll refer to as Windy Hollow, which includes a mix of low-income homeowners and renters. When my friend arrived, she said, "I've been in *this* neighborhood plenty of times." It never occurred to me that there might be open DCF cases in my neighborhood. However, when my friend made the comment, I was not surprised. Windy Hollow spans approximately two by four city blocks. While my street was quiet and I had good relations with my direct neighbors, I was aware that the neighborhood had its problems along with its strengths, which included a playground and a community garden.

The following fall semester, I began my second-year field placement with DCF in a nearby FSD office. Because of short staffing, the director and assistant director shared the responsibility of serving as my field instructors. Within the first two weeks of my placement, our district office was forced to close for three days because of violent threats to a family service worker (FSW) as well as to our place of work. The threats were made by a man with a history of violence who was known to be dangerous, and police were dispatched to our office for surveillance. The director made an announcement to the staff that they should work from home until notified otherwise. She acknowledged that the event could be "triggering" and stated that staff should take self-care as needed.

The next week, a local sheriff visited our weekly all-staff meeting to provide gun safety education in response to the increasing presence of guns in the homes of clients that FSD serves. During his visit, the sheriff displayed a variety of guns, large and small, and passed around ammunition with which we were to familiarize ourselves. These two incidents in the first weeks of my field placement were unsettling. I did not share my discomfort with anyone. I was the new intern in the office and had not established a strong relationship with the directors or my colleagues with whom I'd just begun to mingle in our grid of cubicles that the director referred to as "the bull pen." In the fast-paced office environment, everyone proceeded with business as usual. Later, after building relationships, I was informed by seasoned FSWs that encouragement from leadership to take self-care was just "double-speak." In the office culture at FSD, employees are valued by their ability to "roll with the punches" and "keep up" with the fast pace of the work.

As my concern for worker safety increased, I began attending our district office monthly safety meeting, where I heard FSWs express frustration around the "risk-intensive" nature of child welfare. Two large men in the district office expressed fear about conducting home visits with families in which there was known gun activity. Some FSWs advocated for bulletproof vests. One FSW shared with me in private conversation that her mother had purchased a bulletproof clipboard that she could carry inconspicuously during home visits.

With this awareness, anytime I shadowed an FSW on a home visit, I inquired first if they were going to Windy Hollow but did not mention that was where I lived. Eventually, I brought it to the attention of the directors that I lived in Windy Hollow and requested that I not be assigned to shadow any FSWs working in my development. The director expressed concern for my safety and disclosed that there was a history of drug and sex trafficking in DCF cases at Windy Hollow. The assistant director commented that, given how small the state is, it is not uncommon for workers to live near clients, sometimes in the same apartment building. I was advised to devise a plan should I come home one day and be identified as a child protection worker by one of my neighbors or their guests. The director suggested that, in such a case, I might pretend I was visiting, get back in my car, and return home later.

Shortly after this conversation, Windy Hollow was identified in our monthly safety meeting as a newly listed "hot spot" because of the presence of youth with DCF histories who were known to be carrying guns there. Windy Hollow was designated a "no-go zone" until otherwise notified. In response to this notice, a long-term FSW shared with the team that she never enters Windy Hollow without a police check-in first. At this time, the directors knew that the no-go.zone was my home, but I had not disclosed to the FSWs with whom I was acquainted that I owned a condo in the neighborhood. The director's earlier suggestion (should I come home and be identified as a child protection worker by a neighbor, I might act like a visitor, leave, and return later) felt like an inadequate safety measure. My safety concerns grew.

CRITICAL INCIDENT: COMPROMISING SELF-INTEGRITY IN SOCIAL WORK PRACTICE

The critical incident I reflect upon in this chapter took place at my field placement with FSD during the first week of the spring term, 2022, during my final semester in the MSW program. The director's expressed objective for my internship was for me to complete as much of the employee onboarding as possible during my designated field hours. On my first day in field, the "New Employee Onboarding Guide: Foundations and Field Requirements" packet was placed front and center on my desk in my cubicle. The director said emphatically, "That's your Bible," and told me (many times) to treat it as such. During my internship, I logged the completion of numerous tasks in the long list of onboarding requirements and devoted myself to completing the onboarding process as efficiently as I could, per the director's instructions.

To meet my field requirements, I put in several hours in FSD over my winter recess. For self-preservation, I gave myself permission to take the last two weeks of the winter recess off to visit my family in the Midwest before beginning the final spring term of the program. The first day I returned to field, the director stated matter-of-factly that she wanted to pair me with a Juvenile Service worker (JSW) on a juvenile justice case that had "some gun involvement." I was interested in juvenile justice work but when I heard "gun," interest turned to dread.

"What do you think?" the director asked in a chipper voice.

"Sounds good. I'm interested in exploring juvenile justice work," I replied casually, not sharing my discomfort. The director had made it clear that she wanted me work-ready upon graduation. Turnover rates are always high at DCF. Offices across the state were short staffed, and workers were stretched thinner than ever due to the pandemic. Shadowing the case would fulfill one of the many new-employee onboarding requirements. I agreed to the request and left supervision with unspoken reservations: I didn't feel safe.

WHY I CHOSE TO CRITICALLY REFLECT UPON THIS INCIDENT

When I chose to critically reflect upon this incident, my initial objective was to better understand why I felt uncomfortable discussing my safety concerns with the director. My reluctance to share my vulnerability with the director may have been due partly to a comment she made in our required fall semester meeting with the assistant director and my field liaison. In that conversation, the director told my field liaison that she was evaluating me for employment—a thought that somehow had not occurred to me in my student mindset at the time. I perceived a strong power differential with the director and assistant director in dual roles as my field instructors. The narratives of seasoned FSWs who had repeated the message that the institution valued productivity over self-preservation lingered in the back of my mind. To admit concerns for my safety in the first semester of my internship felt like a risky confession. I was a Title IV-E student with a three-year employment obligation. The district office where I was placed was a fifteen-minute drive from my home. The next closest district was a fifty-minute commute each way. I was hoping to transition from my internship directly into employment in the district office where I was placed. Practical matters were at stake.

During my time in the MSW program, I began to experience bouts of insomnia. The first notable occurrence presented while I was taking the Child Abuse and Neglect course, which kindled memories of trauma from early childhood and adolescence. The insomnia increased in frequency and duration shortly after my field placement began with DCF, where worker safety is a serious concern and a frequently discussed topic. It was pertinent for me to examine my feelings of unsafety as they were affecting my mental and physical health, which in turn was affecting how I was showing up as an intern as well as how I was progressing as a grad student in the final semester of the MSW program.

In my adult life, I have been aware that I have a long history of not feeling safe in the world. I had a visceral sense of unsafety during crisis work conducted in child welfare. In Stage II of the critical reflection process, I realized that I was no longer concerned with the question of why I felt uncomfortable discussing my safety concerns with the director. I was more interested in the fundamental question of why I had a deep-seated feeling of not being safe in the first place.

Shortly after beginning this critical reflection process, I shared my safety concerns with my field liaison, my adviser, and the directors in the family services district office where I was placed. Given my concerns and my contract obligations, the director asked what I saw myself doing for work in DCF upon graduation. She encouraged me to consider if I was "cut out" for child welfare. The directors later informed me that there were other positions within DCF that did not involve direct service in child welfare for which I could apply to fulfill my Title IV-E contract requirements. I also learned that I could establish a repayment plan of the Title IV-E funds if I chose to cancel my contract.

Since repayment was not a foreseeable option, my intention was to complete my contract agreement. Given that I was obligated to be employed as an FSW for three years upon graduation, I wanted to reflect critically upon my fear for my safety. Understanding and addressing my fear were essential to my ability to provide best practices in service to families and children. It was also essential to my ability to set healthy boundaries for self-preservation as necessary while completing my contract obligations. Another primary intention in my reflective process was to stay consciously in my power and to explore my range of choices, regardless of what might eventuate.

MAIN ASSUMPTIONS THAT EMERGED FROM MY REFLECTION

When I applied for the Title IV-E educational assistance program, I expected child welfare work to be challenging yet rewarding. I believed that my lived experience with numerous incidences of domestic violence, rampant drug and alcohol abuse, poverty and neglect, the incarceration of many family members (including my mother), racism, and other life challenges would allow me to take a relational stance with clients and to be of service in ways that some from more privileged backgrounds may not. I took for granted that my extensive background in yoga and massage therapy would equip me with a level of self-awareness and an extensive toolbox for self-care that would sustain me while I fulfilled my employment obligations.

When I interviewed months in advance for the required second-year field placement with DCF, the director at the district office where I was later placed told me that lived experience could make child protection work more challenging given the triggers in child welfare. Shortly after beginning my internship with DCF, a former professor expressed deep concern that I might experience harm in the profession. I heard both of their concerns. I understood their concerns. And I trusted that I would be okay.

I am an enrolled member of the Santee Sioux Tribe of the Dakota Nation, of the *Oceti Sakowin*, the Seven Council Fires, more commonly known as the Great Sioux Nation. In the Dakota language we have a phrase, *mitakuye oyasin*, which means "we are all related." *Mitakuye oyasin* is a concept of oneness: we are one with the Creator and the creation. *Mitakuye oyasin* is also translated as "all my relatives" and expresses the Dakota aspiration to live in harmony with all kingdoms and nations within creation.

I entered the Title IV-E traineeship with Dakota and yogic perspectives, which are similar in many respects. For example, both believe in a creative consciousness or pure awareness that pervades all and unites all in a profound relationship. The Dakota term for this all-pervading force is *Wakan Tanka*, which is translated as the "Great Mystery." *Wakan* means "sacred" and *tanka* means "great." *Wakan Tanka* points to something that is sacredness and beyond words. When I accepted the Title IV-E scholarship, I knew I was signing on for challenging work in child welfare and believed that a force greater than my limited sense of self supported me.

However, the more I focused on the prevalent dangers of child welfare work, the more I assumed my safety was at risk and could not be guaranteed by DCF. I witnessed ways that child protection work affected long-term FSWs. Secondary trauma was common. I heard it said more than once by DCF employees that they stay because of the trauma bonds they develop in the field. I assumed that I, too, would experience secondary trauma in the field.

Furthermore, with the heavy caseloads and the colonial pace of the work, I assumed that I would not have time to process secondary trauma and that my health might suffer. One FSW under the age of fifty experienced a heart attack that was attributed to job-related stress. Despite my professional background in yoga and massage, I assumed that I would not be able to maintain a lifestyle that afforded adequate self-care to sustain myself in the DCF work culture. In fact, yoga and mindfulness practices were contemptuously dismissed by the FSWs I had met during my internship.

In addition, it was guaranteed that, at times, I would be required to remove children from their homes, a thought that had been a source of moral distress over the entirety of my MSW education, beginning in my first semester in the Child Abuse and Neglect course. Kim Strom-Gottfried, MSW, PhD, of the University of North Carolina–Chapel Hill's School of Social Work claims that moral distress may be especially acute in high-risk settings like those charged with child protection, where "the price of a wrong decision could be life or death" (Janssen, 2016).

My moral distress was complicated by my Dakota identity. The child welfare system has a well-known history of oppressive practice involving the removal of American Indian children from their homes and placing them with non-Indian families, perpetuating cultural genocide (Weaver, 2019). One of my Dakota cousins had been removed from his home as a teen, was placed in foster care with a non-Indian family, and was sexually abused by his foster mother. DCF's history of institutional betrayal of American Indians combined with my family history exacerbated my moral distress, which I could not easily convey at the time or even now.

Finally, I was operating under the assumption that canceling my contract was not an option as I did not have the means to repay the Title IV-E funding, without which I could not have afforded the opportunity to receive an MSW education.

OBSERVATIONS AND DISCUSSION ABOUT
THE PROCESS OF REFLECTION

Feeling unsafe in my child welfare internship at DCF led me to examine my deep-seated fears around my basic security and survival. Practicing the two-stage process of critical reflection made explicit fundamental fears that can be related to my Santee Sioux, Dakota identity. My Dakota grandmother once said, "It's not safe to be too Indian, my girl." During this process, I was compelled to explore my Dakota ancestral history, which includes what Maria Yellow Horse Brave Heart calls historical trauma (HT). Brave Heart (2003) defines HT as "cumulative emotional and psychological wounding, over the lifespan and across generations, emanating from massive group trauma experiences." I briefly outline a few of the historic events that have resulted in HT for many Dakota people.

One key traumatic historic event for the Dakota Nation was the Dakota War of 1862. The war was "an act of survival," in which a fraction of the Dakota Nation chose to fight for food for the mass of the people who were dying of starvation after being coerced into relocating from our traditional homelands in Minnesota (Minnesota Historical Society, n.d.). At the relocation site, the Dakota had no means of hunting, fishing, gathering, or growing their food and were dependent upon government rations that were promised but never delivered.

Approximately 1,658 tribal members, primarily children, women, and elders who were starving and who chose not to fight in the Dakota War, were forcibly marched by the U.S. military to the Fort Snelling concentration camp, which had been erected on a sacred site of the Dakota. It is estimated that "between 130 and 300 Dakota detained in the concentration camp died over the winter of 1862–63, mainly due to measles, other diseases, and harsh conditions" (Minnesota Historical Society, n.d.).

Shortly after the forced march, thirty-eight Dakota men who fought for the basic survival needs of the people were hanged without fair trials "in the largest mass execution in U.S. history," at the order of President Lincoln (Minnesota Historical Society, n.d.). After the mass execution, another 270 Dakota men were transported like cattle from Minnesota to camp McClellan in Davenport, Iowa, where they were imprisoned for three years without adequate shelter until they were shipped from the prison camp to what is now the Santee Sioux Reservation in Niobrara, Nebraska (Minnesota Historical Society n.d.). My Santee Sioux, Dakota grandmother and grandfather were born on the Santee Sioux Reservation and are buried there, along with my aunties, uncles, and my father.

In 1883, the Indian Religious Crimes Code banned Indigenous ceremonies nationwide, violating the religious freedom of Native Americans. This "explicit suppression of Native American spirituality" (Weaver, 2019) criminalized Dakota ceremonies like the Sun Dance, the *wiwanyag wachipi*, which is one of seven sacred rites of the Oceti Sakowin, the Seven Council Fires. The Sun Dance helps the people to remember their oneness with all that is and is central to a Dakota way of life (Brown, 1953). The outlawing of Indigenous spiritual practices outlawed what it means to be Dakota, as a Dakota identity is a spiritual identity.

The consequences of resisting U.S. policy outlawing "Indigenous spiritual expression" were harsh. Tribal people of the Oceti Sakowin "who gathered for Ghost Dance ceremonies at Wounded Knee Creek in 1890 were massacred. Their bodies, initially left frozen on the ground in a blizzard, were later dumped in a mass grave. Congress awarded 30 Medals of Honor to those who conducted the massacre. Likewise, hundreds of spiritual leaders were sent to the Hiawatha Asylum for Insane Indians for practicing their spiritual beliefs" (quoted in Weaver, 2019, p. 43).

Punishment for practicing traditional ways was severe because spiritual practices strengthened tribes and nations and "made them incorruptible" (Weaver, 2019). As such, "the destruction of the native religions that yet lived was viewed by the Indian Bureau as a *political* necessity" (quoted in Weaver, 2019, p. 43, emphasis in original). The religious freedoms of American Indians were not restored until 1978 (when I was eight years old) under the American Indian Religious Freedom Act. However, some Dakota practices, "such as those related to traditional burials, are still prohibited" (quoted in Weaver, 2019, p. 43).

This brief exploration of my ancestral history gave me a deeper understanding of my Dakota grandmother and her words, "It's not safe to be too Indian, my girl." It also helped me to better understand my lifelong feeling that it is not safe for me to be in this world.

NEW THINKING AND IDEAS FOR PRACTICE THAT EMERGED FROM THE SECOND STAGE

The second stage of the critical reflection process inspired me to think about how I might ground my social work practice in Dakota ways of seeing. From a Dakota perspective, our human being is not limited to the body, mind, personality, and ego. A Dakota identity also includes a *nagi*, an individual soul, and a *nagi la*, an indwelling spirit that is one with *Wakan Tanka*, also known as *Nagi Tanka*, the "Great Spirit" immanent in every being (Goodman, 2017). "We're not human beings having a spiritual experience; we are spiritual beings having a human experience" is a common adage heard in yogic communities. This view is similar to the Dakota belief that we are *nagi*, we are souls, "making a journey through the material world" (Goodman, 2017).

According to oral history, the Dakota Nation came "from the stars to the place where the Minnesota and Mississippi rivers meet" (Westerman & White, 2012). In the Dakota language, that place is called *Bdote*, which means "where two waters come together" (Minnesota Historical Society, 2008). *Bdote* and the surrounding lands, now Minneapolis–St. Paul, are sacred to the Dakota. As stated in *The Land of the Dakota*, " 'Minnesota' is derived from the Dakota phrase *Mni Sota Makoce*, Land Where the Waters Reflect the Clouds—and the people's roots here remain strong" (Westerman & White, 2012).

While *Mni Sota Makoce* is the traditional homeland of the Dakota, we originated from the stars. The Dakota people are known as the *Wicanlipi Oyate*, the Star Nation, or "star people." The Dakota came to *Bdote* via the "Canku Wanagi, the 'spirit road', more commonly known as the Milky Way" (Westerman & White, 2012). When the *nagi* leaves the body, it returns to *Wakan Tanka* along that same stellar path (Goodman, 2017).

Traditionally, stars are beaded on the moccasins of newborns because they have returned from the *Wanagi Ta Canku*, the "Path of the Spirits." It is believed that the *nagi* "chooses its parents" and incarnates in its chosen family "for its own reasons" (Goodman, 2017). The nagi chooses its relatives not necessarily because of how well they are doing as humans, but because of how much they are loved as souls.

The Dakota name for children is *wakanyeja*, which means "sacred gift." While the U.S. government has systematically removed Native American children from their homes for decades and has made multiple attempts to destroy our *tiospayes*, our deeply relational extended family networks, the traditional ways of the Oceti Sakowin have survived. Because of this, Dakota children "can still be raised with reverence for the immortality of the soul, and with an understanding of the cosmic significance of tiospaye values" (Goodman, 2017).

My research on historical trauma experienced by the Dakota and this critically reflective process inspired a Dakota theory of practice I might call the *Canku Wanagi*, or "Spirit Road" approach to social work. This Dakota framework, which is a work in progress, may be helpful for clients who have a spiritual orientation and may be adapted for clients who do not. For example, the word "spirit" may be exchanged for "consciousness," "awareness," or "intelligence."

I envision the Canku Wanagi Approach (CWA) as a decolonizing method that is based in a Dakota worldview of oneness. Black Elk, a renowned holy man of the Oceti Sakowin, explains, "It is only the ignorant who sees many where there is only one" (Brown, 1953). CWA observes polarities like "darkness and light" and "feminine and masculine" as two aspects of the One. CWA does not separate spirit from matter or consciousness from form. It aims to restore our relationship with *Nagi Tanka*, the Great Spirit immanent in every being, and our *nagi la*. It trusts the Indwelling Spirit of each client to guide them on their human journey and to support them through their soul growth. As individuals are restored in healthy relationship with their *nagi la*, their families and communities benefit. As healthy family and community networks are restored, individuals are better supported, and greater wholeness results.

CWA is a mindful way of being in the world. In the final weeks of the MSW program, while completing my capstone, my coursework, and my internship, working part-time, becoming a first-time grandmother, and coping with the hospitalization of a loved one, I returned again and again to my breath. Pausing for a moment, placing my hand on my heart, taking a breath, and connecting with my *nagi la* helped me to ground myself in my body and calm my total being. Consciously connecting with my breath and my indwelling spirit, just for a moment, helps me to be present and authentic in all my relations, personal and professional. As a mindfulness practice, CWA supports a relational way of being that builds trust and respect, setting a strong foundation for collaborative partnerships that are generative, spirited, and profound.

A Dakota way of being is a deeply relational way of being in which the people live for one another rather than individual self-serving interests. At times, CWA shifts our individual attention inward to strengthen our connection with *Wakan Tanka*, the Great Mystery, pervading and uniting all things. However, it does not ignore the impact of our external environment or the need for systemic change. Its understanding of our oneness may unite communities in research, advocacy, and policy reform necessary for the creation of effective programs that meet the needs of service users and improve the working conditions of service providers. Only when we view others as separate can we oppress, exploit, and attack the "other" and perpetuate systems in which few benefit at the expense of many. If we wish to decolonize social work practice, we must first "decolonize our minds" (Mitchell, 2018) from the myth of separation.

MY TRANSFORMATIVE LEARNING IN SOCIAL WORK: THE SINGLE STORY

Novelist Chimamanda Adichie warns about "the danger of the single story" (TED, 2009, 0:20). If our perception of a person or country is limited by one narrative, we will fail to see or understand the wholeness of that individual or nation. When a single story presents, we have an opportunity to practice other ways of seeing that honor each person's unique experience.

The single story I heard during my field placement in child welfare is that DCF is a toxic institution, the caseloads are heavy, the workdays are long, and the turnover rates are high, as is the potential for employees to experience harm. All these things are true *and*, as I witnessed, there are caring FSWs who are passionate about child protection and committed to child welfare. They support one another through the challenges of the profession while doing their best to keep children safe and families together.

During my internship at DCF, I experienced fear activations that correlated with extended bouts of insomnia. My insomnia persisted for weeks before I discussed it with my field liaison and field instructors. My internship in child welfare was mentally, emotionally, and physically taxing. And it provided me with an opportunity to critically reflect, to examine my fear, and to notice where I had slipped into a single story of not being safe in the world.

Critically reflecting on how I construct my identity in relation to historical, generational, and complex trauma increased my awareness of when, where, and how I use the term *trauma*. Many of us have survived horrific and heartbreaking life experiences that have left us feeling like victims. For many, those same life challenges instilled in us great empathy and inspired us to be of service to others. From a Dakota perspective, every human experience, no matter how terrible, is an opportunity for the soul to evolve and to realize our human potential. This work gave me courage to embody my spiritual identity more fully and, thereby, to better integrate my personal and professional identities. As a result, I can show up authentically with clients, honor their truth, and help them unlock possibilities that create preferred outcomes for their lives.

CONCLUSION

This critical reflection focused on worker safety in child welfare and uncovered deep-seated fears brought to the forefront of my consciousness during my internship at DCF. It led to a brief exploration of historical trauma as experienced by the Dakota Nation. It shared a Dakota worldview, affirmed Dakota values, and inspired a vision for a Dakota framework to integrate with my social work approach. My transformative learning called me to remain critically conscious of the single story that denies the totality of our human experience and the fullness of our creative expression. With conscious awareness, we have the potential to cocreate a world where multiple possibilities can coexist and all our relatives may live in alignment with their truth and free from harm.

REFERENCES

Brave Heart, M. Y. (2003). The historical trauma response among natives and its relationship with substance abuse: A Lakota illustration. *Journal of Psychoactive Drugs, 35*(1), 7–13. https://doi.org/10.1080/02791072.2003.10399988.

Brown, J. E. (Ed.). (1953). *Black Elk's account of the seven rites of the Oglala Sioux*. Norman: University of Oklahoma Press.

Donoghue, M., & Burbank, A. (2015, August 16). Timeline of a tragedy: Unraveling the 4 VT slayings. *Burlington Free Press*. https://www.burlingtonfreepress.com/story/news/local/2015/0 8/16/timeline-tragedy-unraveling-vermont-slayings/31796559/.

Fook, J., & Gardner, F. (2007). *Practising critical reflection: A resource handbook*. Maidenhead, UK: Open University Press.

Goodman, R. (2017). *Lakota star knowledges: Studies in Lakota stellar theology* (3rd ed.). Mission, SD: Sinte Gleska University Press.

Janssen, J. S. (2016). Moral distress in social work practice: when workplace and conscience collide. *Social Work Today, 16*(3), 18.

Minnesota Historical Society. (n.d.). *Bdote*. Historic Fort Snelling. Retrieved April 3, 2022, from https://www.mnhs.org/fortsnelling/learn/bdote.

Mitchell, S. (2018). *Sacred instructions: Indigenous wisdom for living spiritually based change*. Berkeley, CA: North Atlantic.

TED. (2009, October 7). *Chimanda Ngozi Adichie: The danger of a single story* [Video]. YouTube. https://www.youtube.com/watch?v=D9Ihs241zeg.

Weaver, H. N. (2019). *Trauma and resilience in the lives of contemporary Native Americans: Reclaiming our balance, restoring our wellbeing*. New York: Routledge.

Westerman, G., & White, B. (2012). *Mni Sota makoce: The land of the Dakota*. St. Paul: Minnesota Historical Society Press.

11

PRACTICE RESEARCH AND TRANSFORMATIVE SOCIAL WORK

Evolving Concepts and Social Impact

TIMOTHY SIM AND JAN FOOK

The concept of practice research has been developing in social science–based professions like education and social work over the past few decades (for example, Costley & Fulton, 2019). Since it represents a significant departure from traditional university-led ways of thinking about research, it is crucial to include it in this volume, to flesh out the ways that practice research can be transformative, particularly in its involving of different stakeholders: researchers, practitioners, clients, and their significant others.

The chapter begins with a brief overview of some definitions, the evolution of practice research in social work, the main principles involved in the concept, and how it represents a transformative approach to research. The bulk of the chapter then outlines a unique case example of practice research initiatives after a fateful earthquake in China, to illustrate specific ways in which a practice research approach can be put into practice. This example also demonstrates how, informed by such an approach, university-based academics can form partnerships with practitioners, governments, service users, and local communities to ensure that the practice and research conducted can make immediate, relevant, high-social-impact contributions.

OVERVIEW OF PRACTICE RESEARCH
IN SOCIAL WORK

Practice research is research that emanates directly from a problem or issue experienced in practice and whose results are directly relevant to practice. It is an approach to research, rather than a specific method or design. It can encompass a range of methods and epistemologies, but it recognizes, from the beginning of the research process, the relevance of knowledge that is created through the experiences of practitioners, as well as the salience of clients' voices and their lived experiences.

Practice research in social work reflects and emphasizes the relationships and interactions among researchers, practitioners, and service users; its definition is best described as evolving (Epstein et al., 2015; Julkunena & Uggerhoj, 2016). Fisher et al.'s (2016) entry in the *Oxford Bibliographies in Social Work* is helpful in this regard:

> Practice research focuses heavily on the roles of the service provider and service user who play a major role in defining the research questions and interpreting the findings. Compared to other knowledge production processes that are agency-based, service-focused, client-focused, theory-informed, highly interactive (multiple stakeholders), and designed to inform practice, policy, and future research, practice research makes a unique contribution to the research enterprise. . . . It often involves collaboration among multiple stakeholders in addition to service providers, researchers, service users, educators (funders, policymakers, agency directors, etc.), while taking into account the power dynamics between service users and service providers with respect to inclusiveness, transparency, ethical reflexivity, and critical reflection.

This position and perspective of practice research in social work unwittingly echoes some of the core beliefs of the transformative approach. To further appraise the commonalities between practice research and the transformative approach, let us review an ongoing series of practice research statements since 2008.

WHAT IS PRACTICE RESEARCH?

Timothy Sim started his journey in practice research in social work when Jan Fook invited him to the first International Conference on Practice Research in Salisbury in 2008 (Fook & Evans, 2011). This invitation fundamentally transformed his practice and research career in social work. According to the Salisbury Statement on Practice Research (Salisbury Forum Group, 2011, p. 5):

> Practice research involves curiosity about practice. It is about identifying effective and promising ways in which to help people; and it is about challenging troubling practice through the critical examination of practice and the development of new ideas in the light of experience. It recognizes that this is best done by practitioners in partnership with researchers, where [researchers] have as much, if not more, to learn from practitioners as practitioners have to learn from researchers. It is an inclusive approach to professional knowledge that is concerned with understanding the complexity of practice alongside the commitment to empower and address social justice issues, through practice. Practice research involves the generation of knowledge of direct relevance to professional practice and therefore will normally involve knowledge generated directly from practice itself in a grounded way.

This statement defining practice research was expanded in the Helsinki Statement (Helsinki Forum Group, 2014) with a specific focus on the principles and values of establishing partnerships and relationships between research and practice. Specifically, a set of goals was articulated for practice research in social work (Julkunena & Uggerhoj, 2016, 6–7):

> (a) research that critically describes, analyzes, and develops practice; (b) a process in which curiosity, critical reflection, and critical thinking need to be reflected by researchers, practitioners, and service users; (c) a commitment to locally based collaboration between researchers/ research settings and practitioner/practice settings in the planning, generating, and disseminating of research; and (d) a participatory and

dialogue-based research process designed to develop practice while vali-
dating different types of expertise within the partnership.

The New York Statement of Practice Research emerged out of deliberations from three international conferences on defining and operationalizing practice research and continued the construction of the social
science and social philosophy foundation of practice research (Epstein
et al., 2015). It sought to expand the dialogue on practice research to
include more international voices while also searching for linkages
with the evolving process of defining the mixed-methods approach to
evidence-informed practice. This statement provided a platform for
the Fourth International Conference on Practice Research planned for
Hong Kong in 2017. The Hong Kong Statement of Practice Research
focused on the contexts and challenges of carrying out practice research
in East Asia and beyond, as well as raising pertinent questions about the
development of practice research and the role of practitioners and service users in practice research (Sim, Austin, et al., 2019). The Melbourne
Statement of Practice Research (Joubert et al., 2023) highlights that
practice research is where practice meets research; it is about promoting
a sense of curiosity about practice that also challenges current wisdom
through a partnership among practitioners, researchers, service users,
and social work students, often in the context of social justice issues.
Inevitably, this requires practice research in social work to use diverse
research methods to respond to the challenges faced by practitioners
and to answer practice-based questions.

   The foregoing definitions embody key themes that occur in the
subsequent literature regarding practice research. Practice research is
relational and negotiated, with an emphasis on collaborative relations
among researchers, practitioners, service users, and the organizations
that support them. The kind of knowledge being developed is grounded
in context, it is concrete but also complex, and it is holistic. Multiple perspectives are needed in order to elicit the foregoing knowledge, which is
potentially transdisciplinary in nature. Practice research embraces inclusion and rigor, so that it can make an impact on the direct contexts and
stakeholders involved, including service users, practitioners, academics,
educators, students, and policy makers.

HOW IS PRACTICE RESEARCH TRANSFORMATIVE?

Practice research is an alternative way of conceptualizing research that transforms the more traditional tendency to polarize the two main research paradigms as oppositional: quantitative or qualitative. This questioning of the traditional paradigmatic split also means refashioning deep epistemological assumptions about what constitutes legitimate knowledge; how legitimate knowledge is created; and what is regarded as important knowledge. It means refashioning how research is conceived and how the structures and arrangements that support it are designed. The traditional split between researcher and practitioner, and the unequal power relations this implies, must be reconceptualized to allow for more dialogue between the different social worlds occupied by each group. Adopting a practice research framework therefore means changes in the underlying assumptions about the nature of knowledge and its creation, whose knowledge is valued, and the social arrangements and structures that support these changes. Practice research is potentially transformative in that it equalizes power imbalances (in line with a critical approach) but also allows for an inclusive approach to knowledge making (Fook, 2002). Practice research values multiple sources of knowledge and ways of knowing, working across sectors, underpinning transdisciplinary research that is increasingly being applied to resolve various problems associated with real-world situations and complex socioecological problems (Sim, Young, et al., 2019) such as pandemics, poverty, and natural disasters.

In the following section, Tim presents and reflects on a high-social-impact transdisciplinary practice research project in China after an earthquake. This case study aims to highlight the transformation that happened at different levels for different stakeholders, including service users, practitioners, and governments, as well as the Chinese social work field involved. Special attention is paid to the way social work academics and practitioners can practice and research transformatively on complex issues in the unique Chinese context after an earthquake. Acknowledging the centrality of context in transformative practice must be included in ongoing development of the approach (Fook, 2022).

CASE STUDY: A TRANSDISCIPLINARY PRACTICE RESEARCH PROJECT THE WENCHUAN EARTHQUAKE

Unlike typical research projects, this Chinese practice research project did not begin with a literature review or hypothesis formulation, nor was there an invitation by practitioners or governments for consultation. It was a spontaneous response to a fateful earthquake in the Sichuan province of mainland China. This unique longitudinal social work practice research program evolved over a decade from 2008 and 2018, using a transdisciplinary approach.

THE BIG WENCHUAN EARTHQUAKE

A magnitude 8 earthquake struck without notice on May 12, 2008, at about 2:28 p.m., as students were waiting for their teachers in their classrooms and workers were about to return to their offices and factories. Ninety thousand people were killed and missing, and 350,000 were injured. Homes, hospitals, schools, power supplies, transportation, and communication systems were destroyed for millions. The hardest hit were the rural villages and towns. Secondary hazards such as aftershocks, serious landslides, and floods continued to plague the villages at the epicenter in the Wenchuan County of Sichuan Province. Between 2010 and 2013, the villagers were forced to evacuate. As recently as 2019 August, nine people were killed, thirty-five people remained missing in a landslide, and more than two thousand houses collapsed as a result of heavy rain.

As a foreign social work academic with access to the most severely affected areas because of my connections with local universities, I quickly found out that the conventional social work and psychotherapeutic approaches I was teaching were of little relevance. The local villagers were mostly unfamiliar with social work or psychotherapy. They spoke local dialects, which I could barely understood. More than half the villagers in many of the remote areas at the epicenter were of Tibetan or Qiang ethnic minority groups. They have their unique religious beliefs and cultural practices, particularly related to death and mourning and making sense of a natural disaster. To compound the situation further, the local villagers soon found academics untrustworthy. Academics who were opportunistic and unscrupulous entered the fields immediately after the earthquake to collect research data, such as regarding posttraumatic stress disorder. They came in droves and left once they got what they needed. When I arrived two weeks after the earthquake, there was already a widespread dictum: Be cautious around dogs, fire, and psychotherapists after the earthquake. Be cautious of dogs as they may have bitten a corpse and may spread disease; be cautious of fire as the temporary tents may catch fire easily; be cautious of psychotherapists as they may harm you. I quickly realized the context was unfamiliar, challenging, and volatile. I was politely told off by the primary school principal that I should not approach his students, and if I intended to carry out any "interventions," I must do so outside the school compound, regardless of local government support. However, I had the highest respect for the principal, who was fiercely protecting his 222 surviving students when the other half had perished.

We were humbled by the challenges confronting the local people after a horrific natural disaster, as well as by their resilience in bouncing back. We had no ambitious research agendas, no hypothesis, and definitely no theoretical framework. We observed and were present to support the local villagers respectfully and sensitively for two weeks at a time, over an extended period of six months. During this time, we were guided by basic social work values of service, dignity and worth of the person, the importance of human relationships, integrity, and so on, with a focus on understanding the needs of marginalized and vulnerable groups, such as those who have been injured, disabled, or bereaved, those living in great financial difficulties, women, older people, children, and members of certain minority groups (Twigg, 2004). The use of basic relationship-building skills based on person-centered therapy, particularly empathy, genuineness, and unconditional positive regard, guided our relationship building. However, we were often challenged by our own interpretation of professional social work ethics related to interaction with the local people. For instance, despite their lack of resources, they would insist on providing meals for us when we visited. They would be offended if we did not eat the meals. We were offered cigarettes, and it would be rude to reject their offer. We were expected to drink rice wine with an alcohol content of close to 50 percent if we were to engage the local people. After the earthquake, all people, regardless of position or creed, would use the same makeshift toilets, literally dug-out drains, and would bathe in the same makeshift "open-concept" shower rooms. Where, practically speaking, were professional boundaries? I was challenged to my core and tried to make sense of the professional and personal values in conflict. While the basic social work values were helpful in guiding me, I found myself constantly challenged and stretched beyond the familiar and maneuvered carefully (Sim, 2009). As time passed, we respectfully developed some projects and programs for meeting the needs of the marginalized and vulnerable groups. All these were developed in collaboration with the local people and capitalized on the local cultural and political resources, such as organizing a traditional dance gala a few days before the earthquake anniversary. Over more than seven years, we developed a Chinese psychosocial work model in post-disaster contexts using constant feedback from service users, including schoolchildren, their parents and teachers, and local governments and other professionals (Sim & Dominelli, 2017). We called this the SICHUAN model (DOCUinc, 2015).

THE SICHUAN MODEL

In developing this post-disaster psychosocial social work model, we used the acronym S-I-C-H-U-A-N to organize six interlinked concepts through critical reflection based on the practice wisdom acquired during that time, discussion with workers, and service users' feedback:

[S] Step-by-step
[I] Involvement
[C] Contextually respectful
[H] Help people achieve self-help and mutual help
[U] United effort
[A-N] Add no trouble, no chaos, and no harm

This model emphasizes a step-by-step approach for social workers and mental health practitioners to promote local participation and involvement inclusively after a disaster; employ culturally relevant ways of being, knowing, and coping; promote self-help and mutual help; adopt transdisciplinary approaches among stakeholders; and reflexively uphold the highest standards of ethical professional behaviors. Let us briefly elaborate the model with a focus on the way this practice research model is in sync with the transformative approach.

1. *Step-by-step.* This first principle is aptly captured by a famous Chinese adage made popular by the leader Deng Xiao-Ping, who modernized the Chinese economy in the 1980s: "Mo zhe shi tou guo he," or "Cross the river by feeling the stones under one's foot step by step." Uncannily, Deng was from Sichuan. The gist of this dictum is to take a calm and steady approach in the face of fierce challenges. This was a particularly useful reminder for a foreign academic like me who, even though I am Chinese, had little understanding of the context and did not speak the dialect. Instead of imposing my own theoretical frameworks, which were mostly occidental, and conjuring ludicrous hypotheses or conjectures, I respectfully learned to understand the contexts, including the political, cultural, spiritual, and socioeconomic, that continued to evolve dynamically after the earthquake. In fact, the geophysical context after the earthquake continued to evolve and needed some years to stabilize. The villages continued to be threatened by the forces of nature, and the old, women, and children were living in constant fear and anxiety. Despite expensive engineering projects and negotiations to relocate the villagers, it took at least six years for the landslides and floods to lessen. Meanwhile, the psychosocial work projects and programs we developed with the villagers helped to transform the stress and anxiety they were experiencing into hope and possibilities. These projects capitalized on their community connectedness and cultural heritage, as well as our long-term commitment and relationships (Sim & Cui, 2015).

2. *Involvement.* This second principle of involvement is bidirectional and fiercely relations based. While engaging the villagers in developing our plans, social work practitioners, practitioners, and academics must also be involved in the day-to-day living of the villagers. Beyond relationship building, professionals and academics can discover what the local people already have, despite the earthquake's having destroyed almost all of what they once loved and possessed, including their closest family members. Here's an example: On the first winter after the

earthquake, as I was walking on the temporary road, I was amazed at the traditional Guo Zhuang (harvest) dance the village women were performing. Mesmerized by the unison, the potential group dynamics, and the physical and psychological benefits of this traditional dance, we started involving the village women, with the support of local government, in planning events and functions to promote the psychosocial well-being of the villages and communities. Over a period of five years, the entire town, comprising eight villages, began to incorporate traditional dance more in their official occasions and school curricula and eventually developed a self-help group and organization (Sim, Lau, et al., 2019).

3. *Contextually relevant and respectful.* Ng (2012) suggested that social work in China is not and will not be the same as social work practiced elsewhere in the world, given China's political and cultural considerations. Unless social work academics and practitioners are contextually relevant and respectful, they will miss many possibilities to develop models of social work education and practice (Yuen-Tsang & Wang, 2002). Given the political context, the Chinese government plays a strong and directive role in the development of social welfare as well as the social work profession (Tsang & Yan, 2001; Bai, 2014). Wang (2011) believed that social work in China could be embedded within the civil affairs system, gradually transferring the civil affairs work into professional social services. With their understanding of the service users' needs and respective communities' concerns, social workers and academics could play the roles of mediators and advocates, which many other disciplines could not. A case in point would be Chinese social work academics acting as mediators to deflect and resolve the many conflicts that arise from the complex, explosive, and capricious social conditions that often accompany a major disaster, making valuable contributions in fostering communication between grieving parents and the local government (Chen, 2009).

Considering the cultural context, Sichuan, like other Chinese provinces, is rich and diverse. Its varied geographical terrain makes each county's climate very different. Demographically, Sichuan is known for its mix of cultural minority groups, including the Zang, Qiang, Yi, Naxi, Lipo, and A-Hmao. In considering transformative social work in trying conditions after a natural disaster, social workers could consider what rich resources and heritage the contexts are endowed with, instead of trying to impose and import what is foreign and probably unsustainable. In other words, the need for social work academics and practitioners to be respectful and relevant is a sine quo non for successful transformative social work.

4. *Help people achieve self-help and mutual help.* Psychosocial programs aim to improve social and psychological aspects of people's well-being (Psychosocial Working Group, 2003). They are usually community-based interventions that aim to restore security, independence, and dignity to individuals in affected communities, promote communities' resilience, and prevent psychiatric morbidity and further social disruption (Becker, 2007). Interventions that narrowly focus on mental health problems like psychological trauma run the risk of overlooking aspects of social context that are vital to well-being (Psychosocial Working Group, 2003). One way of restoring security, independence, and dignity to individuals is promoting self-help and mutual help by focusing on their contexts and maximizing their resources and resiliencies. These principles guided many of the initiatives we made in helping the marginalized and vulnerable groups in our decade-long program, such as parents in bereavement, parents whose children were disabled in the earthquake, children and older people who were left behind when their able-bodied family members had to leave home to work over extended periods, and so on. One case in point is the transformation of three male teachers who lost their spouses and their children during the earthquake and resorted to heavy drinking. No psychotherapy or counseling was provided as they were averse to these Western models. Instead, we spent many evenings sharing the famous local shao-kau (BBQ) and beer, organized a local trip that provided respite for them during sensitive festivities like Chinese New Year, and developed team-building exercises with their colleagues. In a nutshell, we strengthened the natural group that was evidently providing support and solace to these teachers. Eventually, we embarked on a book-writing project, when one of them was afraid that memories of the horrific earthquake were becoming faint. This book project lasted six years and helped the men bring to closure a

terribly painful life journey, sharing the pains and sorrows that they had not told anyone after the earthquake. Their lives have been transformed by the earthquake. We have continued to keep in touch after all these years, and it has been a privilege to see their lives further transformed after remarrying. This book is currently available on the internet.

5. *United effort.* Given the unique contexts of social work in China, collaboration between academics and practitioners, across disciplines and borders, among school authorities, local governments, and funders, was essential to respond to service users' needs and feedback (Sim & Dominelli, 2017). Cournoyer (2004) advocated a collaborative stance characterized by openness and critical thinking among academics, practitioners, and clients to highlight "many ways of knowing, each of which may contribute to the body of evidence necessary to help practitioners provide competent and effective services" (p. 5). A poignant example is the social workstations we set up in six schools where there had been a high casualty rate (Sim, 2009, 2011). The input from practitioners, including consultants, social workers and therapists, school principals, teachers, and parents, often enriched the thinking and challenged the assumptions of the academics, including the project director and local supervisors. The integration of theory and practice, along with documentation of practice by this author and local supervisors, helped practitioners to validate and promote their practice. Together, members of the team sharpened one another's understanding and practice in an important but underdeveloped social work practice domain—disaster management.

This united effort in post-disaster response and recovery is also relevant in the pre-disaster stages of disaster management: mitigation and preparedness. In another transdisciplinary research project in China, we found that for a transdisciplinary project to be successful, *guanxi*, or relationship, is paramount in the local context. The most important factors in sustaining commitment and achieving project objectives are the potential for new insights and unique learning experiences and the opportunity to take part in salient activities and events that engage stakeholders. However, political considerations and cultural differences can hinder the development of a transdisciplinary research project (Sim, Young, et al., 2019).

6. *Add no trouble, chaos, and harm.* Doing no harm, self-determination, and respect for human dignity are held as sacrosanct, universal ethical principles in social work (Sewpaul, 2015) and in this decade-long program. However, their interpretations are often mediated by culture and context and extend the boundaries of moral relativism (Sewpaul & Henrickson, 2019). Hence, social work academics (e.g., Hugman, 2008) have questioned whether a common ethical framework is possible or even desired since many forms of social work practice are culturally and geographically specific. Several social work ethical models, approaches, frameworks, and theories have been proposed (e.g., Banks, 2012; Caron et al., 2020). Although helpful when managing ethical issues, these frameworks and models often place the responsibility for shortcomings on individuals who make decisions as independent actors (Weinberg, 2010; Sewpaul & Henrickson, 2019). Banks (2008) echoed this critique and asserts that ethical judgment can never be abstracted from the context in which the decision is taking place. In using the transformative approach and carrying out practice research, ethical considerations are a dynamic and difficult consideration. A case in point involved a voluntary group providing rehabilitation services for students after the earthquake and using their services to promote themselves on personal websites. This happened in one of the schools where we set up a social workstation. We shared the case and invited commentaries in a book edited by Banks and Nøhr (2012). We concur with the commenters Larson and Drolet (pp. 42–45) that in a country where social work is a fledgling profession, social workers must ensure that the best interests of vulnerable populations are served. Social workers are expected to be advocates not only for their clients but for all those who are disadvantaged and marginalized, like those who have been adversely affected by a natural disaster. However, the actions of social workers should be tempered by a pragmatic and reasoned approach that leads to positive outcomes rather than the mere enforcement of a moral stance.

SOCIAL IMPACT AND TRANSFORMATIVE PRACTICE IN THE DISASTER MANAGEMENT PRACTICE FOR SOCIAL WORK IN CHINA

The post-disaster community psychosocial capacity–building program developed after the 2008 Wenchuan earthquake in China's Sichuan Province was awarded a three- out of four-star rating for its considerable research impact by the Hong Kong Government University Grants Committee in its research assessment exercise 2020. Research impact was defined as the demonstrable contributions, beneficial effects, valuable changes, or advantages that research qualitatively brings to the economy, society, culture, public policy or services, health, environment, or quality of life, whether locally, regionally, or internationally, that extend beyond academia. Impact in this context includes (a) positive effects on, constructive changes in, or benefits to the activity, attitude, awareness, behavior, capacity, opportunity, performance, policy, practice, process, or understanding of an audience, beneficiary, community, constituency, organization, or individuals, or (b) the reduction or prevention of harm, risk, cost, or other negative effects.

As a result of this program, the SICHUAN model is now used to improve the psychosocial well-being of communities severely affected by disasters. The program's integration of cultural and local resources has proved to be a desirable practice for efficacious community psychosocial capacity building. Over time, this transdisciplinary practice research model has generated sustained psychosocial changes in the communities where it has been adopted and has led to changes in the actions of stakeholders, particularly local governments, funders, and community organizations. It has also facilitated social work in subsequent disaster management in China: the model was duplicated successfully after another earthquake occurred in Ludian County of Yunnan Province on August 3, 2014.

Based on the SICHUAN model and reiterative practice reflection and formative evaluations, the program developed a series of psychosocial assessment and intervention tools for rural communities in post-disaster situations in China. It specifically focused on children (Sim & Chen, 2015), women (Sim et al., 2019), older people (Cui & Sim, 2017), and teachers (Sim et al., 2019) who suffered great losses, injuries, and bereavements. These psychosocial assessments and interventions, the first of their kind in mainland China, were clearly effective and received resoundingly positive feedback from the communities affected.

One of the exceptional aspects of this model lies in the optimal use of local resources and cultural heritage to heighten the resilience of individuals, families, and communities in post-disaster situations (Cui & Sim, 2017; Sim & Chen, 2015; Sim & Dominelli, 2017; Sim et al., 2019). This is in contrast to conventional post-disaster psychosocial interventions focused on individuals and pathologies. For example, the SICHUAN model uses local cultural resources such as the traditional Tibetan dance Guo Zhuang, the New Year picture, or Nianhua, and narrative documentation (Sim, 2015; Sim & Chen, 2015; Sim & Dominelli, 2017; Sim et al., 2019; Cui & Sim, 2017) to provide psychosocial support for vulnerable groups. Moreover, the model involves close collaboration with stakeholders, including the affected individuals, their family members, community leaders, local government, and professionals from a range of backgrounds, who guide and inform both research and practice as the processes unfold (Cui & Sim, 2017; Sim, 2015; Sim & Chen, 2015; Sim & Dominelli, 2017; Sim et al., 2019). Our SICHUAN model is considered "good practice" internationally (Bragin, 2011).

Most post-disaster psychosocial capacity–building programs are unsustainable, are focused on the individual, and pay little attention to the local cultural and political context. This is particularly the case in rural communities, where there are many vulnerable inhabitants. The team developed a social work psychosocial program taking a novel approach that emphasizes the use of cultural heritage and local resources and involves a range of stakeholders. The program enhances the transformation of social work in China and practice in disaster management by adopting a transdisciplinary approach (i.e., a multidisciplinary collaboration across sectors).

Through top-down and bottom-up initiatives of various stakeholders, the program has had an impact on the following stakeholders.

Local government. As a result of the Chinese government's recognition of its positive impact on the local communities, the program received additional funding of $142,000 from the Shenzhen Ministry of Civil Affairs to develop its work and establish a local post-earthquake psychosocial capacity–building model from 2014 to 2016. In 2016–2017, the Wenchuan local government provided additional funding of $15,000 to the Wenchuan Li Chuan Social Work Service Centre, an NGO that was created to oversee the program. This funding was used to continue providing services in the area of the earthquake epicenter and to establish the program in the nearby town of Xuankou. The program represented a groundbreaking development for community social services in the region. It has changed the way the Wenchuan Yingxiu government engages with women villagers, who were invited to contribute to the local culture by reviving the traditional Guo Zhuang dance.

Funders. The project received approximately $1,456,900 from 2013 to 2017 from seven organizations and the Chinese government. When the project ended, the major donor, MINDSET, the philanthropic arm of the Jardine Matheson group, published a booklet titled "Breaking Ground on Broken Ground." It describes the impact of the program: "Eight-year social work programs are rare in rural China. Fortunately, the commitment of Dr. Timothy Sim and continued faith and funding from MINDSET allowed the Programme to run its course and for the wounds of the people to begin healing. By the end, residents of the Yingxiu region went from having little to no idea what a social worker was to regarding them as family" (MINDSET, 2018).

Schools. The principal of the Yingxiu Primary School acknowledged, "In all the school inspections and evaluations of Yingxiu Primary School in recent years after the horrific earthquake, our students have performed outstandingly despite the horrific loss [222 out of 500 students died in the 2008 earthquake]. Other than the contributions of our teachers, the contribution of the Social Workstation is paramount." Considering the program's impact, I was appointed as the honorary principal of Wenchuan Yingxiu Primary School (Hong Kong Polytechnic University, n.d.a).

Villagers. Children, women, teachers of the bereaved, seniors, ethnic minorities, and people who were disabled by the earthquake were our focus. The program helped to improve their psychosocial capacity and quality of life by capitalizing on their cultural and community resources via collaboration with various stakeholders (Chang, 2016). In 2016, a parent whose daughter was disabled during the earthquake wrote a letter to the program staff in which she noted, "You used social work, psychology, sociology, and a range of professional knowledge in an integrative manner, and effectively incorporated examples and cases to help us appreciate the legal and policy implications for our particular situations. This helped us to plan our roads ahead. Most importantly, through the range of activities and programs you implemented, we have helped parents in our group [whose children were disabled in the earthquake] to benefit from mutual help and mutual learning."

Model replication. The psychosocial toolkits generated by the practice research project were adopted by local social workers after the 2014 Ludian earthquake. I was appointed as a committee member by the Ministry of Civil Affairs to coordinate the training and supervision of sixty social workers appointed by the local and central government using the SICHUAN model as a central framework. Applying the SICHUAN model, the Ludian Zhaotong Hospital established the first ever "post-disaster medical social workstation" in mainland China, serving 375 patients who were severely affected by the earthquake. As the Ludian Zhaotong Hospital notes, the station "continues to promote medical social work even after The Hong Kong Polytechnic University concluded its project in the hospital. Meanwhile, the post-disaster medical social workstation has gone beyond the boundaries of the hospital to the community, which has been highly endorsed by the local government."

Social work in China. Before 2008, Chinese social workers were excluded from China's disaster management systems. Our research and practice improved the capacity and skills of social workers in disaster management and provided policy makers and the public with evidence that revised their understanding of the profession. The Department of Civil Affairs of Sichuan Province set up the first "special disaster social work team" on July 15, 2015 to provide immediate post-disaster services to the province. Of the appointed nineteen supervisors and twenty-two social workers, nine were members of the program (Hong Kong Polytechnic University, n.d.,b).

CONCLUSION

Tim was transformed on a personal and professional level by this program. He firmly believes that while there is a place for conventional research, practice research could transform different stakeholders in different contexts. For effective social work and psychotherapy practice, the person of the social worker and the therapist is always emphasized. In practice research, the person of the practice researcher is likewise crucial. Practice researchers should be engaging, relationship oriented, inclusive, contextually sensitive, reflective and respective, and reflexively ethical. Above all, they collaborate to transform and are themselves transformed in the process of collaboration.

For both Tim and Jan, linking the idea of a practice research approach with a transformative perspective is itself transformative. It leads us to refocus on integrating the formerly disparate (and implied unequal) worlds of practice and research in ways that are more inclusive of different viewpoints and experiences. It also leads us to revisit our fundamental assumptions about the nature of knowledge, how it is created, and what types of knowledge and whose knowledge a valued. In this way, it shares possibilities with newer trends in social work thinking, especially with regard to decolonizing social work (Clarke & Yellow Bird, 2021), questioning Eurocentric epistemologies and ontologies, and refashioning post-anthropocentric worldviews (Bozalek & Pease, 2021) in order to be mindful and careful of our whole environments.

REFERENCES

Bai, J. R. (2014). What is the role of social work in China? A multi-dimensional analysis. *Advances in Social Work, 15*(2), 495–506. https://doi.org/10.18060/16441.

Banks, S. (2008). The social work value base: Human rights and social justice in talk and action. In A. Barnard, N. Horner, & J. Wild (Eds.), *The value base of social work and social care* (pp. 25–40). Maidenhead, UK: Open University Press.

Banks, S. (2012). *Ethics and values in social work* (4th ed.). Basingstoke, UK: Palgrave Macmillan.

Banks, S., & Nøhr, K. (Eds.). (2012). *Practising social work ethics around the world: Cases and commentaries.* New York: Routledge.

Becker, S. M. (2007). Psychosocial care for adult and child survivors of the tsunami disaster in India. *Journal of Child and Adolescent Psychiatric Nursing, 20*, 148–155. https://doi.org/10.1111/j.1744-6171.2007.00105.x.

Bozalek, V., & Pease, B. (2021) *Post-anthropocentric social work: Critical posthuman and new materialist perspectives.* London: Routledge.

Bragin, M. (2011). Clinical social work in situations of disaster and terrorism. In J. R. Brandell (Ed.), *Theory and practice in clinical social work.* Thousand Oaks, CA: Sage.

Caron, R., Lee, E. O. J., & Sansfaçon, A. P. (2020). Transformative disruptions and collective knowledge building: Social work professors building anti-oppressive ethical frameworks

for research, teaching, practice and activism. *Social Welfare, 14*(3), 298–314. https://doi.org
/10.1080/17496535.2020.1749690.

Chang, S. (2016, May 17). Eight years after: Closing the door on the past. *China Daily,
Hong Kong Focus*, pp. 8–9. http://www.chinadaily.com.cn/hkedition/2016-05/17/content
_25314329.htm.

Chen, T. (2009). Social workers as conflict mediator: Lessons from the Wenchuan earthquake.
China Journal of Social Work, 2(3), 179–187. https://doi.org/10.1080/17525090903211721.

Clarke, C., & Yellow Bird, M. (2021) *Decolonizing pathways towards integrative healing in social
work*. London: Routledge.

Cournoyer, B. R. (2004). *The evidence-based social work skills book*. Boston: Allyn & Bacon.

Costley, C., & Fulton, J. (Eds.). (2019). *Methodologies for practice development: Philosophy, reflection and research*. London: Sage

Cui, K., & Sim, T. (2017). Older people's psychosocial needs in a disaster rural community of
China: An exploratory study. *Natural Hazards, 85*(3), 1577–1590. https://doi.org/10.1007
/s11069-016-2649-6

DOCUinc. (2015). Building back better in disaster management: The Hong Kong Polytechnic
University Department of Applied Social Sciences [Video]. Vimeo. https://vimeo.com
/128756640.

Epstein, I., Fisher, M., Julkunen, I., Uggerhoj, L., Austin, M. J., & Sim, T. (2015). The New York
statement on the evolving definition of practice research designed for continuing dialogue:
A bulletin from the Third International Conference on Practice Research (2014). *Research
on Social Work Practice, 25*, 711–714. https://doi.org/10.1177/1049731515582250.

Fisher, M., Austin, M. J., Julkunen, I., Sim, T., Uggerhöj, L., & Isokuortti, N. (2016). Practice research. In E. Mullen (Ed.), *Oxford Bibliographies in Social Work*. Oxford: Oxford
University Press. https://mackcenter.berkeley.edu/sites/default/files/publications/practice
research-_oxford_publication.pdf.

Fook, J. (2002). Theorising from practice: Towards an inclusive approach for social work
research. *Qualitative Social Work, 1*(1), 79–95. https://doi.org/10.1177/147332500200100106.

Fook, J. (2022). *Social work: A critical approach to practice* (4th ed.). London: Sage.

Fook, J., & Evans, T. (2011). The Salisbury statement on practice research. *Social Work and Social
Science Review: International Journal of Applied Research, 15*(2), 76–81. https://ejournals.bib
.uni-wuppertal.de/index.php/sws/article/view/2/10.

Helsinki Forum Group. (2014). Helsinki statement on social work practice research. *Nordic
Social Work Research, 4*(Suppl.), 7–13. https://doi.org/10.1080/2156857X.2014.981426.

Hong Kong Polytechnic University Department of Applied Social Sciences (n.d.a). News
and Events, Dr. Timothy SIM appointed as the Honorary Principal of Wenchuan Yingxiu
Primary School, Sichuan, China. Retrieved May 22, 2022, https://www.polyu.edu.hk/apss
/news-and-events/737-dr-timothy-sim-appointed-as-the-honorary-principal-of-wenchuan
-yingxiu-primary-school-sichuan-china.

Hong Kong Polytechnic University Department of Applied Social Sciences (n.d.,b) Website:
News and Events, Special disaster social work team in Sichuan, China. Retrieved May 22,
2022, https://www.polyu.edu.hk/apss/news-and-events/696-special-disaster-social-work-team
-in-sichuan.

Hugman, R. (2008). Ethics in a world of difference. Ethics and Social Welfare, 2(2), 118–132. https://doi.org/10.1080/17496530802117474.

Joubert, L., Webber, M., Uggerhøj, L., Julkunen, I., Yliruka, L., Hampson, R., Simpson, G., Sim, T., Manguy, A. M., & Austin, M. J. (2023). The Melbourne statement on practice research in social work: practice meets research. Research on Social Work, 33(4), 367–374. https://doi.org/10.1177/10497315221139835.

Julkunena, I., & Uggerhoj, L. (2016). Negotiating practice research. Journal of Teaching in Social Work, 36(1), 6–10. https://doi.org/10.1080/08841233.2016.1119625.

MINDSET Limited. (2018). Breaking ground on broken ground. Hong Kong: MINDSET.

Ng, G. T. (2012). Disaster work in China: Tasks and competences for social workers. Social Work Education, 31, 538–556. https://doi.org/10.1080/02615479.2011.581277.

Psychosocial Working Group. (2003). Psychosocial interventions in complex emergencies: A framework for practice. https://www.eldis.org/document/A17612.

Salisbury Forum Group. (2011). Salisbury statement on social work practice research. Social Work and Society, 9, 4–9. https://ejournals.bib.uni-wuppertal.de/index.php/sws/article/view/2/10.

Sewpaul, V. (2015). Politics with soul: Social work and the legacy of Nelson Mandela. International Social Work, 59(6), 697–708. https://doi.org/10.1177/0020872815594226.

Sewpaul, V., & Henrickson, M. (2019). The (r)evolution and decolonization of social work ethics: The global social work statement of ethical principles. International Social Work 62(6), 1469–1481. https://doi.org/10.1177/0020872819846238.

Sim, T. (2009). Crossing the river stone by stone: Developing an expanded school mental health network in post-quake Sichuan. China Journal of Social Work, 2(3), 165–177. https://doi.org/10.1080/17525090903211713.

Sim, T. (2011). Developing an expanded school mental health network in a post-earthquake Chinese context. Journal of Social Work, 11, 326–330. https://doi.org/10.1177/1468017311409495.

Sim, T. (2015). Bouncing back together. Beijing: Social Sciences Academic Press. [沈文伟. (2015). 一起重生. 社会科学文献出版社] (in both Chinese and English).

Sim, T., Austin, M., Abudullah, F., Chan, T. M. S., Chok, M., et al. (2019). The Hong Kong Statement on Practice Research 2017: Contexts and challenges of the Far East. Research on Social Work Practice, 29(1), 3–9. https://doi.org/10.1177/1049731518779440.

Sim, T., & Chen, H. Q. (2015). Post-disaster psychosocial work toolkit for working with children. Beijing: Social Sciences Academic Press (in Chinese). [沈文伟、陈会全. (2015). 灾后儿童心理社会工作手册. 社会科学文献出版社

Sim, T., & Cui, K. (2015). Psychosocial needs assessment and interventions in a Chinese postdisaster community. Health and Social Work, 40(4): 329–332. https://doi.org/10.1093/hsw/hlv061.

Sim, T., & Dominelli, L. (2017). When the mountains move: A Chinese post-disaster psychosocial work model. Qualitative Social Work, 16(5), 594–611. https://doi.org/10.1177/1473325016637912.

Sim, T., Lau, J., Cui, K., & Wei, H. H. (2019). Post-disaster psychosocial capacity building for women in a Chinese rural village. International Journal of Disaster Risk Science, 10(2), 193–203. https://doi.org/10.1007/s13753-019-0221-1.

Sim, T., Young, J., Lau, J., & Cui, K. (2019). Initiating transdisciplinary research in China: A case study. *International Journal of Environmental Sciences & Natural Resources*, 22(1). https://juniperpublishers.com/ijesnr/pdf/IJESNR.MS.ID.556080.pdf.

Tsang, A. K. T., & Yan, M. C. (2001). Chinese corpus, Western application: The Chinese strategy of engagement with Western social work discourse. *International Social Work*, 44(4), 433–454. https://doi.org/10.1177/002087280104400404.

Twigg, J. (2004). *The good practice review: Disaster risk reduction—Mitigation and preparedness in development and emergency programming.* London: ODI.

Wang, S. B. (2011). Embeddedness development of China social work. Social Science Front, 4, 206–222.

Weinberg, M. (2010). The social construction of social work ethics: Politicizing and broadening the lens. *Journal of Progressive Human Services*, 21(1), 32–44. https://doi.org/10.1080/10428231003781774.

Yuen-Tsang, W. K. A., & Wang, S. B. (2002). Tensions confronting the development of social work education in China: Challenges and opportunities. International Social Work, 45, 375–388. https://doi.org/10.1177/0020872802045003366.

12

JUMPING IN, BECOMING IMMERSED IN EXPERIENCE, AND TAKING NOTES

A Swimmer's Guide to Teaching Transformative
Social Work Research

BRENDA SOLOMON

Maybe it is because, in my youth, I loved to swim, was a certified lifeguard, and worked poolside for many years that I approach teaching research methods as I do.

How do you describe swimming without getting into the water? There is only so much you can say about swimming before you just have to get in! And once in the water, there is not much left to say about the ways a swimmer can enhance the buoyancy of their body and the ability to stay afloat. It seems that everyone does something similar yet particular to whatever they have been told and know about floating and their ability to prop themselves up and propel themselves through the water. What is left after that is a tale of techniques, one's refined approach to the water, and lots of practice.

I teach advanced research in a MSW program at the University of Vermont, where I am an associate professor. My ideas about research were largely formed by my doctoral studies in sociology, particularly my association and identification as an institutional ethnographer—and, as I said, from my years at the pool.

As an institutional ethnographer, I focus on the conventions of everyday life. Institutional ethnography is an approach to inquiry whereby the ethnographer works with key informants to map social relations and account for the ways texts mediate and arrange people's actions to create a kind of taken-for-granted way of going about things (see DeVault, 2006; Rankin, 2017; Smith, 1987, 1990a, 1990b, 1996, 1999, 2005). Dorothy E. Smith (1987), the scholar credited with forming institutional ethnography, describes the approach as starting from within a problematic and accounting for the way things are put together that call for a particular way of doing things. Rather than trying to achieve some sort of detached observation of what is, or lingering in the multiplicity of experience to account for what may be, institutional ethnographers are interested in taking account of the way we go about our lives, making connections between organizing texts and people's actions. Questions like the following frame my inquiry: Why are things as they are and not some other way? What is at play to arrange things so that they operate the way they do? How is it that the way things operate at one site connect with and seem to fit with the way things operate at other sites? How do things work in common and become interconnected? How do experiences that could be vast and complicated get shaved down through textual and discursive mediations to become easily recognized and known in much less complicated terms? To make things work, a lot has to be worked out and made simple, so that things can be repeated and accomplished with less forethought and anticipation, with an emphasis on meeting established expectations. An institutional ethnographer is interested in these processes that operate largely without notice.

Applying an institutional ethnographer's sensibility, you have to wonder how accepted social understandings of swimming and staying afloat overwhelm the swimmer, define what is possible, and limit their experience of the water, in much the same way as social work research methods define and limit what is possible for a student's experience of data. What has already been wrung out of the possibilities that await those jumping in for the first time? What social limits have been established before one's feet touch the water or, in the case of learning research, one's eyes meet a subject's gaze?

Still there is a first time (to jump in), and therein lies the opportunity— to extend possibility, suggest attention to vastness and to the fullness of experience, and renew an interest in one's own processes and how one can use them to accomplish something not tried before. And so, with a splash, goes the focus of this paper: here is where I enter with my class on research methods. Underwater? Actually, yes. I think that accounts for it very well.

But let's back up for a minute. Let me say a few words about the problematic I am underscoring and aim to address in this research class: (1) What does it mean to take a transformative stance toward research? (2) What terms of engagement do I establish with students in keeping with transformative social work? (3) What instructions do I give to students just before they jump in?

WHAT DOES IT MEAN TO TAKE A TRANSFORMATIVE STANCE TOWARD RESEARCH?

To take a transformative stance is to call into question what we take for granted in the field, from the values we support to the accepted knowledge and practices. It is to question common ideas that arrange action, as well as the actions themselves. In research, it is to examine critically the questions we ask, the methods of data collection and analysis we use, and the ways we represent and interpret data in expanding contexts for making truth claims and producing knowledge. Informed by critical approaches from various standpoints (see Collins, 1990; Crenshaw, 1994; DeVault, 2021; Luken & Vaughan, 2021; Naples, 2003; Smith, 2005), an interest in decolonizing research paradigms (see BlackDeer, 2021; Held, 2019; Rowe et al., 2015), and transformative and critical constructionist views of research (see Burr, 2003; Fook, 1996, 2011, 2019; Gergen, 2009; McNamee, 2010; Witkin, 2001, 2010), transformative researchers examine *what is* to guide observation and analysis toward *what may be*, in terms of a more just and inclusive future.

With students, in class, I begin a conversation about research by challenging the assumptions of difference between practice and research that commonly set research knowledge apart from practice knowledge. Since master's-level social work students who are learning research usually have a fair amount of practice knowledge, this assumption about the difference between practice and research suggests that they are starting from scratch. Challenging this supposition, I ask students to consider more directly how the steps social work practitioners take in clinical settings mirror the processes of research. Placing the processes side by side shifts the terrain for students, and with little guidance they connect what they know from practice to research methods, particularly related to practices of observation and analysis, and taking a reflexive account of the position and standpoint of the researcher. My interest in transposing practice knowledge to research and minimizing the distinction between the two is well articulated by Jan Fook (1996, 2011) in developing her practice approach, critical reflection, for research. Jan's approach elaborates the reflexive account of the research process in social work.

In addition to emphasizing practice processes for research, I uphold the centrality of practice data for research; I consider narrative and observation in relation with others as primary sources of data for collection and analysis in social work research. Narrative data generated through social work practice events such as a clinical session, a home visit, a family or school meeting, and other everyday data-gathering opportunities that are central to social work practice should be considered no less central to social work research. They should be used to account for what social workers do and to inform and guide the profession.

WHAT TERMS OF ENGAGEMENT DO I ESTABLISH WITH STUDENTS IN KEEPING WITH TRANSFORMATIVE SOCIAL WORK?

I think of teaching transformative social work research as an ongoing attempt to dislodge students from the long-standing suppositions of research that discourage them from their own sense of how to do research derived from their practice knowledge. I seek to create opportunities for students to assert their research in transformative terms, to resist taking knowledge for granted or to take histories of accepted ways of producing knowledge as fact.

With a good deal of uncertainty swirling about, it is my experience that students come to the first class eager to get on with it. It seems that their intrigue with the idea of becoming a researcher and doing research prevails. They want to know what they should know, and for the most part they want to do it well.

As social workers earning an MSW, my students are largely set to be practitioners. The MSW is considered the terminal degree in the field. After an MSW, you can become licensed and, with continuing education of various sorts, have a very successful career in social work. While a PhD is possible, it is not necessary for practice. However, to contribute to the field through research and publishing, one typically needs the training associated with a PhD. Thus, the training we provide our MSW students toward informing the field and beyond is more ambiguous; it is less defined, mapped out, or clearly articulated.

If my students most likely will not continue on to a PhD, how can I best assist them, first, to understand themselves and their work beyond their everyday practice of social work toward being knowledge producers for the field and, second, to see that they are viable, capable, and competent knowledge producers able to meet their obligation to the field and their profession? Many students consider research a bit of a mystery, and one they are not sure they need or want to explore, so it takes some doing to get them to the edge of the pool, let alone to jump in. Research methods might seem more a burden and less a contributor to their future life's work.

Further complicating students' foray into research, my students are being schooled in transformative social work, which is less clearly articulated and defined within the field and, therefore, may require even more commitment on their part to learn and apply. All told, I try to impress upon students the opportunity they have to inform the field—that their published papers and projects would go a long way toward establishing a transformative social work approach to research and knowledge production. They do share my interest in that.

Thus, my aim is to make my class relevant and useful to students, helping them to see that they are important to knowledge production in our field and are quite able to meet that demand. My focus, before they get started, is to set the terms of engagement by emphasizing what they already know about practice and transformative social work in relation to research.

So, at the point when they are at the water's edge, about to begin an exploration of their relationship to research, I believe it is important to make several suggestions:

1. *Research is not a mystery.* You know this already. You take care to set up your work in ways that are consistent and trustworthy. You think and reason about the complicated experiences of people's everyday

lives as they unfold before you in practice settings, sometimes as people are throwing things at each other or at you. Research is a luxury—a practitioner's dream. You get to gather experience as data and examine it at your leisure, not at critical moments. You can use research methods to examine how you and others make decisions or what better paths you or others could have taken; you can map out your actions or discursive practice to show just how things can be done to the betterment of more people more often.

2. *Research is more like practice than you have been led to believe.* What makes research research is how you go about accounting for your process and arriving at findings and interpretations so that they are recognizable to others; usually research is published so others can read and refer to it. You have all had experiences that parallel the elements of research. You can do this.

3. *The more you see research like practice, the more this course will make sense to you and be useful to your practice.* The big division between research and practice keeps you from benefiting from the act of doing research and keeps you from being a viable player in informing your profession and the social sciences. (I don't know who that works for, but it does not work for you or what is important to you in this work.)

4. *Considering the connection between research and practice, you, as social workers, not only understand something about data collection but bring a great deal of insight to the endeavor.* You work with people, trying to understand their plight in order to take action to be of some help to them; your main tools are talk, observation, and a lot of knowing about how things work. Considering the limited time we have together to focus on research, we will not begin our discussion about research methods where the disciplines typically begins: how to gather data. You are data-gathering machines; you don't need a lot of time figuring out how to gather and record data. You have ample experiences with data collection and recordkeeping that should inform your research, so we will build on to what you already know.

You are starting out ahead of the game by what you know about practice and how you practice. Your expertise should help inform research practice. You should be noting your accounts of your work to contribute to the field.

WHAT INSTRUCTIONS DO I GIVE TO STUDENTS JUST BEFORE THEY JUMP IN?

Before you ask someone who doesn't know how to swim to jump into the water, you have to be sure you can save them if they don't find a way to stay afloat. It is serious business, and you should know what you're doing. A bad experience could foreclose someone's relationship with the water.

When I ask students to jump in, I am suggesting that I will be there for them. They have to sense that they can count on my knowledge of transformative social work research and my ability to help them do it. I have seen too many students who enter my classroom reluctant to participate, if not in full-fledged fear of research. So I do understand the responsibility I have, and I take care to conduct myself in a way intended to gain my students' trust.

During the very first class, I present students with the first in a series of data-gathering events. They all experience the event together and then are told to record the event without further direction other than the following:

> In social work, we spend a good deal of time presenting cases; typically the case represents our work with an individual, a family, or a community. It is common, when presenting a case, to wonder what we've accented or left out and how our report of a case would mirror or contrast with someone else's telling of the same case. We usually present a case to access other professionals' analysis of the situation, to see what they see and hear in our presentation that might fill in the gaps or recast something we've believed about the case.
>
> At the end of class, each week for the first six weeks of this course, together, as a class, you will watch a clip from an American movie. The clip will depict a commonplace American family event—dinner. In this way, you will all have access to the same case, event, or clip and be able to do what is rarely possible in social work practice: experience the same case, at the same time, together. You will each take account, keep account, and glean what is there and what to make of what is there, individually. Please bring your account to the next class. We will begin each class with a review of your individual accounts from the clip presented the week before.

With that, and no further instruction, I suggest they indulge the possibilities and just dive in!

JUMPING IN: BECOMING IMMERSED IN THE EXPERIENCE AND TAKING NOTE

After their first attempt at observation and recordkeeping, students usually come to class very energized and excited to know how their work compares with their colleagues' and whether it meets some kind of established notion of research.

Each student has an opportunity to present and discuss aspects of their notes in class, drawing attention to the elements of observation and analysis that characterized their dive into the project. As I look at their notes and listen to them talk about their process, I note four areas for their consideration, presented here as questions:

1. How did they account for data and record their observations?
2. What did they record related to what was going on in the clip (particular to dinner, family, and the American family dinner)?
3. How did their account of the clip relate to their professional position and training, generating accounts, suppositions, and interpretations of data?
4. How did their account of the clip relate to their personal experiences and standpoint, generating accounts, suppositions, and interpretations of data?

Considering that the class was engaged in the same jumping-in process and students were reviewing one another's work as they completed their own, how did their recordkeeping and observations related to these four areas of observation compare and contrast with their classmates'?

Note that social workers usually attend to matters that lend themselves to personal as well as professional interpretation. Social workers know about family life from having studied family process, but no less they also know about family life from being in a family themselves. Further, as this class takes place in the United States, it is expected that there are common understandings about family particular to Western society, directed by standards and promoted by various social institutions such as schools. Dorothy Smith (1993), Nancy Naples (2003), and Gerald de Montigny (1995), among others, have explained pervasive ideological practices used within and across institutions to locate and categorize children and families. Critical race theorists underscore differential racializing practices related to these processes (see Zamudio et al., 2010), and other critical scholars have focused attention on a history of colonizing practices toward indigenous peoples (see Pihama & Lee-Morgan, 2019). These social practices common to Western society locate families, and attention paid to families, in terms of their proximity to Western ideals.

While people's experiences of themselves and their family are complex, citizens and scholars alike are meant to use common ways of making sense to locate and categorize family life so that social imperatives are interwined with their intimate knowledge of their own circumstance. Thus, looking at the clips I assign in class calls for a professional sense of the situation, but invariably enlists a personal way of making sense of things as well. Whether or not it is fully acknowledged and accounted for in field notes and discussed in class, people's personal experience of family, within a history of American society, has a bearing on their view of their own lives and the lives of those they encounter—in this case, in a movie clip at dinner.

A FEW MORE WORDS ABOUT ORGANIZING OBSERVATIONS BY PROFESSIONAL AND PERSONAL STANDPOINT

My focus on professional and personal standpoint derives from Gerald de Montigny's *Social Working*. De Montigny (1995) dedicates a chapter to the standpoint of social workers as members of the supposed professional class. In this connection, he points to the tension that exists when one's personal standpoint does not align with the class-based suppositions of becoming a professional. He notes that one is expected to reconcile these differences and convey a settled professional stance, on the assumption that who one is as a professional is who one is as a person. To be a professional is to assume a particular way of being that denies the ways a social worker's personal history may be in tension with the history of the profession.

I remember during my social work training trying to come to terms with this problem of self as social worker. While jobs are nine to five, becoming a professional means taking a position within society that suggests a way of living. As a social work educator, I find it even less likely that this tension can ever be resolved. My interest is in drawing out that tension and being fully cognizant of how it operates in our practice and in our sense of ourselves as practitioners. It has been a useful way to focus student attention on intersections of experience (Crenshaw, 1994) and professional performance (Butler, 1997). Personal and professional referents offer meaningful contexts for considering and articulating one's position in relation to processes of observation, analysis, and claims making. Also, it provides a way of expressing views to expand conceptualizations of professional standpoint.

FIRST JOTTINGS

From the first review of field notes in class, what stands out is that without direction about standards of note taking, there is quite the range of expression. Some of what students recorded as experience, as well as their methods for recording experience, was nowhere near what I would have anticipated with my no-bars-held call to account for their experience of the movie clip. For instance, one student accounted for action and exchanges among family members by drawing various shades of the rainbow flowing between objects and people. Another student used color primarily to express the feelings of the various people in the scene. Someone wrote as if the field notes were a journal to themselves or to the people in the clips. One student wrote only about the person they most identified with in the scene. Another student said they could only write as if they were the social worker and used jargon from their place of employment to describe action and dialogue between family members. Another drew cartoon characters in blocks of action or drew images that represented various feelings generated from the clip. More in line with what I think of as field note, many other students wrote about the scene emphasizing action or relationships. Some were more concerned with the physical space where the dinner took place, or the table setting and seating arrangements. Some wrote out the entire dialogue as fast as possible; others focused on who initiated dialogue and what the dialogue was about. Some described facial reactions and glances across the table. They also noted who was responsible for the food, who served the food, and who was responsible for children eating the food, especially vegetables. Students also noted what they saw within the dialogue and the action: what the family dinner seemed to mean to the family, how financial means seemed to limit the family dinner experience, where there was conflict, empathy toward a child, an alliance between siblings, stereotypical roles of husbands and wives and of family members representing diverse groups, the burden on women to work and make dinner, the lack of gratitude between family members, a father's struggle to assert his presumed position as head of household, and the mother's say in what can be said at the table.

This exercise allowed me to point out the layers of observation related to how we conceptualize what is there and, particularly, social workers' orientation to the observation. For instance, in a social work research course, you seldom get a record of the furniture or the overbites or an account of various postures; you get social relations, familial problems, parental discord, and social expectations of daughters and sons and mothers and fathers. In this way, professional training and terminology organize observation at the point of observation. Through this process of reviewing student field notes, I can show how interpretation may be layered but nonetheless already in play at the point of observation. Pointing out segments from their notes, I encourage students to identify layers of interpretation, the observer in the observation, and what arranges their attention within their professional and personal observations.

NAVIGATING THE WATERS: NOTICING AND NAMING YOUR APPROACH AND TAKING DIRECTION

The first review of field notes in class allows students to have a hearty discussion about their approaches to data collection and recordkeeping. Going forward, building on this discussion, I focus their attention on their process, further elaborating on the several levels of observation and analysis I referred to in the previous section. In their individual reviews of the remaining clips, I ask them to consider the following questions as they take notes over the next five weeks of data collection.

COLLECTING DATA

Notice your process of being in the water and staying afloat. How are you observing, listening, and recording events as data? How do you physically do it? What works best for you? How do your methods compare with those of others in the class? How do your methods compare with what you are learning about accepted data-gathering practices in research?

MAKING OBSERVATIONS OF AMERICAN FAMILY DINNER CLIPS

What is happening in the clip? What are people doing? What are people saying? What is the context for talk and action? Who is talking to whom? How do you account for what is happening? What arranges the site under study? Our notions of family? Our notions of dinner clips? What is there that you did not expect to see or hear? What is missing that you expected to see or hear? These questions about note taking and observation are, for the most part, common to the teaching of social science qualitative methods and books on the subject (see Creswell, 2018; Emerson et al., 1995).

ACCOUNTING FOR PROFESSIONAL STANDPOINT

How do you use your professional training in transformative social work intentionally to observe and form suppositions and interpretations that may shape data? How does your professional training in transformative social work shape the words you use and how you write? In contrast, how do powerful practices and discourses in the profession inadvertently arrange your attention and account for the words you use and how you write, generating unintended interpretations that may shape data?

ACCOUNTING FOR PERSONAL STANDPOINT

How do your personal sensibilities inform your observations to form suppositions and interpretations that may shape data? How do your personal sensibilities shape the words you use and how you write your remarks? How might you use your personal interpretations intentionally, to contribute to your research process and generate knowledge useful to the field? How might you mitigate the impact of your unintended use of personal interpretations related to your research processes and knowledge production?

Together, these levels of attention and analysis further set the terms of engagement and direct students' awareness of themselves in three ways: as participants in the research process, or researchers; by means of their professional interests in the data, as social work researchers in general and transformative social work researchers in particular; and as researchers occupying various standpoints and social categories with an array of personal experiences and backgrounds. By bringing these layers of processing and sense making into focus, students can take account of the complexity of their observations in more precise ways, locating and detailing the intricacies of experience with greater clarity as they write their field notes and discuss them with one another.

Over the next several weeks, students continue observation and field note taking on the remaining movie clips. Also, they continue to meet and discuss their observations and field notes in various groups, in and out of class. After six movie clip reviews, students write a preliminary memo that addresses several areas: data-collection practices; emergent areas of interest, interpretation, or hunches; issues and concerns in the field related to data-collection practices; and what surprised them or caught them off guard that they are still grappling with. In the memo, students select two areas of interest and provide several excerpts from their field notes to support their emergent analysis. The concluding section of the memo is for bullet-point statements to remind themselves of what is important going forward and to shape the direction of their later work. This memo is modeled after Professor Sari Biklen's, found in her revered instruction on qualitative research methods and elaborated in several of her books on the subject (see Bogdan & Biklen, 2007).

After the instructor's and peers' reviews of their memos, students develop one area of interest into a research proposal and present that in a later class.

At these junctures of taking notes, writing memos, and forming research proposals, students are encouraged to continue noticing the interplay among their note-taking practices, observations of family at dinner, and use of professional and personal knowledge and experience, as well as how their observations are situated in relation to those of their classmates. This repeated set of interests and observations become touchstones for their ongoing individual work and discussions about their work with one another.

STAYING IN YOUR OWN LANE AND SWIMMING TOGETHER: STUDENTS AS INDIVIDUAL CASES AND THE CLASS AS A WHOLE FOCUSING ON TIED PROCESSES OF NOTICING AND NAMING

Strung together, student field notes may serve as data points to help shed light on the data-gathering practices of students as a whole in class. By noting the details of each student's actions step by step and accounting for what each student had to say about what happened in the clips, students began to note the contours of their meaning making as a group. They noted how their observations and interpretations were similar to one another's, related to practice experiences and training rooted in transformative social work. They noted how their ways of representing what they experienced and how they made sense of things were related to their position as students of a particular generation. They could also see points of difference related to particular ways of conceptualizing common phenomena in the field. For instance, one student noted that in each clip there was an "outsider," another student referred to the same set of observations as taking an outside position, yet another called it scapegoating, and a fourth student labeled it as rebellion. These students were taking note of the same set of data points and had similar notions of what was taking place, yet their ways of orienting to the data were slightly different. This led to even more discussion about what contributed to their related but different conceptualizations. For some, it derived from a specific practice experience or the use of terminology within the profession that they regularly referred to in clinical settings. For others, it was a matter of how they experienced the phenomenon in their own lives or how it was conceptualized among their friends and thus was associated with important contexts for meaning making that left lasting impressions.

As the students together explored the relationship between their observations and how they accounted for those observations, they became less invested in getting what they thought might be the "correct meaning" and instead became more interested in what guided their own and others' noticing and meaning making. Their understanding of the processes they were engaged in was no longer academic or derived from textbook instruction but came out of their own experiences with one another. From their discussions, students found that accounting for their own process was central to telling what they found; it was one connected event. Noticing and naming were knotted together to produce the event of telling what is there.

In this way, as a class, their attention shifted away from how their work was the same or different from their classmates' and toward how they accounted for their work or what went into the claims they made. They became interested in one another and themselves in the process of research in ways they had not expected; they became authentically interested in the research endeavor and in themselves and each other as researchers. They found their way together, not in some surface way that had them trying on methods as one does T-shirts at a flash sale, but more in the way one finds a new favorite pair of jeans that are sure to become more comfortable with time. In these moments, I think students began to feel comfortable; they trust and appreciate the process, themselves, and one another in a way that one might call transformative.

Through these conversations among themselves, students began to analyze their field notes in earnest. They studied where their note taking may have shifted to use jargon from the field and what that may have implied. They noted where their observations of the dinner clips rubbed up against, contrasted with, or reinforced their personal sense of family dinner, and then considered these accounts compared to those of their classmates. They noted where their classmates conceptualized a set of observations in ways that contrasted with their own and tried to sort out what seemed to account for that difference. In turn, these considerations led to further conversations among students about their overall observations of the families in the clips and what these observations suggested in terms of social work understanding of family process, American family traditions, and the expression and resistance of familial and cultural imperatives. They also discussed how the modern American movie portrayed the American family, considering how it reinforced and resisted standards of family life beginning with social categories of difference by race, class, gender, and sexuality.

All at once, they were swimmers, and it was a beautiful thing.

CHARTING A COURSE OF ACCOUNTABILITY: THE DISCERNING USE OF THE PERSONAL AND PROFESSIONAL IN OBSERVATIONS AND MEANING MAKING

When teaching research, I amplify the worth of practice knowledge and the types of data generated through practice or narrative. While I do not encourage sweeping claims from data collection and analysis, I believe that student observations can contribute broadly to understanding in the field, calling into question accepted knowledge and practices and putting forward more useful conceptualizations of experience that may benefit more people, more often. In order to make claims, it is commonly understood that people need to take account of themselves in their inquiries. As I see it, my task is to show how knowledge is situated and, at best, how researchers can offer a robust yet partial account of what they experience from their vantage point as observers and sense makers. These notions of partial objectivity (Harding, 1995, 2017) and situated knowledge (Haraway, 1988, 1991, 1997) are well established in the social sciences and are associated with earlier references to standpoint, critical race theory, and decolonizing practices to elevate indigenous approaches to inquiry.

Deferring to my institutional ethnography roots, I am interested in providing an experience for students that shows how problems of objectivity and subjectivity get worked out in practice. My aim is to show what comes into play as researchers take notes, interpret actions, and assign meaning. At the start, I invite students to become subjects of their own inquiry and to sort out among themselves, for themselves, what accounts for observations and analyses. To liberate the researcher from obligations to uphold or contest abstract standards, I emphasize the researcher's obligation to show the complex ways professional knowledge and personal experience affect their actions and come to bear in their claims. Accounting for intentional and unintentional use of both personal and professional experience in their practice allows for a more nuanced way to engage themselves in their work and to bring forward and consider experience for the purposes of making claims about what is there (observation) and what happened (analysis).

By overseeing their own process through the practitioner problematic of personal and professional standpoint established in class, students may draw, with some refinement and precision, lines of accountability and act with purpose to use aspects of self and social worker to enable more complex accounts of their work.

Being aware of their processes of observation and analysis in relation to that of their classmates as well, students can refine practices of discernment, act with greater intention, and take steps to amplify some aspects of their professional training and personal standpoint and mitigate others. They may form an intimate sense of themselves as researchers capable of accounting for complex observations, interpretations, and analyses particular to their stance as social workers and in relation to their personal lives as well. This process should lend itself to detailed and traceable observations and analyses that are potent and may be offered with vigor to contribute to and expand what is taken for knowledge in their field.

TOWELING OFF AND THOUGHTS BEFORE GETTING BACK IN THE WATER

You can never jump in again the way you did that first time; that said, you can bring that awareness of being new to your work each time you enter it. As you had to be that first time, you can be fully present to experience. You can continue to refuse to be complacent or resigned to what is. You can stay interested in how things are put together, amazed by what could be, and drawn in yet again to consider those possibilities.

REFERENCES

BlackDeer, A. A. (2021). From settler colonialism to self-determination: An Indigenous perspective on decolonizing social work. https://www.bu.edu/ssw/files/2021/03/Final -Decolonizing-SWK-PPT.pdf.

Bogdan, R., & Biklen, S. K. (2007). *Qualitative research for education: An introduction to theories and methods* (5th ed.). New York: Pearson.

Burr, V. (2003). Social constructionist research. In *Social constructionism* (pp. 149–177). London: Routledge.

Butler, J. (1997). *Excitable speech: A politics of the performative*. New York: Routledge.

Collins, P. H. (1990). Black feminist thought in the matrix of domination. In *Black feminist thought: Knowledge, consciousness, and the politics of empowerment* (pp. 221–238). New York: Routledge. http://www.hartford-hwp.com/archives/45a/252.html.

Crenshaw, K. (1994). Mapping the margins: Intersectionality, identity politics, and violence against women of color. In M. A. Fineman & R. Mykitiuk (Eds.), *The public nature of private violence* (pp. 93–118). New York: Routledge.

Creswell, J. W. (2018). *Qualitative inquiry and research design: Choosing among five approaches*. Thousand Oaks, CA: Sage.

de Montigny, G. A. (1995). *Social working: An ethnography of front-line practice*. Toronto: University of Toronto Press.

DeVault, M. (2006). Introduction: What is institutional ethnography? *Social Problems, 53*(3), 294–298. https://doi.org/10.1525/sp.2006.53.3.294.

DeVault, M. (2021). Elements of an expansive institutional ethnography: A conceptual history of its North American origins. In P. Luken & S. Vaughan (Eds.), *The Palgrave handbook of institutional ethnography* (pp. 11–34). Cham, Switzerland: Palgrave Macmillan.

Emerson, R. M., Fretz, R. I., & Shaw, L. L. (1995). *Writing ethnographic fieldnotes*. Chicago: University of Chicago Press.

Fook, J. (1996). *The reflective researcher: Social workers' theories of practice research*. St. Leonards, NSW: Allen & Unwin.

Fook, J. (2011). Developing critical reflection as a research method. In J. Higgs, A. Titchen, D. Horsfall, & D. Bridges (Eds.), *Creative spaces for qualitative researching* (pp. 55–64). https:// doi.org/10.1007/978-94-6091-761-5_6.

Fook, J. (2019). Reflective models and frameworks in practice. In C. Costley & J. Fulton (Eds.), *Methodologies for practice research.* (pp. 57–76). Thousand Oaks, CA: Sage.

Gergen, K. J. (2009). *An invitation to social construction* (2nd ed.). Thousand Oaks: Sage.

Haraway, D. (1988). Situated knowledges: The science question in feminism and the privilege of partial perspective. *Feminist Studies, 14*(3), 575–599. https://doi.org/10.2307/3178066.

Haraway, D. (1991). A cyborg manifesto: Science, technology, and socialist-feminism in the late twentieth century. In *Simians, cyborgs, and women: The reinvention of nature* (pp. 149–181). New York: Routledge.

Haraway, D. (1997). The presence of vision. In K. Conboy, N. Medina, & S. Stanbury (Eds.), *Writing on the body: Female embodiment and feminist theory*. New York: Columbia University Press.

Harding, S. (1995). "Strong objectivity": A response to the new objectivity question. *Synthese,* *104,* 331–349. https://doi.org/10.1007/BF01064504.

Harding, S. (2017). *Whose science? Whose knowledge?* Ithaca, NY: Cornell University Press.

Held, M. B. E. (2019). Decolonizing research paradigms in the context of settler colonialism: An unsettling, mutual, and collaborative effort. *International Journal of Qualitative Methods, 18,* 1–16. https://doi.org/10.1177/1609406918821574.

Luken, P., & Vaughan, S. (2021). (Eds.), *The Palgrave handbook of institutional ethnography.* Cham, Switzerland: Palgrave Macmillan.

McNamee, S. (2010). Research as social construction: Transformative inquiry. *Saúde & Transformação Social* [Health & social change], *1*(1), 9–19.

Naples, N. A. (2003). Epistemology, feminist methodology, and the politics of method. *Feminism and method: Ethnography, discourse analysis, and activist research* (pp. 13–34). New York: Routledge.

Pihama, L., & Lee-Morgan, J. (2019). Colonization, education, and Indigenous peoples. In E. McKinley & L. Smith (Eds.), *Handbook of Indigenous education* (pp. 19–27). Singapore: Springer.

Rankin, J. (2017). Conducting analysis in institutional ethnography: Analytical work prior to commencing data collection. *International Journal of Qualitative Methods, 16,* 1–9. https://doi.org/10.1177/1609406917734484.

Rowe, S., Baldry, E., & Earles, W. (2015). Decolonising social work research: Learning from critical Indigenous approaches. *Australian Social Work, 68,* 296–308. https://doi.org/10.1080/0312407X.2015.1024264.

Smith, D. E. (1987). *The everyday world as problematic.* Toronto: University of Toronto Press.

Smith, D. E. (1990a). *Texts, facts and femininity: Exploring the relations of ruling.* New York: Routledge.

Smith, D. E. (1990b). *The conceptual practices of power.* Toronto: University of Toronto Press.

Smith, D. E. (1993). The Standard North American Family: SNAF as an ideological code. *Journal of Family Issues, 14*(1), 50–65. https://doi.org/10.1177/0192513X93014001005.

Smith, D. E. (1996). Telling the truth after postmodernism. *Symbolic Interaction, 19,* 171–201. https://doi.org/10.1525/si.1996.19.3.171.

Smith, D. E. (1999). *Writing the social: Critique, theory and investigations.* Toronto: University of Toronto Press.

Smith, D. E. (2005). *Institutional ethnography: A sociology for people.* Lanham, MD: AltaMira.

Witkin, S. L. (2001). The measure of things. *Social Work, 46*(2), 101–104. https://doi.org/10.1093/sw/46.2.101.

Witkin, S. L. (2010). An introduction to social constructions. In S. L. Witkin (Ed.), *Social construction and social work practice: Interpretations and innovations* (pp. 13–37). New York: Columbia University Press.

Zamudio, M., Russell, C., Rios, F., & Bridgeman, J. L. (2010). *Critical race theory matters: Education and ideology.* New York: Routledge.

13

A TRANSFORMATIVE APPROACH TO
ENVIRONMENTAL SOCIAL WORK EDUCATION

SIDDHESH MUKERJI, KATE GANNON, AND ERIN MACKENZIE

I n our era of planetary crisis, it is critical that social work respond to the needs of the people and environments that have faced—and increasingly face—severe disruption. This necessitates a rigorous, transformative approach to environmental social work education. This chapter outlines our vision for such an approach. We begin by defining *environmental social work education* and noting relevant disciplinary literature. We then discuss our vision of transformative environmental social work education, which integrates multiple theoretical frameworks; offers opportunities for practice; is vision-focused; is explicitly justice-oriented; and centers self-care and community care as foundational values. The goal of this discussion is to offer readers a starting point upon which to design a transformative environmental social work course.

ENVIRONMENTAL SOCIAL WORK EDUCATION

We use the term *environmental social work* to refer to the perspectives and methods by which the field has understood its role in responding to the global ecological crisis. Krings et al.'s (2020) and Ramsay and Boddy's (2017) analyses identify multiple frameworks and areas of focus that comprise environmental social work. These include environmental justice, sustainability, ecospirituality, ecofeminism, natural disaster response, natural resource conservation, food (in)security and (in)justice, human/ environment and human/nonhuman-animal relationships, and more. Environmental social work is a broad and multifaceted undertaking, necessarily so considering the vastness of the problems to which it relates. Thus, perhaps it is fitting to understand environmental social work as a question: "What can social workers do to respond to the massive upheavals to human and nonhuman life caused by anthropogenic environmental breakdown?"

Environmental social work education refers to curricula and pedagogies that center this question. Current social work literature describes a variety of methods for integrating an environmental focus into social work education. Drolet et al. (2015), for example, suggest guiding students to create mind maps (i.e., diagrams that connect aspects of the environment, such as places, cultural beliefs, and community resources) and inviting guest speakers who connect environmental action to social work practice. Boetto and Bell (2015), too, offer general curricular suggestions, such as helping students to develop ecological literacy, concern for communities affected by environmental injustices, and environmental service-learning projects. And Androff et al.'s (2017) case examples illustrate how partnering with community organizations may enable social work students to contribute to environmental initiatives, including "farmer's markets in food deserts, community gardens in homeless shelters, and political advocacy against mining" (p. 399).

A TRANSFORMATIVE APPROACH TO ENVIRONMENTAL SOCIAL WORK EDUCATION

The aforementioned examples are part of a larger body of literature on environmental social work, which sometimes claims a "transformative" approach to education and practice. Jones (2010), drawing on the educational theorist Jack Mezirow, offers an excellent definition of transformative learning, noting that it "is about the nature of change, about the processes through which we produce a shift in the way we see and make meaning of the world" (p. 73). Based on our own academic, educational, and lived experiences, we believe that a transformative environmental social work education (1) integrates multiple theoretical frameworks; (2) offers opportunities for practice; (3) is vision-focused; (4) is explicitly justice-oriented; and (5) centers self-care and community care as foundational values.

INTEGRATING MULTIPLE THEORETICAL FRAMEWORKS

A transformative environmental social work course necessarily integrates multiple theoretical frameworks. The all-encompassing breadth of the ecological crisis means that any single framework may illuminate only a fraction of the whole reality. A more holistic understanding of the problems and potential responses demands the use of multiple frameworks that complement, expand on, and challenge each other. Comparing and moving among frameworks helps students assess the strengths and limitations of varying perspectives on the ecological crisis. This creates more flexible practitioners by encouraging innovative ways of seeing problems and responses.

In the paragraphs that follow, we offer three examples of theoretical frameworks suitable for a transformative environmental social work course. First, we discuss environmental justice, which already occupies an important place in social work. Second, we reflect on ecospirituality, which sees issues from an existential perspective that often receives little attention in social work discourse. Third, we introduce a regenerative bioregional approach that stretches social work's boundaries.

Example One: Environmental Justice

Environmental justice has functioned as a movement, a value, and a framework for decades and has only relatively recently attracted social work's attention. While earlier examples of relevant activism exist (see Mann, 2011), one largely agreed upon marker for the beginning of the environmental justice movement in the United States is the 1982 organizing of the African American community of Warren County,

North Carolina, against toxic dumping (McGurty, 2009). Later, at the turn of the millennium, the National Association of Social Workers began to acknowledge environmental justice's importance for the field by passing a resolution that called practitioners to act against environmental racism and exploitation as part of their professional mandate (Kahn & Scher, 2002; National Association of Social Workers, 2003). Susan Kemp (2011), Lena Dominelli (2013), and other social work scholars heeded this call by urging the field to emphasize environmental justice as a value and a framework. Subsequently, the Council on Social Work Education (2015) incorporated environmental justice as a core competency in its *Educational Policy and Accreditation Standards*. While this shift corresponded with increased scholarly attention to environmental justice (and, more broadly, environmental social work [see Krings et al., 2020]), it is unclear to what extent social work programs have integrated environmental justice into their curricula.

While social work literature describes environmental justice in various ways (see Dominelli, 2013; Erickson, 2018; Philip & Reisch, 2015), a particularly clear and inclusive definition is found in Vermont bill S. 148, introduced by Senators Ram Hinsdale, Campion, Hardy, Lyons, Pearson, Perchlik, and Pollina (An Act Relating to Environmental Justice in Vermont, 2021). The bill states that environmental justice "means all individuals are afforded the right to equitable access to environmental benefits; proportionate distribution of environmental burdens; fair and equitable treatment and meaningful participation in decision-making processes and the development, implementation, and enforcement of environmental laws, regulations, and policies" (pp. 7–8). Importantly, S. 148 emphasizes that environmental justice necessarily addresses colonialism, systemic racism, and other forms of structural oppression while recognizing "the unique needs of individuals of all race, color, income, class, ability status, gender identity, sexual orientation, national origin, ethnicity or ancestry, religious belief, or English language proficiency" (p. 8). This definition clarifies that environmental justice concerns the oppressive (usually race-based) or just distribution of environmental burdens (e.g., exposure to toxicity, lack of access to green spaces) and benefits (e.g., clean air and water, proximity to open natural areas).

Environmental justice offers social workers a proven and practicable methodology. Abundant real-life examples of activism, consciousness raising, community organizing, and policy change demonstrate how social workers may contribute to environmental justice efforts (see Erickson, 2018; Krings et al., 2014; Rambaree, 2020). One compelling example is the ongoing work of Little Village Environmental Justice Organization (LVEJO), which has effectively fought for improved environmental conditions in the primarily Mexican American and Latino/Latinx communities of Little Village and Pilsen in Chicago. For more than two decades, LVEJO has offered "toxic tours" of industrial sites in and near Little Village as a way of raising public consciousness about environmental racism in Chicago (Lyons, 2022). LVEJO's successes include organizing community members to force the shutdown of a coal plant that caused respiratory illnesses and deaths among neighborhood residents, lobbying the city to increase neighborhood access to public transportation, and transforming polluted plots of land into a community garden and a bustling recreational park (LVEJO, 2014).

The obvious overlap of environmental justice issues and social work values creates a logical starting point for practitioners to address environmental problems. While it may be possible to argue that other guiding principles for environmental action (sustainability, conservation, etc.) are the domain of other professions (i.e., "best left to someone else"), the relevance of environmental justice to social work is apparent because of its emphasis on oppression, racism, and the (un)just distribution of power, benefits, and burdens. Thus, while environmental justice concerns only specific aspects of environmental breakdown, it is a powerful entryway for social workers to respond to the ecological crisis.

Example Two: Ecospiritual Social Work

This crisis calls for humanity to reassess the dominant narrative that has shaped our ways of relating to each other and the Earth. Within social work, there has emerged an interest in ecospirituality as a critical theoretical perspective and ethical framework for responding to environmental breakdown (Dylan & Coates, 2012; Gray & Coates, 2013). Ecospiritual perspectives reference contributions from a diverse array of disciplines and cultural traditions, weaving together spiritual and ecological insights about the relational qualities necessary to actualize sustainable environmental transformation (Vaughan-Lee, 2013).

Ecospirituality represents the profound meaning that we derive from our personal embodied experience of intimate kinship with the more-than-human world. At the heart of an ecospiritual perspective is a core shift in values away from human-centeredness and dualistic interpretations of reality toward a more holistic worldview based on interconnection and community well-being (Gray & Coates, 2013). As we reflect on these values, we transcend our sense of a separate self and inevitably develop a desire to act based on our mutual reliance and accountability to others and Earth. In practice, ecospirituality can lead social workers to focus more on root causes (e.g., worldview, qualities of relationship, ways of being) rather than symptom reduction (e.g., technological quick fixes, false green solutions), to be more mindful of the importance of community and responsibility for others in program development and delivery, and to be more politically aware and active in the pursuit of justice for all.

Responding to the complex challenges surrounding the climate crisis will undoubtedly require creativity, innovation, and authentic social transformation at all levels. In recent years, many faith-based organizations have become a force in sustainable community development and raising awareness for climate action. The growing Bahá'í faith maintains a global network of grassroots organizations that share the goal of advancing a peaceful and equitable civilization (Bahá'í International Community [BIC], 2022.). Central to their efforts is the principle of interdependence, which perceives humans and nature as a conscious unified whole, infinitely differentiated in form and function yet united in purpose, like cells in the human body (Bahá'í Faith, 1987). This principle calls for an expansion of empathy and concern in regard to progress: "the welfare of any one segment of humankind, it becomes clear, is inextricably bound up with the welfare of the whole" (BIC, 2019, p. 2). The Bahá'í faith is dedicated to addressing unjust patterns of human interaction to forge a coherent ethic for building a collective conservation consciousness.

Currently, the Bahá'í International Community (BIC) is active in the United Nations Environmental Program and the Commission on Sustainable Development. The BIC offers insights learned at the local level (along with Bahá'í teachings) that can contribute to global policy discourses and the collective shaping of attitudes needed to advance environmental action. At the local level, Bahá'í practitioners around the world build communities' capacity to contribute to their own well-being and promote sustainable development, especially during times of crisis. FUNDAEC, a Bahá'í-inspired organization in Colombia, works with local populations to create self-sufficient food systems that embrace local ancestral knowledge, empower communities, enhance resilience, and therefore reduce poverty and inequality (BIC, 2020). Drawing on decades of experience, FUNDAEC focuses on four areas of local food production: the creation of home gardens, the cultivation of more extensive agricultural plots, improved food processing, and the distribution and marketing of food. This approach has had socioeconomic, environmental, and health advantages, such as reducing carbon emissions by shrinking supply chains and producing localized foods. According to María Cristina Mosquera, director of the Food Production Initiative, people are inspired to unite to channel their collective efforts into a common cause, "realizing, just as plants grow, so do the bonds of friendship, and their abilities as individuals and as a community" (BIC, 2020, para. 15).

In addition to the example that Bahá'í offers, other faith traditions, such as Unitarian Universalism, also demonstrate ecospiritual principles. The Unitarian Universalist (UU) community maintains a core practice of caring for the interdependent web of life, seeing itself as one thread in the fabric of all existence (Unitarian Universalist Association, 2022). For decades, UUs have served as activists in direct action campaigns and demonstrations, as advocates at the United Nations, and as organizers with GreenFaith, 350.org, Greenpeace, and other organizations (Unitarian Universalist Ministry for the Earth, n.d.). The Unitarian Universalist Association (UUA), a member network of more than a thousand congregations, is committed to intersectional climate action work that starts with the elimination of poverty and inequality. Since 2001, the UUA Green Sanctuary program has provided resources for more than 230 congregations to engage in transformational activities that enhance spiritual connection and celebration, Earth stewardship and sustainable development, and social action grounded in the realities, needs, and leadership of frontline communities.

These examples demonstrate an ecospiritual approach that may inform social work education. Courses may integrate spiritual, ecological, and place-based analysis, especially as it relates to cultural context, power, local knowledge, and the experience of hope, belonging, and purpose. Contemplative activities may support students to reflect on the meaning of interdependence in their approach and strengthen their intuitive, embodied understanding of this central ecological insight. This expanded view of self can ripple out into new dimensions of possibility for restorative practice, regenerative care, and community resilience. From this foundation, practitioners can envision diverse, locally relevant possibilities for social action that sustains relationships among communities, future generations, and the Earth in the midst of ongoing uncertainty and increasing complexity.

Example Three: A Regenerative Bioregional Approach

Ecospirituality and environmental justice are frameworks already found in social work literature. In addition to the familiar frameworks, a transformative social work education would include approaches that stretch the boundaries of the field. A regenerative bioregional approach offers such an opportunity. This section provides some basic background about bioregionalism, describes its potential, and offers a case example of this framework actualized in practice.

Bioregionalism refers to the idea that when a community's cultural and economic activities are in alignment with the thriving of its regional, natural ecosystem(s) (i.e., bioregion), this has positive ramifications locally, globally, and for the future of humanity. This notion is not new and, when discussing bioregionalism, it is important to emphasize that many Indigenous peoples have long known how to maintain sustainable and regenerative relationships between their communities and ecosystems. Examples abound of Indigenous regenerative efforts, including the reforestation of degraded areas in the Brazilian Amazon (Schmidt et al., 2021), sustainable agricultural land management (Barndon, 2020), protecting nonhuman animal species (Krupnick, 2022), strengthening food security (Goodluck, 2022; Sutherland, 2022), and defining our vision of planetary health (Redvers et al., 2022).

While these ideas are the original domain of Indigenous peoples across the world, the term *bioregionalism* was coined in 1975 by Allen Van Newkirk, founder of the Institute for Bioregional Research (McGinnis, 1999). Bioregionalism, as a field, has since evolved in the marketplace of ideas through the contributions of many thinkers, notably Peter Berg (1982, 1987, 2009) and, more recently, Joe Brewer (2021). Interpretations of bioregionalism are diverse and intertwined, with applications that relate to complexity research, cultural evolution, economics, political science, and social justice.

For our purposes, regeneration in the context of bioregionalism means reversing damage to a natural ecosystem. A real-life example of a regenerative bioregional approach can be found in the efforts of Sebastião and Lélia Deluiz Wanick Salgado. When Sebastião, a preeminent photographer, returned to his home in Brazil after time abroad as a photojournalist, he discovered that the tropical forest in which his home was nestled had been almost completely razed. In its place sprawled a lifeless wasteland. Sebastião and Lélia were intensely bereaved, and Sebastião struggled with deep depression. Lélia hatched an ingenious idea: they would reforest their property with their own hands. Over the course of the next twenty years, they planted more than two million trees (Vidal, 2015). This act of reforestation had unexpected, cascading regenerative effects. Scores of species of birds returned, along with dozens of species of mammals, amphibians, and reptiles. Hundreds of species of other native plants reappeared and flourished. Sebastião and Lélia had profoundly regenerated the local ecosystem. Given the arresting success of this project, the couple went on to found the Instituto Terra, or Earth Institute, which engages in ongoing environmental education, research, and restorative efforts (Instituto Terra, n.d.).

While these are incredibly important outcomes in their own right, it would be fair to ask, "Why should this be the concern of social workers?" Social workers are stationed throughout society, working in service of marginalized populations and unheard voices. They can serve as liaisons among scientists, policy makers, and individuals. Therefore, they may be uniquely positioned to organize communities to protect and regenerate the natural ecosystems upon which they depend. Social workers, who already serve as brokers among individuals, organizations, and political entities, may also coordinate efforts to connect and empower individuals, communities, and bioregions.

Practically, how could such a regenerative bioregional approach fit into social work education? One starting point may be to integrate content on helping communities establish sustainable and regenerative relationships with their local ecosystems. This relates to the concept of *ecological literacy* found elsewhere in environmental social work scholarship (e.g., Boetto & Bell, 2015; Jones, 2010). A regenerative bioregional approach requires a skill set that includes, but goes beyond, ecological literacy. We use the term *ecological proficiency* to describe some of the methods that environmental social workers may use when taking a regenerative bioregional approach. Ecological proficiency includes (1) identifying the ecosystem (and its unique characteristics and needs) within which a community exists; (2) assessing ways the ecosystem needs support (e.g., focusing on areas damaged by deforestation, development, or pollution) with the help of local experts who possess specialized knowledge of the land, including scientists and Indigenous communities; (3) identifying and analyzing relationships between the community and the ecosystem to assess whether they are sustainable or exploitative (e.g., sustainable forest management versus unsustainable logging); and (4) acting as a liaison between communities and experts to work toward improved human/ecological conditions.

Such an endeavor requires a vision for the future, a love for other people(s) and their unique strengths and contributions, and a deep respect for the land and the diverse human ways of being connected with that land. With imagination, dedication, and collaboration, the Salgados—two people with no prior training—achieved results that vitally benefited the ecosystem and human life in their area. Such successes spark our imagination. We can imagine curricula that train social workers to identify their bioregions, regenerate ecosystems, and protect the diverse cultural identities found in each area. We can imagine social workers contributing to ecologically regenerative community values that are passed down generationally. We can imagine a social work that creates bioregional regeneration forums, conventions, websites, and other platforms for practitioners to collaborate with one another and across disciplines, locally and internationally. In a world in which ecosystems and human systems are deteriorating at a rate with which governments cannot keep pace, we can imagine a social work that contributes to ecological and human thriving with agility, local specificity, international coordination, and a spirit of love and collaboration.

OPPORTUNITIES FOR PRACTICE

Frameworks such as these may provide edification and inspiration, but they must be put into practice for "transformation" to occur. Jones (2010) makes the important point that "most transformative learning theorists agree that such learning can be said to have truly occurred only when it produces action based on the newly transformed frames of reference" (p. 75). A transformative environmental social work education incorporates opportunities for students to actualize values and frameworks in the arena of real-life practice.

As noted earlier, environmental social work literature already suggests a variety of methods for engaging students in practice (e.g., Androff et al., 2017; Boetto & Bell, 2015; Drolet et al., 2015). The approach that we, at the University of Vermont, have taken is to establish field internship collaborations with local environmental organizations whose work overlaps with social work activities. The International Federation of Social Workers' (IFSW) list of fifteen "social work activities" includes several that clearly relate to environmental action, such as "empowerment/ anti-oppressive practice, community [organizing], advocacy/social action, conscientization, (and) political action" (Hare, 2004, p. 412). With these areas of connection in mind, the work of our field education coordinator (J. Sienkewicz, personal communication, February 25, 2022) includes building internship opportunities for students with organizations such as the Vermont chapters of 350, Rights and Democracy, and the Northeast Organic Farming Association.

VISION-FOCUSED

Along with concrete action, the ecological crisis urges us to envision alternative futures and develop the capacity to improvise, adapt, and transform in our daily lives. A pressing challenge for practitioners today is "to continuously re-imagine the future, not as a place we are going to, but one we are creating today" (Miller, 2018, p. 177). In practice, a vision-focused approach empowers the imagination and enhances our ability to prepare, recover, and innovate as changes occur. Similar to a solution-focused approach, this helps us consciously deemphasize problem dialogues in favor of constructing a desirable future that can transform people's sources of hope and motivation into meaningful action. In this case, "vision" functions as a verb because it is an iterative process of inquiry and discovery, an ever-evolving exploration of multiple possible futures.

The Manabí Será (which translates as "Manabí will be") initiative led by Grupo FARO and UNESCO provides a powerful example of a visioning process. This initiative was formed to address the problems of geographic, social, political, and economic fragmentation in the Manabí province of Ecuador. The Futures Literacy Lab methodology, a three-phase creative exploratory framework that includes a collective art-making process, engaged citizens in a generative conversation about the future. This resulted in the shared vision statement, "innovation inspired by identity" (Miller, 2018, p. 176), that continues to inspire actions that have contributed to community restoration and the preservation of cultural knowledge in the region. For example, after a recent earthquake on the peninsula, a group of young Manabí activists led an innovative infrastructure reconstruction project that built off the strength of this region's renewed vision and values.

The Manabí Será initiative is one example of a visioning process, but there are many ways to utilize this approach to reimagine environmental social work practice. One way a transformative environmental social work education could support students to harness this process is through experiential exercises. Working in small groups, students can identify a local environmental issue and elaborate on a vision that responds to the situation, both in the present and into the future. Students can reflect on how their visions are affected by subjective emotions and experiences and by the views, values, and opinions shared throughout society. Reflective prompts (Which specific actions/values are needed today to shape that vision? Whose vision is missing in that future?) can help us examine the power and nuances of anticipatory assumptions and expectations, a process that students can take turns facilitating. Importantly, encouraging students to express this vision through visual, musical, and embodied art extends visioning practice beyond the limits of spoken language. These activities can support students not only to consider alternative pathways inside existing systems but also to conceive totally new societal structures and approaches.

JUSTICE AS AN EXPLICIT ORIENTATION

The necessity to move beyond existing approaches is clear when one considers the history of environmental action. Referring to the early environmental movement in the United States, Philip and Reisch (2015) note that the focus on protecting wildlife and wilderness areas "mirrored the interests of the movement's initial supporters—privileged white populations who wanted to retain their ability to enjoy outdoor recreational opportunities, particularly in the nation's new national parks" (p. 474). The well-documented (see Colman, 2021; Wernick, 2020; Willet et al., 2020) role of "big green" environmental groups in perpetuating white supremacy, colonization, and manifold forms of discrimination and marginalization demonstrates how practices touted as "pro-environment" may, in fact, be anti-justice. Social work educators must carefully consider this legacy lest we advance an environmental ethic that is by and for the socially dominant.

A transformative environmental social work education centers theory and practice that are concurrently pro-environment and pro-justice. Perspectives that heed both of these needs are rare in social work, perhaps because of the field's historical tendency to interpret "person in environment" in strictly human, social terms (Coates & Gray, 2012; Zapf, 2008). However, in addition to strengthening its own perspectives, social work can draw on resources from other fields and interdisciplinary approaches. The "just transition" framework, for example, applies a distributive-, procedural-, and restorative-justice lens to environmental action (McCauley & Heffron, 2018). Just transition calls for a shift away from an extractive fossil fuel economy (i.e., it is pro-environment); however, it posits that this shift must occur in a way that redistributes power to address oppressive environmental realities (e.g., the land dispossession of Indigenous peoples) and include diverse voices when deciding on environmental priorities and actions (Climate Justice Alliance, 2019). This concurrently pro-justice and pro-environment approach is an example of how transformative environmental social work education can—and must—explicitly center justice.

SELF-CARE AND COMMUNITY CARE AS FOUNDATIONAL VALUES

Focusing on topics such as environmental injustice and ecological collapse necessitates intentional, proactive self-care and community care. In addition to the direct consequences of climate change on mental health (see Dumont et al., 2020; van Nieuwenhuizen et al., 2021), bearing witness to the state of our planetary crisis is, for many, an intensely emotional experience of anxiety, grief, depression, and despair (Fritze et al., 2008; Panu, 2020). Transformative environmental social work education must emphasize self- and community care in order to be ethical (i.e., considerate of students' and educators' well-being) and effective (i.e., prompting action, not burnout).

A variety of self-care methodologies may be suitable for tending to climate-related emotions. The All We Can Save Project's (n.d.) resource list illustrates several examples, including climate-aware therapy, emotional methodologies (e.g., Joanna Macy's *The Work That Reconnects*, Good Grief Network), somatics, climate conversations, and climate-specific mindfulness retreats. Furthermore, a transformative environmental social work course is an opportunity to introduce practice modalities for actualizing one's chosen values (e.g., climate activism) in the face of aversive emotions (e.g., climate-related despair), such as acceptance and commitment therapy (Hayes et al., 2016).

Self-care methods for tending to one's emotional experience, while essential, may promote an individualistic, relationally inadequate view of well-being (Sambile, 2018). Emotions are not simply intrapersonal phenomena but, rather, arise in interrelationship. Instead of implying that caring for emotions is solely the responsibility of individuals, transformative educators can proactively nurture a classroom community in which each member contributes to the well-being of the other members. By centering language and practices that encourage compassion, listening, and mutual support (e.g., beginning class with small-group discussions that help students to bond personally, inviting students to lead relaxation exercises), the classroom culture can serve as a powerful context for actualizing care on the individual and community levels.

CONCLUSION

The social work classroom, we believe, is a powerful context for galvanizing transformative environmental action. Thus, we hope that this chapter has provided a starting point upon which to design a course. This course will help transform consciousness by integrating and comparing multiple theoretical frameworks, such as environmental justice, ecospirituality, and regenerative bioregionalism. It will urge students not only to reflect and discuss but also, crucially, to engage in applied practice. It will guide them to examine present realities and future possibilities with creative vision. This course will simultaneously center the needs of natural eco-systems while challenging the systems of oppressions that affect individuals and communities. And it will invite students, educators, and the classroom community to nurture care and action in an era when our care and action are so urgently needed.

REFERENCES

All We Can Save Project. (n.d.). *Resources for working with climate emotions*. Retrieved February 5, 2022, from https://www.allwecansave.earth/emotions.

An Act Relating to Environmental Justice in Vermont, S. 148. (2021). https://legislature.vermont.gov/Documents/2022/Docs/BILLS/S-0148/S-0148%20As%20Introduced.pdf.

Androff, D., Fike, C., & Rorke, J. (2017). Greening social work education: Teaching environmental rights and sustainability in community practice. *Journal of Social Work Education*, *53*(3), 399–413. https://doi.org/10.1080/10437797.2016.1266976.

Bahá'í Faith. (1987). *The Bahá'í statement on nature*. https://www.bahai.org/documents/bic-opi/bahai-statement-nature.

Bahá'í International Community. (2019). *Unity in action: Reclaiming the spirit of the sustainable development agenda*. https://www.bic.org/sites/default/files/bic_unityinaction_statement_2.pdf.

Bahá'í International Community. (2020, November 10). *Top UN organizations discuss food security with BIC and grassroots actors at social forum*. https://www.bic.org/news/top-un-organizations-discuss-food-security-bic-and-grassroots-actors-social-forum.

Bahá'í International Community. (2022). *Development*. https://www.bic.org/focus-areas/development.

Barndon, G. (2020, July 21). Indigenous regenerative land management included in agricultural program at TAFE: A new land management training course combines indigenous conservation methods with western agricultural practice. *ABC Premium News*. https://www.abc.net.au/news/2020-07-21/indigenous-regenerative-land-education-course-at-tafe/12268326.

Boetto, H., & Bell, K. (2015). Environmental sustainability in social work education: An online initiative to encourage global citizenship. *International Social Work*, *58*(3), 448–462. https://doi.org/10.1177/0020872815570073.

Brewer, J. (2021). *The design pathway for regenerating Earth*. Barichara, Colombia: Earth Regenerators.

Climate Justice Alliance. (2019). *Just transition principles*. https://climatejusticealliance.org/wp-content/uploads/2019/11/CJA_JustTransition_highres.pdf.

Coates, J., & Gray, M. (2012). The environment and social work: An overview and introduction. *International Journal of Social Welfare, 21*(3), 230–238. https://doi.org/10.1111/j.1468-2397 .2011.00851.x.

Colman, Z. (2021, February 5). Environmental groups' greatest obstacle may not be republican opposition. *Politico.* https://www.politico.com/news/magazine/2021/02/05/environmental -movement-racial-reckoning-green-diversity-465501.

Council on Social Work Education. (2015). *Educational policy and accreditation standards.* Alexandria, VA: Author.

Dominelli, L. (2013). Environmental justice at the heart of social work practice: Greening the profession. *International Journal of Social Welfare, 22*(4), 431–439. https://doi.org/10.1111 /ijsw.12024.

Drolet, J., Wu, H., Taylor, M., & Dennehy, A. (2015). Social work and sustainable social development: Teaching and learning strategies for "green social work" curriculum. *Social Work Education, 34*(5), 528–543. https://doi.org/10.1080/02615479.2015.1065808.

Dumont, C., Haase, E., Dolber, T., Lewis, J., & Coverdale, J. (2020). Climate change and risk of completed suicide. *Journal of Nervous and Mental Disease, 208*(7), 559–565. https://doi.org /10.1097/NMD.0000000000001162.

Dylan, A., & Coates, J. (2012). The spirituality of justice: Bringing together the eco and the social. *Journal of Religion & Spirituality in Social Work: Social Thought, 31*(1–2), 128–149. https://doi.org /10.1080/15426432.2012.647895.

Erickson, C. L. (2018). *Environmental justice as social work practice.* New York: Oxford University Press.

Fritze, J. G., Blashki, G. A., Burke, S., & Wiseman, J. (2008). Hope, despair and transformation: Climate change and the promotion of mental health and wellbeing. *International Journal of Mental Health Systems, 2*(1), 1–10. https://doi.org/10.1186/1752-4458-2-13.

Goodluck, K. (2022, February 10). Indigenous farmers are "rematriating" centuries-old seeds to plant a movement. *Popular Science.* https://www.popsci.com/environment/indigenous-farmers -rematriation/.

Gray, M., & Coates, J. (2013). Changing values and valuing change: Toward an ecospiritual perspective in social work. *International Social Work, 56*(3), 355–367. http://dx.doi.org /10.1177/0020872812474009.

Hare, I. (2004). Defining social work for the 21st century: The International Federation of Social Workers' revised definition of social work. *International Social Work, 47*(3), 407–424. https://doi.org/10.1177/0020872804043973.

Hayes, S. C., Strosahl, K. D., & Wilson, K. G. (2016). *Acceptance and commitment therapy.* New York: Guilford.

Instituto Terra. (n.d.). *Applied scientific research.* https://institutoterra.org/pesquisa-cientifica -aplicada/.

Jones, P. (2010). Responding to the ecological crisis: Transformative pathways for social work education. *Journal of Social Work Education, 46*(1), 67–84. https://doi.org/10.5175 /JSWE.2010.200800073.

Kahn, M., & Scher, S. (2002). Infusing content on the physical environment into the BSW curriculum. *Journal of Baccalaureate Social Work, 7*(2), 1–14. https://doi.org/10.18084/1084-7219.7.2.1.

Kemp, S. P. (2011). Recentring environment in social work practice: Necessity, opportunity, challenge. *British Journal of Social Work*, *41*(6), 1198–1210. https://doi.org/10.1093/bjsw/bcr119.

Krings, A., Spencer, M. S., & Jimenez, K. (2014). Organizing for environmental justice: From bridges to taro patches. In C. S. Ramanathan & S. Dutta (Eds.), *Governance, development, and social work* (pp. 206–220). New York: Routledge.

Krings, A., Victor, B. G., Mathias, J., & Perron, B. E. (2020). Environmental social work in the disciplinary literature, 1991–2015. *International Social Work*, *63*(3), 275–290. https://doi.org /10.1177/0020872818788397.

Krupnick, M. (2022, February 20). 'It's a powerful feeling': The Indigenous American tribe helping to bring back buffalo. *Guardian*. https://www.theguardian.com/environment/2022/feb/20 /its-a-powerful-feeling-the-indigenous-american-tribe-helping-to-bring-back-buffalo.

LVEJO. (2014). *Our accomplishments*. http://www.lvejo.org/our-accomplishments/coal-plant -shutdown/.

Lyons, K. (2022, February 23). A Chicago neighborhood is redefining toxicity in pursuit of environmental justice. *YES! Magazine*. https://www.yesmagazine.org/environment/2022/02 /23/chicago-environmental-justice-pollution.

Mann, S. (2011). Pioneers of U.S. ecofeminism and environmental Justice. *Feminist Formations*, *23*(2), 1–25. https://doi.org/10.1353/ff.2011.0028.

McCauley, D., & Heffron, R. (2018). Just transition: Integrating climate, energy and environmental justice. *Energy Policy*, *119*, 1–7. https://doi.org/10.1016/j.enpol.2018.04.014.

McGurty, E. (2009). *Transforming environmentalism: Warren County, PCBs, and the origins of environmental justice*. New Brunswick, NJ: Rutgers University Press.

Miller, R. (Ed.). (2018). *Transforming the future: Anticipation in the 21st century*. New York: Routledge.

National Association of Social Workers. (2003). Environmental policy. In *Social work speaks* (6th ed., pp. 116–123). Washington, DC: NASW Press.

Panu, P. (2020). Anxiety and the ecological crisis: An analysis of eco-anxiety and climate anxiety. *Sustainability*, *12*(19), 7836. https://doi.org/10.3390/su12197836.

Philip, D., & Reisch, M. (2015). Rethinking social work's interpretation of "environmental justice": From local to global. *Social Work Education*, *34*(5), 471–483. https://doi.org/10.1080 /02615479.2015.1063602.

Rambaree, K. (2020). Environmental justice in the case of the Chagos marine protected area: Implications for international social work. *Sustainability*, *12*(20), 8349. https://doi.org /10.3390/su12208349.

Ramsay, S., & Boddy, J. (2017). Environmental social work: A concept analysis. *British Journal of Social Work*, *47*(1), 68–86. https://doi.org/10.1093/bjsw/bcw078.

Redvers, N., Celidwen, Y., Schultz, C., Horn, O., Githaiga, C., Vera, M., . . . & Rojas, J. N. (2022). The determinants of planetary health: An Indigenous consensus perspective. *Lancet Planetary Health*, *6*(2), e156-e163. https://doi.org/10.1016/S2542-5196(21)00354-5.

Sambile, A. F. (2018). Energy exchange: The urgency to move from self-care to community-care in student affairs. *Vermont Connection*, *39*(1), 7. https://scholarworks.uvm.edu/tvc/vol39/iss1/7.

Schmidt M. V. C., Ikpeng, Y. U., Kayabi, T., Sanches, R. A., Ono, K. Y., & Adams C. (2021). Indigenous knowledge and forest succession management in the Brazilian Amazon: Contributions to reforestation of degraded areas. *Frontiers in Forests and Global Change, 4.* https://doi.org/10.3389/ffgc.2021.605925.

Sutherland, L. (2022, February 1). Indigenous hunter-gatherers in Cameroon diversify food sources in the face of change. *Mongabay.* https://news.mongabay.com/2022/02/indigenous-hunter-gatherers-in-cameroon-diversify-food-sources-in-the-face-of-change/.

Unitarian Universalist Association. (2022). *Climate and environmental justice.* https://www.uua.org/environment.

Unitarian Universalist Ministry for the Earth. (n.d.). *Our history.* Retrieved February 22, 2022, from https://www.uumfe.org/resources/green-sanctuary/.

van Nieuwenhuizen, A., Hudson, K., Chen, X., & Hwong, A. R. (2021). The effects of climate change on child and adolescent mental health: Clinical considerations. *Current Psychiatry Reports, 23*(12), 1–9. https://doi.org/10.1007/s11920-021-01296-y.

Vaughan-Lee, L. (Ed.). (2013). *Spiritual ecology: The cry of the earth.* Point Reyes, CA: Golden Sufi Center.

Vidal, J. (2015, July 7). Sebastião Salgado focuses on big picture with parable of reforestation in Brazil. *Guardian.* https://www.theguardian.com/global-development/2015/jul/27/sebastiao-salgado-fredrick-shoo-reforestation-brazil-tanzania.

Wernick, A. (2020, August 11). Green groups grapple with a history of racism and exclusion. *World.* https://theworld.org/stories/2020-08-11/green-groups-grapple-history-racism-and-exclusion.

Willett, J., Tamayo, A., & Kern, J. (2020). Understandings of environmental injustice and sustainability in marginalized communities: A qualitative inquiry in Nevada. *International Journal of Social Welfare, 29*(4), 335–345. https://doi.org/10.1111/ijsw.12456.

Zapf, M. K. (2008). Transforming social work's understanding of person and environment: Spirituality and the "common ground." *Journal of Religion and Spirituality in Social Work: Social Thought, 27*(1–2), 171–181. https://doi.org/10.1080/15426430802114200.

14

THE SOUNDSCAPES OF SOCIAL WORK

ALEXANDER BOBELLA

Our contemporary soundscape is inimitably different from any historically experienced by humanity. Old, familiar sounds linger: birds flit through the forest, calling one another; wind howls across plains or tumultuous seas; tree creak, and crack, and fall; rain pitters and patters; insects buzz and chirp; stomachs rumble with hunger, and knees pop with strain. These sounds are often identified in literature as "natural sounds" (Schafer, 1994; Salvari et al., 2019), born from the natural environment and embodying primordial forces of corporeal existence (Schafer, 1994). They are unique to our geographic context and inspire both poetry and religion.

Relatively new sounds, brought by industrialization and evolving as relentlessly as their catalyst, intermingle. These sounds often overshadow or silence natural sounds, drowning them out with volume or replacing them entirely. Many sounds within our contemporary acoustic sphere are pleasing; most are not. Their volume, measured in decibels (dB), ranges drastically: the ambient noise level in a quiet room is approximately 28–33 dB, a floor fan is 38–70 dB, and the average chainsaw buzzes at approximately 110 dB (Chepesiuk, 2005). Long-term effects of exposure to the industrialized soundscape are poorly legislated: hearing protection is required in occupational settings that reach 85 dB, but nonauditory health impacts begin to manifest with daily exposure of as low as 45 dB (Fink, 2017). Areas throughout the United States with loud soundscapes often have higher populations of Asian, Black, and Hispanic Americans, representing long-standing systemic oppression that reduces health outcomes for vulnerable populations while defying their human rights (UN UDHR articles 24–27) and their civic participation (Casey et al., 2017; Emmet & Francis, 2015).

It would be trite of me to say that sound is ubiquitous in human experience, although it is by no means ubiquitously experienced. So, too, would it be banal for me to suggest that sound is ubiquitously referenced and studied throughout literature, scholarship, and art; yet, despite its presence, sound is woefully underrepresented in discussions of social work. While sound ordinances maintain quiet hours in communities across the world to control volume and curtail sound pollution—as they have for centuries (Schafer, 1994, pp. 189–190)—many professional fields leave aural experience unconsidered when it should be a fundamental consideration.

In this chapter, I assert the potential for soundscape consideration in social work policy, practice, scholarship, and pedagogy. Soundscapes— the focus of soundscape ecology—can be understood as "sounds . . . emanating from a given landscape to create unique acoustical patterns across a variety of spatial and temporal scales" (Pijanowski et al., 2011). The theory of soundscapes was formalized by R. Murray Schafer, whose influential book *The Soundscape: Our Sonic Environment and the Tuning of the World* (1994) has substantially informed my ideas and writing throughout. The field of soundscape ecology, focused on human experiences of sound, is small but not without success: for example, the U.S. National Park Service recognizes soundscapes as an important natural resource of parks and has taken both social and scientific measures to protect them (National Park Service, 2023). The first part of this chapter describes complications that arise from the oppressive contemporary soundscape; the second part provides suggestions for social work practice, policy, pedagogy, and further research.

Ultimately, I seek to generate a basic understanding of, and pedagogical interest in, the integration of soundscape theory into various dimensions of social work. The field of social work and the clients served by social workers are done a great injustice by the underestimation of sound: its inclusion in social work curricula and daily practice considerations may prove instrumental to social work's stated mission of pursuing social equity and justice (NASW Code of Ethics). Where applicable, I draw clear links to four critical components of transformative social work practice as I understand the field: critical social constructionism, the strengths perspective, human rights, and the pursuit of social justice.

The first part of this chapter serves as a literature review describing two complementary ontologies of sound: (1) that sound is a physical phenomenon with physiological consequences and (2) that sound is a socially controlled construct and phenomenon that reflects cultural and social values. Both ontologies operate under an assumption that the industrialized soundscape is detrimental to physical, emotional, and spiritual health. They also assume that there are deep inequities and structural oppressions creating and perpetuating unjust soundscapes and that social worker knowledge and engagement with the aural landscape on all levels can yield socially just, transformative change on all levels of society. The second part of this chapter situates social workers within a vision of an equitable, human-oriented soundscape that acknowledges the nuance of power and oppression in everyday lived experience.

Social constructionism plays an integral role in deconstructing the social effects of soundscapes. It is a difficult theory to define, grounded in postmodernity. Social constructionism holds that societal norms are born from social perception and expectation rather than describing something essential in nature—that the assumptions we hold as reality, even the theory of social constructionism itself, are created by humans and are therefore variable, mutable, and potentially oppressive. These societally born structures, such as race or gender, are keenly felt in lived experience as they are used to justify and perpetuate oppression and marginalization (Witkin, 2011). The second component of this chapter creates room for variable social constructions, acknowledging the breadth of potentially beneficial soundscapes. Also part of this discussion will be the strengths perspective, an ideology built on empowering social work clients to recognize their own strengths and resources as a source of resilience and growth (Hartling, 2010), along with the protection of human rights and the pursuit of social justice. Small auto-ethnographic sections have been included largely to convey the intimacy and constitutive nature of aural experience.

DEVELOPING AN INTEREST IN SOUND

My scholarly interest in sound began when I stumbled across an article in the *Atlantic* that described the curation of sound in restaurant spaces; fine-dining restaurants in the 1940s through the early 1990s managed noise levels by covering their walls and floors in heavy carpet, their windows in heavy drapes, and their tables in thick linen cloth (Wagner, 2018). Such luxurious and plush environments absorb sound waves before they reverberate, reducing overall volume in dining spaces; while this luxury was certainly informed by cultural mores such as class, this control of the aural environment was a response to the harsh soundscape brought by industrialization. Thompson (2002) points to a cultural disassociation between sound and space that developed after the advent of sound-controlling technologies, resulting ultimately in the reduction and commodification of sound. In this aurally commodified environment, the unique soundscape of each place became standardized and tidied. Modernity introduced the buzzing of artificial lights and the rumble of mechanized cookery to restaurant spaces; in this new soundscape, "reverberation now became just another kind of noise, unnecessary and best eliminated" (p. 3).

In the late 1990s, restaurants began prioritizing easy-to-clean and aesthetically pleasing open-floor plans, resulting in architecture that caused sound to reverberate and increase in volume (Wagner, 2018). I am personally familiar only with these newer, louder restaurant settings. I was raised in an area of New Jersey that brushes against the noisy New York metropolitan area on one side and the Watchung Reservation on the other. My mother, born in Queens, often brought my siblings and me to Manhattan, where we acclimated to the roar of midday Broadway traffic; my father made us familiar with the sounds of nature and of New England when we visited his mother in New Hampshire. Both worked long hours in demanding fields that provided us economic comfort but left them neither energy nor wherewithal to worry over cooking each night, and we consequently dined out several times weekly. Many of my early memories are set in restaurants: eating out was our most regular family activity.

Reading in the *Atlantic* that restaurants have been moving toward louder and louder soundscapes in the past twenty-five years validated my childhood experience and my current aversion to loud spaces (Wagner, 2018). I gravitate toward silence. A brief interlude between the first and second parts of this chapter more deeply investigates silence. Ultimately, this chapter has almost as much to do with silence as it does with sound.

I am white, ostensibly male, and was raised in an upper-middle-class environment that allowed me education and travel with which to critically examine and compare soundscapes. I have rarely been exposed to soundscapes that are overtly hostile or threatening. I have no fear of or aversion to silence, as many do. This experience is unique and privileged. Future study would do well to include the voices of other communities, and I would like to caveat everything written here as arising from my own understanding (albeit informed by research).

The express purpose of this chapter is to broadly demonstrate the pan-human aural experience, tying it concretely to the field of social work. Thus, a great deal of information has been strategically omitted to align this discussion with social work; further study must be undertaken to reincorporate those omitted items and demonstrate their importance. I intend for this chapter to be the first in a field of aural social work, redefining the profession toward multisensoriality, but it is also intended to contribute to the broader field of ecological or environmental social work.

DEFINING SOUND: ACOUSTICS AND PSYCHOACOUSTICS

A sound is a molecular vibration that travels through the air and is received by cochlea within the ear; this vibration runs along the basilar membrane, which is broken into constituent parts that respond best to a specific "characteristic frequency" (CF) in the sound wave. The basilar membrane engages "the cochlea from the inner ear via the inner hair cells and the auditory nerve, through the brainstem and midbrain, to the primary auditory cortex" (Oxenham, 2018). Much is still unknown about the mechanisms of human hearing: the nonlinear processing nature of the cochlea and technological limitations determining cochlea size pose challenges to research.

A great deal of psychoacoustic research delves into what is known as the "cocktail party problem": how do we maintain a conversation at a cocktail party, distinguishing the words of whoever is speaking from other noises in the soundscape? Important information for social work includes that speech is specially intelligible among other sounds; hearing is greatly affected by signal-to-noise ratio (SNR); hearing is aided tremendously by binaural listening (listening with both ears); and what sounds the ear perceives change according to where attention is focused (Bronkhorst, 2015).

The most obvious social work application for this physiological understanding of sound involves efficacy of hearing function. Every client that we interact with as social workers is affected by or at risk of hearing loss; social work must consider how hearing loss defies the above observations. Bronkhorst contends that the mind is more attuned to sentences or recognizable words than other sounds: this is moot when an individual cannot hear much at all, and hearing impairment is often associated with "a reduced ability to hear out or segregate sounds, such as someone talking against a backdrop of other sounds" (Oxenham, 2018). Binaural listening assists in the processing of interpreting information, but hearing loss is often not experienced equally in both ears and compensating for a less finely tuned hearing ability may increase the psychological strain of listening (Bronkhorst, 2015). SNR is affected greatly by variables in the physical context that are often difficult to control. Perhaps most frightening, recent research has revealed that while paying close attention in an effort to hear increase's the ability to discern and separate sounds, the strain caused by focusing too closely while experiencing late-in-life hearing impairment accounts for roughly 8 percent of new dementia cases each year (Johns Hopkins, 2021).

Prolonged, regular exposure to loud noises can lead to hearing loss, but hearing impairment can also be caused by age, genetic mutation, exposure to therapeutic drugs, smoking, chronic illness—or it can occur suddenly, unexpectedly, and inexplicably (Cunningham & Tucci, 2017). Hearing loss can also be hidden, not physically acute enough to appear in hearing tests yet sufficient to cause lifestyle interruption (Oxenham, 2018). Exposure to loud noises inordinately affects individuals in working-class positions: reports show that 90 percent of coal miners experience hearing impairment by the age of fifty-two (Chepesiuk, 2005), and a noise assessment of three Nigerian tobacco production plants found that the quietest had a mean volume of 96.15 dB, well above the international workplace safety threshold (Wang et al., 2020). Lower-income or structurally oppressed neighborhoods often border loud industrial, transportation, or commercial sites that put their residents at risk of hearing loss. Hearing loss has been closely linked to poverty, likely a consequence of inadequate medical access: 6.9 percent of children in Peru experience hearing impairment, compared to 3.1 percent in the more resourced United States (Czechowicz et al., 2010). Hearing loss is significantly more common in white people than in any other racial group (Emmet & Francis, 2015; Lin et al., 2012).

Individuals with hearing loss or impairment face unique challenges that social work might ameliorate. Physically, hearing loss can affect balance and health, leading to increased hospitalization rates and overall frailty. Social effects are dire: hearing loss, especially later in life, can cause social isolation, depression, and, as mentioned, dementia (Cunningham & Tucci, 2017). Hearing loss has also been shown to reduce educational, income, and professional outcomes, leading to increased rates of poverty: one study indicated that "hearing loss increased the likelihood of low income over 1.5-fold" (Emmet & Francis, 2015). An interesting study has been proposed (but not yet undertaken) that will integrate sound and deaf studies, understanding nonauditory physiological effects of sound on individuals with hearing impairment; this line of study will yield insight into the ubiquity of soundscapes even when they are not auditorily experienced (Fridner & Helmreich, 2015).

There are other dangerous physiological responses to sound that we must be aware of as social workers. Consistent exposure to noise levels of 45 dB or more may increase stress hormones, hypertension, obesity, cardiac disease, and mortality (Fink, 2017). Intense sound can, by virtue of its nature as a vibration, "cause headaches, nausea, sexual impotence, reduced vision, impaired cardiovascular, gastrointestinal and respiratory functions" (Schafer, 1994, p. 184). The effect of noise on pregnant mothers and fetal development is debated; some sources suggest that loud noise levels can damage fetus hearing in utero and that loud noises may even stimulate contractions (Chepesiuk, 2005). Exposure to loud noises, and a loud living environment, also affects children: behavioral and health issues arise from consistent exposure at a young age, and noisy learning environments significantly reduce learning outcomes (Chepesiuk, 2005; van der Kruk et al., 2017).

Social work actions to prevent hearing loss and to minimize negative outcomes for hearing impaired individuals will be discussed in detail in the second part of this chapter. The field of social work is uniquely situated to conceptualize socioeconomic and sociocultural factors that create risk of hearing impairment, to instate or encourage measures that reduce potential damage to hearing, and to ensure the well-being of individuals living with hearing impairment. Social workers also interact with diverse clients from across the demographic spectrum: whoever is served, there is benefit in understanding how the contemporary soundscape affects physiological well-being.

DEFINING SOUND: SOCIAL CONSTRUCTIONS OF SOUND AND THE SOUNDSCAPE

It is important to reemphasize that the soundscape of daily living was once driven by natural sounds, many of which (although not all) were quiet or, if loud, short. Soundscapes were largely unique to their specific geographic environment, and rural environments differed widely from urban environments. It would not be incorrect to say that natural sounds are biologic in nature inasmuch as they are discrete and interruptible: natural sounds have a life span of their own in which "they are born, they flourish, and they die" (Schafer, 1994, p. 78)

The advent of industrialism rapidly brought into the soundscape a myriad of new sounds that were louder and more sustained than the sounds they overpowered; silenced by these new sounds, many older sounds have been further diminished by the slow encroachment of the industrial realm into the natural—between 1970 and 2021, North America's bird population fell by 2.9 billion. Insects, mammals, other wildlife, and the ecology itself have similarly been replaced by human products and muted in the soundscape (Schafer, 1994). Acoustically minded building materials homogenize sound among locations, reducing geographic and cultural character (Thompson, 2002). Sound has become commodifiable and controllable by architects and by the music industry, abstracting experience from the natural soundscape entirely (Schafer, 1994; Thompson, 2002). The "flat line" was introduced: "an artificial construction," the flat line appeared in the ceaseless white noise from a generator or the unfeatured rumble of a car engine as "the noise of the machine became a 'narcotic for the brain,' and listlessness increased in modern life" (Schafer, 1994, pp. 79).

We are left with "noise." What noise is or what qualifies as noise is culturally contingent and socially constructed: the most cited understanding of noise is that it is "unwanted sound" (Schafer, 1994, p. 182; Chepesiuk, 2005). Noise is subjective and received differently by different people in different contexts: urbanites are often off put by the unusual soundscape of rural locations.

The social construction of noise goes beyond personal experience. Societies and communities worldwide have responded to ambient noise levels (which are rising in volume over time, although how much is difficult to quantify) by creating noise pollution policies and ordinances that determine acceptable sonic behavior. Many cultures and groups in warm climates, for instance, observe siesta by discouraging noisiness during hours in the afternoon; other locations specify certain times of day where certain noises born of cultural identity or vestigial from history are allowed or scheduled, such as a law in Bonn, Germany, that limits the beating of objects (i.e., rugs and mattresses) to weekdays between 8 a.m. and 12 p.m. (Schafer, 1994, p. 198). Anti-noise activists advocate for reduced noise levels by increasing policy constraints, referring to "secondhand noise ... [as] 'a civil rights issue'" (Chepesiuk, 2005). One such advocacy group, the Noise Pollution Clearing House (https://www.nonoise.org/index.htm), based in Montpelier, Vermont, speaks of noise control as both a civil and a human rights concern, maintaining a robust record of noise-related legislation throughout the United States.

Noisy environments have a demonstrable effect on social organization and behavior outside of policy. I have already mentioned the soundscape of restaurants; contemporary restaurants have created noisier soundscapes, at least in part because noisy environments encourage individuals to drink more (perhaps from yelling over the din), act less inhibited, and spend more money (Pomranz, 2018; Wagner, 2018). Sound is similarly used in retail settings to control shopper behavior and increase sales (Knoferle et al., 2011; Milliman, 1982). It is clear, at least in business settings, that the power inherent in sound is manipulated in the interest of capital.

Learning outcomes are reduced significantly for children exposed to noisy environments (Chepesiuk, 2005; van der Kruk et al., 2017). Individuals experiencing PTSD or anxiety-related disorders are also at risk and may be traumatized by unexpected loud noises, catalyzing autonomic stress response (Rouwand Erfanian, 2018). Social segregation is enforced by the soundscape in the form of redlining and home affordability near noisy locations, organizing the geopolitical composition of society while putting systemically oppressed individuals at greater risk of noise pollution–related health risks (Casey et al., 2017).

DEFINING SOUND: SONGS OF SPIRIT

As I have mentioned, sound and the soundscape are panhuman experiences. While so far I have dwelled on the dire circumstances of the contemporary soundscape, I would be remiss not to momentarily delve into natural sounds. Schafer (1994) writes that natural sounds maintain an important connection to human experience, evidenced by the prolific use of natural sounds throughout religion, spirituality, and art. There is no shortage of whispers on the wind, silence in the forests, or wrath in the shout of thunder; the natural soundscape heralds a natural order greater than humanity, from which humanity is inextricable. Some human sounds are even theorized to echo the sounds of nature, languages and sounds inspired by or onomatopoeic for sounds in our natural soundscape (Schafer, 1994, p. 41). Sound can also be crafted to inspire spiritual experience: the ringing of a bell, the clamor of an organ, the collectivity of a choir, or the hush of a chant all serve to shorten distance experientially and theologically between the divine and the human (Eliade, 1987; Schafer, 1994, p. 52; Schuon, 2005).

Resources specifically focusing on the psychological benefit of natural soundscapes are scant, but do exist. One study found that soundscapes rich in natural sources cause marked decreases in stress and annoyance, while soundscapes without natural sounds and safety indicators caused increases in vigilance and autonomic alertness (Buxton et al., 2021). Studies and frameworks designed for nature-based rehabilitation also speak to the healing power of natural soundscapes (Cerrwén, 2016).

Nearly all sources I have cited throughout this chapter advocate for curtailing the sounds of industrial life and reinvigorating the natural soundscape. This call to action is usually to reduce negative health outcomes created by noise pollution and hearing loss; but the emotional, psychological, and spiritual benefit of quieter soundscapes cannot be ignored. Social work is, as a profession, in a position to restore generative soundscapes in clients' daily experience. The emerging field of environmental social work encourages the protection and revitalization of natural soundscapes, acknowledging both the importance of sound in human experience and the role that human sound plays in destabilizing natural environments. A mounting body of evidence shows that anthropogenic sound contributes to environmental degradation and decreased biodiversity (Sordello et al., 2019), proving soundscape ecology a key priority in environmental protection measures. This chapter reinforces the role of sound as a neglected component of the environment that must be included for a better ecological approach to social work. There is clearly an ethical obligation to preserve the natural environment, and natural soundscapes, for their value beyond human interaction.

INTERLUDE: A MOMENT OF SILENCE

It is not easy to find silence in an industrialized landscape.

In the short time I lived in London, I plotted several walking routes through the city. My favorite and most traveled journey wove around an established path known as the Queen's Walk, skirting along the Thames from The Strand to Tower Bridge. The cacophony of urban life followed me as I traveled until the last step of my journey: Southwark Cathedral.

Any discussion of sound is incomplete without acknowledgement of silence, and silence was my primary objective when I reached Southwark Cathedral. Western culture has come to view silence as a negative phenomenon, an absence of the positive force that is sound: noise and sound are indicative of life and of animation, whereas silence "is the rejection of human personality" that "modern man . . . avoids . . . to nourish his fantasy of perpetual life" (Schafer, 1994, p. 256). Because sound is intrinsic to human experience from both within and without our corpus, silence is emblematic of a reality beyond human conceptualization or understanding. Silence, especially to Western sensibility in an industrialized landscape, is "beyond the realm of the possible, of the attainable" (Schafer, 1994, p. 257).

It is precisely because silence is alien that silence has power. Historical examples abound of designated cultural spaces in which silence is cultivated: they are often spiritual in nature, taking the form of churches or synagogues, monuments or memorials, sacred groves or secluded shrines (Schafer 1994). These spaces are culturally imbued with reverence, often carefully curated through architectural or landscape design (or a purposeful lack thereof) to manipulate sound and inspire specific emotional responses.

In the dim quietude of Southwark Cathedral, it felt as if the world slowed and the thrum of urban life dissipated entirely. Religious ascetics throughout the world have and continue to seek silence; Frithjof Schuon (2005) tells us that "silence . . . has been called a 'Name of the Buddha'" and that "the name *Allâh* . . . is the Peace that silences all the sounds of the world, whether around us or within us" (pp. 60, 72). The silence that I found in Southwark was nothing short of sacred—or, put in scholarly secular terms, the silence I found in Southwark Cathedral created within me an experiential rupture so profoundly different from my typical modernized existence that the vast and noisy homogeneity of my personal cosmology acquired dimension (Eliade, 1987).

Schafer writes that "just as man requires time for sleep to refresh and renew his life energies, so too he requires quiet periods to regain mental and spiritual composure. At one time stillness was a precious article in an unwritten code of human rights" (Schafer, 1994, p. 253–254). He suggests that Western culture must reacquaint itself with silence by understanding it not as an absence of sound but as a positive force of its own. We meditate not to drain our minds of sound, but to fill our minds with silence.

In the remainder of this chapter, I return to the soundscape to discuss policy, practice, and scholarly considerations that can aid social workers in ameliorating the stressors imposed by the industrial soundscape. Silence will always be implicit; it is already present in social work dialogue, in deliberate silence with clients, or as a catalyst of spiritual moments. As social work begins to embrace aural experience as a paramount consideration in the pursuit of social justice and equity, it is imperative that silence always be lightly held within view.

MOVING FORWARD: AURAL SOCIAL WORK

My intention throughout this chapter has been to emphasize the integral role of sound in every facet of lived experience, while illustrating two ontological constructions of the contemporary soundscape (physical sound and socially determined soundscapes/noise pollution) that create physiological, emotional, and psychological stress. The importance of the natural soundscape as a quasi-spiritual natural resource has been articulated, as has the slow elimination of silence. In the remainder of this chapter, I envision a healthier, more equitable soundscape that requires engagement from social workers on all levels, providing recommendations and practice skills.

I must note again that the ideal aural environment is culturally and personally contingent: societies and individuals have unique perspectives and needs that are served by different soundscapes. Social work is obliged by NASW Code of Ethics clause 1.03 to promote the self-determination of clients whenever possible, acknowledging the diversity of socially constructed aural values; the field is also tasked by NASW Ethics Code clause 1.05 to practice cultural competence by recognizing cultural perspectives on sound and on silence, suppressing practitioner assumptions to respect authentic client needs.

Remaining mindful of multivocality and alternative perspectives is best achieved with social work relational skills, the strengths perspective, and critical self-reflection. Creating space for clients to articulate their own ideal soundscape allows both social worker and client to collaboratively take stock of preexisting sounds and strengths that can be cultivated and used to build a foundation for transformative change, preserving the character and respecting the needs of individuals, communities, and their local soundscapes (Madsen & Gillespie, 2014). To achieve a truly collaborative relationship that prioritizes client self-designation, it is necessary that we social workers practice critical self-reflection models that elucidate our own experiences, biases, values, and their effects (Fook, 2016).

Research on soundscapes has been undergoing a scholarly shift away from studying sound in physical space (acoustics) to studying sound as it is perceived and experienced by humans (soundscapes); more than just of scholarly interest, this shift in academic focus represents changes in power away from strictly scientific priorities to multivocal, interdisciplinary, human-oriented priorities (Pijanowski et al., 2011; Schafer, 1994). Movement has been made toward this new scholarly paradigm, but policy and social service–related fields have not kept pace: soundscapes are largely undervalued in social service provision, and policy measures seek only to contain the negative effects of sound at the highest safety threshold lest dangerous soundscapes interfere with economic development. To actualize the dream of a healthier soundscape, social work must embrace soundscape ecology as being fundamental to human experience and not simply a facet of economic development.

Bearing in mind the variation of desirable soundscapes and the representational shift of power that soundscape study catalyzes, I now return to the previously discussed ontologies of physical sound and social soundscapes to provide recommendations based upon them. Some proposed recommendations are directly actionable in social work practice; others will be policy or paradigmatic shifts that social workers would do well to advocate for at community, organizational, and policy levels. Where possible, I will refer to existing measures that are already being taken toward healthier soundscapes.

SOCIAL WORK RESPONSES TO PHYSICAL SOUND

I have already mentioned the wealth of policy interventions that exist worldwide to curtail sound pollution or restrict noise to certain times of day. To many scholars, they are not enough (Chepesiuk, 2005; Fink, 2017). Although the U.S. National Park Service recognizes natural soundscapes as a resource in need of conservation, decibel levels in protected areas throughout the United States are frequently exceeded (Buxton et al., 2017), implying the need for even stronger control of noise pollution than currently exists. Given that most noise near protected areas is caused by development, transportation, and tourism, the protection of natural soundscapes will require a paradigmatic shift away from ideologies that perceive environmental assets as commodities. This protection should be extended and individualized for interested Indigenous communities and reservations, where noise pollution is currently recorded to be lowest among racial groups in the United States (Casey et al., 2017). School environments should similarly be protected from noise and acoustically designed to stifle harmful noises, preserving UDHR Article 26 by ensuring noise does not interfere with education (Chepesiuk, 2005).

More research should be undertaken to understand exactly at which decibel ranges sound becomes detrimental to both auditory and nonauditory health, and more research should be done into the mechanisms of human hearing. Current standards of acceptable volume levels are limited mostly to occupational settings, leaving the details of ambient physiological effect hazy, and occupational standards of health do not account for other variables like emotional or energetic state or for the variation in soundscapes that fill occupational settings (Fink, 2017). The connection between hearing loss and dementia also bears further investigation.

Electroacoustic devices, such as hearing aids, must continue to be refined to counter the effects of hearing loss, and electroacoustic devices should be more easily accessible for individuals that want them, in compliance with UDHR Article 27. Hearing assistance devices are often prohibitively expensive, underinsured, stigmatized, and geographically inaccessible, leading to disparate rates of hearing aid usage among racial and gender groups (Nieman et al., 2016; Widen et al., 2011). Several U.S. states have begun passing legislation that ensures Medicare-covered hearing aids for individuals who would benefit from them; similar legislation must be encouraged and written to ensure the evolving support of individuals affected by hearing loss. One such example is Vermont House Bill 266, which was signed into law in May 2022.

We must remain keenly aware of hearing-impaired individuals self-designating whether they want electroacoustic devices or would benefit from service instead. Services and community spaces must be established, or preexisting services broadened, to generatively accommodate hearing-impaired individuals. Individuals with hearing loss or impairment, especially those of increased age, are at great risk of isolation and depression brought on by their hearing difficulties; ensuring their participation in society is required by UDHR Article 27. Such services must have acoustically oriented physical environments; employ individuals trained in working with hearing-impaired individuals; provide sign-language translation services, psychoeducation, and American Sign Language classes; establish community-oriented programming; and offer hearing-loss prevention education and measures.

Social work education must inform students of how ubiquitous hearing loss is in industrialized areas both inside and outside of the United States. Students should be aware of their aural environment and of the physiological consequences of overexposure to loud sounds. Pedagogues may consider introducing simple measures throughout practice classes that elucidate aural experience, such as those described by Schafer in his chapter on listening, such as ear cleaning exercises (it's less odd than it sounds) or soundwalks (Schafer, 1994, pp. 205–213).

SOCIAL WORK RESPONSES TO CONSTRUCTED SOUNDSCAPES

Responding to socially constructed soundscapes is significantly more difficult than responding to their physiological effects. This is in large part because healthy soundscapes are incredibly variable by individual; because research on the psychological, emotional, and spiritual consequences of sound are largely underdeveloped (although not entirely, as evidenced by soundscape ecology); and because what research does exist is not yet grounded in a robust evidence-based framework that would be accepted for legislative change. Whatever the case, a paradigmatic shift is needed wherein the organization of society prioritizes generative soundscapes over economic goals.

Obvious policy reforms to clean the social soundscape might include creating larger buffer zones for naturally protected areas (Buxton et al, 2017; National Park Service, 2023) or enforcing noise ratings on consumer products like vacuums and dishwashers for informed purchasing (Fink, 2017). Less obvious policy measures might limit the use of items that create loud noises (such as firecrackers) to avoid psychological disturbance; create assistance programs that allow vulnerable individuals to access good housing and services in healthy soundscapes that suit them (ensuring UDHR Article 25; Emmet & Francis, 2015; Lin et al., 2012); or create and preserve easily accessible natural soundscapes in the form of parks, designated low-volume areas with reduced ambient noise, or urban gardens. Such spaces would ensure that UDHR Article 24 is protected. Legislation must also recognize that different cultures produce different soundscapes; soundscapes are expression of character, not reason for stigma.

Practice settings should be modulated based on the desired sound-scape of clients. Client involvement in determining soundscape will not only improve quality of service, but empowering clients with the strengths perspective also enables them to consider soundscapes in their own lives and take greater control of their aural circumstance. Technological innovation has made the creation of specific soundscapes easier. Relationally building knowledge of soundscapes will yield important practice insights, and established therapeutic models such as nature-based rehabilitation (Cerwén et al., 2016) and music therapy (Tang et al., 2020) provide useful frameworks for the active manipulation of sound in therapeutic settings. Silence should be actively considered and pursued where appropriate when working with clients (Hill et al., 2003).

Students in academic and pedagogic settings should be introduced to soundscape ecology and exposed to a variety of soundscapes for integration into their practice. Interdisciplinary sources on soundscapes—especially those speaking to the psychological, emotional, or spiritual dimensions of sound—should be introduced in all pedagogic settings. Soundscapes must be always at the forefront of social work perception for holistic, human-oriented practice: it may be that the field of social work would benefit from the creation of specialized aural social workers who can assist in the navigation of soundscape-related work in organizational and practice settings.

More qualitative research must be done to explore the various sound-scapes of life and the nuanced perceptions of them. Interdisciplinary study must be pursued with other professional fields to approach soundscapes holistically. Technological sounds and the electric soundscape warrant a great deal of study and may prove the way forward in controlling noise pollution while creating generative soundscapes.

CONCLUSION: MOVING TOWARD SOUNDSCAPE DESIGN

Schafer wrote *The Soundscape* (1994) to generate an interdisciplinary movement that conceives of the world as a musical composition of myriad sounds that can be controlled and arranged with certain goals in mind; being a composer, his focus was largely on artistic and acoustic fields of knowledge. Referring to the intentional soundscape as acoustic design, he is careful to note that it "should never become design control from above. It is rather a matter of the retrieval of a *significant aural culture*, and that is a task for everyone" (Schafer, 1994, p. 206).

Soundscapes are omnipresent: it is the responsibility of social workers to engage with present soundscapes and lead communities in deconstructing and improving their soundscapes as suits their needs and values. Failing to do so allows present inequities, oppressions, and human rights violations perpetrated through aural negligence to continue. To satisfy values stated in the NASW Code of Ethics, it is imperative that the field of social work and its numerous professionals integrate soundscape ecology into every consideration of social work practice, pedagogy, research, advocacy, and policy reform. To continue ignoring the impact of sound on clients and its potential to harm or oppress is to defy the values that fundamentally undergird social work. We must act.

REFERENCES

Bronkhorst, A. W. (2015). The cocktail-party problem revisited: Early processing and selection of multi-talker speech. *Attention, Perception & Psychophysics, 77*(5), 1465–1487. https://doi.org/10.3758/s13414-015-0882-9.

Buxton, R. T., Pearson, A. L., Allou, C., Fristrup, K., & Wittemyer, G. (2021). A synthesis of health benefits of natural sounds and their distribution in national parks. *Proceedings of the National Academy of Sciences, 118*(14), e2013097118. https://doi.org/10.1073/pnas.2013097118.

Buxton, R. T., McKenna, M. F., Mennitt, D., Fristrup, K., Crooks, K., Angeloni, L., & Wittemyer, G. (2017). Noise pollution is pervasive in U.S. protected areas. *Science, 356*(6337), 531–533. https://doi.org/10.1126/science.aah4783.

Casey, J. A., Morello-Frosch, R., Mennitt, D. J., Fristrup, K., Ogburn, E. L., & James, P. (2017). Race/ethnicity, socioeconomic status, residential segregation, and spatial variation in noise exposure in the contiguous United States. *Environmental Health Perspectives, 125*(7), 077017. https://doi.org/10.1289/EHP898.

Cerwén, G., Pedersen, E., & Pálsdóttir, A. M. (2016). The role of soundscape in nature-based rehabilitation: A patient perspective. *International Journal of Environmental Research and Public Health, 13*(12), 1229. https://doi.org/10.3390/ijerph13121229.

Chepesiuk, R. (2005). Decibel hell: The effects of living in a noisy world. *Environmental Health Perspectives, 113*(1), A34–A41. https://doi.org/10.1289/ehp.113-a34.

Cunningham, L. L., & Tucci, D. L. (2017). Hearing loss in adults. *New England Journal of Medicine, 377*(25), 2465–2473. https://doi.org/10.1056/NEJMra1616601.

Czechowicz, J. A., Messner, A. H., Alarcon-Matutti, E., Alarcon, J., Quinones-Calderon, G., Montano, S., & Zunt, J. R. (2010). Hearing impairment and poverty: The epidemiology of ear disease in Peruvian schoolchildren. *Otolaryngology–Head and Neck Surgery, 142*(2), 272–277. https://doi.org/10.1016/j.otohns.2009.10.040.

Eliade, M. (1987). *The sacred and the profane: The nature of religion* (W. R. Trask, Trans.). Orlando, FL: Harcourt.

Emmett, S. D., & Francis, H. W. (2015). The socioeconomic impact of hearing loss in US adults. *Otology & Neurotology, 36*(3), 545–550. https://doi.org/10.1097/MAO.0000000000000562.

Fink, D. J. (2017). What is a safe noise level for the public? *American Journal of Public Health, 107*(1), 44–45. https://doi.org/10.2105/AJPH.2016.303527.

Fook, J. (2016). *Social work: A critical approach to practice.* Thousand Oaks, CA: Sage.

Friedner, M., & Helmreich, S. (2015). Sound studies meets deaf studies. *Senses and Society, 7*(1), 72–86. https://doi.org/10.2752/174589312X13173255802120

Hill, C. E., Thompson, B. J., & Ladany, N. (2003). Therapist use of silence in therapy: A survey. *Journal of Clinical Psychology, 59*(4), 513–524. https://doi.org/10.1002/jclp.10155.

Johns Hopkins. (2021, November 12). *Hearing loss and the dementia connection.* Bloomberg School of Public Health. https://publichealth.jhu.edu/2021/hearing-loss-and-the-dementia-connection.

Knoferle, K. M., Spangenberg, E. R., Herrmann, A., & Landwehr, J. R. (2011). It is all in the mix: The interactive effect of music tempo and mode on in-store sales. *Marketing Letters, 23*(1), 325–337. https://doi.org/10.1007/s11002-011-9156-z.

Lin, F. R., Maas, P., Chien, W., Carey, J. P., Ferrucci, L., & Thorpe, R. (2012). Association of skin color, race/ethnicity, and hearing loss among adults in the USA. *Journal of the Association for Research in Otolaryngology, 13*(1), 109–117. https://doi.org/10.1007/s10162-011-0298-8.

Madsen, W. C., & Gillespie, K. (2014). *Collaborative helping: A strengths framework for home-based services.* Hoboken, NJ: Wiley.

Milliman, R. E. (1982). Using Background music to affect the behavior of supermarket shoppers. *Journal of Marketing, 46*(3), 86–91. https://doi.org/10.2307/1251706.

Noise Pollution Clearing House. (2022). *Noise Pollution Clearinghouse.* https://www.nonoise.org/index.htm.

NASW. (n.d.). *National Association of Social Workers (NASW).* NASW - National Associacion of Social Workers. Retrieved June 14, 2021, from https://www.socialworkers.org.

Nieman, C. L., Marrone, N., Szanton, S. L., Thorpe, R. J., & Lin, F. R. (2016). Racial/Ethnic and Socioeconomic Disparities in Hearing Health Care Among Older Americans. Journal of Aging and Health, 28(1), 68–94. https://doi.org/10.1177/0898264315585505

National Park Service. (2023, January 17). *A symphony of sounds.* https://www.nps.gov/subjects/sound/index.htm.

Oxenham, A. J. (2018). How we hear: The perception and neural coding of sound. *Annual Review of Psychology, 69*, 27–50. https://doi.org/10.1146/annurev-psych-122216-011635.

Pijanowski, B. C., Villanueva-Rivera, L. J., Dumyahn, S. L., Farina, A., Krause, B. L., Napoletano, B. M., Gage, S. H., & Pieretti, N. (2011). Soundscape ecology: The science of sound in the landscape. *BioScience, 61*(3), 203–216. https://doi.org/10.1525/bio.2011.61.3.6.

Rouw, R., & Erfanian, M. (2018). A Large-Scale Study of Misophonia. *Journal of Clinical Psychology, 74*(3), 453–479. https://doi.org/10.1002/jclp.22500.

Salvari, V., Paraskevopoulos, E., Chalas, N., Müller, K., Wollbrink, A., Dobel, C., Korth, D., & Pantev, C. (2019). Auditory categorization of man-made sounds versus natural sounds by means of MEG functional brain connectivity. *Frontiers in Neuroscience, 13.* https://www.frontiersin.org/article/10.3389/fnins.2019.01052.

Schafer, R. M. (1994). *The soundscape: Our sonic environment and the tuning of the world.* Rochester, VT: Destiny.

Schuon, Frithjof. (2004). *Prayer fashions man: Frithjof Schuon on the spiritual life* (J. S. Cutsinger, Ed.). Bloomington, IN: World Wisdom.

Sordello, R., Flamerie De Lachapelle, F., Livoreil, B., & Vanpeene, S. (2019). Evidence of the environmental impact of noise pollution on biodiversity: A systematic map protocol. *Environmental Evidence, 8*(1), 8. https://doi.org/10.1186/s13750-019-0146-6.

Tang, Q., Huang, Z., Zhou, H., & Ye, P. (2020). Effects of music therapy on depression: A meta-analysis of randomized controlled trials. *PloS One, 15*(11), e0240862. https://doi.org/10.1371/journal.pone.0240862.

Thompson, E. (2002). *The soundscape of modernity: Architectural acoustics and the culture of listening in America, 1900–1933.* Cambridge, MA: MIT Press.

van der Kruk, Y., Wilson, W. J., Palghat, K., Downing, C., Harper-Hill, K., & Ashburner, J. (2017). Improved signal-to-noise ratio and classroom performance in children with autism spectrum disorder: A systematic review. *Review Journal of Autism and Developmental Disorders, 4*(3), 243–253. https://doi.org/10.1007/s40489-017-0111-7.

Wagner, K. (2018, November 27). How restaurants got so loud. *Atlantic.* https://www.theatlantic.com/technology/archive/2018/11/how-restaurants-got-so-loud/576715/.

Wang, X., Orelaja, O. A., Ibrahim, D. Sh., & Ogbonna, S. M. (2020). Evaluation of noise risk level and its consequences on technical operators of tobacco processing equipment in a cigarette producing company in Nigeria. *Scientific African, 8,* e00344. https://doi.org/10.1016/j.sciaf.2020.e00344.

Widen, S., Bohlin, M., & Johansson, I. (2011). Gender perspectives in psychometrics related to leisure time noise exposure and use of hearing protection. *Noise & Health, 13*(55), 407–414. https://doi.org/10.4103/1463-1741.90299.

Witkin, S. L. (2011). *Social construction and social work practice: Interpretations and innovations.* New York: Columbia University Press.

15

TOWARD A TRANSFORMATIVE APPROACH TO THE CONCEPT OF RISK IN SOCIAL WORK

TUCKER BOYD

The concept of risk provides a commonly understood framework for social work practice, yet there are problems with it from a transformative social work perspective. A risk-based conceptualization potentially supports a neoliberal idea of selfhood and so is potentially at odds with transformative values such as relationality, a resistance to modernist ways of thinking, and an openness to the use of imagination and creativity in visioning social possibilities. This chapter considers the implications of Kemshall's (2002) and Webb's (2006) argument that social work has shifted from a needs-based to a risks-based profession. It begins with a brief review of the dominant approach to risk within social work. At a macro level, its negative consequences are manifested in the rise of defensive practice and a culture of blame. At a micro level, these consequences are demonstrated by the popularity of concepts such as empowerment, trauma, strengths, and resilience, which I argue are examples of governmentality meant to enforce neoliberal selfhood. The bulk of this chapter is concerned with exploring a transformative approach to the concept of risk in social work.

A BRIEF REVIEW OF RISK

Risk is not a new concept. In the eighteenth century BC, the Code of Hammurabi encouraged risk management by holding engineers accountable for poor home construction (Stalker, 2003). Later, maritime insurers used the Renaissance Latin word *riscum* to describe assessing the likelihood of ship-related disasters (Stalker, 2003). Though risk is not new, how societies live with risk, or perhaps more accurately how societies live with uncertainty, has changed considerably over time.

For example, from the Middle Ages until the Enlightenment, Western societies generally attributed outcomes to divine intervention. Early modernity replaced God with science, so risk became "scientized" (Stalker, 2003). Statistics emerged during this period. Whereas in previous eras, outcomes were up to God's will, and therefore almost all unknowable, Enlightenment science distinguished risk ("conditions in which the probability estimates of an event are known or knowable") from uncertainty ("when probabilities were inestimable") (Lupton, 1999, qtd. in Stalker, 2003, p. 213).

The expansion of what could be known was significant, but so too was the weight of what could not. Though science was (and is) a powerful balm to ease the burden of living with risk and uncertainty, it also necessarily involves "[seeing] risk as risk, which can no longer be transformed into certainty through religion or magic" (Stalker, 2003, p. 215). While in early modernity, future progress was expected to "cure" or "at least mitigate" still existing hazards, in later modernity this promise became less convincing (p. 141). Risk began to "connote less opportunity for gain and more possibility of loss" (Gephart et al., 2009, p. 141).

Social work, which has been described as a "modernist enterprise" (Hyslop, 2012, p. 406) and as a "child of modernity" (Howe, 1994) finds its origin in the West during this period and was influenced by modernist ideas. It follows then that modern social work, being born in this period, would be preoccupied with risk and would strive to control it, consistent with the modernist view of "science as the harbinger of truth through reason" (Hyslop, 2012, p. 406), a preoccupation with progress, and a shift from tradition and religion toward secular individualism (Webb, 2006). It is out of this context that the contemporary culture of blame within social work arises.

EVIDENCE-BASED PRACTICE AND
A CULTURE OF BLAME

"Culture of blame" is a phrase used throughout social work literature (see Parton, 1996) to refer to increasing levels of regulation and punishment within human services. Some scholars argue this culture of blame is due to high-profile cases of social workers' failing to control risk, particularly in child welfare (Whittaker & Havard, 2016) and probation (Tuddenham, 2000). Negative media coverage of these incidents presents an image of social workers as incompetent or negligent, which fuels outrage within the public and leads to support for "regimes of audit" and "risk assessment" as well as an "insurgence of empiricism" (Stanford, 2010, p. 1066). Webb (2002) argues that evidence-based practice (EBP), a hot topic within contemporary social work, is an example of empiricism designed to address the "counterfactuals" that so often follow negative, high-profile events. Using the child abuse case of Victoria Climbie, Webb (2002, p. 48) explains counterfactuals as questions such as "what would have happened if things had happened differently?" or "what would have happened if Victoria's injuries had been given a higher priority by Haringey's child protection team?" Counterfactuals are, of course, mostly unanswerable: "one can never observe counterfactuals, nor assess empirically the validity of any modeling assumptions made about them." Said another way, risk is very difficult to predict in hindsight.

Still, evidence-based practice "purports to offer certainty, facility, predictability and stability" (Stanford, 2010, p. 1066). It is also used to dictate "best practice," which social workers are mandated to follow and held accountable for any failure to do so. It is not clear that the imposition of empiricism and a culture of blame actually translates to higher-quality social work interactions. Defensive practice, a term defined by Harris (1987, p. 162) as "practices which are deliberately chosen in order to protect the professional worker, at the possible expense of the well-being of the client" has increased as a result of these trends (qtd. in Whittaker & Havard, 2016, p. 1160). Stanford (2010) describes the practice environment brought on by EBP and a culture of blame as "defensive" and "morally timid" (p. 1067).

MORALIZING AND INDIVIDUALIZING RISK TO DETERMINE WORTHINESS AND ENFORCE NEOLIBERAL SELFHOOD

So far, a risks-based social work has been critiqued because of its cultivation of a culture of blame and subsequent rise in defensive practice. A risks-based social work might also be criticized for its role in "privat[izing]" (Rose, 1999) and "moral[izing]" (Gephart et al., 2009) risk, then operationalizing it to determine who is "worthy" of quality social work services and "discipling" social work clients into adhering to a narrow neoliberal selfhood.

Let us start with the argument that risks-based social work privatizes and moralizes clients' risk identities in order to determine their worthiness for quality social work interventions. Stanford (2010) observed that among the social workers in their sample, quality interventions were rationed based on the outcome of weighing a client's "at-risk" versus their "a-risk" identities. Examples of at-risk identities could include vulnerability and isolation, while a-risk identities could include anger and violence (p. 1074). "Having moralized their clients' risk identities in terms of them being innocent and/or at fault, good and/or bad," social workers would determine whether the client was "deserving of them taking a stand on their behalf" (p. 1076). When one considers the significant pressures social workers might feel to manage risk effectively, and the extreme judgment and consequences they might face if they fail to do so (the culture of blame), it is not difficult to imagine that social workers would be willing to take practice risks only with clients they deem generally low-risk. This is not to excuse the practice. This is a significant departure from the National Association of Social Workers' (NASW) Code of Ethics in the United States, which describes social work's mission and client base as "to enhance human well-being and help meet the basic human needs of *all people*, with particular attention to the *needs and empowerment of people who are vulnerable, oppressed, and living in poverty*" (NASW, 2021, preamble, emphasis added). It is only to point out yet another insidious function of risk as it is understood and responded to within dominant contemporary social work.

The next argument is that risks-led social work "disciplines" social work clients into a narrow, neoliberal selfhood. To describe this view, it is necessary to define two terms, starting with neoliberalism. *Neoliberalism* can be defined in many different ways but generally refers to political and economic policies that became widespread, particularly in the West but also globally, following the end of the dominance of Keynesian economics. Webb (2006) offers the following attributes as defining elements of neoliberalism: "the rule of the market; cutting public expenditure on social services and reducing the safety net for the poor; de-regulating systems that diminish profit; privatizing public enterprises; and eliminating the concepts of the public good and of community, replacing them with those of individual responsibility and choice" (p. 17).

The second term to be defined is governmentality. Michel Foucault used the term *governmentality* to refer to a "modern approach to social regulation and control." Foucault argued that in modern times, it is no longer fashionable for governments to govern through "excessive intervention by the state." In accordance with the neoliberal principles of individual responsibility and choice, governments must find a way to create "docile bodies" without public expressions of state power. This new form of state power can be referred to as "governmentality": a "neoliberal approach to political rule that endorses individual freedom and rights" and "uses regulatory power to monitor and manage people while pursuing goals of neoliberalism" (Gephart et al., 2009, p. 146).

Governmentality theorists suggest that under neoliberalism, the worthy citizen "should be autonomous" and "self-regulating" (Gephart et al., 2009, p. 147). Developing an autonomous neoliberal self is central to the larger neoliberal project of "endorsing individual freedom and rights" through small (or invisible) government (p. 146). In support of this aim, Beck (2006) argues that neoliberalism advocates for the "privatization of risk," defined as "individuals bear[ing] the responsibility associated with risk decision making" (p. 60). Rose (1999) helpfully adds that the privatization of risk reflects a larger neoliberal "regime of self where competent personhood is thought to depend upon the continual exercise of freedom, and where one is encouraged to understand one's life, actually or potentially, not in terms of fate or social status, but in terms of one's success or failure acquiring the skills and making the choices to actualize oneself" (p. 256, qtd. in Beck, 2006, p. 60).

Consider the contemporary popularity of concepts such as strengths, resilience, trauma, and empowerment in social work education, policy, and practice. Though understandings and practices of these concepts vary, they each tend to focus on individual characteristics consistent with cultivating the neoliberal self. With this context in place, perhaps social workers' evaluation of clients' a-risk versus at-risk identities is a way of evaluating their neoliberal selfhood. It begs the question: how much of risks-led social work practice is oriented toward the production and enforcement of conforming neoliberal subjects?

Seen in this way, risks-led social work poses a significant threat to social work's core values, particularly those concerned with social justice, human rights, human relationships, and professional integrity. Adopting a transformative approach to risk in social work is of critical importance if the field is to realize these values in practice. The rest of this chapter is an early effort toward identifying ideas that might shape a transformative approach to risk, beginning with one of critical importance: imagination.

SOCIAL WORK AS SPECULATIVE FICTION: THE IMPORTANCE OF IMAGINATION

Are we brave enough to imagine beyond the boundaries of "the real" and then do the hard work of sculpting reality from our dreams?

—WALIDAH IMARISHA, IN THE INTRODUCTION TO *OCTAVIA'S BROOD*

In the introduction to Adrienne Maree Brown's and Walidah Imarisha's brilliant anthology *Octavia's Brood* (2015), Imarisha writes: "Whenever we try to envision a world without war, without violence, without prisons, without capitalism, we are engaging in speculative fiction" (p. 3). As a member of a profession committed to "challeng[ing] social injustice" (NASW Code of Ethics) and promoting the "empowerment and liberation of people" (IFSW Code of Ethics), one might assume that more had been written connecting social work with speculative fiction, but there is a dearth of literature on the topic. This chapter contributes to expanding social work's consideration of speculative fiction, and of imagination more broadly, by applying images and ideas from Octavia E. Butler's 1993 novel *Parable of the Sower* to a transformative social work approach to risk.

Dominant approaches to risk, like many modernist ideas, have a tendency to restrict the imagination. As the slogan commonly associated with Margaret Thatcher, a significant figure in the development of neoliberalism in the UK, goes: "There is no alternative." In the case of risk, the current approach, even when its limitations are acknowledged, can be pardoned on the grounds that at least risk assessment and management are clear and readily operational. Situations involving risk within social work are often highly emotional. This may be due to their provoking a worker's or service user's fundamental fears, such as death, or, in the context of a culture of blame, because of the potential punitive action that could follow if risk is mismanaged. In these highly emotional situations, the certainty offered by empiricism, even if it is a false certainty, has real value.

Barnetz (2015) proposes that imagination, specifically a "social work imagination" (van Wormer, 2002, p. 21, qtd. in Barnetz, 2015, p. 251), can be exercised to challenge those dominant ideas that resist questioning. As Barnetz shows, through the use of imagination in challenging social Darwinism, the current risk regime need not be left unexamined. Imagination, as exemplified by speculative fiction, may be one way to destabilize the hold that dominant approaches to risk have on "the truth."

The work of the artist, regardless of the medium, is to "bring an image to life." This phrase is often narrowly interpreted to refer to the physical product that an artist creates, but it can also refer to new ways of seeing and understanding that an artist provokes, and therefore brings to life, within their audience. This act of imagination that art invites is an essential component of the development and adoption of a transformative approach to risk. As Barnetz (2015) notes:

> The war against the current cultural structure cannot be waged by means of critical intellectual analysis alone. To existing social injustice and oppression, it is not enough to theoretically analyze the factors that may explain those situations, and it is not adequate simply to demonstrate the human price of such social realities. A central part of the struggle for

social change is, therefore, over the human ability, as well as the courage, to imagine. (pp. 258–259)

To imagine beyond the boundaries of "the real," as Imarisha suggests, demands new images and metaphors for a transformative social work approach to risk. It is unreasonable to ask social workers to abandon dominant approaches to risk without the beginnings of an alternative, just as it is unethical in psychotherapy for a therapist to support a service user in reevaluating old coping mechanisms without supporting the person in developing new ones. I propose that one such image for guiding a transformative social work approach to risk lies in Octavia E. Butler's prescient work of speculative fiction, *The Parable of the Sower*.

Butler's novel opens with a dream. The novel's protagonist, Lauren Olimina, dreams of a door, which she comes to while flying. As she pushes through, she is enveloped in flames. When Olimina does not wake up, the dream progresses to a memory. In this memory, Olimina's stepmother teaches her that before she was born, the sky was empty of stars.

"Why couldn't you see the stars?" Lauren asked, innocently. "Everyone can see them."

"City lights," her stepmother responded. "Lights, progress, growth. All those things we are too hot and too poor to bother with anymore."

Butler's novel takes place in an imagined 2020s and 2030s, when the United States and many countries around the world have succumbed to climate disaster and rampant economic inequality. "When I was your age, my mother told me that those stars, the few stars that we could see, were windows into Heaven," Olimina's stepmother said. "Windows for God to look through and keep an eye on us."

These lines of dialogue bring to the fore an essential question throughout the rest of the book, a question that I believe is at the heart of a transformative approach to risk: What is lost when we cannot see the stars? Lauren's stepmother implies that whatever is lost from losing sight of the stars, it is not as great a loss as losing the "blaze of light that cities used to be."

Lauren thought about this and said, "I'd rather have the stars. The stars are free."

"I'd rather have the lights back myself," her stepmother said. "The sooner the better. But we can afford the stars."

A SOCIAL WORK IN RELATIONSHIP TO THE STARS

The viewpoints on the stars represented by Olimina and her stepmother are reflective of a larger social, intellectual, political, and cultural debate between what we may refer to as postmodernism and modernism (also known as positivism and structuralism) (Freedman & Combs, 1996). A full review of this debate is beyond the scope of this chapter, but any discussion of contemporary social work, particularly the current risk regime within social work, must consider the profound impact that this ontological, epistemological, and phenomenological debate has had on how risk is currently understood and experienced.

Olimina's defense of the stars, in defiance of her stepmother, who would "rather have the lights back," represents a postmodern position that is at the core of a transformative approach to risk. The stars, so long as they are visible, can be interpreted as symbols of resistance to modernist thinking and as openings through which new ways of conceptualizing and interacting with risk might emerge. With these meanings in mind, the stars might serve as useful imagery to guide social workers' imaginings of a transformative approach to risk. A transformative approach to risk then might be thought of as part of a larger social work in defense of, or in relationship to, the stars.

The task of this chapter is to consider a transformative approach to risk in social work. So far it has been established that this approach aligns itself with a postmodern worldview. A next question might be: What do I mean by the approach's "aligning itself with a postmodern worldview"?

Many scholars have devoted their energies to the difficult task of defining postmodernism. Despite these efforts, postmodernism remains famously resistant to definition. Some describe postmodernism as an ideology, animated by ideas such as a rejection of the modernist focus on order and by a skepticism of singular, "objective" truth (Freedman & Combs, 1996; Klages, 2001); others describe postmodernity as a set of conditions brought on by a particular stage of capitalism (Harvey, 1989). For the purposes of a transformative approach to risk in social work, postmodernism serves as an animating force that drives attention toward "the stars"—in other words, those aspects of social work practice and imagination that modernist thinking has left behind. Rather than a prescriptive set of beliefs that I implore all social workers to adhere to and practice, a transformative approach to risk, in the image of postmodernism and the stars, aims first and foremost to promote spaciousness for the purpose of imagination. This spaciousness provides not only intellectual "room to grow" but also an invitation to creativity and experimentation, all-important characteristics of a transformative approach to risk. As Olimina says, it is the stars' freedom that distinguishes them from the city lights.

ON THE OTHER SIDE OF 'THE REAL'

Ralph Waldo Emerson, an influential figure in the mid-nineteenth century Transcendentalist movement in the United States, said: "The stars awaken a certain reverence because though always present, they are inaccessible" (from *Nature*, 1836). Risks, like the stars, are omnipresent, and though it might be too extreme to argue that they are inaccessible, there is reason to believe that they are uniquely challenging to predict and manage (Beck, 1986; Giddens, 1991).

Beck's influential "risk society thesis" argues that "the victories of early modernity," such as an increase in life expectancy and wealth, are "systematically accompanied by the social production of risks" (1986, p. 19). This is poignantly described by Butler in the discussion between Olimina and her stepmother, as the remarkable discovery of electricity in early modernity led to the advent of light pollution and the subsequent obscuring of the stars in late modernity. Other examples of late modern risks that have their origin in early modernity include the risk of nuclear war (brought on by the incredible discovery of nuclear fission) and chemical and hazardous waste contamination of the soil and food supply. These late modern risks, according to Beck (1986) and Giddens (1991) are unique in that they transcend borders, pose generational consequences, and may be latent for many years, requiring experts to warn of their danger. These unique aspects of late modern risks lead Jaeger et al. (2001) to argue that "rationality," perhaps the most highly esteemed capacity within modernism, "is not able to help us fully understand and respond to the risk society" (qtd. in Stalker, 2003, p. 216). The basic modernist premise, "the expectation of progress and continual improvement," is increasingly improbable as more and more of late modern life is shaped by the "dark side of progress" (qtd. in Stalker, 2003, p. 216).

Interestingly, while the stars warrant "reverence" because of their prevalence and inaccessibility, social workers report experiencing fear in the face of risk (Stanford, 2010). Not only is fear associated with defensive practice, defined by Harris (1987, p. 162) as "practices which are deliberately chosen in order to protect the professional worker, at the possible extent of the well-being of the client," but bell hooks (2000, p. 93) suggests in *All About Love* that fear "is the primary force in upholding structures of domination. It promotes the desire for separation, the desire not to be known." Fear is a poisonous response to risk in social work. It threatens perhaps the most fundamental building block of any social work interaction: relationship. How have two great unknowns, the stars and risk, come to invoke such contradictory emotional responses?

The question of risk within social work is essentially a question of how to live with our own smallness. As is all too familiar to many of the people social workers work with and care for, life is a fragile enterprise. It can be ended or upended without notice and seemingly without reason. The modernist approach to risk, which dominates in late modern social work, is governed by the basic assumption that "risk can be managed" (Stalker, 2003, p. 218). I do not believe a transformative approach to risk should aim to refute this claim in its entirety. Of course, there are risks that can be more or less managed, sometimes very accurately. For example, diligent mask wearing and social distancing were found to "flatten the curve" of COVID-19 infections (Li et al., 2020), and taking preexposure prophylaxis as recommended has been found to reduce the risk of getting HIV through sex by more than 99 percent (Centers for Disease and Control and Prevention, 2021). Social workers have a responsibility to communicate these risk mitigation strategies, in fulfillment of their ethical obligations to competence (NASW Code of Ethics) and professional integrity (IFSW). But even in these cases, when risk management strategies are particularly effective, there remains the possibility that the worst outcome may occur. And these cases are often the exception rather than the rule; social work clients frequently face situations where risk assessment and mitigation are more complex and less effective.

What if social workers practiced from the belief that not all risks are knowable? A modernist orientation treats the unknown, at best, as evidence of how far society still has to go and, at worst, as failure. It is no wonder, then, that risk in late modern society is frequently framed in "negative terms" (Stalker, 2003, p. 213). A transformative approach might learn from the stars, whose unknowability produces curiosity, awe, and inspiration. Risk taking is an everyday practice, core to the human experience, and particularly relevant to navigating late modern life. How could the current, fear-driven response to risk, which grows from an increasingly indefensible belief that risk can be managed, be transformed by an acknowledgment of the limitations of human knowing and control? I do not claim to have any answers to this question. The difficulty of acknowledging and living with uncertainty and the limitations of human knowing and control are age-old challenges that concern many world religions. I only mean to identify a line of thinking that modernism has excluded, I believe to the detriment of social workers and clients, and to invite transformative social workers to imagine beyond.

But transformative social workers need not be rudderless in this imagining. Here, too, Butler's novel has much to teach us. As part of navigating an increasingly uncertain and violent world, Olimina, the novel's protagonist, establishes a religion, called Earthseed. She aims to spread Earthseed as widely as possible, hoping it might offer an alternative to her father's [Christian] God, or to any religion that offers a sense of certainty. "A lot of people seem to believe in a big-daddy-God or a big-cop-God or a big-king-God. They believe in a kind of super person. A few believe God is another word for nature. And nature turns out to mean just about anything they happen not to understand or feel in control of" (1993, p. 43). In contrast, Earthseed teaches that "God is change." A core verse of Earthseed expands on change as *the* guiding force in a world that resists prediction and certainty: "All that you touch you change. All that you change changes you. The only lasting truth is change. God is change." Olimina admits that hers is not an easy God to follow. Accepting the limitations of human knowing and control—in other words, accepting human smallness—is no small task, particularly in an environment that privileges knowing and control to such a high degree. But there may be rewards for acknowledging the limitations of human knowing and control with regard to risk in social work. Social work is a deeply human practice that involves responding to a full range of human emotion and experience in others and in oneself. Modernism has driven social work "from depth to surface," toward a "focus on task and process at the expense of value" (Stalker, 2003, p. 220). A transformative approach to risk in social work is uniquely positioned to heed Imarisha's call to "imagine beyond boundaries of 'the real' " and to "do the hard work of sculpting reality from our dreams." In the words of Octavia E. Butler, "so be it, see to it."

REFERENCES

Barnetz, Z. (2015). The role of radical imagination in social work education, practice, and research. *Journal of Teaching in Social Work, 35*(3), 251–261.

Beck, U. (1992). *Risk society: Towards a new modernity.* Thousand Oaks, CA: Sage.

Bertilsson, M. (1990). Review essay: The role of science and knowledge in a risk society: comments and reflections on Beck. *Industrial Crisis Quarterly, 4*(2), 141–148.

Brown, A. M., & Imarisha, W. (Eds.). (2015). *Octavia's brood: Science fiction stories from social justice movements.* Chico. CA: AK Press.

Butler, O. E. (1993). *Parable of the sower.* New York: Four Walls Eight Windows.

Centers for Disease and Control and Prevention. (2021). *PrEP effectiveness.* https://www.cdc.gov/hiv/basics/prep/prep-effectiveness.html.

Douglas, Mary. (1966). *Purity and danger.* London: Ark Paperbacks.

Douglas, Mary. (1982). *Natural symbols: Explorations in cosmology.* New York: Pantheon.

Douglas, Mary. (1985). *Risk acceptability according to the social sciences.* New York: Russell Sage Foundation.

Douglas, Mary. (1986). *How institutions think.* Syracuse: Syracuse University Press.

Douglas, Mary. (1992). *Risk and blame: Essays in cultural theory.* London: Routledge.

Douglas, Mary, and Aaron Wildavsky. (1982). *Risk and culture: An essay on the selection of technological and environmental dangers.* Berkeley, CA: University of California Press.

Emerson, R. W. (1836). *Nature.* James Munroe and Company.

Freedman, J., & Combs, G. (1996). The narrative metaphor and social constructionism: A postmodern worldview. In *Narrative therapy: The social construction of preferred realities* (pp. 19–41). New York: Norton.

Gephart, R. P., Van Maanen, J., & Oberlechner, T. (2009). Organizations and risk in late modernity. *Organization Studies, 30*(2–3), 141–155.

Gibelman, Margaret. (1999). The search for identity: defining social work, past, present, future. *Social Work, 44*(4), 298–310.

Giddens, A. (1991). *Modernity and self-identity.* Cambridge: Polity.

Harris N. (1987). Defensive social work. *British Journal of Social Work, 17*(1), 61–69.

Harvey, D. (1989). *The condition of postmodernity: An enquiry into the origins of cultural change.* Hoboken, NJ: Wiley-Blackwell.

hooks, b. (2001). *All about love: New visions.* New York: William Morrow.

Howe, D. (1994). Modernity, postmodernity, and social work. *British Journal of Social Work,* 24(5), 513–532.

Hyslop, I. (2012). Social work as a practice of freedom. *Journal of Social Work,* 12(4) 404–422.

International Federation of Social Workers (IFSW). (2014). *Global definition of social work.* https://www.ifsw.org/what-is-social-work/global-definition-of-social-work/.

Jabareen, Yosef. (2009). *Building a Conceptual Framework: Philosophy, Definitions, and Procedure.* International Journal of Qualitative Methods. 8(4), pp. 49–62.

Kemshall, H. (2002) *Risk, social policy and welfare.* Buckingham, UK: Open University Press.

Klages, M. (2001). *Postmodernism.* University of Colorado, Boulder. https://www.webpages.uidaho.edu/~sflores/KlagesPostmodernism.html.

Li, T., Liu, Y., Li, M., Qian, X., & Dai, S. Y. (2020). Mask or no mask for COVID-19: A public health and market study. *PLoS ONE,* 15(8).

Lupton, D. (1999). *Risk.* London: Routledge.

McEvoy, Jamie, Susan Gilbertz, Matthew Anderson, Kerri Jean Ormerod, and Nicolas Bergmann. (2017). *Cultural Theory of Risk as a Heuristic for Understanding Perceptions of Oil and Gas Development in Eastern Montana, USA.* National Library of Medicine, 4(4) 852–859.

National Association of Social Workers (NASW). (2021). *NASW code of ethics.* https://www.socialworkers.org/About/Ethics/Code-of-Ethics/Code-of-Ethics-English.

Parton, N. (1996). Social work, risk and "the blaming system." In N. Parton (Ed.), *Social theory, social change and social work* (pp. 98–114). London: Routledge.

Pollack, Shoshana. (2010). *Labelling Clients 'Risky': Social Work and the Neoliberal Welfare State,* 40 1263–1278.

Rose, N. (1999). *Powers of freedom: Reframing political thought.* Cambridge: Cambridge University Press.

Schwarz M, Thompson M. *Divided We Stand: Redefining Politics, Technology, and Social Choice.* University of Pennsylvania Press; Philadelphia: 1990.

Stalker, K. (2003). *Managing risk and uncertainty in social work: A literature review. Journal of Social Work,* 3(2) 211–233.

Stanford, S. (2010). "Speaking back" to fear: Responding to the moral dilemmas of risk in social work practice. *British Journal of Social Work,* 40(4), 1065–1080.

Tuddenham, R. (2000). Beyond defensible decision-making: Towards reflexive assessment of risk and dangerousness. *Probation Journal,* 47(3), 173–183.

United Nations. (1948). *The Universal Declaration of Human Rights.* From: https://www.un.org/en/udhrbook/pdf/udhr_booklet_en_web.pdf

Wallace, John and Bob Pease. (2011). *Neoliberalism and Australian Social Work: Accommodation or Resistance?,* 11(2), 132–142.

Webb, S. A. (2006). *Social work in a risk society: Social and political perspectives.* New York: Palgrave Macmillan.

Whittaker, A., & Havard, T. (2015). Defensive practice as 'fear-based' practice: Social work's open secret? *British Journal of Social Work,* 46(5), 1158–1174.

Witkin, Stanley. (2012). *Social Construction and Social Work Practice.* Columbia University Press. 13–38.

III

SPECIFIC MODELS
AND STRATEGIES

16

CRITICAL REFLECTION IN ENVIRONMENTAL/ ECOLOGICAL SOCIAL WORK PRACTICE

ERIN MACKENZIE

A t a time when our social work practice and hope for collective transformation feel challenged on a daily basis, embodying and integrating a living critical reflection process is necessary for understanding how to navigate uncertainty in a rapidly changing environment. In this chapter, I demonstrate the importance of integrating critical reflection into daily social work practice that aims to be transformative, socially just, and emancipatory and to move beyond the limits of neoliberal, colonial, modernist, racial capitalist, and dualistic interpretations of reality. Additionally, I will discuss how this integration is particularly important for social work practice within environmental, ecological, or climate justice grassroots organizational settings and projects.

To ground my definition of critical reflection, I must first ask, what prompts me to embark on this journey? As an emerging practitioner of transformative social work in these times of planetary crisis, I feel called to cultivate more creative and compassionate engagement with the world and its many inhabitants, while supporting others to do the same. To me, critical reflection is a transformative practice necessary for addressing complex challenges and for learning from the meaning we attribute to our embodied experiences in an interconnected and emergent socioecological environment.

As Jan Fook and Fiona Gardner explain (2007, p. 17), the process of critical reflection can feel unsettling in that it is "one of shaking up assumptions to surface those that may be hidden for a variety of reasons . . . the image that comes to mind is of dice being thrown, with little ability to predict how and even when they will fall, and what face will show." The unsettling aspect of this process also implies that there is not a predetermined framework for evaluating or stratifying the more bedrock assumptions that emerge. Therefore, the critical aspect of this process becomes the degree of discomfort or unease that arises to spark inspiration and give life to the learning journey. As Fook emphasizes, "how the process is facilitated, and the learning environment created, are therefore both (extremely) crucial" (Fook & Gardner, 2007, p. 17). In my experience, a willingness to be vulnerable and open to the depth of our embodied emotions during the process results in a more personally meaningful and sustainable felt sense of transformational learning..

With this insight, we critically examine our experience in relation to the broader sociocultural context, leading us to unearth assumptions about the powers that story the landscape of our bodily and earthly experience. As a result, we engage in the continuous discovery of less limiting interpretations of possible and potential futures. Therefore, in practice situations that center environmental justice, critical reflection has the potential to transform the underlying worldview that connects, roots, and sustains unseen harmful systems of relating that inevitably inform organizational processes in a neoliberal cultural climate.

In the paragraphs that follow, I use Fook and Garder's (2007) two-stage model to demonstrate the transformative potential of a critical reflection practice, particularly in an interdisciplinary environmental social work context. This model involves examining a specific incident that is significant to learning, reflecting on the underlying assumptions, and using the new awareness that arises to develop principles for future practice. I therefore provide a brief description of my critical incident, the main assumptions that emerged, new thinking and ideas for my future practice, and observations about this entire two-stage reflection process. Lastly, I discuss ways to sustain this living reflection practice, particularly through attunement with my embodied feelings, to help illuminate how to practice in a time when practice often feels ambiguous and tricky. I discuss how this may help cultivate new, more liberating, ways of thinking, seeing, and being together on Earth. In this connection, I discuss the emancipatory potential of critical, future-oriented approaches to practice that emphasize creativity and place-based awareness.

CRITICAL INCIDENT

My critical incident, which occurred during my MSW field placement, centers around an exchange with my on-site field instructor during a phone call to discuss our grassroots organizing project. The project was centered around climate justice and public engagement with frontline communities. Together, we decided to create some language for how we would describe the project to frontline community liaisons in meetings. Knowing that verbal expression is not my strength and that I was new to this practice setting context, I felt it was important to engage in a collaborative meaning-making practice to guide our work journey and discuss our shared principles. Previous to the discussion, I had been feeling unsettled about my role and the project's justice structure.

We decided that I would read the bulleted document I created and then discuss it. I was reading the process-focused section of the outline when I reached a note I had left marked with an asterisk, explaining that it was "just a curiosity." The note said: "Would communities like to lead listening sessions themselves? For example, safe/sanctuary spaces, intentional support from peers, inter-community strength/connection, and cultivating partnerships (working alongside)." While I was speaking, my supervisor stopped me to express a different direction. In response, I blamed "social work" for the discrepancy: "I think I'm just injecting too much social work into this [project language and description]." I also apologized, immediately assuming fault. Afterward, my reaction to blame the field created increasing confusion, leaving me frequently unsettled about my role as a social worker in this context.

THE MAIN ASSUMPTIONS THAT EMERGED FROM THE STAGE ONE REFLECTION PROCESS

In stage one of my critical reflection, I discovered that I was inadvertently devaluing and compartmentalizing my personal knowledge and emotional experience in this context. By not addressing my authentic experience, I cut myself off from being able to deeply process the situation and thus provide myself with the care and respect I needed. By blaming my reaction on social work and then choosing this incident for critical reflection, I assumed that I could resolve the situation by creating distance from the painful embodied aspect of my experience.

I discovered that by living through the painful feelings without recognizing them, I continue to rob myself of the power that can come from using those feelings to fuel some movement beyond them. As a result, I have condemned myself to relive that pain over and over whenever something resonant triggers it, which ultimately creates a cycle of suffering. This also perpetuates disconnection from my strengths and devalues what I have to offer. This helped me to see that I was constructing a binary in relation to my strengths and perceived weaknesses, rather than seeing these traits as co-constituted and entangled with each other. This bifurcated way of categorizing defined my strengths within a hierarchical structure. This helped me to see how modernist frames of reference create the illusion of deficiency or opposing forces in my thinking and continue to undermine my critical inquiry.

By revealing this binary, I saw that I was assuming that a "managerial interpretation" would help to resolve and prevent a recurrence of these unsettled feelings in relation to my strengths and social work practice in this context. Managerial thinking is reflected in most neoliberal professional interactions, along with a tendency to place ourselves above or outside of a situation. This type of thinking assumes linear cause-and-effect relations, based on "unicausal" (as opposed to multicausal) thinking. "It is a type of culture of management: we assume that by properly reviewing a situation, working out the causes of the problem (blaming), we can therefore design policies/practices/protocols that will prevent a similar problem occurring. In effect, we manage the situation" (Fook, 2012, p. 229). The problem with our inner manager is that it potentially closes down dialogue, openness, and collaboration for further soul searching.

Considering that the goal was to center community justice in our work, and both my supervisor and I have privileged identities (white, able-bodied, etc.), a reflexive practice would benefit our ability to address the ways we are perpetuating oppressive systems of relations, even unconsciously (whiteness, paternalism, ableism, etc.). Looking at how power was situated and constructed in this organizational context revealed an underlying culture of professionalization in alignment with patriarchal power relations and the impact of neoliberalism on a nonprofit's ability to participate effectively in equitable community organizing processes (Alexander & Fernandez, 2021; Morley & O'Bree, 2021). This professionalized frame of reference became entangled with my interpretation of available ways to feel and respond in this situation. As a result, I continued to assume a fixed, identifiable, and reductionist definition of my environmental social work practice.

While sitting deeply with the painful emotions that arose from this incident, I was able to connect sources of meaning from my personal history. In exploring previous life situations in which similar feelings of pain had manifested, I discovered that my reaction was connected to my experiences with physical violence, emotional abuse, and bullying, as well as growing up fairly isolated with an extremely sensitive nervous system and divergent mental processing. I was also reminded of my previous experiences as a graphic artist in corporate work settings, where intense pressure to perform and conform at the expense of one's well-being was commonplace and expected. So, my tendency to protect, decenter, and devalue the vulnerable embodied aspect of my experience is relatively strong, along with a desire to avoid rejection and preserve connection at all costs. Similarly, I continued to assume that my heightened ability to sense subtle dimensions was untrustworthy and ineffective, and I assumed that I could find a way to manage this confusion through further critical reflection. This uncovered all of the times when I felt something unsettling but ignored it, which was upsetting and difficult to accept.

Looking deeply at how I let myself become disconnected from this intimate dimension of myself revealed that this aspect of the incident was ultimately what was infuriating and painful about my experience. By choosing this incident and attempting to intellectualize and manage the feelings that arose, I assumed I was not allowed to feel hurt by my supervisor's response and ongoing relational style. As a result, my supervisor and I were not able to really address how harmful power dynamics came into our everyday work processes on a deeper subconscious level. It is possible that this continued to inject a status quo and essentialized interpretation of justice into our work, roles, and interactions, which risks perpetuating a complicit colonial mindset about work and associated power dynamics.

Finally, by not seeing that I have oppressed identities in this particular material time frame and context (neurodivergent, sensory-processing sensitivity/disorder, gender nonconforming, etc.), in addition to privileged identities (white, able-bodied, middle-class, educated, etc.), I continue to limit my ability to challenge the status quo, which in turn also perpetuates the oppressive assumptions I wish to unearth and challenge. This deep assumption denies the many different forms of power I feel that I have and accommodates my refusal to take on an oppressed identity. Therefore, the main assumptions that emerged from stage one revealed where our Western culture's modernist, neoliberal, racial capitalist, and colonial frames of mind sneaked into my interpretations of myself and experience. These deeply embedded assumptions have a trickster-like quality, in that they create the illusion of being critical or transformative, yet all the while, separation, reduction, and control unconsciously permeate and evolve within the unseen dimensions of our work and relationships. Michael Yellow Bird (2015), an Indigenous social work scholar, refers to this kind of practice as "coyote social work."

NEW THINKING AND IDEAS FOR PRACTICE THAT EMERGED FROM THE STAGE TWO REFLECTION

Stage two of this reflection process helped me to decipher and articulate the influence of personal life experiences and feelings that arose in this incident. I was also able to own my unique embodied emotional experience in an accepting social environment. Central to this was a willingness to be vulnerable and held by a group of trusted and caring peers, which then created space for me to look at the places I didn't want to look. During the process, one of my classmates pointed out that I used the words *find* and *create* interchangeably to describe how I might navigate similar situations in the future (e.g., I will find/create spaciousness before and during difficult meetings). This helped me to see how I was still trying to find a solution, rather than actually feeling my way into, and through, changed thinking.

Through further reflection, I realized that in this particular incident I was already feeling emotionally sensitive because of an incident with my dog earlier in the week. She had injured her leg while chasing a rogue coyote. Possibly, this was more of a coincidence, given that during my initial internship interview and subsequent meetings, I felt relationally unsettled. From the beginning, there were many instances in which I ignored the emotional aspect of my meaning-making process. However, by feeling through my unique emotional experience in this incident, I was able to see that other, previously unimagined, ways of relating are possible within this more embodied dimension of practice, such as the intimate kinship connection I have with my dog. This hard-to-describe experience of animal-human connection may point to many other ways of feeling our relationships differently, along with new unexplored vistas of human experience (Fook, 2014). Thus, I propose a "post-humanist epistemology of the unknown," which is more aligned with the value of multispecies interdependence for social work practice within an all-encompassing ecological environment (Boetto, 2017). This thinking acknowledges an embodied justice that is important to all living organisms, and therefore always exists in dialogue, without favoring humans (or individual actors or groups) as the central recipients or managers of Earth's natural resources (Boetto, 2017).

This expanded thinking supports moving beyond the limits of words to our shadow dimensions of place and imagination, where my creative strengths become inseparable from my social work strengths and unique embodiment. This personal theory of practice is best described as "be the space you wish to feel (see) in the world" and "don't let the coyote in; learn to converse instead." In this case, "coyote" refers to maintaining an awareness of trickster relations or trickster social work practice that operates on unseen dimensions and creates the illusion of transformation.

Therefore, during this stage of the process, it is important to understand how our unprocessed trauma may be operating on unseen dimensions. As Resmaa Menakem (2017), points out, the trauma associated with whiteness "is a classic example of what therapists call gaslighting, getting people to override their own experience and perceptions by repeating a lie over and over," and then proving it with still more misdirection. Eventually, the lies are widely accepted as essential facts of life, like birth, death, and gravity, and become taken for granted (p. 68). As Menakem emphasizes (p. 13), "we need to understand our body's process of connection and settling. We need to slow ourselves down and learn to lean into uncertainty, rather than away from it. We need to ground ourselves, touch the pain or discomfort inside our trauma, and explore gently" with compassion. Rather than trying to flee, we must stay present with our bodily and emotional discomfort. Not necessarily reliving it or trying to understand it cognitively, but rather providing attention and care, which can open up space for new bodily feelings and thoughts.

Going forward, we need to cultivate an ongoing self-awareness and mindfulness practice to pay attention to the thinking that arises in connection with certain bodily sensations. This can help us see the shift in unsettled emotions and new thinking that leads to feelings of release, joy, hope, or a form of "lightness." I found that this also means opening up to feelings of enjoyment during stage two of the reflection process, further helping me to see how anger, sadness, and joy are not separate entities but come from the same place. As a result of this change in my thinking, I have developed a deep appreciation for this place of limbo and confusion, where the rational and emotional minds meet in creative tension. After lingering in that vulnerable place for a while, I began to see how it creates space to ask the necessary deeper questions, so other ways of feeling and being can emerge—where we channel feelings like anger, listen to it, give it care, and then turn it into a radical act of love and poetry that has the potential to unsettle and instigate future transformation. This is how I learned where the emergent potential is to continuously transform and negotiate the meaning, form, and location of my (our) power, with respect to my embodied perception of safety in any given situation.

Stage two of my reflection process became about what Mezirow (2000) conceptualizes as "transforming our epistemologies, liberating ourselves from that which we are embedded, making that which is object into subject, so that we can 'have it' rather than 'be had' by it" (p. 25). Here is where the human "self" is created and re-created, with a greater understanding of the assumptions supporting our concepts, beliefs, and feelings and those of others. In my practice, I will describe this as a continuous "way-finding" process of "creative and mysterious ongoingness and becomingness" that explores alternative, more liberating, ways of feeling and being human together.

OBSERVATIONS, DISCUSSION, AND SUSTAINING
A CRITICALLY REFLECTIVE FUTURES PRACTICE

Critical reflection, if trusted with the full force of our embodied being, brings us to a point of unsettledness that I have found necessary for understanding how the transformation process works in its mysterious ways. This process requires us to listen deeply and to feel into new territories with humility, vulnerability, courage, and compassion. To find a situational sense of negotiated and equitable "settledness" among the "always unsettled." This is a continuous conversation and dialogue with the many diverse voices present at any given moment (both human and more-than-human). And possibly, from this place of unsettledness, we can relocate and harness the power and creativity of our earthly sociological imagination.

Learning how to integrate critical reflection into ecological social work practice can be the conduit for advancing transformative change within social work, thus requiring "a fundamental reorientation of the philosophical base, including ontological, epistemological, and methodological aspects" that challenges both students and teachers (Boetto, 2017). This can contribute to transformative learning and perspective transformation that can also provide a way forward for developing a different frame of reference for envisioning alternative and sustainable futures, well-being, and the Earth as a holistic entity.

This kind of critical reflection can help us conduct an inquiry in a way that gets us lost and unsettles our notions of ourselves beyond the idea that we are the primary knowers of the world or its primary subjects. This kind of reflection understands that we can only meet the material world halfway because, possibly, we are known by the world as much as we know. For this reason, any reference to holistic transformation or a sustainable future must embrace all forms of knowledge, communication, and intelligence on Earth. This realization has helped me to sense that rational thinking, by itself, might not be able to help social workers understand and prepare for the magnitude of the change we humans face. The growing complexity of the world calls for creative and expanded approaches to practice that can work with the unknown and unseen dimensions, especially in these hyper-digitally connected times.

How might we move beyond our own notions of what's possible toward what Donna Haraway (1998) calls "natureculture"—the inseparability of nature and culture in the shaping of our world and its future? I will continue to consider framing my social work practice as a creative practice that requires active engagement with the environment to produce a sense of shaping imagination happening through matter. The knowledge that arises from this sensual experience is a poetic space that starts with my body. These new worlding explorations introduce a poetics of embodied place and demonstrate the role of imaginative thinking in mediating environmental knowledge and transformation. I will bring more of this spatial, place-based awareness to my critical reflection practice in order to examine the invisible discourses and texts that give meaning to our contextually situated organizing practices. Continuous inquiry into this dimension can bring new thought to a community's material and affective layers, debated histories, and inescapable relation to global flows of power. In a grassroots nonprofit organization centering justice, this kind of active engagement with knowledge is a necessary act of relational accountability to the people historically marginalized by neoliberal and colonial systems.

In letting this reflection settle, I have found that I am learning to adopt a more performative standpoint that is based on a simultaneous understanding, thinking, feeling, observing, and theorizing practice of entangled engagement with the interdependent multispecies world in which we interact. This ambiguous stance can create an exploratory space in which the terms of social interaction and behavior need to be experienced as an experiment. I intend to apply this stance of uncertainty to adopt other modes of knowing to analyze those aspects of the human condition that science cannot easily illuminate.

Therefore, I hope to continue learning about future-oriented approaches to critical reflection that involve an ongoing examination of assumptions and emotions about possible futures, and an exploration of new roles, perspectives, and ways to act on new insights (Pouru-Mikkola & Wilenius, 2021). Donna Haraway (1998) insists on placing a metaphorical reliance on the sensory system of "vision" to help avoid binary oppositions. This means attending to the embodied nature of all vision-based discourses to "reclaim the sensory system that has been used to signify a leap out of the marked body and into a conquering gaze from nowhere".

This gaze often attempts to control, own, or have power over, as it defines objectivity, inscribes and marks bodies, and claims what is seen and not seen, all while escaping representation or accountability. In the United States, this gaze controls the future and often represents the "unmarked positions of man and white." (p. 581).

Introducing a critically reflective approach to futures-based social work might help us keep a keen eye on the power relations of possible futures and the potential "colonial" aspects of privileged groups' making decisions about the future for everyone (Nissen, 2020). This practice is concerned with widening the voices that participate in defining and creating what a successful future might be. Thus, integrating a feminist new-materialist futures lens into the critical reflection process has the potential to transform the interconnected dimension of today's challenges as well as the eco-sociological imagination, with particular attention to the everyday practices, social relations, and place-based spaces of creativity and social reproduction. This might point to a materialist rewriting of practice, and possibly of social work education as a whole.

Finally, while reflecting on our efforts to decolonize during this time, we might concur with Indigenous thinkers who understand that decolonization is something the Earth undertakes on its own accord. Possibly, decolonization might be understood as a biocultural process that cannot be grounded solely in human terms. Instead, decolonial praxis is seen as a matter of energy, molecules, and material conditions coming together for specific beings to take form (Snaza, 2020). Possibly, this more-than-human world "resists being reduced to a mere source of consumption because it is not mother, matter, or mutter, but coyote, or a figure of the always problematic . . . an always potent tie between meaning and bodies" (Haraway, 1988, p. 596). Thus, our aspirations for accountability necessitate seeing the Earth as a "coded trickster" with whom we must learn to converse. And, to decolonize the human, we must sense and feel ourselves differently.

REFERENCES

Alexander, J., & Fernandez, K. (2021). The impact of neoliberalism on civil society and nonprofit advocacy. *Nonprofit Policy Forum*, 12(2), 367–394. https://doi.org/10.1515/npf-2020-0016.

Boetto, H. (2017). A transformative eco-social model: Challenging modernist assumptions in social work, *British Journal of Social Work*, 47(1), 48–67. https://doi.org/10.1093/bjsw/bcw149.

Fook, J. (2012). The challenges of creating critically reflective groups. *Social Work with Groups*, *35*(3), 218–234, https://doi.org/10.1080/01609513.2011.624375.

Fook, J. (2014). The meaning of animals in women's lives: The importance of the "domestic" realm to social work. In T. Ryan (Eds.), *Animals in Social Work* (pp. 18–31). London: Palgrave Macmillan.

Fook, J., & Gardner, F. (2007). *Practising critical reflection: A resource handbook*. Maidenhead, UK: Open University Press.

Haraway, D. (1988). Situated knowledges: The science question in feminism and the privilege of partial perspective. *Feminist Studies*, *14*(3), 575–599. https://doi.org/10.2307/3178066.

Menakem, R. (2017). *My grandmother's hands: Racialized trauma and the pathway to mending our hearts and bodies*. Las Vegas, NV: Central Recovery.

Mezirow, J. (2000). Learning to think like an adult: Core concepts of transformation theory. In J. Mezirow & Associates (Eds.), *Learning as transformation: Critical perspectives on a theory in progress* (pp. 3–33). San Francisco: Jossey-Bass.

Morley, C., & O'Bree, C. (2021). Critical reflection: An imperative skill for social work practice in neoliberal organisations? *Social Sciences*, *10*(3), 97. https://doi.org/10.3390/socsci10030097.

Nissen, L. (2020). Social work and the future in a post–COVID 19 world: A foresight lens and a call to action for the profession. *Journal of Technology in Human Services*, *38*(4), 309–330, https://doi.org/10.1080/15228835.2020.1796892.

Pouru-Mikkola, L. & Wilenius, M. (2021) Building individual futures capacity through transformative futures learning. *Futures*, *132*. https://doi.org/10.1016/j.futures.2021.102804.

Snaza, N. (2020). Biopolitics without bodies: Feminism and the feeling of life. *Feminist Studies*, *46*(1), 178–203. https://doi.org/10.1353/fem.2020.0017.

Yellow Bird, M. (2015, July). Evidence-based healing practices older than Columbus [Video]. https://www.youtube.com/watch?v=At72EOwtf5M.

17

TRANSFORMATIVE SOCIAL WORK EDUCATION

Using Critical Reflection to Develop Culturally Safe Practice

CHRISTINE MORLEY AND RATNA BEEKMAN

We live in times that are often described as uncertain and unprecedented (see, for example, Afrouz, 2021, p. 561). The global climate emergency, coinciding with the COVID-19 global pandemic, which has unfolded against the ongoing assault of neoliberalism and related growing authoritarianism, has produced new forms of inequality and injustice. Within this context, social work must be transformative if it to be useful in responding to emerging and future social problems (Morley, 2020b; Morley et al., 2020).

Transformative education involves cultivating "deep learning that confronts and challenges taken-for-granted assumptions" (Morley et al., 2020, p. 5). According to Giroux (2011, p. 3), transformative education "is essential for a democratic society and fundamental to creating the conditions for producing citizens who are critical, self-reflective, knowledgeable, and willing to make moral judgments and act in a socially responsible way." Since most social work value statements, education standards, and codes of ethics discuss social work as having a mandate to foster "social justice, human rights, collective responsibility and respect for diversities" (see, for example, IFSW, 2014), transformative education is essential to help students think beyond hegemonic discourses that lead to victim blaming, justify inequality, and obscure the structural causes of oppression (Morley & O'Bree, 2021).

According to O'Sullivan et al. (2002, p. 11), "Transformative learning involves experiencing a deep, structural shift in the basic premise of thought, feelings, and actions" (see also Greenhill et al., 2018; Mezirow, 1991). Informed by the work of Habermas, Mezirow (2003, p. 58) asserts that transformative learning "transforms problematic frames of reference—sets of fixed assumptions and expectations (habits of mind, meaning perspectives, mindsets)—to make them more inclusive, discriminating, open, reflective, and emotionally able to change." Cranton (2002, p. 64, cited in Jones, 2009, p. 10) provides a clear outline of this process: "At its core, transformative learning theory is elegantly simple. Through some event, which could be as traumatic as losing a job or as ordinary as an unexpected question, an individual becomes aware of holding a limiting or distorted view. If the individual critically examines this view, opens herself [sic] to alternatives, and consequently changes the way she sees things, she has transformed some part of how she makes meaning out of the world."

Bass et al. (2017) argue that "self-awareness, reflection, critical reflection, reflexivity and reflective practice" are core components that facilitate transformative learning (p. 231). They see critical reflection as a higher-order skill, involving examination of values, beliefs, and assumptions that inform practice, that is essential to transformative learning and education. They suggest it is necessary to reflect both inwardly (on personal/professional beliefs) and outwardly (on broader social/political conditions) to help develop changes in perspective that enable learning to be transformative. Fook (2016) adds postmodernism, deconstruction, and critical social theory to this mix as essential ingredients for transformative learning (see also Beres, 2019, p. 281). Brookfield's (see, for example, 2005) work, too, in synthesizing insights from a range of critical theorists (including Marx, Gramsci, Foucault, Habermas, and Marcuse), has been used to inform critically reflective pedagogies that cultivate transformative learning in social work (Morley, 2020a).

Brookfield (2005) adopts critical theories over other approaches because they explain "not just how the world is but also how it might be changed for the better" (p. 7). A better world, Brookfield posits, is one in which "adult education can contribute to building a society organized according to democratic values of fairness, justice, and compassion" (pp. 7–8). Transformative education, informed by critical theory involves "learning to recognize and challenge ideology . . . learning to uncover and counter hegemony, learning to unmask power, learning to overcome alienation . . . learning to pursue liberation, learning to reclaim reason, and learning to practice democracy" (p. 39). Pedagogic innovations such as critical reflection, therefore, have a "transformative impetus" that enables students to engage with the "powers of critical thinking so that they can critique the interlocking systems of oppression embedded in contemporary society" (p. 353). From this perspective, transformative education is "highly directive" and "inherently political" as it focuses on emancipatory outcomes and freedom as primary goals of critical theories (p. 354).

Bay and Macfarlane (2011, p. 756) similarly observe that critical education provides a "transformative process [that] generates . . . alternative approaches [that promote] practices of freedom, autonomy and social responsibility." Carrington and Selva (2010) similarly emphasize the important contribution that critical theories make to transforming knowledge. Fook (2004) concurs, asserting that critical reflection as a process assists with deconstructing and reconstructing ways of knowing and thinking, and that this can lead to change that enables transformative social work practice. For the process of critical reflection to be transformative, Fook (2004, p. 22) argues that individuals need to overcome "feelings of fatalism" that disrupt a sense of agency to enact change. She considers that by changing these thoughts, the process of critical reflection can liberate individuals from unhelpful constructions. Furthermore, she considers that when individuals locate their experiences within social environments, critical reflection can result in action that brings forth change within broader communities, creating transformative possibilities (Fook, 2004).

Jones (2020) identifies critical reflection and dialogue as essential features of transformative learning. Das and Anand (2014) suggest that critical reflection can transform learning to be deeper and more meaningful, enabling new insights to occur by exploring values and knowledge. However, they note that "whilst most social work educators are committed to the use of reflective processes and can identify when transformative learning occurs, the challenge is to identify and describe the processes involved" (Das & Anand, 2014, p. 111). Similarly, they note that "there is limited detailed description of processes that promote a more critical form of reflection and reflexivity for teaching and learning" (p. 110, citing Pawar et al., 2004, and Wehbi, 2009). Gardner (2021, p. 154), too, observes that "what [transformative education] actually looks like in a practical, real world, sense" is not well articulated. She asks: "How, in other words, does this play out in the lives of students (i.e. the process of transformation) and what, if anything, is happening in the classroom that supports this change?"

Hence, while there is a growing body of literature that suggests that critical reflection can foster transformative learning among social work students, less is known about how this occurs. With few exceptions (see Fook & Beres, 2019, the research on critical reflection as a transformative pedagogic process is largely written from the perspective of educators, with little known about students' perspectives on engaging in transformative learning in social work. This chapter contributes to addressing these gaps by (1) exploring how Ratna (a former student of Christine) engaged in a critically reflective research project that resulted in transformative learning and (2) reflecting on Ratna's experience of being supervised by Christine, who was trying to facilitate transformative education. Our reflections emerged in the context of Ratna's Honors project aiming to improve culturally safe practice in social work.

CULTURAL SAFETY AS A TRANSFORMATIVE PRACTICE

Culturally safe practice involves working across difference and necessitates critical reflection on one's own positionality. While we are aware of the critiques that exist about the use of the terms *safe* or *safety*, particularly in relation to creating "safe [teaching] spaces" that potentially limit the effectiveness of critical pedagogies and transformative learning (see, for example, Arao & Clemens, 2013; Gayle et al., 2013), the term (and concept) '*cultural safety* is used here intentionally, as it is widely adopted and preferred, particularly in countries like Australia and New Zealand (Curtis et al., 2019; Duthie, 2019). The preference for cultural safety lies in the fact that the concept is Indigenous developed and led and acknowledges power imbalances as a barrier to effective practice (Laverty et al., 2017). Unlike other practices, such as cultural competence, cultural safety seeks to restore power imbalances through a process of critical reflection in which the practitioner explores how their own cultural foundations may affect service delivery. Laverty et al. further explain that the practitioner strives for a critical awareness of difference, demonstrating an under-standing of decolonizing practice by acknowledging these inherent power dynamics. The practitioner actively implements this self-critical stance by allowing the recipients of care to define what safety means. Culturally safe practice, then, occurs when the recipients of a service are involved in the decision-making process of their care and support needs. Therefore, a defining and distinguishing feature of cultural safety is its position-ing of the practitioner as a critically reflective agent, which enhances our understanding of our own cultural beliefs and assumptions that affect our practice. This awareness enables the development of alterna-tive ways of knowing, being, and doing (Bennett et al., 2011). Similar to the gap in knowledge about how critical reflection results in transfor-mative learning, Ratna's research aimed to transform social work prac-tice by developing a framework detailing how to meaningfully embed culturally safe principles.

Ratna's research had clear transformative intent in seeking to improve practitioners' cultural safety literacy. She recognized that social workers have participated in policies and practices that have resulted in discrim-ination against and oppression of Aboriginal and Torres Strait Islander peoples (Bennett, 2013). She contended that improving culturally safe practice of non-Indigenous workers would contribute toward addressing social work's colonialist history and decolonizing practice. She further elaborates the transformative aims of her research below.

RATNA

Legislation and policies have unjustly affected Aboriginal and Torres Strait Islander peoples, and health professionals (including social workers) have played an active role in causing harm (Bennett, 2013; Briskman, 2014; Sousa & Almeida, 2016). Social workers' participation in harmful prac-tices has resulted in Aboriginal and Torres Strait Islander peoples' feeling suspicious and distrustful toward social workers (Australian Association of Social Workers, 2016; Bennett, 2013; Briskman, 2014). However, because of the intergenerational disadvantages experienced by many Aboriginal and Torres Strait Islander peoples, a disproportionate number come into contact with social work services (Green & Baldry, 2013; Mendes, 2005). These relationships remain contentious for both social work practitioners and Aboriginal and Torres Strait Islander peoples. This has been exacerbated by colonizing forms of social work that valorize Western knowledge systems and practices (Bennett, 2015; Green & Baldry, 2008). Social workers need to action a clearer plan for decolonizing practice and develop culturally appropriate service delivery (Walter et al., 2011) in order to contribute to improving the health and well-being of Aboriginal and Torres Strait Islander peoples (Griffiths et al., 2016; Saggers et al., 2011).

CHRISTINE

Fook (2004) observes that critical reflection can be effective in working with Aboriginal students because they sometimes find mainstream social work curriculum to arise from a different worldview. For learning to be meaningful, Fook (2004, p. 28) suggests, "we must engage in a process of developing their own version of social work from their own sets of experiences . . . reconstructing their identities as Aboriginal social workers, [and] developing a picture of Aboriginal Social Work along the way"—a process that Fook acknowledges results in simultaneous transformation of her own framework.

CHRISTINE'S CRITICAL INCIDENT

BACKGROUND AND CONTEXT

I assumed Ratna might have something like Fook's (2004) approach in mind for her research. I had known Ratna for a number of years, and she had impressed me as an undergraduate. She was very bright, conscientious, an excellent contributor to class discussion, and in my view, a student who understood the purpose and vision of critical social work. I had invited her to attend lectures on critical reflection, which Das and Anand (2014) assert can enable deconstruction through the questioning of power and dominant discourses.

I had also specifically discussed Ratna's research project with her and was struck by her excitement and enthusiasm for improving culturally safe social work practice. The project she had outlined aligned with my interests of advancing critical practice and decolonizing social work, and I was keen to review her proposal.

CRITICAL INCIDENT DESCRIPTION

When I started reading Ratna's research proposal, I began to feel concerned. There were statements about Aboriginal social work practitioners that assumed homogeneity. She talked about "building trusting and respectful relationships with Aboriginal social work practitioners" to gain their knowledge, which sounded instrumental, contrived, and exploitative (albeit inadvertently). The proposed design to conduct face-to-face interviews seemed to have been developed without consultation with Aboriginal people, and even though the process included open-ended questions, I remained concerned about research about Aboriginal people that was owned and controlled by a non-Indigenous researcher who was going to be involved (although unconsciously) in potentially appropriating Aboriginal peoples' knowledges, which has happened too often, usually without appropriate attribution (Bennett, 2013).

I felt ungenerous for judging Ratna's first attempt so harshly and somewhat worried that my feedback would crush her enthusiasm or not be perceived as helpful. Damianakis (2020, p. 2026) notes that "student receptivity is a frequently cited barrier to successful implementation of transformative learning practices, noting that students not ready to transform will resist." I worried about this, but overwhelmingly, I felt a sense of responsibility to provide critical feedback. I recognized this was an opportunity for us both to engage in transformative education. As Duthie (2019, p. 114) suggests, "non-Indigenous social work educators . . . have a responsibility to . . . step up, embrace, and contribute to learning and teaching in the Indigenous space."

INITIAL REFLECTION

Jones (2020) suggests that the process of critically reflecting on assumptions that are usually not questioned is potentially transformative and involves exposing learners to new perspectives. He provides an example from his own teaching in which transformative learning strategies were used to ensure that issues of culture and racism were considered critically, rather than remaining unquestioned.

The process of critical reflection often begins with a "disorientating dilemma" (Damianakis et al., 2020; Greenhill et al., 2018; Mezirow, 1990, 2012) that ultimately leads to a shift in consciousness. Students have used the term *cultural border crossing* (Damianakis et al., 2020, p. 2018) to describe new learning, both figuratively and literally, that emerged during the process of transformative learning.

Jones (2020) suggests: "Transformation becomes possible where an experience that is incongruent with our existing meaning structures leads to critical reflection upon previously taken-for-granted assumptions" (p. 491). However, "simply reflecting upon or even changing one's meaning perspective is not sufficient for transformative learning to have taken place. Action is also required, in the sense of the enactment of the altered perspective in the social world" (p. 492). To support transformation and facilitate action, clear and open communication between teacher and students is required (Das & Anand, 2014; Parra et al., 2015). Educators' modeling of the process of deconstruction and critical questioning is also recommended (Brookfield, 2017; Das & Anand, 2014).

I reread Ratna's proposal with a view to inviting her to consider issues of culture, power, ethnocentrism, and privilege. I inserted questions into her proposal to prompt critical reflection, such as:

- How might this practice be considered cultural appropriation of Aboriginal knowledge to benefit non-Indigenous practitioners?
- How might expecting Aboriginal practitioners to read and comment on transcripts load them with a burden to contribute to your research?
- What's in it [i.e., participation] for Aboriginal people?
- How might stating that "Aboriginal people have different knowledge" serve to other them and their experiences? How might you instead seek to decenter whiteness in social work?

While much adult learning is self-directed, with "fully participatory, inclusive [and democratic] conversations" being possible, Brookfield (2005, pp. 357–358) suggests that sometimes a more strongly interventionist approach is needed, requiring the educator to adopt a leadership role to bring a critical perspective into the dialogue. This process requires brave conversations that use critical pedagogy intentionally (Jones, 2020) and that capture the tension between experimentation and risk (Brookfield, 1995, p. 42) as educators to try to understand and simultaneously challenge students' experiences in ways that create possibilities for transformative learning. In practical terms, Jones (2020, p. 497) suggests "this means being prepared to create disruptive, disorienting learning experiences, and equipping students with the skills required to then use those challenging experiences to look critically at society, but also to examine their own taken-for-granted assumptions and worldviews through critical reflection"; bell hooks similarly describes the need to confront students with the injuries of privilege and prejudice (Noble, 2020). Kumashiro talks about the need to teach through crises that are created by confrontation (Kaighin, 2020).

"Speaking authentically" is central to facilitating this type of transformative education (Brookfield, 2017). Hence, the final comment in my feedback was along the lines of "I don't think this research can proceed without a team of Aboriginal practitioners—who would need to lead it." Like Beres (2019, p. 285), I felt a bit "vulnerable . . . about providing this feedback, as there is no guarantee students will understand or appreciate the feedback in the spirit it is offered, but I was also cognizant that this is an essential component of transformative teaching." I also concur with Duthie (2019, p. 115), who argues that "non-Indigenous academics [students and practitioners] need to take responsibility for their own learning of Indigenous history and ways of Knowing, Being, and Doing," rather than expecting Aboriginal people to educate non-Indigenous practitioners.

RATNA'S CRITICAL INCIDENT

RESPONSE TO FEEDBACK

While it was unsettling and confronting to receive this feedback, it was important to uncover dominant ways of thinking. Reading the feedback, which initially provoked a strong emotional reaction, actually motivated me to further engage with the critical reflective process. It strengthened my commitment to find and learn new ways of thinking. By reflecting on the feedback, I was able to shift my thinking. Fortunately, like the students in Damianakis's (2020) study, I recognized that being asked the hard questions, being challenged in a supportive way, and stepping out of my comfort zone were part of the transformative learning necessary for me to advance this research.

I think it is important to mention that my supervisor supported me through this process by modeling critical reflection. I was provided with a safe, trusting, nonjudgmental environment to explore some of those inherent assumptions. I also felt that Christine had treated me respectfully and as a colleague. Das and Anand (2014) note that the minimization of power relations between academic staff and students helps to build a relationship that cultivates transformative learning. Being personally ready for change and having a safe and supportive environment and relationship with my supervisor meant that I could begin to locate unconscious biases and assumptions, reconsider dominant beliefs, and start the process of "unlearning" to develop new ways of viewing.

INITIAL REFLECTION

My initial thinking about interviewing Aboriginal social work practitioners and documenting their perspectives was grounded in dominant Western practice frameworks. My awareness of the need to change the research became a critical incident for me. As Carrington and Selva (2010) note, locating and reflecting on unknown prejudices can highlight the need to deconstruct knowledge, which provides opportunities for transformation.

My initial approach was driven by my first placement in a family intervention service. Here I observed other workers' culturally ignorant practices that were inconsistent with my values of nonjudgment and respect for all persons. There was a dichotomy between workers' being encouraged to practice within a "culturally inclusive" model and, at the same time, being required to work using Western models of practice. This resulted in tensions for workers, whereby they reverted to their default, dominant cultural approach, which at times resulted in oppressive practices. Aboriginal families were assessed and judged from a Western perspective, with workers making comments such as "they've gone on sorry business or walkabout for however long, as they do"; and "how are we supposed to help them if they don't understand our systems?" I felt personally challenged by these views and wondered how we could bolster culturally inclusive practice.

My initial response was to seek answers from Aboriginal practitioners who had been successful in integrating their cultural knowledge into practice. My intention was to gain their perspectives to guide non-Indigenous practitioners, like me, who may seek to partner in the struggle against colonization. This new understanding, I thought, would also be relevant for how we work with Aboriginal and/or Torres Strait Islander peoples and families in the service user context, thereby contributing to improved culturally appropriate services.

Reflecting on this and having learned more about the true history of Australia and Aboriginal and Torres Strait Islander cultures, I made two key assumptions: (1) I had a different view from white Australians and (2) coming from another country, and thereby privileging my identity, I could approach the learning from a different, non-Australian perspective. Enthusiastically, I drafted an initial proposal to justify this method of research, outlining my intentions and motivations. My supervisor feedback on this draft proposal then prompted a process of critical reflection to challenge my own dominant cultural views. To discover that my use of language was oppressive, dominant, and at times discriminatory was confronting and required deeper analysis.

METHODOLOGY

Critically reflecting on my own experiences as a social work practitioner became a focus of this research and, as such, I became the sole research participant. I used a qualitative research approach, underpinned by a critical constructivist paradigm (Denzin & Lincoln, 2011), in which I examined how my experiences were shaped by social and cultural constructions of Aboriginal and Torres Strait Islander peoples. Using a critically reflective paradigm, I focused on exploring and analyzing how

I made meaning of personal experiences and how I positioned myself in the experience, exploring alternative perspectives (Fook & Gardner, 2007). To conceptualize possibilities for change, I used postmodern theories to examine my participation in discourses and my use of language (Morley, 2014b). Changing my participation in the discourses required a critical postmodernist approach, which provided the space to develop new ways of thinking about my responses to these constructs and find ways to reject dominant paradigms (Fook, 2016; Morley, 2014b; Morley & Macfarlane, 2012).

The study was premised on the idea that the new knowledge generated from critical reflection on self can have broader implications for the ways other practitioners work (Morley, 2014a, p. 70) and thus held transformative possibilities. It employed Fook's (2016, p. 128) model of deconstruction/reconstruction, with a specific focus on the critical incident technique for developing new knowledge. The main research question for the study became: How might critical reflection enhance culturally safe practice?

After identifying a critical incident, the first step in the critical reflection process involves a process of deconstruction, questioning the implicit assumptions that underpin practice, with the aim of exposing how we hold onto dominant discourses (Morley, 2016, p. 28). I then embarked on a process of reconstruction to develop alternative ways of thinking (Fook, 2016). This process enabled me to find alternative ways of knowing, thinking, and doing, thereby creating and gaining new knowledge and rejecting universal knowledge as the norm (Fook & Gardner, 2007). Developing new knowledge from reflecting on my critical incident allowed me to make changes to my thinking and my approach to practice. This addressed the aim of this research by contributing to improving practice approaches toward cultural safety.

DECONSTRUCTION

Initial deconstruction of my narrative revealed little consideration for cultural diversity or power. Through critical reflection, prompted and guided by my supervisor, I became aware of several implicit assumptions made based on ethnocentric and hegemonic discourses. For example, I recognized that I had positioned myself as the expert in designing a research project about Aboriginal practitioners, without culturally appropriate consultation. Thus, even though my approach stemmed from genuine curiosity, by projecting my views onto others, I risked objectifying Aboriginal people (Hollinsworth, 2006; Land, 2015). I realized how my approach to the research was embedded within dominant discourses (Fook, 2016). My narrative was shaped by assumptions that doing research with Aboriginal practitioners as a non-Indigenous worker would be a positive step toward integrating practice and working together.

Positioning myself as "coming from another country" legitimized my intentions to learn (as a non-Australian) about Aboriginal culture and enabled me to construct myself as different from white Australians. Seeing myself as different (from the racists and colonizers) enabled me to reinforce my perception of myself as nonracist. I also assumed that Aboriginal practitioners would want to partner with me to share their cultural knowledge with non-Indigenous people for the "greater good" of social work practice. This reproduces the invisible position of privilege and power that often remains unchallenged (Fredericks, 2008; Moreton-Robinson, 1999). Justifying my research by assuming that Aboriginal practitioners preferred to share knowledge with someone from another country, rather than with white Australians, permitted me to privilege my learning and access to cultural knowledge, even if used for the benefit of my practice and the practice of other non-Indigenous social work practitioners (Briskman, 2014, p. 73).

The aim of this research was to enhance my own and other non-Indigenous practitioners' knowledge; consequently, I did not consider the benefits (or detriments) for Aboriginal people. I assumed that Aboriginal practitioners would be happy to educate non-Indigenous practitioners, thereby placing the responsibility for the cultural education of non-Indigenous people on Aboriginal people (Green et al., 2013). These identified assumptions were based on my genuine belief, at that time, that I could contribute to creating a more culturally inclusive social work environment by incorporating new knowledge from an Aboriginal perspective (Green et al., 2016).

Critical reflection reveals this assumption as flawed since Indigenous people are the most (over)researched population worldwide and historically (Fredericks, 2008). Research is often done *to* Indigenous peoples, which has resulted in their objectification, with questionable benefit for them (Briskman, 2014; Yu, 2011). The homogenizing of Aboriginal people and presenting of their culture as one voice creates a false perception and ignores their diversity (Cowlishaw, 2014, p. 65; Paradies et al., 2008). I essentialized Aboriginal people as having "the right way," which I wanted to know about, so that I could replicate it and "do" culturally safe practice—thereby contradicting the principles of culturally safe practice.

My failure to recognize how research should respond to the interests and needs of Indigenous peoples and local communities (Australian Institute of Aboriginal and Torres Strait Islander Studies, 2017; Yu, 2011) was of great concern to me. Deconstruction of the incident has highlighted how my initial approach to the research proposal was limited and has forced me to rethink the ways in which I seek to gain cultural knowledge.

RECONSTRUCTION

Reconstruction enabled me to reinterpret my narrative, change my thinking, and develop alternative views (Fook, 2016; Morley & O'Connor, 2016). I put aside my initial work and started again. Interrogating the colonizing approach I had unwittingly adopted challenged the invisible discourses that were deeply rooted in my initial approach. Highlighting my position as a non-Indigenous researcher and its assumed power, control, and privilege made me question how my role could undermine and suppress Aboriginal people (Fredericks, 2008). Through this learning, and by challenging my position of dominance, I recommitted to anti-colonizing practice. This included ensuring that I did not unintentionally appropriate knowledge from Aboriginal people (Fredericks, 2008) and emphasizing that research involving Aboriginal people should aim to bolster their interests (Briskman, 2014, p. 218; Butler & Butler, 2015, p. 8). Developing my aptitude for cultural safety by problematizing the role of non-Indigenous researchers was transformative, pointing to new approaches and understandings in social work practice.

Positioning myself as a non-Indigenous researcher, I realized the need to learn more about my own positionality and how this affects my practice. Reflecting on my own Dutch cultural background (not just ethnicity, but social class, gender, sexuality, age, ability status, and other forms of difference) enabled me to value diversity and reject homogenizing views of Aboriginal and Torres Strait Islander peoples.

Rejecting binary thinking and questioning dominant views allowed me to explore different perspectives, which made me rethink the responsibility to gain cultural knowledge. By taking responsibility for educating myself about the impacts of racism and colonization on Aboriginal and Torres Strait Islander peoples, as well as their diverse histories and knowledge, I let go of expecting Aboriginal and Torres Strait Islander peoples to act as educators of non-Indigenous people (Duthie, 2019; Green et al., 2016; Hendrick & Young, 2018). Reconsidering my position as a white, non-Indigenous social worker provided new insights into how I might be able to help, support, and assist in research, while simultaneously recognizing that collaboration needs to be led and defined by Aboriginal people and needs to be of benefit to them (Bennett, 2015; Briskman, 2014). This approach is consistent with cultural safety, which identifies decolonizing methods of research as ways to improve practice and better respond to cultural diversity (Ramsden, 2002). It became clear that taking a critically reflective approach to the research, thereby improving and changing non-Indigenous practice, might benefit Aboriginal and Torres Strait Islander peoples by creating more culturally safe spaces.

OUTCOMES AND DISCUSSION

Throughout this journey I kept a journal, and through a process of critical reflection, I questioned and examined my own positionality and implicit assumptions, linking these with my values of becoming a critical and culturally safe practitioner. As with the students in Damianakis et al.'s (2020) study, my own experience of transformative learning "involved conflict, deeply felt emotions and tensions (ie: disorienting dilemmas)," yet by the end of the research process, the "growth" was "positive" and "felt justified" (p. 2025). The transformative research process allowed space to unpack and reflect on the culture, positionality, dominant social constructs, and hegemonic assumptions embedded within my social biography, challenge dominant views and unconscious biases, and look for alternative approaches to create and develop new knowledge and ways of thinking about how to embody culturally safe practice.

Ultimately, the critical reflective process highlighted the dominant ways of thinking in my initial account, which, if left uncovered and unchallenged, could contribute to the continuation of domination and power inequalities (Bender et al., 2010; Fook, 2002, p. 41). Critical reflection provided me with significant opportunities for transformative learning by developing practices more aligned with my espoused values (Fook, 2016).

By offering practical strategies to generate new understanding, my intention is to contribute to existing social work knowledge around critical reflection and cultural safety, particularly from the perspective of a learner engaged in this process. I hope I have demonstrated how engaging in critical reflection can enhance one's understanding of self and work toward becoming a culturally safe practitioner—and person.

CONCLUSION

This chapter has attempted to provide an example of how critical reflection can foster transformation and, in particular, how it might be used to foster culturally safe practice. Ratna has articulated her own transformative process for becoming a culturally safe social work practitioner that can be instructive for other non-Indigenous practitioners who are committed to becoming allies of Aboriginal and Torres Strait Islander peoples in the struggle for justice against ongoing racism and colonization. Transformative education enabled Ratna to develop and embody culturally safe practices that are committed to acting in solidarity (as a non-Indigenous person) with Aboriginal and Torres Strait Islander peoples. Her research makes an important contribution to improving culturally safe practices and outlines a critically reflective approach to decolonizing social work.

Consistent with Mezirow, we have argued that intentional transformative educational practice has the potential to create students and practitioners who "are more open, inclusive and critically aware." Ultimately, we concur with Jones (2020, p. 497) that a "critically transformative approach to social work education might help to create the foundation for future social work practice which is oriented toward the progressive and emancipatory." This is particularly important within contemporary contexts that are increasingly divided, complex, and uncertain.

REFERENCES

Afrouz, R. (2021). Approaching uncertainty in social work education, a lesson from COVID-19 pandemic. *Qualitative Social Work, 20*(1–2), 561–567. https://doi.org/10.1177/1473325020981078.

Arao, B., & Clemens, K. (2013). From safe spaces to brave spaces. In L. Landreman (Ed.), *The art of effective facilitation: Reflections from social justice educators* (pp. 135–150). Sterling, VA: Stylus.

Australian Association of Social Workers. (2016). *Preparing for culturally responsive and inclusive social work practice in Australia: Working with Aboriginal and Torres Strait Islander peoples.* https://www.aasw.asn.au/document/item/7006.

Australian Institute of Aboriginal and Torres Strait Islander Studies. (2017). *Guidelines for ethical research in Australian Indigenous studies (GERAIS).* https://aiatsis.gov.au/research/ethical-research/guidelines-ethical-research-australian-indigenous-studies.

Bass, J., Fenwick, J., & Sidebotham, M. (2017). Development of a model of holistic reflection to facilitate transformative learning in student midwives. *Women and Birth, 30,* 227–235. https://dx.doi.org/10.1016/j.wombi.2017.02.010.

Bay, U., & Macfarlane, S. (2011). Teaching critical reflection: A tool for transformative learning in social work. *Social Work Education, 30*(7), 745–758. https://doi.org.10.1080/02615479.2010.516429.

Bender, K., Negi, N., & Fowler, D. (2010). Exploring the relationship between self-awareness and student commitment and understanding of culturally responsive social work practice. *Journal of Ethnic & Cultural Diversity in Social Work, 19*(1), 34–53. https://doi.org/10.1080/15313200903531990.

Bennett, B. (2013). The importance of Aboriginal and Torres Strait Islander history for social work students and graduates. In B. Bennett, S. Green, S. Gilbert, & D. Bessarab (Eds.), *Our voices: Aboriginal and Torres Strait Islander social work* (pp. 1–25). South Yarra, Australia: Palgrave Macmillan.

Bennett, B. (2015). Stop deploying your white privilege on me! Aboriginal and Torres Strait Islander engagement with the Australian Association of Social Workers. *Australian Social Work, 68*(1), 19–31. https://doi.org/10.1080/0312407X.2013.840325.

Beres, L. (2019). Valuing critical reflection and narratives in professional practice wisdom. In J. Higgs (Ed.), *Practice wisdom: Values and interpretations* (pp. 277–288). Leiden, Netherlands: Brill Sense.

Béres, L., & Fook, J. (2019). *Learning critical reflection: Experiences of the transformative learning process.* London: Taylor & Francis Group.

Briskman, L. (2014). *Social work with Indigenous communities: A human rights approach* (2nd ed). Alexandria, Australia: Federation Press.

Brookfield, S. (1995). *Becoming a critically reflective teacher.* San Francisco: Jossey-Bass.

Brookfield, S. (2005). *The power of critical theory for adult learning and teaching.* Maidenhead, UK: Open University Press.

Brookfield, S. (2017). *Becoming a critically reflective teacher* (2nd ed.). San Francisco: Jossey-Bass.

Butler, W. B., & Butler, N. (2015). From fear and division to true reconciliation. In C. Fejo-King & J. Poona (Eds.), *Reconciliation and Australian social work: Past and current experiences informing future practice* (pp. 7–32). Torrens, Australia: Magpie Goose.

Carrington, S., & Selva, G. (2010). Critical social theory and transformative learning: Evidence in pre-service teachers' service-learning reflection logs. *Higher Education Research & Development, 29*(1), 45–57. https://doi.org.10.1080/07294360903421384.

Cowlishaw, G. (2014). Racial positioning, privilege and public debate. In A. Moreton-Robinson (Ed.), *Whitening race: Essays in social and cultural criticism* (pp. 59–74). Canberra, Australia: Aboriginal Studies.

Cranton, P. (2002). Teaching for transformation. *New Directions for Adult and Continuing Education, 93*, 63-71. https://doi.org/10.1002/ace.50.

Curtis, E., Jones, R., Tipene-Leach, D., Walker, C., Loring, B., Paine, S. J., & Reid, P. (2019). Why cultural safety rather than cultural competency is required to achieve health equity: A literature review and recommended definition. *International Journal for Equity in Health, 18*(174). https://doi.org/10.1186/s12939-019-1082-3.

Damianakis, T., Barrett, B., Archer-Kuhn, B., Samson, P. L., Matin, S., & Ahern, C. (2020). Transformative learning in graduate education: Masters of social work students' experiences of personal and professional learning. *Studies in Higher Education, 45*(9), 2011–2029. https://doi.org/10.1080/03075079.2019.1650735.

Das, D., & Anand, J. C. (2014). Strategies for critical reflection in international contexts for social work students. *International Social Work, 57*(2), 109–120. https://doi.org/10.1177/0020872812443693.

Denzin, N., & Lincoln, Y. (2011). *The handbook of qualitative research* (4th ed). Thousand Oaks, CA: Sage.

Duthie, D., (2019). Embedding Indigenous knowledges and cultural safety in social work curricula. *Australian Social Work, 72*(1), 113–116. https://doi.org/10.1080/0312407X.2018.1534978.

Fook, J. (2002). *Social work: Critical theory and practice*. London: Sage.

Fook, J. (2004). Critical reflection and transformative possibilities. In L. Davies & P. Leonard (Eds.), *Social work in a corporate era: Practices of power and resistance* (pp. 16–30). London: Routledge.

Fook, J. (2016). *Social work: A critical approach to practice* (3rd ed). London: Sage.

Fook, J., & Gardner, F. (2007). *Practising critical reflection: A handbook*. Maidenhead, UK: Open University Press.

Fredericks, B. (2008). Making an impact researching with Australian Aboriginal and Torres Strait Islander peoples. *Studies in Learning, Evaluation, Innovation and Development, 5*(1), pp. 24–33. https://eprints.qut.edu.au/224906/.

Gardner, P. (2021). Contemplative pedagogy: Fostering transformation learning in a critical service-learning course. *Journal of Experimental Education, 44*(2), 152–166. https://doi.org.10.1177/1053825920952086.

Gayle, B. M., Cortez, D., & Preiss, R. W. (2013). Safe spaces, difficult dialogues, and critical thinking. *International Journal for the Scholarship of Teaching and Learning, 7*(2). https://doi.org/10.20429/ijsotl.2013.070205.

Giroux, H. (2011). *On critical pedagogy*. New York: Continuum.

Green, S., & Baldry, E. (2008). Building Indigenous Australian social work. *Australian Social Work, 61*(4), 389–402. https://doi.org/10.1080/03124070802430718.

Green, S., & Baldry, E. (2013). Indigenous social work education in Australia. In B. Bennett, S. Green, S. Gilbert, & D. Bessarab (Eds.), *Our voices: Aboriginal and Torres Strait Islander social work* (pp. 166–180). South Yarra, Australia: Palgrave Macmillan.

Green, S., Bennett, B., & Betteridge, S. (2016). Cultural responsiveness and social work—a discussion. *Social Alternatives*, 35(4), 66–72.

Green, S., Bennett, B., Collins, A., Gowans, B., Hennessey K., & Smith K. (2013). Walking the journey: The student experience. In B. Bennett, S. Green, S. Gilbert, & D. Bessarab (Eds.), *Our voices: Aboriginal and Torres Strait Islander social work* (pp. 207–229). South Yarra, Australia: Palgrave Macmillan.

Greenhill, J., Richards, J. N., Mahoney, S., Campbell, N., & Walters, L. (2018). Transformative learning in medical education: Context matters, a South Australian longitudinal study. *Journal of Transformative Education*, 16(1), 58–75. https://doi.org.10.1177/1541344617715710.

Griffiths, K., Coleman, C., Lee, V., & Madden, R. (2016). How colonisation determines social justice and Indigenous health: A review of the literature. *Journal of Population Research*, 33(1), 9–30. https://doi.org/10.1007/s12546-016-9164-1.

Hendrick, A., & Young, S. (2018). Teaching about decoloniality: The experience of non-Indigenous social work educators. *American Journal of Community Psychology*, 62(3–4), 306–318. https://doi.org/10.1002/ajcp.12285.

Hollinsworth, D. (2006). *Race and racism in Australia* (3rd ed.). South Melbourne, Australia: Social Science Press.

International Federation of Social Workers. (2014, July). *Global definitions of social work*. https://www.ifsw.org/what-is-social-work/global-definition-of-social-work/.

Jones, P. (2009). Teaching for change in social work: A discipline-based argument for the use of transformative approaches to teaching and learning. *Journal of Transformative Education*, 7(1), 8–25. https://10.1177/1541344609338053.

Jones, P. (2020). Critical transformative learning and social work education. In C. Morley, P. Ablett, C. Noble, & C. Cowden (Eds.), *The Routledge handbook of critical pedagogies for social work* (pp. 489–500). London: Routledge.

Kaighin, J. (2020). Embedding the queer and embracing the crisis: Kevin Jumashiro's anti-oppressive pedagogies for queering social work education and practice. In C. Morley, P. Ablett, C. Noble, & S. Cowden (Eds.), *The Routledge handbook of critical pedagogies for social work* (pp. 333–344). Abingdon, UK: Routledge.

Land, C. (2015). *Decolonizing solidarity: Dilemmas and directions for supporters of indigenous struggles*. London: Zed.

Laverty, M., McDermott, D., & Calma, T. (2017). Embedding cultural safety in Australia's main health care standards. *Medical Journal of Australia*, 207(1), 15–16. https://doi.org/10.5694/mja17.00328. https://www.mja.com.au/system/files/2017-06/10.5694mja17.00328.pdf.

Mendes, P. (2005). The history of social work in Australia: A critical literature review. *Australian Social Work*, 58(2), 121–131. https://doi.org/10.1111/j.1447-0748.2005.00197.x.

Mezirow, J. (1990). Fostering critical reflection in adulthood: a guide to transformative and emancipatory learning. San Francisco: Jossey-Bass.

Mezirow, J. (1991). *Transformative dimensions of adults learning*. San Francisco: Jossey-Bass.

Mezirow, J. (2003). Transformative learning as discourse. *Journal of Transformative Education, 1*(1), 58–63. https://doi.org/10.1177/1541344603252172.

Mezirow, J. (2012). Learning to think like and adult: Core concepts of transformative learning theory. In E. W. Taylor & P. Cranton (Eds.), *The Handbook of Transformative Learning: Theory, Research and Practice.* (pp. 73-95). New York: Wiley.

Moreton-Robinson, A. (1999). Unmasking whiteness: A Gooris Jondal's look at some Duggai business. In B. McKay (Ed.), *Unmasking whiteness: Race relations and reconciliation* (pp. 28–37). Brisbane, Australia: Griffith University.

Morley, C. (2014a). *Practising critical reflection to develop emancipatory change: Challenging the legal response to sexual assault.* Abingdon, UK: Routledge.

Morley, C. (2014b). Using critical reflection to research possibilities for change. *British Journal of Social Work, 44*(6), 1419–1435. https://doi.org/10.1093/bjsw/bct004.

Morley, C. (2016). Critical reflection and critical social work. In B. Pease, S. Goldingay, N. Hosken, & S. Nipperess (Eds.), *Doing critical social work: Transformative practices for social justice* (pp. 25–38). Crows Nest, Australia: Allen & Unwin.

Morley C. (2020a). The contribution of Stephen Brookfield's scholarship to teaching critical reflection in social work. In C. Morley, P. Ablett, C. Noble, & S. Cowden (Eds.), *The Routledge handbook of critical pedagogies for social work* (pp. 523–535). Abingdon, UK: Routledge.

Morley C. (2020b, February 24). *Reactivating social work practice as an emancipatory project: The role of critical theory, pedagogy and reflection.* International keynote for University of British Columbia Ninetieth Anniversary, Vancouver.

Morley, C., Ablett, P., & Noble, C. (2020). Introduction: The imperative of critical pedagogies for social work. In C. Morley., P. Ablett, C. Noble, & S. Cowden (Eds.), *The Routledge handbook of critical pedagogies for social work* (pp. 1–16). Abingdon, UK: Routledge.

Morley, C., & Macfarlane, S. (2012). The nexus between feminism and postmodernism: Still a central concern for social work. *British Journal of Social Work, 42*(4), 687–705. https://doi.org /10.1093/bjsw/bcr107.

Morley, C., & O'Bree, C. (2021). Critical reflection: An imperative skill for social work practice in neoliberal organisations? *Social Sciences, 10*(3), 1–17. https://doi.org/10.3390 /socsci10030097.

Morley, C., & O'Connor, D. (2016). Contesting field education in social work: Using critical reflection to enhance student learning for critical practice. In I. Taylor, M. Bogo, M. Lefevre, & B. Teater (Eds.), *Routledge international handbook of social work education* (pp. 220–231). Abingdon, UK: Routledge.

Noble, C. (2020). Bell hooks trilogy: Pedagogy for social work supervision. In C. Morley, P. Ablett, C. Noble, & S. Cowden (Eds.), *The Routledge handbook of critical pedagogies for social work* (pp. 501–511). Abingdon, UK: Routledge.

O'Sullivan, E., Morrel, A., & O'Connor, M.A. (2002). *Expanding the boundaries of the transformative learning: Essays on theory and praxis.* Londong: Palgrave Macmillan.

Paradies, Y., Harris, R., & Anderson, I. (2008). *The impact of racism on Indigenous health in Australia and Aotearoa: Towards a research agenda.* Cooperative Research Centre for Aboriginal Health.

Parra, M. O., Gutierrez, R., & Aldana, M. F. (2015). Engaging in critically reflective teaching: From theory to practice in pursuit of transformative learning. *Reflective Practice, 16*(1), 16–30. https://dx.doi.org/10.1080/14623943.2014.944141.

Pawar, M., Hanna, G., & Sheridan, R. (2004). International social work practicum in India. *Australian Social Work, 57*(3), 223-236. https://doi.org/10.1111/j.1447-0748.2004.00150.x.

Ramsden, I. M. (2002). Cultural safety and nursing education in Aotearoa and Te Waipounamu. (doctoral dissertation, Victoria University of Wellington, New Zealand). https://www.nzno .org.nz/Portals/0/Files/Documents/Services/Library/2002%20RAMSDEN%20I %20Cultural%20Safety_Full.pdf.

Saggers, S., Walter, M., & Gray, D. (2011). Culture, history and health. In R. Thackrah & K. Scott (Eds.), *Indigenous Australian health and cultures: An introduction for health professionals* (pp. 1–21). Sydney: Pearson Australia.

Sousa, P., & Almeida, J. L. (2016). Culturally sensitive social work: Promoting cultural competence. *European Journal of Social Work, 19*(3–4), 537–555. https://doi.org/10.1080/13691457 .2015.1126559.

Walter, M., Taylor, S., & Habibis, D. (2011). How white is social work in Australia? *Australian Social Work, 64*(1), 6–19. https://doi.org/10.1080/0312407X.2010.510892.

Wehbi, S. (2009). Deconstructing motivations: challenging international social work placement. *International Social Work, 52*(1), 48-59. https://doi.org/10.1177/0020872808097750.

Yu, P. (2011). *The power of data in Aboriginal hands.* Paper presented at the conference Social Science Perspectives on the 2008 National Aboriginal and Torres Strait Islander Social Survey. Canberra: Australian National University.

18

LINKING POLITICAL ACTION, CRITICAL THINKING, AND VALUE-DRIVEN LEARNING

A Proposed New Paradigm for Teaching Social Work for Social Change

LIA LEVIN, ADAYA LIBERMAN, DEDI BUZAGLO,
DOR ROBINZON, AND RONI ZILKA

The up-to-date definition of social work emphasizes the profession's role as promoting social justice, social development, and human rights while seeking to place individuals, systems, groups, and communities as relevant target audiences for the intervention of social workers (IASSW & IFSW, 2014). Accordingly, academic programs for social work education around the world have undergone changes, integrating new courses and materials associated with policy practice, activism, and social change (Weiss-Gal, 2016).

This trend raises questions regarding teaching methods in social work: Are traditional approaches suitable for teaching policy practice and social action? Can teaching policy practice and social action propose new principles not only for the contents of social work education but also for the spirit and approach of instruction in social work? This chapter lays the foundations for a new paradigm for teaching social work that is essentially political; the central practice it imparts is changing harmful social policy.

In order to understand the foundations of the proposed teaching paradigm, it may be helpful to first review the principles of some of the paradigms that currently dominate social work education programs (Levin, 2019).

THE MODERNIST-POSITIVIST PARADIGM

According to Doll (2015), the epistemological premise of this paradigm is that phenomena are closed, constant, and reducible. The intersection between modernism—characterized by an aspiration for rationality, expertise, and intelligence—and the positivist position turns the scientific and empirical examination into an ideological starting point that excludes other possibilities of observing social events and situations (Payne, 2015). Within the modernist-positivist paradigm, teachers are perceived as neutral, rational, objective persons who are the proprietors of knowledge (Fook, 2003). When learning in such a milieu, social work students may adopt a professional identity that is more concerned with class status and the level of expertise attached to it than with assessing the social, institutional, and organizational context in which it is consolidated (Horkheimer et al., 2002).

THE CRITICAL PARADIGM

This paradigm includes radical theories alongside postmodern theories. According to its advocates, the modernist convention is intended to neutralize, conceal, or hide differences between people, by force and in the name of "universal truths" (Parton, 2009). The critical paradigm offers a shift to a flexible examination of different alternatives in response to different situations, based on historic realism rooted in assumptions about power relations (Linstead & Thanem, 2007). It is argued that, in comparison with the critical paradigm, the modernist-positivist paradigm offers simpler coherent and logical modes of study and is therefore also used to teach critical theories (Giroux, 2001).

The critical pedagogy of Paolo Freire seeks to create an educational model that exposes the sociopolitical character of the production of knowledge. Freire (2013) analyzes the way the traditional education system works and points out that over time, students ask fewer and fewer questions and adopt what he calls "passive consciousness." His conclusion is that the more students accept the passive role that is imposed on them, the more they tend to adapt to the world as it is and adopt conformist views. As an alternative, Freire suggests a pedagogy of liberation based on dialogue and the development of a critical-activist political consciousness among students (Roberts, 2015). According to this view, it is imperative to ask how any learning situation can contribute to a change in power structures in favor of the weakened, subordinated, and oppressed. It follows that critical pedagogy has a clear political agenda (McLaren, 1995).

The teaching paradigm proposed in this chapter is based on the supposition that in order to develop new teaching approaches, it is possible, and perhaps even recommended, to dwell in the interface areas between currently available educational paradigms and not be confined by their closed sets of assumptions. This paradigm is presented below, through answers to key questions that address its ontological, epistemological, and methodological foundations (Guba & Lincoln, 1994).

A PROPOSED NEW PARADIGM FOR TEACHING SOCIAL WORK FOR SOCIAL CHANGE: REALISTIC REFLECTIVE ACTION

ONTOLOGICAL QUESTIONS: WHAT IS THE NATURE OF REALITY IN AND OUTSIDE THE CLASSROOM?

Realistic Reflective Action (RRA) is guided by a "value-driven realism"— the acceptance of a discourse that contains different narratives about reality but simultaneously assumes the existence of a carefully selected number of über-principles representing currently dominant professional values in social work. In this paradigm, "reality" is the values that can be discussed and debated, but their *relevance* to learning and practice in social work is the only predetermined subject in any dialogue. So, from an ontological point of view, only values are set a priori. In the classroom, various aspects of social problems are raised and discussed openly, as are solutions to them; the only assumption regarding common knowledge concerns the unwavering adoption of equality, social justice, and fairness as leading professional values (O'Brien, 2011). In RRA, all discussions are conducted on a platform that treats these values as fundamental, in the sense both that they are largely agreed upon by all of those present and that they make it possible to distinguish between good and bad: between a good policy and a bad policy, and between good solutions and bad solutions.

Naturally, the decisiveness that realist thinking bears may reduce the scope of discussion in the classroom. At the same time, the reliance on it is vigilant, deliberate, and based on two central considerations. The first is that the need to categorize situations as "desirable" and "undesirable," "plausible" and "unacceptable," is a catalyst for exposing personal positions and discussing them in depth and, in an atmosphere of candid debate, can assist in the exposure of personal attitudes and their mutual reexamination (Mackie, 1990). The second relates to the diversity among students. Students may be characterized by major differences in terms of personal and cultural backgrounds, political tendencies, professional status, and more. The prior agreement on a discourse of predetermined values enables a common starting point for initiating dialogue and action. In addition, social work students are accustomed to relating to a common denominator of values that is organic and inherent to their professional choice. Their ability to quickly position themselves across various value discourses works in favor of the educational process in this case.

CRITICAL THINKING AND THE RECOGNITION AND DEEP APPRECIATION OF MULTIPLE PERSPECTIVES

This aspect of the RRA's ontological foundations is complementary to the previous principle. Anything that transcends a value-driven realism and touches on the content of different attitudes regarding social phenomena is perceived as legitimate and as an opportunity for mutual learning of all those present in the classroom, teacher and students alike. Complex local and global realities contain endless narratives about the encounter between politics, structural processes, and individual attributes. A change in policy that ignores this richness risks confining learning to superficial levels. This, in turn, may damage the process of change itself, promote policies that are inapplicable across a wide range of contexts, and/or contribute to the shallowing of the social discourse. Thus, in learning sessions based on RRA, there is thorough adherence to the ability to offer different ways of looking at the same issue. All perspectives are discussed in a nonjudgmental manner, in order to facilitate the creation of new perspectives arising from the encounter between participants (teacher and students) within the given framework of values.

EPISTEMOLOGICAL QUESTIONS: WHAT CAN BE LEARNED? WHAT IS THE NATURE OF THE RELATIONSHIP BETWEEN THE LEARNER AND THE SUBJECT LEARNED?

In RRA, the subject matter to be learned is the way social realities are interpreted by the students, teacher, policy makers, and communities who stand to be affected by the change of policy students aspire to generate. Thus, learning is motivated by naturalistic observation of diverse, dynamic, and changing interpretations of the world, with the goal of better understanding the ramifications of harmful and discriminatory policies on different groups in society. Other goals include gaining better insight into the determination and preservation of policy, and listening to the insights of people affected by the policy and the creative solutions that they and others have to offer. Thus, for students, decisions made in the practice of changing policy are not only a result of choosing between the alternatives presented by academic literature or the teacher. The direct encounter with individuals outside the classroom, with the clear instruction to listen to them and learn from them in order to make better decisions, helps students avoid idealizing or demonizing them and delineates the policy arena within its complexity. Dialogue with these agents occurs at each of the following stages: selecting the subject for intervention, defining the problem accurately, creating partnerships, implementing the change, and evaluating its outcomes.

METHODOLOGICAL QUESTIONS: HOW DO WE KNOW WHAT WE BELIEVE CAN BE KNOWN?

Following the ontological and epistemological principles described above, the method in the classroom guided by RRA refers to the "truth" that different actors within the policy arena express, as well as to the ways in which they choose to describe or implement the implications of this "truth" in their social world as knowledge to be uncovered. Under a paradigmatic presumption that all that can be learned about social phenomena is the way different people interpret them, exposing a wider range of perspectives is perceived as the most effective way to learn more about such phenomena and tackle them. According to the principles of RRA, these perspectives are reviewed and discussed without predetermined hierarchy. This reconnects students' understanding of the politics of knowledge creation with the political aspects salient in all spheres of social problems and social policy—from the basic worth accorded to knowledge to the actual resources allocated toward correcting social injustices. From this reconnection emanates the justification to regard all learning activities as necessarily entailing political action.

THE POLICY PRACTICE CLINIC: A SOCIAL WORK EDUCATION PROGRAM GUIDED BY RRA

RRA will be typified through a description of the Policy Practice Clinic operating in Tel Aviv University, Israel, for the past eight years. The clinic's main goal is to convey knowledge and skills to its graduates so that they can influence social policy, conceptualize and consolidate theoretical and practical models in the area of policy practice, and link and interconnect academic, government, and civil institutions and organizations that wish to realize the role of Israel as a welfare state. As part of the curriculum, students engage in one year of practical work toward policy change that is guided, analyzed, and processed through class discussions and theoretical learning sessions. Students work at the clinic in small, closely mentored groups. The selection of policy issues to be promoted by students is based primarily on their interests and motivations.

STUDENTS' EXPERIENCES OF LEARNING IN THE CLINIC: MAIN THEMES

To learn about how students experience a learning program that is guided by RRA, a participatory action research (PAR; Kemmis et al., 2014) was conducted. At its core were these questions: How did students experience their studies in the clinic? What do they think about the method of study? What effects did studying in the clinic have on them? In accordance with the principles of PAR, students who took part in the clinic actively participated in the design and implementation of all stages of research (McIntyre, 2008).

Twenty-six of the fifty-three students who had completed their studies in the clinic at the time of data collection comprised the sample of interviewees. Most were women and Jewish; their average age was twenty-four. In order to ensure full participant anonymity, the exact number of men and students from non-Jewish ethnic minorities (Palestinian, Druze) is not specified. Participation in the interviews was voluntary and required signing an informed consent form. The research received the approval of Tel Aviv University's Ethics Committee prior to data collection.

Data were collected using semi-structured in-depth interviews (Kallio et al., 2016). Transcripts of interviews were analyzed using thematic analysis according to the principles suggested by Strauss and Corbin (1998). In order to minimize the risk of social desirability bias (Bergen & Labonté, 2020) or any conflict of interest, transcripts were fully anonymized before data analysis, and identifying information of participants was kept only by research assistants who had no vested interest in the clinic. Letters attached to quotations replace the real names of interviewees.

Theme I: One Truth Versus Multiple Realities

Describing their learning experience in the clinic, most students chose to begin by situating their studies in the context of other, prior experiences. Common to most of the students' narratives was that before studying in the clinic, they had felt that something was missing from their studies, although they were not able, at the time, to identify precisely what that something was. It had to do with types of knowledge they wished to be exposed to and a more egalitarian relationship they were looking for in the classroom. Participant D shared an experience that had prompted her toward enrolling in the clinic:

> I remember one of the first lessons in another course. . . . I read the
> article before the lesson. . . . Then I looked at the Power Point based on

the article, and I saw that something was missing. . . . I raised my hand and asked about this, and the reaction was strange. It was very, very defensive . . . as if I had undermined something. I did not understand what exactly, but it was this little event that made me suspicious regarding the way knowledge is conveyed . . . In the end, it is always mediated.

Most students pointed to the lack of teaching combined with practice, or experience-based learning, in the field of activism and policy change. They reported sensing a skewed balance between "frontal, unidirectional" (T) teaching and "hands on learning, where you can actually be part of what you are learning about" (N). It was emphasized that as long as learning remains theoretical, knowledge is not attached to a role model from whose conduct in practice students can draw insights and inspiration: "You feel like they are telling you about something you are supposed to do, that you wish yourself to do, but you do not see it. Everyone talks about it, but you hardly see it anywhere. You do not have the opportunity to examine yourself in [handling] it" (F).

Given this backdrop, students brought a variety of expectations to the clinic. These expectations were sometimes far-reaching: "I wanted it to be everything that all the other courses were not" (R). Perhaps as a result of this broad spectrum of anticipation, most students described a dialectic of desires with which they had initially come to the clinic: "On the one hand, I came because I wanted to receive tools. Something practical. I wanted someone to tell me, 'You have to do so and so to change policy.' On the other hand, part of the motivation was to be in a place that was building something new, asking questions, entering unfamiliar spaces" (H).

As learning in the clinic progressed, this dialectic seemed to be addressed, and most students experienced a balance between the various types of learning the clinic had to offer. As L said, "Everything was questionable, apart from our intention. It was clear to us from the beginning what kind of agenda we wanted to promote: more egalitarian, more just, more democratic." Or, as described by S, "We learned not only how to think, but also what to do to make achievements, good results."

For students, when the dialogue with the teacher was more consistent with a participatory approach, their ability to find a balance between what we termed "value-based realism" and critical thinking, between theory and practice, and between voicing their attitudes and intently listening to those of others was enhanced. Students who felt that they underwent the process of seeking such a balance described how insights derived from it influenced them in other spaces of study outside the clinic and in their work as social workers after graduation:

> When we learned that you have to ask "why?" something special happened to me. . . . As [the teacher in the clinic] said, when you ask "why?" all the time, the mind gets used to not taking anything for granted . . . although it can be difficult. Everyone is afraid of changes . . . but it does connect with my values and those of my profession. . . . I could no longer avoid wanting to change. . . . It's irreversible. . . . To this day I'm like that in my work as a social worker . . . and then I become my own motivation to act. It's pretty cool, and at the same time confusing . . . because my morality directs me, but it is mine and of my profession . . . and on the other hand I try to doubt and understand everything. . . . Time that passes teaches me to find balance. (K)

Theme II: Change Versus the Status Quo

Most of the students described the process of studying in the clinic as a turning point in the path of their professional education. This turning point involved experiences both of growth and of destabilization. Tensions deriving from this experience touched upon four issues. One dealt with the conjunction between the aspiration for comprehensive structural social change and the decision-making process in the clinic, which was sometimes based on pragmatic considerations aimed at achieving specific policy changes within one school year. In this vein, Z shared: "In retrospect, you can view everything as 'all or nothing' and wait for the desired dramatic change, but in the meantime, there is a system and people are waiting and in great need of help. So you can't stay stuck in your deliberations, you act, and your actions reveal the balances you need to find."

A second issue mentioned by students concerned their unique position within the policy-change arena and included a simultaneous need for the protection, or "margin of error," conserved for them as students and their wish to be perceived early on as capable members of the change-making community. Q recounted:

> We said, "Well, if we mess it up seriously, at worst, we ruin her [the teacher's] reputations (Laughter)." And then, we were instructed, "Every letter goes out on your behalf." . . . we thought they [policy makers] would say we were cheeky, we thought it could harm us. . . . The shock came when we were actually listened to and changes began to happen. That was empowering, but at the same time came with what I experienced as almost paralyzing responsibility. In short, being a student who changes policy within a project like the clinic is a major [life] changing place.

A third issue arose from instances in which students were exposed to weaknesses or failures in social service systems or developed harsh criticism toward them, while at the same they began to imagine their future within these very systems as prospective social workers. For students, graduating from the clinic and entering the social work professional field brought renewed insights on this subject. Participant A said in this context: "Only when I became a social worker myself did I understand . . . something that she [the teacher] had been trying to tell us the whole time . . . that it was not me against the system. I am the system. . . . And that . . . is scary but also fantastically optimistic."

A fourth issue raised by students had to do with the awkwardness some of them felt when trying to situate themselves in the learning atmosphere prevalent in the clinic that was previously unfamiliar to them. In this connection, S noted: "I am not sure it was considered how strange it is suddenly to speak with a lecturer so directly, and even argue sometimes, or feel that it is indeed possible to express a different attitude." T added: "Partners and all, in the end she [the teacher] gave us our mark." It seemed that when students graduated from the clinic and became social workers, their attempts to continue to implement the principles on which the clinic is based, primarily the challenging of hierarchies, provided them with additional understanding. In this respect, many shared sentiments similar to J's, who explained that "the learning process in the clinic did not end when I graduated. I don't think it has even ended yet."

D gave an instructive example of this:

Now [as a social worker] I have the authority and supposedly the knowledge. I learned and don't forget that the most harmful thing I can do is to stifle other voices or disregard them. Therefore, my job is to expose them [social service users] to as many ways as possible to make the change and to as many people as possible who make changes in different areas, using different approaches and creating an atmosphere of dialogue. Even if it does not come easy, I ask questions with them.

CONCLUSION

The integration between the principles of RRA and students' experiences in a program guided by these principles offers some insights and ideas for further developing the paradigm and additional venues through which it may evolve. The main assumptions of RRA, although never explicitly described to the students as presented in this chapter, have been identified by them and expressed in their learning experience and its long-term effects. Students' appreciation of the change in their relationship with knowledge and the way it was created or offered to them resulted primarily from criticism, and sometimes unnamed emotions, they felt toward traditional teaching and learning methods. They described the absence of practical learning for policy change that is explicitly deemed political and discussed in axiological terms as a lack of diversity in approaches to knowledge, its formulation, and its consumption.

The statements of the students interviewed point to what can be characterized as parallel processes between the way RRA was consolidated and the dialectical position into which the students were introduced. The "gray area" between existing paradigms within which the proposed paradigm lies is unfamiliar and uncharted terrain with which the students had to cope. We can question whether it is at all possible to create new paradigms of teaching and learning that object to hierarchy, under the auspices of higher education systems idiosyncratically structured as hierarchies (Preston & Aslett, 2014). We should reflect upon what preconditions are needed in order to make room for this. This, in turn, points to the essential positioning of those who act upon RRA as having a role in attempting to change the system in which they operate, from within. Presumably, "activist" educators can benefit from communicating and supporting one another not only in terms of sharing and developing new teaching methods but also in terms of the personal, emotional, and professional consequences of treading outside familiar paths. It will likely be beneficial to integrate students into any future move to allow the proposed or similar paradigms to develop, as well as into research and empirical efforts to examine its effects on them in the short and long term.

ACKNOWLEDGMENTS

This work was supported by a grant from the Committee for Budget and Planning of the Council for Higher Education in Israel as part of the Shosh Berlinski Award for Special Contribution to the Community.

We would like to heartily thank Mr. Ran Melamed for his continuous partnership in thought and action for the development of the Policy Practice Clinic over the years.

REFERENCES

Bergen, N., & Labonté, R. (2020). "Everything is perfect, and we have no problems": Detecting and limiting social desirability bias in qualitative research. *Qualitative Health Research*, *30*(5), 783–792.

Doll, W. E. (2015). *A post-modern perspective on curriculum*. New York: Teachers College Press.

Fook, J. (2003). Critical social work: The current issues. *Qualitative Social Work*, *2*(2), 123–130.

Freire, P. (2013). *Education for critical consciousness*. New York: Bloomsbury.

Giroux, H. A. (2001). *Theory and resistance in education: Towards a pedagogy for the opposition*. Westport, CT: Bergin & Garvey.

Guba, E. G., & Lincoln, Y. S. (1994). Competing paradigms in qualitative research. In N. K. Denzin & Y. S. Lincoln (Eds.), *Handbook of qualitative research* (pp. 105–117). Thousand Oaks, CA: Sage.

Horkheimer, M., Adorno, T. W., & Noeri, G. (2002). *Dialectic of enlightenment*. Stanford, CA: Stanford University Press.

International Association of Schools of Social Work (IASSW) & International Federation of Social Workers (IFSW). (2014). *Global definition of social work*. https://www.iassw-aiets.org /global-definition-of-social-work-review-of-the-global-definition/.

Kallio, H., Pietilä, A. M., Johnson, M., & Kangasniemi, M. (2016). Systematic methodological review: Developing a framework for a qualitative semi-structured interview guide. *Journal of Advanced Nursing, 72*(12), 2954–2965.

Kemmis, S., McTaggart, R., & Nixon, R. (2014). *The action research planner: Doing critical participatory action research*. Singapore: Springer.

Levin, L. (2019, April). *Walking between the lines: Towards a new teaching paradigm in social work education for sustainability*. Paper presented at the University Alliance for Sustainability Conference, Berlin.

Linstead, S., & Thanem, T. (2007). Multiplicity, virtuality and organization: The contribution of Gilles Deleuze. *Organization Studies, 28*(10), 1483–1501.

Mackie, J. L. (1990). *Ethics: Inventing right and wrong*. London: Penguin.

McIntyre, A. (2008). *Participatory action research*. Thousand Oaks, CA: Sage.

McLaren, P. (1995). *Critical pedagogy and predatory culture: Oppositional politics in a postmodern era*. New York: Routledge.

O'Brien, M. (2011). Equality and fairness: Linking social justice and social work practice. *Journal of Social Work, 11*(2), 143–158.

Parton, N. (2009). Postmodern and constructionist approaches to social work. In R. Adams, L. Dominelli, & M. Payne (Eds.), *Critical practice in social work* (2nd ed.; pp. 220–229). Basingstoke, UK: Palgrave.

Payne, M. (2015). *Modern social work theory*. Oxford: Oxford University Press.

Preston, S., & Aslett, J. (2014). Resisting neoliberalism from within the academy: Subversion through an activist pedagogy. *Social Work Education, 33*(4), 502–518.

Roberts, P. (2015). *Paulo Freire in the 21st century: Education, dialogue, and transformation*. New York: Routledge.

Strauss, A., & Corbin, J. (1998). *Basics of qualitative research: Procedures and techniques for developing grounded theory*. Thousand Oaks, CA: Sage.

Weiss-Gal, I. (2016). Policy practice in social work education: A literature review. *International Journal of Social Welfare, 25*(3), 290–303.

19

BRIDGING THE GAP BETWEEN CRITICAL REFLECTION AND PROFESSIONAL PRACTICE

SHACHAR TIMOR-SHLEVIN, TAMAR AHARON, SHARON SEGEV, SHANI MAZOR, AND EMILY ISHAI

One of the main concerns of critical and transformative academic teaching in social work is preparing students to cope with the challenges of integrating critical practice into the field, which is mainly characterized by conservative and neoliberal professional perspectives (Timor-Shlevin & Benjamin, 2021). Without such preparation, social work students might find it difficult to translate critical notions into "real life" practice, and there is a risk that their critical thought will be limited to the realm of theory. This chapter focuses on the tension between hegemonic and critical rationalities, which is recognized as a fundamental impediment to critical practice (Payne, 2014), and demonstrates how processing it enabled social work students to develop contextualized critical practices and professional perspectives. This chapter thus offers a broad conceptualization of critical reflection processes that can bridge the gap that currently exists between critical analysis and critical practice. To this end, we present an undergraduate social work course that used a collaborative inquiry group to explore critical participatory practices, and analyze how processing the tension between hegemonic and critical perspectives enabled the students to engage in critical practice in a hegemonic context.[1] We begin by introducing the tension between hegemonic and critical perspectives and the gap between critical analysis and critical practice in the construction of critical reflection processes.

THE TENSION BETWEEN HEGEMONIC
AND CRITICAL PERSPECTIVES

The theoretical foundation of social work is characterized by a tension between conservative and critical perspectives (Payne, 2014). The conservative line of thought demonstrates a tendency to reduce structural social problems to personal problems of individuals, emphasizing people's sole responsibility for their distress (Krumer-Nevo & Benjamin, 2010). In the past three decades, the sweeping effects of the neoliberal discourse have bolstered these components of conservative thought, enabling it to reinforce its hegemonic hold over social services and social work practice (Timor-Shlevin & Benjamin, 2021). Neoliberal thought emphasizes market rationality and advocates a commitment to reducing public spending and government intervention in the market and in citizens' lives (Pavolini & Klenk, 2015). Thus, neoliberal social policies use the notion of sole responsibility as the moral justification for cost reduction reforms (Evetts, 2009). In many countries, conservative and neoliberal thought provide the hegemonic underpinnings of social policies, services, and practices (Brodkin, 2011; Ferguson, 2008; Malin, 2020).

At the other end of the scale, the critical perspective in social work provides a structural interpretation of social distress that critiques the intrapsychic interpretation common to conservative approaches and builds critical theory of practice to counter unjust social conditions and promote social justice (Fook, 2016). Nonetheless, the hegemonic hold of conservative and neoliberal perspectives in the field of social services may operate as an impediment to critical practice (Payne, 2014). Recent studies have demonstrated that, in the face of these hegemonic constructions of normative professional practice, social workers who attempt to promote critical practice face harsh criticism from their teammates and managers (Timor-Shlevin, 2021) and often choose to practice critically under the organizational radar (Lavee, 2021; Prior & Barnes, 2011). While critical perspectives and practices are not one size that fits all social problems and professional processes to the same extent, the tension between hegemonic and critical perspectives draws attention as an impediment to critical practice (Timor-Shlevin et al., 2023).

   To address this discursive impediment, some critical scholars of social work have turned to critical reflection processes, which are considered a key tool in teaching critical practice (Fook & Gardner, 2007; Morley & Dunstan, 2013). Yet the current construction of critical reflection processes fails to fully connect reflexive critical analysis with professional practice, leaving the practical operation of critical social work outside of its models (Fook & Kellehear, 2010; Tretheway et al., 2017). The next section will discuss this lacuna.

CRITICAL REFLECTION PROCESSES
AND CRITICAL PRACTICE

Critical reflection builds on critical theory, which analyzes social processes to expose the underlying power dynamics that construct social reality and the distribution of social resources (Horkheimer, 1972). These oppressive mechanisms are usually concealed by veils of neutrality and social habits, and thus must be exposed and reconstructed. Therefore, critical reflection involves developing an awareness of structural mechanisms in order to resist their underlying influence (Morley, 2014a). Reflexive attention can address personal beliefs, interpersonal dynamics, and collective perspectives and assumptions (Chiu, 2006). Thus, critical reflection provides social workers with valuable materials for the reconstruction of oppressive social constructs at different value levels. For instance, when a middle-class social worker identifies her own feelings of superiority over a service user who is a single mother living in poverty, critical reflection may allow her to identify, deconstruct, and reconstruct the commonly accepted value ladder of social status that triggers her sense of superiority. Since oppressive social constructions are often implicit, critical social work points to the value of acknowledging their existence and naming their effects on people, both as a therapeutic process and for the promotion of social justice (Krumer-Nevo, 2020).

   In practical terms, critical reflection processes spiral among awareness of personal and relational thoughts and feelings, the deconstruction of their hegemonic meanings, and their reconstruction in light of critical perspectives (Morley, 2004). Fook and Gardner (2007) describe a detailed process of critical reflection in which they use critical questions to highlight the everyday contextualized meanings and costs of the hegemonic construction of reality. This method enables the reconstruction of common truths in a new, critical manner. Curtis and Morley (2019) point to the significance of acknowledging the underlying, subtle ways in which social workers themselves contribute to the construction of the social order. Such acknowledgment may expose the nuanced levels of hegemonic operation and enable social workers to develop professional perspectives that are less influenced by the hegemonic rationality. For example, in a qualitative study with social work practitioners, critical reflection was associated with changes in their perceived agency in ways that allowed them to formulate future interventions (Morley, 2014b). Thus, critical reflection should be an established component of critical social work education because it enables a critical analysis of the current social order, which in turn may allow social workers to resist hegemonic constructions.

Nonetheless, research on the process of linking critical reflection processes and critical practice remains underdeveloped (Tretheway et al., 2017). Morley (2014b) highlights the goal of using critical reflection to develop social workers' own critical perceptions. Likewise, Fook and Gardner's (2007) well-known model culminates in social workers' connecting critical insights with ideas regarding their practice. The construction of this model points to the achievement of critical reflection in the realm of insights, ideas, and intended actions. It is apparent, then, that critical reflection is often conceptualized as belonging to the sphere of perceptions and intended practices, while its translation into the sphere of practice remains ambiguous, with the result that current critical reflection models fall short in providing social workers with specific guidelines for the promotion of critical professionalism in hegemonic fields. Considering the absence of a clear model that connects critical reflection processes with professional practice, this chapter describes a collaborative educational process that focused on critical participatory practice in youth social work. In what follows, we describe our experience as members of a participatory inquiry group (Heron & Reason, 1997).

THE PARTICIPATORY INQUIRY GROUP

This chapter describes a learning process that took place in 2016 during an academic course titled Critical Participatory Practices in Youth Social Work. Attempting to incorporate an experiential practical participatory process into the course, the lecturer invited the students to take part. Following an open discussion, fifteen female students chose to study the applicability of critical participatory practices, building on their field training experience, and we set up a collaborative research group based on the participatory inquiry approach (Heron & Reason, 1997).

PARTICIPATORY INQUIRY

Participatory inquiry was introduced by Heron and Reason (1997) and is commonly considered a branch of the critical stream of collaborative action research (Reason & Bradbury, 2001). It is based on a group of common stakeholders who meet to explore a shared area of interest. The process of participatory inquiry takes place through cycles of experience, reflection, and co-processing that are repeated for several rounds. After the research topic is initially defined, the group members take part in an experiential phase in the field that provides them with direct experience of the research topic, and they write about it reflectively. In the process described here, the first decision we made was to write about our encounter with critical participatory practices, which took place simultaneously at the theoretical level in the course, at the practical level in our field training, and during our collaborative inquiry process.

In the next step, the group met again to discuss the reflective material collected by its members. In this phase, the insights gained by the group on the research topic were shared and discussed in light of the literature to refocus the research. The product of the research consisted of the knowledge that was created, summarized, and processed by the group after several rounds of experience and reflection. The data collected with this method consisted of the participants' personal reflections and the shared discussions (Heron & Reason, 2006).

THE STRUGGLE OVER PROFESSIONALIZATION

In the discussion sessions held during this process, we noted the complexity of creating participatory practices. In some cases, professionals at the various field training agencies marked participatory practices as unprofessional, while in others, the field agencies' common working procedures were paternalistic and participatory practices were unfamiliar. Discussing these experiences, we realized that we were encountering a tension familiar from the critical participatory practice literature: on the one hand, these practices are considered valuable and necessary (Timor-Shlevin & Krumer-Nevo, 2016), while on the other, they are rarely accepted in the field (Alfandari, 2017). Based on the conceptualization that emerges from the literature regarding the tension between hegemonic and critical approaches in social work (Ferguson, 2008), we understood the difficulties we were encountering as part of the discursive tension that reflects a struggle over professionalization (Timor-Shlevin & Benjamin, 2021). Following from this understanding, we decided to focus our inquiry on this tension and write about our experiences of coping with it.

We held four rounds of experience, reflection, and discussion during the course. Each participant wrote six reflections; in addition, we recorded and transcribed the four group discussions. The materials collected included ninety reflective documents written by the students in addition to the transcripts of the four joint discussions. After we completed the course and our undergraduate social work degrees, the lecturer invited the group members to continue the process and analyze the materials that had been collected. Six participants from the original group decided to join, and we began the analysis phase of the project. Along the way, two participants left the group, and today we are a group of four social workers and the course lecturer.

DATA ANALYSIS

The data analysis was conducted jointly by the group members, with each reflection analyzed by at least two participants and discussed in joint meetings. We used thematic analysis to analyze the reflective materials in three phases (Braun & Clarke, 2006). The first phase was an introduction to the reflective materials. We ensured that each participant would analyze only the reflections written by other members of the group. In the second phase, the reflections were coded into initial categories that directly described the students' experiences as well as various barriers they faced when they sought to engage in critical participatory practice. Examples of these initial codes are "confusion and apprehension in the face of partnership," "my position as a student," and "boundaries and partnership." In the third phase, these categories were analyzed in group discussions to combine central themes that more broadly expressed the students' experience across a more limited number of themes. Here we describe in detail the theme we called "addressing the tensions," which demonstrates both the barriers we encountered and the ways in which we processed them.

ETHICAL CONSIDERATIONS

Establishing a research group within an academic course as part of our studies raised several ethical questions. The first was whether to disclose the project to the field training agencies. This project took place as an integral component of the undergraduate social worker degree, in which students' field training experiences are regularly discussed in theoretical courses. Therefore, after discussing this issue with a senior researcher in the department, we decided there was no need to inform the field agencies about the project. Nevertheless, the project was publicly discussed on three occasions with field agency members, who emphasized their positive opinion regarding the ways it highlighted the need to further develop critical discussion between the university and the field agencies. The second ethical question concerned the power imbalance between the course lecturer and the students. Addressing these power relations has been an integral part of our process as a participatory inquiry group, enhancing our learning regarding the complex manner in which power plays a part in participatory practices (Heron & Reason, 2006). A third ethical issue was the possibility that nonparticipation in the group would be detrimental to the students' course grades. Therefore, to ensure that participation would be voluntary, we decided that the course grade would be determined only by a fully anonymized exam. Participation in the research group proved to be genuinely voluntary, with fifteen of thirty students choosing to take part during the course. Next, we discussed how to encourage authentic reflexive writing in light of our concern that writing unpleasant content about the course lecturer or the instructors in the field could have affected the lecturer's attitude toward the students. Considering this concern, we decided together that the lecturer would not read the reflective materials until after completing the grading process in order to allow open and honest writing. The lecturer accompanied our process in consultation with an expert in the field of qualitative action research and received assistance in reflecting and bracketing the ethical and methodological issues (Moustakas, 1994). Finally, all members of the original research group provided their written consent to participate in this research. All names used here are pseudonyms.

CONTEXT: ISRAELI FIELD TRAINING AND CRITICAL PARTICIPATORY PRACTICE

In Israel, a bachelor's degree grants a professional license to practice social work. A key element of undergraduate social work studies consists of field training, which constitutes approximately one third of all degree requirements and in which students must receive a passing grade. Critical participatory practice is an established tradition in social work and is based on a critical rationality that challenges traditional hierarchical relationships between social workers and service users (Van Bijleveld et al., 2015). Nevertheless, since one of the basic tenets of critical participatory practice is challenging hegemonic power relations, the professional participatory stance is considered to be weakly positioned in the field of social services (Timor-Shlevin, 2023), as became evident in our direct experiences in the field training. Thus, the main questions that drove our participatory inquiry were the following: (1) How do social work students experience the tension between critical participatory practices and the professional perspective in their field training? (2) How does the reflective process enable students to address and process these tensions?

ADDRESSING THE TENSIONS BETWEEN CRITICAL AND HEGEMONIC PERSPECTIVES

The reflective materials clearly illustrated the hegemonic barriers to critical participatory practices and the creative ways in which the students addressed and processed these tensions to enable critical practice. Addressing and processing these barriers involved four milestones that can be viewed as elements of an evolving spiral process. We termed these milestones (1) removal of doubt, (2) critical perspectives, (3) agency and action in a complex space, and (4) the emergence of critical professionalism.

REMOVAL OF DOUBT

This milestone consisted of the personal and professional confusion that arose when students encountered the tensions between the critical and hegemonic professional discourses. For example, many scholars consider that the common conservative construction of therapeutic relations as hierarchical inhibits participatory practices (Timor-Shlevin & Krumer-Nevo, 2016). Thus, when students attempted to introduce participatory practice into the field, the inherent tension between the common paternalistic professional position and students' participatory ideas raised doubts in students that hindered them from engaging in participatory practice. Consider the following case from Tamar's third reflection, which presents personal and professional questions that may arise when doubt is created:

> One of the teenagers I worked with told me once that he was tired of talking and asked if we could play ping-pong outside. I agreed, and from that day on, we played ping-pong. He had hardly spoken to anyone until then, but now he began to create new relationships with other kids in his [boarding] house. He was happier and more engaged and confident. The social worker asked me if the ping-pong sessions were what he *really* needed. I told her that we had made the decision together and he was flourishing. I understood that what she was really asking was

"is it professional?" Then I began to wonder what makes conversations while playing ping-pong less professional. Is "professional" only what is defined as such, for example a conversation in a closed room, conducted in a conservative, acceptable way? These questions made me doubt myself. What if I had chosen to play ping-pong with him as an easy way to be with him? Perhaps I was denying him the professional assistance he deserved? And perhaps the ping-pong conversations were more convenient for me and not genuinely participatory. After considering these points, I shared some of these thoughts with him, and we decided to meet in the therapy room one week and at the ping-pong table the next for the duration of the therapy. These decisions again made me wonder about participatory practices. Are they therapeutic? What was my professional responsibility in this participatory process, and how much responsibility could I take upon myself? Was sharing responsibility professional? To what degree should responsibility be shared?

In this case, we can see how the encounter with conservative questions evoked Tamar's doubts regarding her own motives and professional responsibility. It is also evident that she experienced difficulties on two fronts: first, the power relations between her and the teenager with whom she was working, and second, the suspicious attitude of her supervisor, who was in a stronger power position. This process raised difficult questions regarding her own motives, conduct, and professional notions of participatory practice.

Learning processes should take place in spaces in which it is safe to raise questions and express doubts. In our case, we considered the professional questions raised at the stage of *removal of doubt* to enable the development of two fundamental themes: first, the acknowledgment of the hegemonic opposition to participatory practice, and second, the specific professional qualities of participatory practice. The next milestone in the process consisted of the critical exploration of the questions raised by the doubts revealed in the previous step.

CRITICAL PERSPECTIVES

This milestone consisted of the critical examination of the students themselves, participatory practice, the hegemonic professional discourse, the power relations present in field training, and society as a whole. Let us consider the following excerpt from Dana's second reflection:

> Today's lesson left me with a strong sense of doubt—can participatory practice really be therapeutic for adolescents? Am I capable of engaging in it? Or is it only wishful thinking on my part? On the one hand, I think we should listen to the teenagers we work with and believe that there is no point in forcing them to engage in processes they don't want to engage in. Their voices are the most important thing in the process. On the other hand, I have some hesitation in the face of actual participatory practice. After all, sometimes teenagers don't know what they want to change, or how to do it, and sometimes they expect us to tell them, to show the way. Should I abandon participation in such cases? And besides that, I find myself talking a lot about how we build therapeutic encounters with no power relations, but do I really act in this way? *No.* Many times I make decisions alone and not with them. Sometimes this is due to a lack of time to ask their opinions, sometimes other team members don't agree with the participatory approach, and sometimes I think they're not ready to express their opinion on certain things, which is quite paternalistic, but . . . at other times it's just because I want to do things my own way.

The student described the difference she experienced between the conservative discourse, which provides clarity, order, and professional boundaries, and the participatory discourse, which is more fluid and complex and requires her to conduct a constant, intense dialogue with teenagers about the therapeutic process itself. This critical perspective allows her to make room for complexity. She understands that at times conservative practice is appropriate and recognizes that the conservative discourse may limit participatory practice in order to maintain a more secure and boundary-based position. Such an understanding can be confusing and exhausting when we want to identify with a clear professional position.

The next case, from Efrat's fifth reflection, presents another level of a critical perspective:

> I was attending a planning, intervention, and evaluation committee meeting[2] held to discuss a young girl I work with, and some of the other social workers were talking about how young I was and saying that maybe

this was too complicated a case for a student to be dealing with. Immediately I felt what it was like when power relations are weighted against you and realized that the same power that was directed at this young girl was now directed at me. After I processed these feelings, I talked to my supervisor about them. I was trying to explain my feelings of being diminished and disempowered, but she took everything I said and used it against me, as if I didn't understand anything. After this conversation, I thought a lot about the power we have as "experts" to disempower others, to damage people's self-confidence. I think that what happened was paternalistic at two levels: first, towards this young girl, because her voice was silenced at that committee meeting, and second, towards me, because my opinion and ability to say anything in favor of that girl were also diminished.

In the early stages of our process, confusion and doubt were evident, but here we can see how Efrat conducted a mature critical examination of what took place, identifying the underlying forces that operated around her and finding ways to address them by talking about the situation with her supervisor. Although this conversation was not successful, her choice to discuss the issue presented a new option of addressing some of the forces that inhibit critical participatory practices and moving into a dialogue with them. Her choice to speak with the supervisor brings us to the next milestone: agency and action.

Agency and Action in a Complex Space

This milestone consists of critical operations that questioned and problematized the hegemonic construction of professionalism, as the next case, from Tamar's sixth reflection, demonstrates:

I remember a situation in which I joined one of the teenagers while he was carrying out his kitchen duties. It felt very natural. . . . However, the response of the other youth workers was surprising. They didn't understand why I had done it, and now, as I think about it, I guess that in joining this guy as he did his kitchen duties, I had shattered their firm conception of the power relations between staff and youth, which was apparently fundamental to their practice. Later, in a conversation with one of the youth workers, I asked her about her surprise, and we talked about authority and how she thought that a distanced position would give her greater authority. I said that in my view closeness enabled authority more than distance did. I felt that I had managed to translate participatory theory into participatory practice not only with the teenagers, but also within the space of the agency, with other staff members. It felt very good to be able to turn the staff's opposition into a conversation in which this youth worker and I acknowledged the complexities of authority and participatory practice and processed them together.

What is special about this case is the student's ability to identify the barriers to participatory practice—e.g., the youth worker's distress over her closeness to the teenagers and changes in formal power relations—and talk about them. From the conservative perspective, closeness that goes beyond the commonly accepted standards of authoritarian relationships is a threat to professionalism (Krumer-Nevo & Benjamin, 2010). The ability to identify and name these barriers allowed the student to use the critical reflective view of herself to create a space for challenging thinking about participatory practice. In the next case, Netanela managed to engage in critical practice that contradicted power relations in another way, as the following excerpt from her fifth reflection reveals:

In a group of young women that I facilitated, Iris mentioned that it was difficult to be a Caucasian Jew[3] at school. Other girls joined in and described the local power structure, explaining why they needed to maintain a threatening image so no one would "mess with them." I asked her if I would have belonged to the mainstream group or a marginal one if I had been a student at their school. They said I would certainly have been in the mainstream group. I asked what characterized those in the mainstream and after a brief discussion they concluded that it might be related to money. We started talking about my situation versus theirs. We are nearly the same age, but I had almost completed my social work degree and was facilitating this program, while they were struggling every day to complete their high school matriculation, be accepted into training programs, support themselves, overcome a lack of confidence and still enter the labor market, and so on. I told them that my parents had paid for my degree studies while I struggled not to feel too guilty. We laughed a little about me being a rich snob. I asked them why they thought I was telling them about this. I think I was also asking myself this question. They all stared at me and looked very curious. I told them that I wanted them to know they were not unsuccessful, incompetent, or at fault. They often felt extreme guilt about where they were in their lives. I said that unfortunately, our starting position in life has great significance in terms of where we are currently. We talked about their parents' immigration to Israel, life in the periphery, and the meaning of growing up in a marginalized group. About the difficulty of making a living. We talked about how money is not everything in life, but how the ability to pay for your child's academic education does make life easier. I explained that I did not say this to brag or to show that I was superior to them. I also faced difficulties in life, different from theirs. But it was important to me that they knew they were not at fault. That they were no less successful. They agreed with me and elaborated on their experience of guilt about their current positions in life. They empowered each other and themselves. I saw that the conversation was meaningful to them. I felt they appreciated that I spoke with them as equals and had the courage to talk about what stood out in our encounter even though it was not pleasant.

In this case, Netanela walked boldly into the territory of the social power structure that was manifested in her group encounter with marginalized young woman. Considering the common tendency to ignore such issues in professional encounters, she and the young women were surprised at her ability to acknowledge their distinct social positions and discuss the emotions evoked by the gaps between them. This case demonstrates the student's ability to creatively open this issue for discussion and shared processing. The next milestone in this process was the development of a broader view of the field, which now consisted of a deeper understanding of ourselves and a critical view of the tense struggle between hegemonic and critical perspectives.

THE EMERGENCE OF CRITICAL PROFESSIONALISM

This milestone is characterized by the formulation of a more nuanced critical professional perspective. Let us consider the next excerpt from Ruth's fifth reflection:

> Initially, I was angry that the managers at the training center feared that if we engaged in participatory practices, they would lose their authority or positions of power. I still feel this way, but now I think that more generally, it is a huge challenge to translate critical participatory theory into practice at the field level. Participatory practice is most needed in places and contexts where we have issues of power relations, but it is difficult to achieve. I think that talking about authority and professionality could reduce the anxious responses to participatory practice. We should make clear that participatory practice is not about abandoning professionalism. Rather, it indicates a more nuanced and complex level of professionalism.

This excerpt reveals the process through which the student went, moving between a threatening experience that raised self-doubt through the ability to examine herself and the field and engage in professional practice aimed at challenging and widening hegemonic perspectives. The reflective space created by the research group provided a safe place in which to address the tensions between the critical and hegemonic perspectives. In turn, this process enabled the formation of critical professional positions that contextually addressed the hegemonic field. We understand the process of addressing the hegemonic–critical tension as a spiral, i.e., not a linear process that culminates in the development of a critical professional perspective. Further hegemonic impediments will arise and be subjected to additional rounds of doubt, critical perspectives, practical engagement, and professional construction. In the closing section, we use our findings to discuss the conceptualization of the process of linking critical reflection and critical practice.

DISCUSSION

Existing models of critical reflection processes culminate in the development of critical professional perspectives but lack a component that facilitates their implementation in practice (Tretheway et al., 2017). Acknowledging that the social work field is not divided dichotomously into critical and hegemonic practices, our aim in this chapter is to expand critical reflection models to address the challenge of promoting critical practice, given the hegemonic impediments. The process we describe here reveals critical practice as an integral part of the spiral of critical reflection. First, in addition to emphasizing personal perspectives that require deconstruction, our processes of critical reflection reveal the nuanced tensions between critical and hegemonic perspectives. Second, we highlight the ways in which the ability to process these tensions makes it possible to invent, experiment with, and experience critical practice in the field, in an ongoing dialogue with common hegemonic perspectives. We contend that in order to translate critical analysis and perspectives into feasible critical practice, practitioners require shared spaces in which to process hegemonic–critical tensions (Testa & Egan, 2016). Through processing, we engage in the conceptual deconstruction and reconstruction of hegemonic perspectives and receive the group support that makes it possible to imagine new critical practices and experiment with them. Our experience of participatory inquiry enabled the creation of a unique opportunity for processing—the experience of critical participatory practice shared by the lecturer and the students. We experienced, on the one hand, the tension in the imbalanced power relations between lecturer and students and, on the other, the critical participatory commitment to challenge these power relations (Timor-Shlevin & Krumer-Nevo, 2016). The need to address this complex tension in a practical manner provided us with direct experience of some feasible ways to develop critical practice in hegemonic contexts. Thus, our first contribution lies in elaborating on the role of a shared space in which to address hegemonic–critical tensions as a fundamental component of critical reflection models that enable the translation of critical reflection into critical practice in hegemonic fields.

At the theoretical level, we suggest broadening existing models of critical reflection by including the translation of critical perspectives into critical practice as a fundamental element of the process. While existing models separate reflectivity and analysis, the development of a professional position, and professional practice, we claim that the relationship between reflection and action is nonlinear. We describe these components as part of the same process, in which the formulation of a professional position and the operation of critical practice follow and reinforce each other. The first step, removal of doubt, marked the tensions between hegemonic and critical perspectives, and the second step addressed these tensions in order to process them. The third step involved granting social workers the agency to practice critical professionalism in the field while taking hegemonic–critical tensions into account—that is, considering the advantages and disadvantages of both hegemonic and critical professional positions to rebuild their critical professional position on firmer ground. Following these experiences of critical practice, the professional perspectives of the students in our study began to emerge in a more contextualized and nuanced manner. Since the current field of social services is still based on conservative and neoliberal positions, further hegemonic–critical tensions will arise in the students' coming encounters in the field, leading to additional cycles of tension processing and the development of new ways to engage in critical practice and further cultivate practitioners' professional perspectives. Thus, critical reflection, the possibility of producing critical practice in the field, and the formulation of a professional perspective all influence and are influenced by one another. This evolving-spiral conceptualization of critical reflection processes sheds new light on the challenges social workers can face in promoting critical professionalism in their daily practice in social services dominated by hegemonic discourses. In addition, it offers a conceptual road map for addressing these challenges within safe shared spaces for critical reflection and analysis, which in turn may enable the sustainable development of critical practice.

We are hopeful that these understandings will connect the field of critical reflection more firmly to the challenges faced by social workers when they seek to translate critical analysis into professional practice. We believe that this contribution reveals critical reflection as a practical and useful tool for the development of sustainable critical social work in a more contextualized, nuanced, and professional manner.

ACKNOWLEDGMENTS

The authors wish to thank Prof. Maya Lavie-Ajay for her insightful and warm support throughout our collaborative inquiry process. We also wish to thank Dana Shemesh, who took part in the analysis of the reflective materials. Finally, we wish to thank the youth study collaborative inquiry group for their open and sincere participation in this process.

NOTES

1. Some ideas in this article have been previously published in Timor-Shlevin et al. (2022).
2. The planning, intervention, and evaluation committees are the main authorities, alongside the courts, involved in child protection decision making in Israel (Israel Ministry of Social Services and Social Affairs, 2014).
3. The Caucasian Jews immigrated to Israel from the Caucasus region of the former Soviet Union, where they were called Mountain Jews (Krumer-Nevo & Malka, 2012).

REFERENCES

Alfandari, R. (2017). Evaluation of a national reform in the Israeli child protection practice designed to improve children's participation in decision-making. *Child & Family Social Work*, 22(S2), 54–62. https://doi.org/10.1111/cfs.12261.

Braun, V., & Clarke, V. (2006). Using thematic analysis in psychology. *Qualitative Research in Psychology*, 3(2), 77–101. https://doi.org/10.1191/1478088706qp063oa.

Brodkin, Z. E. (2011). Policy work: Street-level organizations under new managerialism. *Journal of Public Administration Research and Theory*, 21(2), i253–i277. https://doi.org/10.1093/jopart /muq093.

Chiu, L. F. (2006). Critical reflection: More than nuts and bolts. *Action Research*, 4(2), 183–203. https://doi.org/10.1177%2F1476750306063991.

Curtis, C., & Morley, C. (2019). Banging the same old colonial drum? Moving from individualising practices and cultural appropriation to the ethical application of alternative practices in social work. *Aotearoa New Zealand Social Work*, 31(2), 29–41. https://doi.org/10.11157 /anzswj-vol31iss2id632.

Evetts, J. (2009). New professionalism and new public management: Changes, continuities and consequences. *Comparative Sociology*, 8(2), 247–266. https://doi.org/10.1163/156913309X421655.

Ferguson, I. (2008). *Reclaiming social work: Challenging neo-liberalism and promoting social justice*. London: Sage.

Fook, J. (2016). *Social work: A critical approach to practice* (3rd ed.). London: Sage.

Fook, J., & Gardner, F. (2007). *Practising critical reflection: A resource handbook*. New York: Open University Press.

Fook, J., & Kellehear, A. (2010). Using critical reflection to support health promotion goals in palliative care. *Journal of Palliative Care*, 26(4), 295–302. https://doi.org/10.1177 %2F082585971002600406.

Heron, J., & Reason, P. (1997). A participatory inquiry paradigm. *Qualitative Inquiry*, 3, 274–294. https://doi.org/10.1177%2F107780049700300302.

Heron, J., & Reason, P. (2006). The practice of co-operative inquiry: Research "with" rather than "on" people. In P. Reason & H. Bradbury (Eds.), *Handbook of action research* (pp. 144–154). London: Sage.

Horkheimer, M. (1972). *Critical theory: Selected essays*. New York: Continuum.

Israel Ministry of Social Services and Social Affairs. (2014). *The commission to examine the ministry's policy in relations to children's removal to out-of-home placement and custody arrangements.* Israel Ministry of Social Services and Social Affairs, Jerusalem (in Hebrew).

Krumer-Nevo, M. (2020). *Radical hope: Poverty aware social work.* Bristol, UK: Policy.

Krumer-Nevo, M., & Benjamin, O. (2010). Critical poverty knowledge: Contesting othering and social distancing. *Current Sociology, 58*(5), 693–714. https://doi.org/10.1177%2F0011392110372729.

Krumer-Nevo, M., & Malka, M. (2012). Identity wounds: Multiple identities and intersectional theory in the context of multiculturalism. In R. Josselson & M. Harway (Eds.), *Navigating multiple identities: Race, gender, culture, nationality, and roles* (pp. 187–206). Oxford: Oxford University Press.

Lavee, E. (2021). Who is in charge? The provision of informal personal resources at the street level. *Journal of Public Administration Research and Theory, 31*(1), 4–20. https://doi.org/10.1093/jopart/muaa025.

Malin, N. (2020). *De-professionalism and austerity: Challenges for the public sector.* Bristol, UK: Policy.

Morley, C. (2004). Critical reflection in social work: A response to globalization? *International Journal of Social Welfare, 13*(4), 297–303. https://doi.org/10.1111/j.1468-2397.2004.00325.x.

Morley, C. (2014a). *Practising critical reflection to develop emancipatory change.* New York: Routledge.

Morley, C. (2014b). Using critical reflection to research possibilities for change. *British Journal of Social Work, 44*(6), 1419–1435. https://doi.org/10.1093/bjsw/bct004.

Morley, C., & Dunstan, J. (2013). Critical reflection: A response to neoliberal challenges to field education? *Social Work Education, 32*(2), 141–156. https://doi.org/10.1080/02615479.2012.730141.

Moustakas, Clark. (1994). *Phenomenological research methods.* Thousand Oaks, CA: Sage.

Newman, Andrea, and McNamara, Yvonne. (2016). Teaching qualitative research and participatory practices in neoliberal times. *Qualitative Social Work, 15*(3), 428–443. https://doi.org/10.1177%2F1473325015624500

Pavolini, E., & Klenk, T. (2015). Introduction. In E. Pavoloni & T. Klenk (Eds.), *Restructuring welfare governance: Marketization, managerialism and welfare state professionalism* (pp. 1–5). Cheltenham, UK: Edward Edgar.

Payne, M. (2014). *Modern social work theory* (4th ed). New York: Oxford University Press.

Prior, D., & Barnes, M. (2011). Subverting social policy on the front line: Agencies of resistance in the delivery of services. *Social Policy & Administration, 45*(3), 264–279. https://doi.org/10.1111/j.1467-9515.2011.00768.x.

Reason, P., & Bradbury, H. (2001). Introduction: Inquiry and participation in search of a world worthy of human aspiration. In Reason, P. & Bradbury, H. (Eds.), *Handbook of Action Research: Participative Inquiry and Practice* (pp. 1–14). London: Sage.

Testa, D., & Egan, R. (2016). How useful are discussion boards and written critical reflections in helping social work students critically reflect on their field education placements? *Qualitative Social Work, 15*(2), 263–280. https://doi.org/10.1177%2F1473325014565146.

Timor-Shlevin, S. (2021). The controlled arena of contested practices: Critical practice in Israel's state social services. *British Journal of Social Work, 51*(1), 279–296. https://doi.org/10.1093/bjsw/bcaa059.

Timor-Shlevin, S. (2023). Conceptualizing critical practice in social work: An integration of recognition and redistribution. *European Journal of Social Work, 26*(1), 28–40. https://doi.org/10.1080/13691457.2021.1977250.

Timor-Shlevin, S., Aharon, T., Segev, S., Mazor, S., & Ishai, E. (2022). From critical reflection to critical professional practice: Addressing the tensions between critical and hegemonic perspectives. *Qualitative Social Work, 21*(2), 277–293.

Timor-Shlevin, S., & Benjamin, O. (2021). The tension between managerial and critical professional discourses in social work. *Journal of Social Work, 21*(4), 951–969. https://doi.org/10.1177%2F1468017320949359.

Timor-Shlevin, S., Hermans, K., & Roose, R. (2023). In search of social justice–informed services: A research agenda for the study of resistance to neo-managerialism. *British Journal of Social Work, 53*(1), 23–39. https://doi.org/10.1093/bjsw/bcac131.

Timor-Shlevin, S., & Krumer-Nevo, M. (2016). Partnership-based practice with young people: Relational dimensions of partnership in a therapeutic setting. *Health & Social Care in the Community, 24*(5), 576–586. https://doi.org/10.1111/hsc.12227.

Tretheway, R., Taylor, J., & O'Hara, L. (2017). Finding new ways to practise critically: Applying a critical reflection model with Australian health promotion practitioners. *Reflective Practice, 18*(5), 627–640. https://doi.org/10.1080/14623943.2017.1307721.

Van Bijleveld, G. G., Dedding, C. W. M., & Bunders-Aelen, J. F. G. (2015). Children's and young people's participation within child welfare and child protection services: A state-of-the-art review. *Child & Family Social Work, 20*(2), 129–138. https://doi.org/10.1111/cfs.12082.

20

TRANSFORMATIVE ASSESSMENT
IN SOCIAL WORK EDUCATION

Using Critical Performance Pedagogy as a Creative Strategy

JEAN CARRUTHERS

Traditional, managerial, and technicist forms of assessment have played a significant role in the way we do social work education despite an increase in critically reflective pedagogy. However, new approaches to pedagogy and assessment, more suited to the values of social work, have been incorporated by reconstructing the narrative of curriculum and assessment to make room for critically reflective and reflexive knowledge and skills. Such approaches prioritize a critical, creative, and collaborative investment from students and educators in assessment processes and seek to evaluate students' ability to develop understanding of less tangible practices like critical analysis, critical reflection, and social action. In this chapter, I argue that engaging in critical and postmodern critique and incorporating alternatives to dominant forms of education and assessment are central to transformative social work practice.

Within the higher education context, there are three dominant approaches to assessment: traditional, managerialist, and technicist (see Fraser & Taylor, 2016; Macfarlane, 2016; Morley & O'Connor, 2016). Despite these influences, social work educators have creatively reshaped the use of assessment mechanisms by incorporating critical and creative practices into current processes of assessment (see Morley & Ablett, 2017).

Consequently, when applied to social work education, the process of assessment is most often treated as distinct or separate from the pedagogy used in the education process. This chapter demonstrates how one Australian university social work program has reshaped the curriculum narrative to use traditional mechanisms of assessment in ways that support critically reflective practice.

The vision of social work as an emancipatory project is not easily captured in dominant forms of assessment. When seeking to deliver transformative approaches to pedagogy and assessment, the aim is to demonstrate the attainment of knowledge and skills in critical analysis, critique, critical reflection, and social action. We can acknowledge that the attainment of this kind of knowledge does not necessarily fit neatly into current mechanisms of how we measure learning; however, it is not outside the scope of what is possible when subjected to deconstructive and reconstructive examination (Fook, 2016). For social work education to truly capture learning within transformative spaces, assessment needs to reflect a nuanced examination of theory and practice and an explicit acknowledgment of students' ability to develop new knowledge and theory informed by processes of critical praxis. Transformative alternatives through critical and creative pedagogies are becoming increasingly recognized (see Barak, 2016; Brookfield, 2005; Geisler, 2017; Jones, 2009; Morley et al., 2020); however, most often, they do not extend to the ways we deliver assessment. Transformative education in social work requires a shift in perspective from assessment as "the measurement of learning" to "assessment for [critical] learning," which begins with a critical and postmodern critique of the status quo (Morley & Ablett, 2017, p. 3).

In this chapter, I critically examine traditional, managerial and, technicist approaches influencing pedagogy and assessment and outline critical performance pedagogy (CPP) as an alternative approach to pedagogy and assessment with transformative potential for social work. An example of CPP within an Australian university setting is discussed, specifically showcasing a performance assessment. This approach is offered as a counternarrative fostering critical alternatives, providing one example of transformative assessment in social work education.

CONSTRUCTING NEW NARRATIVES FOR MEASURING TRANSFORMATIVE EDUCATION

There is generally a set of standards that inform the criteria for curriculum and assessment that determine what is deemed "relevant" knowledge and how it fits within the university's prescribed structure. Traditional mechanisms for measuring knowledge, such as criterion-referenced assessment (CRA) forms or assessment rubrics, limited to the measurement of technical or narrowly evidence-based practices, are outdated. Educational outcomes are often determined according to the type of assessment that is deemed most suitable and efficient for academic learning, such as exams, essays, presentations and, or reports. However, the tools utilized in assessment, the ways knowledge is assessed, and by whom are all part of a standardized managerial and technological blueprint (Fraser & Taylor, 2016). Boud and Falchikov (2007, p. 17) observe that "[students] conform to the rules and procedures of others to satisfy the needs of an assessment bureaucracy." If the aim of social work education is to prioritize delivering socially just practice, we need to be incorporating critical and creative approaches to pedagogy and assessment in a way that reshapes the social work education narrative and how we assess students' capacity for critically reflective practice.

Social work practice requires moral, ethical, political, historical, social, theoretical, cultural, and spiritual engagement. Emerging practitioners are required to reflect critically on their own personal, cultural, and political biases, which cannot be reduced to a set of techniques (Morley & O'Connor 2016; Reisch, 2013). Technicist approaches create the view that "practice is somehow unaffected by the dominance of neoliberal, capitalist, colonialist, patriarchal and medicalised influences" (Morley et al., 2014, p. 184). Separating theory development and practice offers little scope for questioning or challenging dominant power relations and discourses by which social work continues to be a colonizing force (Rossiter, 2019). Furthermore, the development of new knowledge, reflexivity, and personal theory as part of students' developing practice framework is omitted (Brookfield, 2005; Fook, 2016). Fundamentally, technicism fails to examine students' capacity for critical praxis (i.e., the ability to link theory and practice in a critically conscious way) and, as such, represents a "politically conservative" or "politically neutral" standpoint (Morley et al., 2014, p. 184).

Assuming that we can separate social work assessment from the aims of transformative practice raises concerns about how we, as educators, challenge students' unquestioned assumptions. This is especially relevant in situations where students are highly proficient in meeting academic expectations but lack critical reflexivity regarding notions of power and privilege. If the aims of social work education are advancing social justice, addressing power, and educating students to be culturally responsive (see Australian Association of Social Workers, 2020), then transformative practice requires us, as educators, to be creative in the ways we coconstruct a more critically reflective and reflexive approach to pedagogy and assessment. Drawing on Mezirow's concept of transformative learning, Kealy (2010) suggests that transformative education and assessment present an opportunity for autonomous thinking and critical reflection to be recognized in the facilitation and measurement of social work in higher education. Thinking critically, we could suggest that the increased transparency provided by curriculum and assessment mechanisms (recognized in traditional approaches to education) can be useful as a means for measuring critically reflective and reflexive knowledge and skills.

TRANSFORMING THE PROCESS OF ASSESSMENT IN HIGHER EDUCATION THROUGH COLLABORATION

The administrative rules of university assessment (e.g., ensuring students' work is their own, avoiding plagiarism, and establishing marking and moderation mechanisms) all focus on student accountability and can be a deterrent to collaborative efforts. Operationally, students are cautioned not to share knowledge with their peers to avoid similarities in essays. A collegial approach of sharing work and resources creates fear among students about charges of plagiarism or collusion, leading to disciplinary action. In addition, educators are reluctant to engage in collaborative approaches to assessment for fear of their inability to measure outcomes "accurately." For this reason, it has become "safer" or "easier" to individualize assessment (Ife, 2012). Inadvertently, this has resulted in promoting values of competition and meritocracy over the values of social work such as emancipatory, democratic, and culturally responsive arrangements (Brookfield, 2005; Morley & Ablett, 2017).

In many accounts, assessment falls short of the aim to develop progressive knowledge that supports sustainability in the field. Boud and Falchikov (2007, p. 3) propose that "assessment is not sufficiently equipping students to learn in situations in which teachers and examinations are not present to focus their attention. As a result, we are failing to equip them for the rest of their lives." Little or no attention is paid to the ways assessment can contribute to deep learning, how assessment inhibits learning, or the provision of informal developmental feedback (Boud & Falchikov, 2007). In addition, students' voices are often excluded from the assessment process (Ife, 2012). Thus, the positioning of students as passive recipients of education (Fraser & Taylor, 2016) extends to their exclusion from any involvement in developing assessment criteria beyond providing feedback in student surveys.

If educators embraced the values of social work within assessment criteria, students would be encouraged to work together, share knowledge among peers, and support one another collectively (Morley & Ablett, 2017). Through this collective engagement, creative responses to complex situations could account for the diverse social, political, and cultural positions students hold and assessment processes would reflect an embodied, critically reflexive approach that fosters transformative engagement in knowledge and skills conducive to practicing social work (Carruthers, 2020; Morley & Ablett, 2017). Furthermore, the assessment space becomes a negotiated space where, through collective critical reflection, new knowledge of how assessment is delivered can be discovered.

TRANSFORMATIVE PEDAGOGY FOR SOCIAL WORK ASSESSMENT: A COUNTERNARRATIVE

New critical and creative forms of assessment have emerged. However, as Walz and Uematsu (2008) caution, being creative in the ways we develop curriculum and assessment is no easy task; they suggest that "creativity requires . . . substantial scholarship, a broad experience, energy, ego, and the courage to go against the status quo and accept the costs of doing so." Creativity requires the courage to "appreciate and direct . . . change" (p. 24). In transformative education, nurturing students' capacity to make critical links between theory and practice, to examine the ways they think about and respond to practice situations, and to develop new knowledge and theory for practice is considered more relevant than developing technical skills and efficiency (Brookfield, 2009; Fook, 2016; Morley & O'Connor, 2016). Transformative learning, according to Brookfield (2003, p. 142) is "learning in which the learner comes to a new understanding of something that causes a re-ordering of the pragmatic assumptions she holds and leads her life in a fundamentally different way." As such, the learner is opened to "alternative social formations" and the suggestion of a form of "democratic socialism" (Brookfield, 2003, p. 142). Within the university setting, students are expected to inform everything they have learned with theory (i.e., an evidence base); however, transformative learning expects more. Within transformative approaches, students draw on critically reflective processes (see Fook, 2016) to uncover new theory for practice in a given context; however, they may struggle to utilize theory creatively in conjunction with generating new knowledge. Critical and creative pedagogies can be useful here.

As a transformative approach to learning, critical pedagogy sees education as "the task of educating students to become critical agents who actively question and negotiate the relationships between theory and practice, critical analysis and common sense and learning and social change" (Giroux, 2007, p. 1). As a counternarrative, critical pedagogy opens possibilities for students to become invested in the ways peda-gogy and assessment can be linked to critical praxis (i.e., thinking crit-ically about the way we link theory to practice) (Carruthers, 2020). Using critical pedagogy to inform assessment makes space for students to engage in processes that encourage critical analysis and collective action as part of the learning process. It encourages educators to be more democratic, as opposed to meritocratic, in feedback loops and processes of assessment, and to imagine new mechanisms for students to assess themselves, each other, and educators (Ife, 2012). This opens the possibility of new forms of assessment that align with a more demo-cratic participatory engagement when developing praxis.

Critical and creative alternatives that respond to the nuances in social interactions, enhance culturally responsive practice, engage students in critical thinking and reflection, and counter the influence of neoliberal social work are becoming more recognized (see Geisler, 2017; Jones, 2009; Morley & Ablett, 2017). Critical performance pedagogy (CPP) is a reasonably new form in social work education that offers a transformative approach to social work education using critical pedagogies and the arts. It was inspired by the efforts of educators who see value in the arts and other alternative forms of knowledge as a platform for critical learning and assessment. The approach incorporates the intentions of critical pedagogy with performative and collaborative strategies, specifically designed to support embodied transformative learning (Carruthers, 2020). Originally used in political studies and autoethnographic research (see Conquergood, 1998; Denzin, 2003), CPP has been reimagined for social work education as a performative approach used to facilitate critical learning, whereby the "performative and political intersect" (Carruthers, 2020, p. 2). As recognized by Denzin (cited in Carruthers & Ablett, 2020, p. 478), "performance pedagogy draws its inspiration from Augusto Boal's [Theatre of the Oppressed (TO)], as well as creative and Indigenous knowledges that are often marginalised in academic settings." Fundamentally, CPP is a foundation for transformative assessment in social work education in which dominant discourses are resisted, counterhegemonic knowledges are utilized, and new ways of knowing are formed.

THE PERFORMANCE ASSESSMENT: A CREATIVE STRATEGY FOR TRANSFORMATIVE EDUCATION

An example of CPP is a performance (i.e., performing arts) based assessment used in a social work program in Australia (see Carruthers, 2020; Carruthers & Ablett, 2020; Morley & Ablett, 2017). It is described as an applied performance approach:

a theatrical form, for students to explore, compare and critique a range of theoretical perspectives associated with social work, making relevant links between theory and practice in a critically conscious way.

Students, as part of a whole-tutorial collaborative assessment, develop a play and perform this in front of their student cohort. Each tutorial group showcases their group's understanding of social work theory and practice, as a way to share knowledge creatively and collectively across the cohort. (Carruthers & Ablett, 2020, p. 478)

The task requires students to "work together during tutorials to contribute to their group's capacity . . . to apply at least three social work specific theories to a practice scenario." The process supports students to "devise innovative ways to present their material creatively in order to engage their peers from other tutorials" (Morley & Ablett, 2017, p. 5). Through collective tutorial engagement, students are involved in learning skills associated with citizenship participation, democratic decision making, and negotiating power and conflict in their efforts to brainstorm ideas, negotiate roles, and make decisions about the case example (Carruthers, 2020). The group decides what theories and creative frame they will use to showcase their learning in the performance presentation. Additionally, students are provided with opportunities to critically reflect through dialogical exchange in tutorials. In some instances, this process supported transformation of students' deeply held assumptions about issues arising in the case study and encouraged new knowledge for practice (Carruthers, 2020; Morley & Ablett, 2017, p. 5).

Existing narratives, such as fairy tales, are used as a creative frame to provide structure to the performance presentation and support embodied theoretical exploration within the performance assessment:

What it looked like was mostly we used existing narratives. . . . We would use a lot of fairytales, [gameshows, reality TV, cultural stories] and other kinds of existing narratives because students only had twenty minutes to present the performance. They did not have a lot of time to introduce characters. Basically, if there was an existing narrative then the audience straight away knew the story or was in that context. Then students were able to make twists and nuances in the narrative that showed they understood the theory. Students actually became the character, so if it was Goldilocks, they became Goldilocks and Goldilocks was part of the case study. For example, in the case study Goldilocks was a homeless girl, who broke into someone's house because she was hungry. The three bears came home, and each bear was a different theory. . . . Basically, the bears [theories] offered Goldilocks ways that she could help herself or what they could do for her from each theoretical perspective and then Goldilocks critiques the theory and says yes that would be helpful or no that is not. (Carruthers, 2020, pp. 119–120)

Students develop the case scenario themselves (with support from their tutor) and use existing narratives to playfully demonstrate their interpretation and embodiment of different theoretical perspectives as they apply and respond to the social justice concerns within the scenario. The creative development and application of a range of theories enable students to form a critical analysis, eliciting culturally relevant and emancipatory responses drawing on critical and postmodern theory to inform their understanding of praxis (Carruthers, 2020). Furthermore, playing out the scenario and applying the theories encourage reflexive thinking to deconstruct students' own taken-for-granted assumptions and support the development of creative and intuitive constructions that are more in line with socially just practice. This supports the development of new theories for practice and a critically reflective approach (Fook, 2016). The performance can thus be seen as a catalyst for reflexivity and emancipatory practice, extending to students working in a multidisciplinary environment, engaging in collaborative practice, and mobilizing for social action (Carruthers, 2020; Morley & Ablett, 2017).

As a form of transformative education practice, the process can be described as "critical analysis in action" or a performative approach for developing critical praxis (Carruthers & Ablett, 2020, p. 112). As an assessment piece, it reflects assessment for critical learning and intentionally resists the desire to reduce assessment to "the measurement of learning," while also recognizing that, in any educational pursuit in academia, measuring success is part of the process (Morley & Ablett, 2017, p. 3). To be responsive to this point, while also honoring the transformative framework, the performance assessment uses a team-teaching and self/peer-evaluation approach to assess student learning (see Carruthers, 2020; Morley & Ablett, 2017).

The collaborative team-teaching approach is used to assess the performance presentation developed by students and presented in the final lecture to showcase students' learning. All students in the cohort attend this event, and all members of the teaching team assess the performances in real time. Team members, including the unit coordinator, are tasked with providing feedback and responding to the criteria. Performances are assessed according to the group's ability to (1) demonstrate theoretical knowledge (i.e., key tenets and assumptions of the chosen theories, including what the theory prioritizes in response to the case scenario; (2) clearly explicate links between theory and practice (i.e., the beginning point of developing critical praxis); and (3) offer a relevant critique of the limitations of each theory as applied to the practice example (Carruthers, 2020). Critical reflection is not currently an aspect of the assessment criteria; however, space for critically reflective dialogue is an important part of formative assessment and could be considered in evaluation.

Within a collaborative team-teaching approach, all members of the teaching team compare notes and come to a "shared consensus about a grade" (Carruthers, 2020, p. 129). As educators are often invested in their own students' performances, the shared approach assists in taking account of the subjective assumptions each tutor will likely hold, given the role they play in facilitating the group's process and performance. As described by Carruthers (2020, p. 129), "if there is a disagreement it tends to be the person who has taught that tutorial . . . whose view is less valued." Alongside this ethical stance, there are pragmatic benefits; for example, "it allows a significant piece of assessment [for the entire cohort of students] to be marked and moderated in three hours" (Carruthers, 2020, p. 129). The approach is a means for educators to model the same collaborative intentions they expect of students in the performance assessment process.

The second part of the grading approach is a self/peer-assessment to assess students' participation and contribution to the development and delivery of the performance (Morley & Ablett, 2017). Students are tasked with evaluating their own and peers' involvement in the performance, which includes developing the case scenario, researching relevant theories, collaboratively engaging to create the play, and delivering the theatrical performance to the cohort (Carruthers, 2020). Students' participation in the collaborative process and their intimate working with the group positions them more favorably than their tutor to evaluate these contributions.

Evaluation questions are targeted toward students' demonstrated ability to (1) contribute actively to their group's capacity to apply theoretical perspectives to a practice situation; (2) undertake tasks as negotiated with their group to prepare for the performance presentation; and (3) work constructively and collaboratively as a collective group member. Unlike traditional approaches to assessment that favor individualism and competitiveness, the CPP approach fosters democratic citizenship where students have the freedom to work together, share knowledge and decision making, and participate actively in collaborative assessment processes.

According to Morley and Ablett (2017, p. 2), collaborative approaches to assessment can provide a sense of connection and belonging that is integral to student engagement. It establishes an expectation for collective engagement within a student-centered partnership arrangement (see Somerville, 1993; Stefani, 1998). Students are encouraged to consider their evaluation of themselves and their peers with social justice values in mind (Morley & Ablett, 2017). This means making equitable decisions, despite whatever conflict or power struggles may have occurred, and recognizing the contributions that they and their peers have made when working collaboratively, as opposed to seeking only individual merit. The opportunity for students to self-assess by reflecting on their experiences encourages the development of critical self-reflection (i.e., reflexive contemplation), which is an important disposition when becoming a social worker. According to Mezirow (2003, p. 62), "foster[ing] the development of skills, insights, and especially dispositions essential for critical reflection—and self-reflection" is important for students to develop reflective judgment, which he sees as an "essential component of democratic citizenship." Additionally, this approach to assessment has the potential to enable students to develop knowledge and skills in assessment and evaluation relevant to critically reflective decision making in their future practice. Although not measured directly, this process of critical reflection is evidenced in their comments in the self/peer evaluation. These comments demonstrate students' ability to challenge normative assumptions and develop a personal theory that informs their own process of assessment for their emerging practice.

According to Wagner and Shahjahan (2015), a challenge to collaborative assessment is that the delivery of learning outcomes is not readily available.

A collective approach challenges and transforms the fundamental premise of learning according to traditional standards. When exposed to unfamiliar processes such as self- and peer-led approaches, students and superiors may react with resistance. This can result in negative feedback for participants as well as in teaching evaluations when conflict occurs because of hurt or uncomfortable feelings (Carruthers, 2020). Morley and Ablett (2017, p. 3) make the point that critically reflective pedagogy in assessment can be "arguably more demanding than reproducing a particular set of facts and techniques." However, transformative approaches such as the performance assessment are "most likely to inspire belonging" because they engage students socially, politically, and collaboratively and instigate the commencement of their development as agents for emancipatory social change.

SOCIAL WORK ASSESSMENT IN HIGHER EDUCATION: SITTING WITH THE TENSIONS

To suggest that transformative pedagogy and assessment can be used in isolation irrespective of the requirements of higher education would be naïve. There are tensions in social work as a teaching modality, a discipline, a professional body, and an emancipatory project (Rossiter, 2019). However, if approaches to assessment that claim to be transformative are designed purely to develop technical knowledge and skills, or are still embedded in metrics-led grading systems with little acknowledgment of the critical implications, the goals of assessment might run counter to the aims of transformative practice (Boud & Falchikov, 2007; Ife, 2012). There are benefits to all forms of assessment if applied through a critical lens. Lymbery (2003, p. 100) suggests that social work's survival as a distinct professional discipline depends on its "ability to reconcile the contradictions between the discourses of competence and creativity, in particular in the context of social work education." Social work as a profession/ discipline/practice is ever-changing and builds upon a diverse range of critical, creative, reflective, intuitive, and Indigenous knowledge that makes it unique and conducive to critical, collaborative, and performative pedagogy and assessment.

CONCLUSION

Social work, in essence, is a value-laden profession working toward social justice and emancipatory change. Thinking critically about assessment fosters the means to reshape our narrative to recognize how transformative learning can be recognized within traditional assessment mechanisms. Using critical performance pedagogy (CPP) as a creative strategy offers a means for critical, performative, and collaborative approaches to pedagogy and assessment. The performance assessment, informed by CPP, demonstrates that creative alternatives support students to develop beyond technical knowledge and skills, with the potential for embodied integration of critical praxis, collaborative practice, mobilizing for social action, and developing capacity for building new knowledge. This chapter has demonstrated how critical and creative approaches to pedagogy and assessment are possible and do support transformative education.

REFERENCES

Australian Association of Social Workers. (2020). *Australian social work education and accreditation standards.* https://www.aasw.asn.au/document/item/13565.

Barak, A. (2016). Critical consciousness in critical social work: Learning from the Theatre of the Oppressed. *British Journal of Social Work, 46*(6), 1776–1792.

Boud, D., & Falchikov, N. (2007). *Rethinking assessment in higher education: Learning for the longer term.* Abingdon, UK: Routledge.

Brookfield, S. (2003). Putting the critical back into critical pedagogy: A commentary on the path of dissent. *Journal of Transformative Education, 1*(2), 141–149.

Brookfield, S. (2005). *Power of critical theory for adult learning and teaching.* New York: Open University Press.

Brookfield, S. (2009). The concept of critical reflection: Promises and contradictions. *European Journal of Social Work, 12*(3), 293–304.

Carruthers, J., & Ablett, P. (2020). Boal and Gadamer: A complimentary relationship towards critical performance pedagogy. In C. Morley, P. Ablett, C. Noble, & S. Cowden (Eds.), *Routledge handbook of critical pedagogies* (pp. 477–488). Abingdon, UK: Routledge.

Carruthers, J. C. (2020). *Performance as a platform for critical pedagogy in social work education* [Doctoral dissertation, Queensland University of Technology]. QUT ePrints. https://eprints .qut.edu.au/205094/.

Conquergood, D. (1998). Beyond the text: Towards a performative culture of politics. In S. J. Dailey (Ed.), *The future of performance studies: Visions and revisions* (pp. 25–36). Annandale, VA: National Communication Association.

Denzin, N. K. (2003). Performing [auto] ethnography politically. *Review of Education, Pedagogy and Cultural Studies, 25*(3), 257–278. https://doi.org/10.1080/10714410390225894.

Fook, J. (2016). *Social work: A critical approach to practice* (3rd ed). London: Sage.

Fraser, H., & Taylor, N. (2016). *Neoliberalization, universities and the public intellectual species, gender and class and the production of knowledge.* London: Palgrave Macmillan.

Jones, P. (2009). Teaching for change in social work: A discipline-based argument for the use of transformative approaches to teaching and learning. *Journal of Transformative Education, 1*(7), 8–25.

Geisler, M. (2017). Teaching note—Theatre of the Oppressed and social work education: Radicalizing the practice classroom. *Journal of Social Work Education, 53*(2), 347–353.

Giroux, H. A. (2007). Democracy, education, and the politics of critical pedagogy. In P. McLaren & J. L. Kincheloe (Eds.), *Critical pedagogy: Where are we now?* (pp. 1–8). New York: Peter Lang.

Ife, J. (2012). *Human rights and social work* (3rd ed.). Cambridge: Cambridge University Press.

Kealy, E. (2010). Assessment and evaluation in social work education: Formative and summative approaches. *Journal of Teaching in Social Work, 30*, 64–74.

Lymbery, M. E. F. (2003). Negotiating the contradictions between competence and creativity in social work education. *Journal of Social Work, 3*(1), 99–117. https://doi.org/10.1177/1468017303003001007.

Macfarlane, S. (2016). Education for critical social work: Being true to a worthy project. In B. Pease (Ed.), *Doing critical social work: Transformative practice for social justice* (pp. 326–338). London: Allen & Unwin.

Mezirow, J. (1997). Transformative learning: Theory to practice. *New Directions for Adult and Continuing Education, 1997*(74), 5–12. https://doi.org/10.1002/ace.7401

Morley, C., & Ablett, P. (2017). Designing assessment to promote engagement among first year social work students. *E-Journal of Business Education and Scholarship of Teaching, 11*(2), 1–14.

Morley, C., & O'Connor, D. (2016). Contesting field education in social work: Using critical reflection to enhance student learning for critical practice. In M. Bogo, I. Taylor, B. Teater, & M. Lefevre (Eds.), Routledge international handbook of social work education (pp. 220–231). Abingdon, UK: Routledge.

Morley, C., Macfarlane, S., & Ablett, P. (2014). *Engaging with social work: A critical introduction.* Cambridge: Cambridge University Press.

Morley, C., Ablett, A., Noble, C., & Cowden, S. (2020). *The Routledge handbook of critical pedagogies for social work.* Abingdon, UK: Routledge.

Reisch, M. (2013). Social work education and the neo-liberal challenge: The US response to increasing global inequality. *Social Work Education, 32*(6), 715–733.

Rossiter, A. (2019). Discourse analysis in critical social work: From apology to question. *Critical Social Work, 6*(1).

Somerville, H. (1993). Issues in assessment, enterprise, and higher education: The case for self, peer, and collaborative assessment. *Assessment and Evaluation in Higher Education, 18*(3), 221–233.

Stefani, L. A. J. (1998). Assessment in partnership with learners. *Assessment & Evaluation in Higher Education, 23*(4), 339–350.

Wagner, A. E., & Shahjahan, R. A. (2015). Centering embodied learning in anti-oppressive pedagogy. *Teaching in Higher Education, 20*(3), 244–254.

Walz, T., & Uematsu, M. (2008). Creativity in social work practice: A pedagogy. *Journal of Teaching in Social Work, 15*(1–2), 17–31.

CONCLUSION

Transformative Practice in Academic Social Work

JAN FOOK

T his book has attempted to cover all arenas of academic practice (teaching, research, management/administration, and outreach), but it seems clear that there are common ideas that inform work in each of them. In addition, there are common challenges that need to be acknowledged and worked with in order for us to keep developing a transformative set of values in a context that increasingly runs counter to them.

In this concluding chapter, I highlight what stands out from these discussions, in order to provide a platform for continuing to craft how we work more relationally for social justice in rapidly changing contexts. I begin with the question of how to be and act transformatively within a neoliberal environment. This is clearly assumed by all discussions in each chapter. Next, I cover some of the age-old issues in social work: the links between individual and society, the links between theory and practice, and the links between practice and research. However, there are other disparities that need to be linked in order for transformative work to be developed, and I dwell on these as well. In the last section, I outline the main suggestions for what, specifically, needs further attention.

TRANSFORMATIVE PRACTICE IN CONTEXT

Most chapters point up the ongoing task of maintaining transformative values in an international, national, and university context that seems increasingly adverse to these. The broader context offers new challenges to social justice values because of both increasing political conservatism and more stringent economic spending regimes. The pandemic has ushered in new types of inequalities and emphasized already existing social disparities. In addition, within universities, the trend is toward less self-government and more centralized control, with initiatives based on economic rationalization. This gives rise to a measurement-oriented culture, antithetical to a more fluid and relationally based way of thinking. These sorts of paradigms are felt all the way down to the level of individual faculty and staff and of course influence student expectations and assessment.

From a transformative perspective, we need to recognize that this context directly influences personal beliefs and individual actions. However, the important word here is *influences*. A transformative perspective demands that we analyze in detail what these influences are, in order not to mistake influence for cause. An important question, therefore, is: Exactly how much individual agency can be exercised in these environments? A crucial step in being transformative is to understand and appreciate the details of how a neoliberal context can influence us so we can devise specific ways of resisting and develop strategies for change. These sorts of questions are pursued in chapter 3, where I explore some of the specific trends of neoliberalism at play in my own university context and outline some ways of appreciating what changes mean for different players, in order to be more inclusive in our approach. I also try to outline a framework for retaining fundamental social justice principles while taking into account how some initiatives may work differently for different people or groups.

In chapter 2 Wanda Heading-Grant provides a hands-on example of how social work values and skills can be used at executive levels in transformative ways. Wanda illustrates beautifully how being relational with colleagues at all levels has allowed her credibility to work in transformative ways. She been allowed "into everyone's business," which is surely one of the things a good social worker needs to be able to do in working with, and within, one's context. Chapter 4, written with Ken Bechtel, Kate Ball Clem, and BC Garvey, demonstrates how an awareness of and care for physical space blossoms into a caring and inclusive social space; as academic staff and administrators, their role is key to this. This chapter reminds us that all our colleagues, as well as students, are part of the context we inherit and create. It is up to all of us to think and act in holistic and inclusive ways to ensure that this environmental context transmits transformational values.

Perhaps the most important point to remember in this section is that in order to practice transformatively, we must work with the whole context. This means not only appreciating how the context influences individuals but also how this analysis can indicate specific strategies for change and how different aspects of the context work together holistically. Chapter 14, by Alex Bobella, illustrates perfectly that although social work is developing an environmental approach, there are still more aspects of the environmental context that need to be incorporated. His analysis of the contribution of sound to our environments, and how this affects people differentially, fills out beautifully this aspect of an evolving environmental social work approach.

This more detailed holistic appreciation of the contexts in which we live and work requires a past, a present, and a future vision: of the past, to understand how the current situation came about and the particular meanings it transmits to those party to its establishment; of the present, to recognize that past visions may need to change; and of the future, to free ourselves from the bonds of the past and establish a fluid basis for moving forward.

MAKING LINKS

As I write this, I am reminded how our taken-for-granted Western academic tradition tends to construct categories, particularly binary ones, to order our world: individual versus society, theory versus practice, practice versus research. Each of these categories carries with it a related infrastructure that reflects and supports this polarized thinking. In recent decades, we have spent a great deal of time and energy trying to remake the binaries as we begin to realize that the world, including ourselves as human beings, does not really work this way. The chapters in this book bring these trends poignantly to light; all, in their own ways, suggest new frameworks and ways of envisioning that embody a more integrated, holistic, open-ended, and mindful way of relating to our environments and our fellow human beings.

One long-standing binary, the individual versus society, is integral to our current conception of the social work profession, which is founded on the concept of "person in society." In chapter 1, Anna Gupta discusses two new theoretical formulations that could help us integrate our understanding of the individual in society. She outlines how the Poverty Aware Paradigm (PAP), developed by Krumer-Nevo in Israel, works to facilitate social workers' understanding of how the structural aspects of poverty manifest at individual levels and how a mindset that incorporates this avoids discriminatory practice. She also shows how another theoretical perspective, the capability approach (CA), also works from a basis of transformative values and easily integrates personal experience with structural contexts. Of course critical perspectives, which have been used in social work for some time in parts of the Western world, also emphasize the integration of the personal and the structural. Perhaps because of their earlier genesis in social work thinking, critical perspectives were connected more with structural thinking, which in the 1970s to the 1990s was seen as the way forward in critiquing individual direct work. As a result, the theoretical potential of critical perspectives in developing the nature of the relationship between the individual person and their broader social context remained underdeveloped. Anna Gupta's coverage of the PAP and CA makes an important contribution to a more detailed understanding of the relationship between the person and their structural environment. Her chapter also addresses another important binary, the gap between theory and practice.

Traditionally, we have perhaps simplistically associated theory with the academy and practice with the field. In this way, theory has been conceptualized as preceding practice, and this correlates with the idea that a university credential must precede effective legitimate professional practice. There are many offshoots of this thinking that further institutionalize it and valorize theory (and what is associated with it) over practice.

Currently, we are becoming more familiar with critiques of this way of thinking, particularly that put forward by classic writers such as Donald Schon (1983), who is commonly regarded as the father of the reflective practice approach. This approach contests the split between theory and practice and argues that integrating the two, through a deep reflection on implicit assumptions inherent in a person's practice, may help to integrate theory with practice. This involves a process of unearthing and creating a person's own practice theory, improving their practice by ironing out potential contradictions with their stated desired values or theories.

Thus reflective practice, and its cousin critical reflection, are now almost becoming a new orthodoxy in social work. However, reflective approaches are included in this volume on transformative social work not because they are now popular, but because they are truly in line with transformative perspectives in destabilizing the fixed categories of theory and practice, providing a way of actually integrating the two in practice. Quite a few of the chapters in this book demonstrate a critically reflective process and illustrate how it can be used in teaching to further a transformative perspective. Christine Morley and Ratna Beekman, in chapter 17, describe in detail how Ratna's critical reflection was transformative for her. Tiffany Tuttle and Erin Mackenzie, in chapters 10 and 16 respectively, illustrate in fascinating detail how a process of critical reflection actually functioned to be transformative in allowing them to develop their own personal theories of practice from their own experiences. In Tiffany's case, she was able to reaffirm her own sense of an Indigenous worldview, which restored her sense of integrity and ability to integrate the meaning of her felt lack of safety in the world, and in child welfare work in particular. In Erin's case, reflecting on a small discrepancy she experienced while on placement in an environmental social work setting allowed her to develop her own approach to environmental social work.

In chapter 7, Danielle Jatlow walks us thoughtfully through an experience of her grandmother's approach to death. She gently and artfully draws out her reflections on people's different needs for certainty and knowing, and how these understandings can be incorporated into the way we work as social workers and as educators. This push for certainty, which I think is part and parcel of our imperative to categorize, is something that needs to be approached with humility and courage, which Danielle embodies so well in her chapter. These stances are, I think, one of the cornerstones of being transformative, and of creating a transformative learning environment.

In chapter 12, Brenda Solomon describes almost poetically how she both models and teaches reflexivity in research. Her image of swimming, how she invites students to immerse themselves in the experience of understanding and entering fully into another person's experience, supports her own personal approach to thinking and being that embodies a transformative approach. The ideas in this chapter integrate nicely with the ideas in chapter 11, written with Timothy Sim. This chapter shows how the idea of practice research challenges the traditional split between practice and research (with research being seen as the domain of academics) by remaking the idea of research along transformative lines. Practice research, with its emphasis on practice-led research and an inclusive (rather than rigidly categorized) approach to different methodologies, is an attempt to bridge the gap between the worlds of practice and research and to produce research that is immediately applicable to current problems. Timothy illustrates this convincingly and movingly with his description of a major research project in China in the aftermath of a devastating earthquake. He describes how he set up partnerships with local people, and how the project evolved into a transferable model for working in the wake of disaster.

It is fitting in this section to return to the idea of the disparities we ourselves might unwittingly construct in the academy. Here I am particularly referring to the split we often assume between academic faculty and administrative staff. This is extensively dealt with in chapter 4, written by two administrative staff, a student, and myself. Academic faculty often assume that the role of staff is secondary to academic work, which is of prime importance. Related to this thinking can be a tendency to dismiss the role of the department chair and other managers, because of faculty ambivalence about power. This can lead to academic faculty seeing students as being the only group that should be empowered, to the neglect of the needs and rights of staff and others in the organizational context. However, if we are to take a transformative view, we need to be mindful of how we create and sustain inequities among all people in the university organization. Power, if we take a more relational, complex, and dynamic constructionist understanding, is not something finite and connected only with official social positions but can be created and changed in relationships. This is part and parcel of being more systematically transformational by being mindful of the whole environment and the differing interests in the contexts within which we all work and relate to one another.

SPECIFIC SUGGESTIONS

In this last section, I detail some of the more specific thinking, strategies, and models that are put forward by the authors in this volume. I have referred to some of these already in that they address specific challenges thrown up in the current environment. Here I want to draw attention to what they offer in terms of more specific ways forward.

In terms of curriculum, a number of very strong chapters detail specific transformative approaches. In chapter 8, JB Barna provides a wonderfully full and detailed account of how to approach a field education program from a relational perspective. JB describes what she means by relationality for both field instructors and students. With regard to relationality for students, she focuses on the need for reflexive self-understanding; she includes an example of a critical reflection from a student that demonstrates not only the transformative potential of this strategy but also how it can be integrated into the supportive classroom teaching of field education. In chapter 13, Siddhesh Mukerji, Kate Gannon, and Erin Mackenzie focus on the teaching of environmental social work, clearly pulling together the different strands and approaches that can make this more effective. Their chapter is extremely helpful in integrating all the differing strands of an environmental approach to provide a more complex and rigorous platform from which an environmental perspective should be taught. Going forward, the approach should (1) integrate multiple theoretical frameworks (environmental justice, ecospiritual social work, and a regenerative bioregional approach); (2) offer opportunities for practice; (3) be vision-focused; (4) be explicitly justice-oriented; and (5) center self-care and community care as foundational values.

Jean Carruthers tackles another issue that needs further work in teaching from a transformative perspective. It is often all too easy to teach the content of a transformative perspective without necessarily modeling the congruent principles in the pedagogical design of a course. Recognizing one of the problematic relationships in teaching transformatively, Carruthers offers, in chapter 20, a strategy for ensuring that assessment and pedagogy are properly linked in a transformative curriculum. She describes a tool, critical performance pedagogy, that is based on collective and collaborative engagement between instructor and students.

Both Lia Levin et al., in chapter 18, and Shacher Timor-Shlevin et al., in chapter 19, detail easily replicable approaches for classroom teaching that articulate the transformative principles as their basis. Chapter 18 describes a new teaching paradigm (a realistic reflective action approach) that aims to link political action, critical thinking, and values-driven learning. The authors of this chapter discuss a foundational epistemology and ontology that include a critical recognition of multiple perspectives and then provide an example, the policy practice clinic, that allows students to experience practice over a year, while processing the experiences in class. The aim is to help them make connections between the broader critiques of critical theory and actual practice.

Chapter 19 addresses a similar issue, what is sometimes seen as a gap between the theory or thinking developed through critical reflection and the actual putting into practice of those new ideas. The authors describe a collaborative inquiry group based on a participatory inquiry approach, whereby participants were able to be involved in successive reflection discussions of their shared practice experiences. The project also included a research aspect, in which the documented reflections were used as data and students participated in the analysis. The analysis resulted in the identification of milestones on the way to developing a critical professionalism, providing helpful detail of the experience of translating reflection into everyday practice.

Several chapters address work outside the curriculum and classroom. Sarah Nunes and Diane Wiener describe, in chapter 6, an initiative designed to reach outside a specific university context to create a profile of the need for disability-related content in social work courses nationally. They set up an alliance of individual academics and practitioners to achieve this, intentionally constructing the group in a transformative way, using a flat structure and ensuring a variety of different perspectives. The chapters by Laura Abrams et al. (chapter 5) and Merlinda Weinberg (chapter 9) focus on the issue of race, perhaps one of the most significant areas to be addressed in current times, given the polarization discussed earlier. Laura and her colleagues describe in detail their efforts to address racism in the school and curriculum and include the differing perspectives of all those involved in the initiative. This is a telling example of an attempt to work together on a very controversial issue, about which there will always be divergent and strong emotions and opinions. It is compelling reading, not just because it is open and honest but also because it models that we need to create a space to air different perspectives and then listen to them if we are move along in this endeavor.

Merlinda's chapter comes to the issue of race from her own research into ethics and her startling realization that, in her research project, it was only racialized social workers who named race as an issue. Given her own Jewish background, this concerned her, but as a transformative social work educator and researcher, she also felt this was an issue that required more exploration. She discusses thorny issues about the role of allies and who has a right to address anti-racism. She ends with a number of recommendations about creating classroom spaces for the discussion of race. This idea of appropriate classroom learning spaces is a recurrent theme in this book and one of immediate concern to all those who are striving to practice a transformative pedagogy.

Clearly, there is more work to be done in developing the theoretical base of a transformative perspective. In particular, I have mentioned the need to constantly rework our understanding of the connection between the individual and society. The Poverty Aware Paradigm and the Capability Approach discussed by Anna Gupta in chapter 1 do this successfully and are known to be highly successful in application. The chapters by Alexander Bobella (chapter 14) and Tucker Boyd (chapter 15) draw our attention to other theoretical ways of reworking a transformative approach. Tucker Boyd's chapter critiques the idea of risk as a basis for social work practice and outlines a wonderful expansive approach that has much more capacity to be transformative. Alexander Bobella develops our approach to environmental social work by introducing the missing element of sound and showing how including this will transform our conception of the environment, and of environmental social work.

In the introduction to this book, we mentioned that indeed there are other theoretical approaches that need to be considered and incorporated into our approach to transformative social work. The development of environmental social work was one. Another was the exploration of Indigenous perspectives (see chapter 10 by Tiffany Tuttle). If this is undertaken as part of a move to decolonize social work, then there will be a greater emphasis on identifying and valuing Indigenous perspectives, but also questioning the epistemological bases of our current social work thinking. In this sense, it supports a more integrated and holistic way of working, with perhaps less rigid categorization of forms of knowledge and processes for developing it. If we are to extend this logic, then we will need to continue developing our thinking in relation to the environment, opening up the relatively restricted anthropocentric vision endemic to much social work thinking until relatively recently.

SO, WHAT IS TRANSFORMATIVE SOCIAL WORK AND WHAT IS THE CONTINUING ENDEAVOR?

Our earlier understandings of transformative social work, as outlined in the introduction, have been reaffirmed by discussions in this book. The basis of fundamental change in a progressive direction, informed by values and principles of relationality, social justice, and critical social constructionist perspectives, underpins the chapters in this book. Newer specific approaches include the further development of environmental perspectives, the inclusion and development of decolonizing and Indigenous approaches, and the incorporation of anthropocentric analyses as part of our future environmental understanding. Newer developments must also include more specific theories and analyses that better integrate our understanding of the relationship between the individual and society and also integrate the worlds of theory, practice, and research in a more complex and fluid way. Teaching and working in a context of polarized and often rigid conceptions means that a transformative approach must incorporate strategies for courageous, generous, nonjudgmental, and reflexive learning environments.

How to cultivate our own reflexivity as academic and staff members of a university is central to achieving this. Being comfortable, but not complacent, with who we are as individual and social beings is vital. It is important to recognize that we are partly formed by historical background, personal biography, and social circumstance, but that we can also exercise some choice about how this plays out in our own lives, now and in the future. Recognizing this complexity can act as a launching point to develop, in a relational way, new ideas for connecting with one another, and together transform the spaces in which we interact, teach, learn, administer, and manage.

REFERENCE

Schon, D. (1983). *The reflective practitioner*. New York: Basic Books.

CONTRIBUTORS

Laura S. Abrams, MSW, PhD, is a professor of social welfare at the UCLA Luskin School of Public Affairs. Her scholarship examines experiences of youth in the U.S. justice system through reentry and the transition to adulthood. She is also interested in critical race theory and transformative approaches to social work education.

Tamar Aharon is a social worker and an MA student in gender studies at Ben-Gurion University. She works as a sexual educator for youth and educational staff and offers group guidance for female teenagers regarding gender, feminism, and leadership. Her research focuses on the construction of masculine identity for men who experience difficulties and anxieties about the dimensions of their genitalia.

Roni Arditi, MSW, Tel Aviv University, is a community social worker in the Makom association, accompanying young women who cannot be reunited with their families.

JB Barna was formerly senior lecturer and BSW program coordinator at the University of Vermont. She spent her first twenty years as the field education coordinator for both the MSW and BSW programs. JB identifies strongly with her practitioner roots and will always keep in her heart the children and families with whom she worked.

Ken Bechtel has served since 2006 as academic support for the undergraduate, graduate, and field programs of the University of Vermont Social Work Department, specializing in graduate student recruitment and retention.

Ratna Beekman is a sessional lecturer in social work, Queensland University of Technology.

Alexander Bobella is a Social Work Case Manager at the University of Vermont Medical Center interested in historical sociology, sociology of contemporary religion, cultural history, structural reform, social justice, and the role of memory studies in contemporary discourse. He hopes that this is the first of many scholarly contributions to the world of social theory and social work literature.

Tucker Boyd is a recent MSW graduate of the University of Vermont. They currently work in homeless services in Vermont, where they aim to realize their belief that our basic needs are human rights.

Dedi Buzaglo, MSW, is a social worker and a student in the thesis-completion track at Bar-Ilan University's School of Social Work. His work and research focus on the relations between humans and other species, ecosocial justice, and moral ideology toward nonhumans and the environment from a posthumanist-ecocentric perspective.

Jean Carruthers, PhD, is a lecturer in social work at the Queensland University of Technology, in the Faculty of Health's School of Public Health and Social Work. She has used the arts, specifically performance art, as a means of embodying critical learning in social work education. Her PhD, "Performance as a Platform for Critical Pedagogy in Social Work Education," outlines the use of critical performance pedagogy, a critical and creative educational approach used in social work education. Her current research is focused on using the arts, particularly drama, to expose novel and innovative directions in teaching critical social work practice.

Kate Ball Clem has been a staff member at the University of Vermont for more than twenty-five years and has served as business manager in the Department of Social Work for more than twenty years. She has a degree in English.

Jan Fook, MSW, PhD, FAcSS, is a professor and chair of the Department of Social Work, University of Vermont, and a visiting professor at Royal Holloway, University of London. She has held professorships in social work and in education in Australia, Norway, the UK, and Canada. She has published widely on critical social work and critical reflection. Her two most recent books are *Learning Critical Reflection: Experiences of the Transformative Learning Process* (edited with Laura Beres, 2020) and *Practicing Critical Reflection in Social Care Organisations* (2022).

Kate Gannon is an MSW graduate student at Syracuse University. Her background in wildlife rehabilitation and interest in runaway cultural evolution as a framework for ecological collapse have informed her contribution to the emerging field of environmental social work.

BC Garvey is a recent graduate of the MSW program at the University of Vermont. They hold an EdM in higher administration from the University of Buffalo and has worked as a financial aid counselor.

Anna Gupta is a professor of social work in the School of Law and Social Sciences, Royal Holloway, University of London. Her research interests include child protection, poverty, and inequality; work with Black and minority ethnic children and families; work in the family courts; children in care and adoption; and the Capability Approach. Throughout her work is a focus on social justice and human rights and on participatory approaches with people who have had lived experience of social work services. She is a coauthor of *Protecting Children: A Social Model* (2018) and a coeditor of *Unaccompanied Young Migrants: Identity, Care and Justice* (2019). She was a coinvestigator on a project, funded by the Economic and Social Research Council (ESRC), exploring the impact of COVID and racial inequalities on the well-being of Black and Asian young people and families and is currently completing a project with the Universities of Siegen and Hamburg on residential care in Germany and England.

Wanda Heading-Grant, PhD, is Carnegie Mellon University's inaugural vice provost for diversity, equity, and inclusion (DEI) and chief diversity officer. She also holds the post of distinguished service professor in the Heinz College of Information Systems and Public Policy at CMU. Dr. Heading-Grant previously served as vice president for DEI at the University of Vermont. Recent recognitions include the Dr. Wanda Heading-Grant Justice Award, named in her honor; the 2019 Women Worth Watching Award from *Profiles in Diversity Journal*; the 2018 University of Vermont Alumni Achievement Award; and the 2018 National Association of Diversity Officers in Higher Education (NADOHE) Individual Leadership Award.

Emily Ishai is a social worker. She works as a graduate community manager at Educating for Excellence, a nonprofit organization in Israel.

Danielle Jatlow, MSW, LICSW, LADC, has been working with adolescents, young adults, and their families for over eighteen years across a variety of contexts—first in San Francisco, then in New York City, and currently in Burlington, Vermont. She is a lecturer in the University of Vermont's Department of Social Work, coordinator of the University's BSW program, and teaches at both the graduate and undergraduate levels. She is currently pursuing her PhD at Simmons University.

Gerry Laviña, MSW, LCSW, is a social worker, the son of Filipino and Honduran immigrants, and a proud Angeleno. As a practitioner, he has been involved in anti-racism, diversity, equity, and inclusion (ADEI) efforts. He served for thirty years as a field education faculty member in the Department of Social Welfare at the UCLA Luskin School of Public Affairs.

Lia Levin, PhD, is a senior lecturer at Tel Aviv University's School of Social Work, and heads the Tel Aviv University Policy Practice Clinic. Her work deals primarily with the research, practice, and theory of social justice, with a particular emphasis on its intersections with epistemic justice and ecosocial justice.

Adaya Liberman, MSW, is a PhD student at Tel Aviv University's School of Social Work. Her work deals with speculative philosophy and its applications to empirical research. Her doctoral research uses a philospeculative approach to show the value of the knowledge of people with dementia.

Erin Mackenzie recently obtained an MSW degree from the University of Vermont. She hopes to continue developing a transdisciplinary skill set that merges her experience as a visual designer with her current social work interests in ecospirituality, futures thinking, and relational justice. As an emerging practitioner, she is committed to learning how to live more compassionately with herself, others, and the Earth.

Shani Mazor is a social worker, working with youth in risk and distress, and an MSW student in the Department of Social Work at the Hebrew University of Jerusalem, Israel.

Dominique Mikell Montgomery, AM, is an assistant professor of social work at the University of Nevada, Reno. Her research interests include the experiences of families affected by the child welfare system, Black studies, and participatory research methods.

Christine Morley, PhD, is discipline head, social work and human services, and a professor of social work at the School of Public Health and Social Work, Queensland University of Technology. She is the author or coauthor of several books in the area of critical social work.

Siddhesh Mukerji is a senior lecturer in social work at Goldsmiths, University of London. His scholarship focuses on socially engaged Buddhism, exploring how Buddhist thinker-activists conceptualize and respond to social and environmental problems. As an educator, he is interested in methodologies that focus on critical societal issues and challenge disciplinary boundaries, such as environmental social work.

Sarah Nunes, NIC, LMSW, has experience working as a dual diagnosis therapist in community mental health and psychiatric emergency room spaces. She obtained her MSW and a Certificate of Advanced Study in Disability Studies from Syracuse University. During her graduate studies, she cofounded—with Dr. Diane R. Wiener—the Alliance of Disability and Social Work (ADSW), for which she serves as managing director. Before becoming a social worker, she worked for more than a decade as a nationally certified American Sign Language interpreter (NIC), providing critical language access, advocacy, and care management throughout New York State for individuals living with substance use disorders and serious and persistent mental illness (SPMI), as well as serving people connected with carceral institutions.

Jason Anthony Plummer, MSW, MUP (Master of Urban Planning), PhD, is a political social worker. His research focuses on identifying the ways in which racism prevents the realization of a functioning democracy, a high quality of life, and a socially just society. He is an assistant professor of social work at California State University, Long Beach.

Dor Robinzon, MSW, is a community social worker.

Nana Sarkodee-Adoo is a recent graduate of the social welfare program at the Luskin School of Public Affairs, UCLA. A proud daughter of Ghanaian immigrants, she received her BS in policy, planning, and development at the University of Southern California and a Master of Public Health from UCLA. During her time at UCLA, she was involved in DEI efforts for both graduate programs and served on the board of the Luskin Black Caucus. She currently works as a research and evaluation coordinator at the Los Angeles County Office of Violence Prevention.

Sharon Segev is a social worker at a center for domestic violence treatment and an MSW student in the Department of Social Work, Tel Aviv University. Her research deals with the relationship between child maltreatment and conflict management styles in relationships.

Timothy Sim is an associate professor and head of the Master of Counselling program at the S.R. Nathan School of Human Development, Singapore University of Social Sciences. He spent eighteen years working at Hong Kong Baptist University and has established himself as an international expert in disaster management, practice research, and systemic family therapy. He has built models of disaster management for various vulnerable groups and conducted large-scale impact assessments of these models, which have been replicated and promoted internationally. For more information, please visit his personal website: https://timothysim316.wixsite.com/my-site.

Latoya Small, MSW, PhD, is an assistant professor of social welfare at UCLA. Her research is centered on addressing disparities in health and mental health for low-income women and children in the United States and abroad. Her scholarship has examined how key social determinants of health are associated with the well-being of women of color in the United States and children in sub-Saharan Africa.

Brenda Solomon is an associate professor in the Department of Social Work at the University of Vermont. Her PhD is in sociology. Her teaching interests include research methodology and transformative practice, and she researches in the area of auto ethnography and child welfare.

Shachar Timor-Shlevin, PhD, is a social work practitioner and lecturer at the Louis and Gabi Weisfeld School of Social Work, Bar-Ilan University, Israel. His research deals with the professionalization processes of social work, focusing primarily on the encounter between the neo-managerial discourse and the critical discourses in social work practice and how this encounter operates in institutionalized spaces of public services.

Tiffany Tuttle is an enrolled member of the Santee Sioux Tribe of the Dakota Nation of the Oceti Sakowin, the Seven Council Fires, more commonly known as the Great Sioux Nation. She holds a Master of Social Work from the University of Vermont (UVM) and a Master of Fine Art in creative writing from Indiana University at Bloomington. She was an inaugural recipient of the First Nations' Scholarship and cofounded the First Nations' Collective (FNC) in the College of Education and Social Services (CESS) at UVM. The FNC makes generous funding available for Indigenous students who would like to pursue a degree at UVM and go on to serve Indigenous communities upon graduation; it also helps to create a holistic environment that supports Indigenous students on campus. Tiffany works part-time with the FNC and has a full-time psychotherapy practice in Vermont. She is a multi-certified yoga teacher, massage therapist, and Reiki master and integrates spirituality and mindfulness into her work.

Nicole Vazquez, MSW, MPP (Master of Public Policy), is an Afro-Latinx, queer, cisgender woman of Mexican American and Panamanian parents. She holds dual master's degrees from UCLA and has more than twenty years' direct practice and administrative experience in both the public and nonprofit sectors. She conducts critical-race-specific trainings and workshops in addition to providing consultation in organizational development and support as the principal at Vazquez Consulting.

Merlinda Weinberg, PhD, is a professor in the School of Social Work, Dalhousie University, where she has been employed for the past ten years. Before that, she had an extensive career in social work management. Her research work on ethics is gaining widespread international recognition. She is the author of *Paradoxes in Social Work Practice: Mitigating Ethical Trespass* (2016).

Diane R. Wiener, LMSW, PhD, cofounded (with Sarah Nunes) the Alliance of Disability and Social Work (ADSW) in 2021. A neuroqueer social worker and activist-educator, she has experience in teaching, counseling, group facilitation, advising, mentoring, disability advocacy, and consulting, as well as in program development and management, leadership, assessment, and supervision. A former social work professor at Binghamton University, she also served as a field instructor for New York University, Adelphi University, Columbia University, and Syracuse University. She was a research professor and the associate director of the Burton Blatt Institute's Office of Interdisciplinary

Programs and Outreach and served as the Syracuse University Disability Cultural Center's founding director. In 2022, she returned to full-time social work practice, serving disabled children and youth and their families at a nonprofit, school-based program in upstate New York.

Rony Zilka, MSW, is currently employed in "121—Engine for Social Change". Her main interests are policy and rights promotion.

INDEX

Printed in the USA
CPSIA information can be obtained
at www.ICGtesting.com
CBHW022342190124
3624CB00006B/474